Abraham Verghese

My Own Country

"ONE OF THE BEST BOOKS OF THE YEAR."
—*Time*

"*My Own Country* is a medical journey into the heart of a community. Walker Percy once called a character 'an old-fashioned physician of the soul.' Dr. Verghese could claim this title as his own. This is a startling and disturbing book, yet as fine and lyrical as anything I've read in a great while."
> —Kaye Gibbons,
> author of *Charms for the Easy Life* and *Ellen Foster*

"Engrossing . . . an empathetic and eloquently written memoir."
> —*New York Newsday*

"*My Own Country* is a book about the effect of the AIDS epidemic in a deeply traditional, non-urban, 'country' setting. But it's also about identity . . . and reminds the reader of what is honorable and charitable in the way humans behave toward each other."
> —*Washington Post Book World*

"Here is that special combination, a worthy subject and a doctor who can write. Verghese's depiction of AIDS in the Bible Belt brings to mind not medical writers but the masters of regional fiction: Bobbie Ann Mason, Reynolds Price, Flannery O'Connor."
> —Peter D. Kramer,
> author of *Listening to Prozac*

"Haunting. . . . A story about AIDS that is intelligent, illuminating and, above all, deeply humane."
—*Dallas Morning News*

"Riveting. . . . *My Own Country* is devastating, inspiring, beautifully written."
—*Detroit Free Press*

"A heartbreaking chronicle of medical and human catastrophe in a microcosm. But *My Own Country* is also an unsentimental and careful meditation on the tenacious craving for a home in the world."
—*Entertainment Weekly*

"A remarkable testament . . . Verghese writes with the novelist's exacting eye [and] an irresistible narrative drive. . . . An astonishing feat."
—Gail Godwin, author of A *Southern Family*

"A rich, literary work of medical anthropology."
—*Chicago Tribune*

"[A] story told from the closely observed heart of an epidemic. Far from being a sociological discourse, it is intensely personal; Dr. Verghese's vulnerability and his lucid prose give this book the emotional momentum of a good novel. . . . This impressive literary debut puts him in the esteemed company of such physician-writers as Sherwin Nuland and Richard Selzer."
—John Irving, *Vanity Fair*

"Abraham Verghese has an impeccable knowledge of his medicine but he also writes lucid, beautiful English prose in the tradition of Conrad and Nabokov. This warm wanderer, in search of home, bares his own soul until the reader is shaken, challenged, repentant, exultant and finally at peace."
—Ferrol Sams, M.D.,
author of *When All the World Was Young*

Abraham Verghese

My Own Country

Abraham Verghese is Professor and Senior Associate
Chair for the Theory and Practice of Medicine at the
Stanford University School of Medicine. He has served
on the faculty at East Tennessee State University, the
University of Iowa, Texas Tech University, and the University of Texas Health Science Center, San Antonio,
where he was the founding director of the Center for
Medical Humanities & Ethics and where he holds an
adjunct professorship. A graduate of the Iowa Writers'
Workshop, he is the author of *The Tennis Partner*, a *New
York Times* Notable Book and most recently a novel,
Cutting for Stone. His essays and short stories have appeared in *The New Yorker*, *The New York Times*, *Sports
Illustrated*, *The Atlantic Monthly*, *Esquire*, *Story*, *Granta*,
The New York Times Magazine, *The Wall Street Journal*,
and elsewhere, and he is a regular correspondent for
TheAtlantic.com. He lives in Palo Alto, California.

www.abrahamverghese.com

My
Own Country

My
Own Country

A Doctor's Story

Abraham Verghese

Vintage Books

A DIVISION OF RANDOM HOUSE, INC.

NEW YORK

Library of Congress Cataloging-in-Publication Data
Verghese, A. (Abraham), 1955–
My own country : a doctor's story / Abraham Verghese.
— 1st Vintage Books ed.
p.   cm.
Originally published: New York : Simon & Schuster, c1994.
ISBN 0-679-75292-7
1. AIDS (Disease)—Social aspects—Tennessee—Johnson City.
I. Title.
[RA644.A25V47 1995]
362.1'969792'00976897—dc20   94-23500
CIP

BOOK DESIGN BY CATHRYN S. AISON

Manufactured in the United States of America

9 E 8

For Steven and Jacob

My
Own Country

THE LONG VOYAGE

Not that the pines were darker there,
nor mid-May dogwood brighter there,
nor swifts more swift in summer air;
    it was my own country,

having its thunderclap of spring,
its long midsummer ripening,
its corn hoar-stiff at harvesting,
    almost like any country,

yet being mine; its face, its speech,
its hills bent low within my reach,
its river birch and upland beech
    were mine, of my own country.

Now the dark waters at the bow
fold back, like earth against the plow;
foam brightens like the dogwood now
    at home, in my own country.

—From *Blue Juniata: A Life*
by Malcolm Cowley

1

S UMMER, 1985. A young man is driving down from New York to
visit his parents in Johnson City, Tennessee.

I can hear the radio playing. I can picture his parents waiting, his
mother cooking his favorite food, his father pacing. I see the young man
in my mind, despite the years that have passed; I can see him driving
home along a route that he knows well and that I have traveled many
times. He started before dawn. By the time it gets hot, he has reached
Pennsylvania. Three hundred or so miles from home, he begins to feel
his chest tighten.

He rolls up the windows. Soon, chills shake his body. He turns the
heater on full blast; it is hard for him to keep his foot on the accelerator
or his hands on the wheel.

By the time he reaches Virginia, the chills give way to a profuse
sweat. Now he is burning up and he turns on the air conditioner, but
the perspiration still soaks through his shirt and drips off his brow. His
lungs feel heavy as if laden with buckshot. His breath is labored,
weighted by fear and perhaps by the knowledge of the burden he is
bringing to his parents. Maybe he thinks about taking the next exit off
Interstate 81 and seeking help. But he knows that no one can help him,
and the dread of finding himself sick and alone keeps him going. That
and the desire for home.

I know this stretch of highway that cuts through the Virginia mountains; I know how the road rises, sheer rock on one side, how in places

the kudzu takes over and seems to hold up a hillside, and how, in the early afternoon, the sun glares directly into the windshield. He would have seen hay rolled into tidy bundles, lined up on the edges of fields. And tobacco plants and sagging sheds with their rusted, corrugated-tin roofs and shutterless side-openings. It would have all been familiar, this country. His own country.

IN THE EARLY EVENING of August 11, 1985, he was rolled into the emergency room (ER) of the Johnson City Medical Center—the "Miracle Center," as we referred to it when we were interns. Puffing like an overheated steam engine, he was squeezing in forty-five breaths a minute. Or so Claire Bellamy, the nurse, told me later. It had shocked her to see a thirty-two-year-old man in such severe respiratory distress.

He sat bolt upright on the stretcher, his arms propped behind him like struts that braced his heaving chest. His blond hair was wet and stuck to his forehead; his skin, Claire recalled, was gunmetal gray, his lips and nail beds blue.

She had slapped an oxygen mask on him and hollered for someone to pull the duty physician away from the wound he was suturing. A genuine emergency was at hand, something she realized, even as it overtook her, she was not fully comprehending. She knew what it was not: it was *not* severe asthma, status asthmaticus; it was *not* a heart attack. She could not stop to take it all in. Everything was happening too quickly.

With every breath he sucked in, his nostrils flared. The strap muscles of his neck stood out like cables. He pursed his lips when he exhaled, as if he was loath to let the oxygen go, hanging on to it as long as he could.

Electrodes placed on his chest and hooked to a monitor showed his heart fluttering at a desperate 160 beats per minute.

On his chest x-ray, the lungs that should have been dark as the night were instead whited out by a veritable snowstorm.

My friend Ray, a pulmonary physician, was immediately summoned. While Ray listened to his chest, the phlebotomist drew blood for serum electrolytes and red and white blood cell counts. The respiratory therapist punctured the radial artery at the wrist to measure blood oxygen levels. Claire started an intravenous line. And the young man slumped on the stretcher. He stopped breathing.

Claire punched the "Code Blue" button on the cubicle wall and an operator's voice sounded through the six-story hospital building: "Code Blue, emergency room!"

The code team—an intern, a senior resident, two intensive care unit nurses, a respiratory therapist, a pharmacist—thundered down the hallway.

Patients in their rooms watching TV sat up in their beds; visitors froze in place in the corridors.

More doctors arrived; some came in street clothes, having heard the call as they headed for the parking lot. Others came in scrub suits. Ray was "running" the code; he called for boluses of bicarbonate and epinephrine, for a second intravenous line to be secured, and for Claire to increase the vigor but slow down the rate of her chest compressions.

The code team took their positions. The beefy intern with Nautilus shoulders took off his jacket and climbed onto a step stool. He moved in just as Claire stepped back, picking up the rhythm of chest compression without missing a beat, calling the cadence out loud. With locked elbows, one palm over the back of the other, he squished the heart between breastbone and spine, trying to squirt enough blood out of it to supply the brain.

The ER physician unbuttoned the young man's pants and cut away the underwear, now soiled with urine. His fingers reached for the groin, feeling for the femoral artery to assess the adequacy of the chest compressions.

A "crash cart" stocked with ampules of every variety, its defibrillator paddles charged and ready, stood at the foot of the bed as the pharmacist recorded each medication given and the exact time it was administered.

The clock above the stretcher had been automatically zeroed when the Code Blue was called. A code nurse called out the elapsed time at thirty-second intervals. The resident and another nurse from the code team probed with a needle for a vein to establish the second "line."

Ray "bagged" the patient with a tight-fitting mask and hand-held squeeze bag as the respiratory therapist readied an endotracheal tube and laryngoscope.

At a signal from Ray, the players froze in midair while he bent the young man's head back over the edge of the stretcher. Ray slid the laryngoscope in between tongue and palate and heaved up with his left hand, pulling the base of the tongue up and forward until the leaf-shaped epiglottis appeared.

Behind it, the light at the tip of the laryngoscope showed glimpses of the voice box and the vocal cords. With his right hand, Ray fed the endotracheal tube alongside the laryngoscope, down the back of the throat, past the epiglottis, and past the vocal cords—this part done almost blindly and with a prayer—and into the trachea. Then he connected the squeeze bag to the end of the endotracheal tube and watched the chest rise as he pumped air into the lungs. He nodded, giving the signal for the action to resume.

Now Ray listened with his stethoscope over both sides of the chest as the respiratory therapist bagged the limp young man. He listened for the muffled *whoosh* of air, listened to see if it was equally loud over both lungs.

He heard sounds only over the right lung. The tube had gone down the right main bronchus, a straighter shot than the left.

He pulled the tube back an inch, listened again, and heard air entering both sides. The tube was sitting above the carina, above the point where the trachea bifurcates. He called for another chest x-ray; a radiopaque marker at the end of the tube would confirm its exact position.

With a syringe he inflated the balloon cuff at the end of the endotracheal tube that would keep it snugly in the trachea. Claire wound tape around the tube and plastered it down across the young man's cheeks and behind his neck.

The blue in the young man's skin began to wash out and a faint pink appeared in his cheeks. The ECG machine, which had spewed paper into a curly mound on the floor, now showed the original rapid heart rhythm restored.

At this point the young man was alive again, but just barely. The Code Blue had been a success.

In no time, the young man was moved to the intensive care unit (ICU) and hooked up via the endotracheal tube to a machine that looked like a top-loading washer, gauges and dials covering its flat surface. Its bellows took over the work of his tired diaphragm.

He came awake an hour later to the suffocating and gagging sensation of the endotracheal tube lodged in his throat. Even as the respirator tried to pump oxygen into his lungs, he bucked and resisted it, tried to cough out the tube. One can only imagine his terror at this awakening: naked, blazing light shining in his eyes, tubes in his mouth, tubes up his nose, tubes in his penis, transfixed by needles and probes stuck into his arms.

He must have wondered if this was hell.

THE MIRACLE CENTER ICU nurses who were experienced—at least in theory—with this sort of fright and dislocation, reassured him in loud tones. Because of the tube passing between his vocal cords and because his hands were tied to prevent his snatching at the tube (an automatic gesture in this setting), he could not communicate at all. With every passing second, his terror escalated. His heart rate rose quickly.

He was immediately sedated with a bolus of morphine injected into one of his lines. He was paralyzed with a curarelike agent, a cousin of the paste used on arrow-tips by indigenous tribes in the Amazon. As the drug shot through his circulation and reached the billions of junctions where nerve met and directed muscle, it blocked all signals and he lay utterly still and flaccid.

The respirator sent breaths into him with rhythmic precision at the rate dialed in by Ray, even throwing in a mechanical sigh—a breath larger than usual—to recruit and keep patent the air sacs in the base of the lung.

THE YOUNG MAN'S PARENTS now arrived at the hospital and were escorted up to their son's bedside. They had been waiting for him at home. Now they stood, I was told, in utter disbelief, trying to see their son through the forest of intravenous poles and the thicket of tubing and wires that covered him, asking again and again *what* had happened. And *why?*

By the next day the pneumonia had progressed. His lungs were even stiffer, making the respirator work overtime to drive oxygen into him. Ray performed a bronchoscopy, sliding a fiberoptic device into the endotracheal tube. Through the bronchoscope he could see the glossy red lining of the trachea and the bronchi. All looked normal. He directed the bronchoscope as far out as it would go, then passed a biopsy forceps through it and took a blind bite of the air sacs of the lung.

Under the microscope, the honeycomblike air spaces of the lung were congealed with a syrupy outpouring of inflammatory fluid and cells. Embedded in this matrix were thousands upon thousands of tiny, darkly staining, flying-saucerlike discs that the pathologist identified as *Pneumocystis carinii*.

The young man had no predisposing illness like leukemia or cancer that would explain this fulminant pneumonia caused by an innocuous organism.

His immune system *had* to be abnormal.

It was clear, though no one had yet seen a case, that he was Johnson City's first case of the acquired immune deficiency syndrome—AIDS.

Word spread like wildfire through the hospital. All those involved in his care in the ER and ICU agonized over their exposure.

The intern remembered his palms pressed against the clammy breast as he performed closed-chest massage.

Claire remembered starting the intravenous line and having blood trickle out and touch her ungloved skin.

The respiratory therapist recalled the fine spray that landed on his face as he suctioned the tracheal tube.

The emergency room physician recalled the sweat and the wet underwear his fingers encountered as he sought out the femoral artery.

Even those who had not touched the young man—the pharmacist, the orderlies, the transport personnel—were alarmed.

Ray worried too; he had been exposed as much as anyone. In the days to follow, he was stopped again and again in the corridor by people quizzing him about the danger, about their exposure. Ray even felt some anger directed at him. As if he, who had done everything right and diagnosed the case in short order, could have prevented this or warned them.

An ICU nurse told me that the young man's room took on a special aura. In the way a grisly murder or the viewing of an apparition can transform an otherwise ordinary abode, so cubicle 7C was forever transformed. Doctors and others in the ICU peeked through the glass, watching the inert body of the young man. His father was seated beside him.

The hometown boy was now regarded as an alien, the father an object of pity.

Ray told me how the parents took the news. The mother froze, staring at Ray's lips as if he was speaking a foreign language. The father turned away, only the sound of his footsteps breaking the silence as he walked out into the corridor and on out into the parking lot, unable to stay in the building where that word had been uttered.

Much later, the father asked, "But *how* did he get it? How could he have gotten this?"

Ray pointed out that he had had no time to get a history: perhaps they could give him some information. Had their son been healthy in the past year and in the days preceding the trip? Lord, yes! (The father did all the answering.) Did he ever use intravenous drugs? Lord, no! And to their knowledge had he ever had a blood transfusion?

No.

Was he married?

No.

Did he live alone? No, he had a friend in New York.

A male friend? Yes . . . they had never met him.

"Oh Lord! Is that what you're saying? Is that how he got it? Is my son a queer?"

Ray just stood there, unable to respond to the father's words.

The father turned to his wife and said, "Mother, do you hear this? Do you hear this?"

She gazed at the floor, nodding slowly, confirming finally what she had always known.

THE MOTHER NEVER LEFT THE ICU or her son's side. And in a day or so, the father also rallied around his son, spending long hours with him, holding his hand, talking to him. Behind the glass one could watch as the father bent over his son, his lips moving soundlessly.

He balked when his son's buddies flew down from New York. He was angry, on the verge of a violent outburst. This was all too much. This nightmare, these city boys, this new world that had suddenly engulfed his family.

Ray tried to mediate. But only when it seemed his boy's death was inevitable did the father relent and allow the New Yorkers near him. He guarded the space around his son, marshaling his protection.

The two visitors were men with closely cut hair. One had a pierced ear, purple suede boots, tight jeans and what the ICU ward clerk, Jennie, described to me as a "New York attitude—know what I mean?"

Jennie said the other friend, clearly the patient's lover, was dressed more conservatively and was in his early forties. She thought he was "a computer person." She remembers the tears that trickled continuously down his cheeks and the handkerchief squeezed in his hand. Jennie thought the mother wanted to talk to her son's lover. He, in turn, needed badly to talk to anyone. But in the presence of the father there was no chance for them to speak.

Three weeks after his arrival, the young man died.

The New Yorkers left before the funeral.

The respirator was unhooked and rolled back to the respiratory therapy department. A heated debate ensued as to what to do with it. There were, of course, published and simple recommendations for disinfecting it. But that was not the point. The machine that had sustained the young man had come to symbolize AIDS in Johnson City.

Some favored burying the respirator, deep-sixing it in the swampy land at the back of the hospital. Others were for incinerating it. As a compromise, the machine was opened up, its innards gutted and most replaceable parts changed. It was then gas disinfected several times. Even so, it was a long time before it was put back into circulation.

ABOUT TWO MONTHS AFTER the young man died, I returned to Johnson City. I had previously worked there as an intern and resident in internal medicine and I was now coming back after completing my training in infectious diseases in Boston. People who knew me from my residency days stopped me and told me the sad story of this young man's homecoming.

But it was not always recounted as a sad story. "Did you hear what happened to Ray?" a doctor asked me. He proceeded to tell me how a young man had dropped into the emergency room looking like he had pneumonia but turning out to be "a homo from New York with AIDS." The humor resided in what had happened to the unsuspecting Ray, the pie-in-your-face nature of the patient's diagnosis.

Some of the veteran ICU nurses, perhaps because this case broke through their I've-seen-it-all-and-more-honey attitudes, astonished me with their indignation. In their opinion, this "homo-sex-shual" with AIDS clearly had no right to expect to be taken care of in our state-of-the-art, computerized ICU.

When I heard the story, the shock waves in the hospital had already subsided. Everyone thought it had been a freak accident, a one-time thing in Johnson City. This was a small town in the country, a town of clean-living, good country people. AIDS was clearly a big city problem. It was something that happened in other kinds of lives.

2

I HAD ARRIVED in America as a rookie doctor in 1980.
At about the same time, HIV, the virus that causes AIDS, landed in the port cities of the United States: New York, San Francisco and Los Angeles. The virus arrived from Africa (perhaps via Haiti) carried in the bloodstream of one or more unsuspecting people who had then passed it on by sharing needles or through sexual intercourse. Like recipients of a biological chain letter, the numbers of carriers mushroomed. Quickly, but without commotion, the virus took root in the immune system of thousands of urban individuals.

It was not in its nature to kill at once. Instead, in the first months of infection, the virus quietly undermined the immune system, latching on to and then destroying the CD4 lymphocyte, the conductor of the immune orchestra. Months and often years would pass before bizarre, fulminant infections by *other* microorganisms—like *Pneumocystis carinii*—revealed the extent to which the immune orchestra had been decimated.

I FIRST CAME TO America from Africa in 1973. War and political unrest had interrupted my medical education in Ethiopia, the land where I was born and where my parents had worked for thirty-five years as expatriate teachers. After a hiatus spent working as an orderly in a succession of hospitals and nursing homes in New Jersey during my first period of American citizenship, I had eventually completed medical school in India and by 1980 had passed all the necessary exams to come back to the United States as a doctor. I considered myself lucky.

My father and mother were born in Kerala, in the south of India, to Christian families that trace their religion back to the apostle Thomas. After Christ's death, "Doubting" Thomas traveled east and arrived on the Malabar coast of India. There, long before St. Peter arrived in Rome, long before Christianity had taken any sort of hold outside of Palestine, "Mar Thoma" converted the south Indian Brahmins he encountered to Christianity. They named their children with Christian names. My surname, Verghese, has the same derivation as Geórgios or George.

The Christianity of my parents was a rigorous and demanding rite with daily prayer, fasting, and church services that became all-day marathons on Good Friday or Christmas.

When my father, George Verghese, graduated from Wilson College in India with a master's degree in physics, he wrote to the Ethiopian Education Ministry inquiring about teaching positions. "I had heard from someone—a relative or friend, I forget—that teachers were being recruited to Ethiopia." In reply he received a letter of appointment; he was to cable his acceptance and prepare to leave within ten days.

Meanwhile, unbeknownst to him, his future bride, Miriam Abraham, had received a letter of appointment to teach in a girls' school in Addis Ababa, the capital city of Ethiopia. She was also a recent physics graduate.

She says: "I wanted to go, but your grandfather had grave misgivings. A single woman going to *Africa* to work! Just imagine! He consulted lots of people. Finally he wrote to Thomas Uncle who was in Nairobi for many years running a tire-retreading business. He asked him about the wisdom of sending an unmarried girl to Ethiopia. Now see how God works: Thomas Uncle wrote back promptly: not only was Addis Ababa a safe place and the job offer good, but he even knew a family—Terese Auntie's family as it turns out—who had moved to Ethiopia from Kenya. Not only that, but he had already written to them about my situation. Soon a letter came from Terese Auntie saying I could stay with them and my father need not worry. All was arranged."

The letter from Terese Auntie went on to say, to my grandfather's satisfaction, that Ethiopia was an ancient Christian country with a Coptic Orthodox faith and a tradition very much like his own.

My mother and father arrived in Addis Ababa a week apart. They were among four hundred other Indian teachers—most of them Christians from Kerala—who would spread out over Ethiopia and teach math, physics, biology or English in the newly built high schools in Ethiopia. Why were all these teachers recruited from one state in India? Emperor Haile Selassie of Ethiopia, shortly after his country was liberated from Mussolini's hold, went on a state visit to India. He traveled to the south of India to see the churches of St. Thomas. He had seen in the early morning, as you can still see today, legions of schoolboys and schoolgirls in uniform making their way to classes. Kerala was then and still is the state with the highest literacy rate in India. This sight had impressed the emperor so much that he had decided to hire teachers from this Christian state to man the new schools he was starting across his country.

On the matter of how my parents met, how they courted, I dare not ask my father. And my mother, though seemingly willing, parts with no significant details. My brothers and I always thought it had something to do with physics.

When my parents tell me the story of their arrival in Ethiopia—the tough times in India, the struggle to get a college education, the word of mouth from friends about jobs overseas, the letters of inquiry to "relatives" abroad, the establishment of a base, the accumulation of a nest egg, the consolidation of resources by marriage, the help and support extended to their younger cousins and more distant "relatives" who wrote asking for advice—I understand the migration of Indians to South Africa, Uganda, Kenya, Tanzania, Mozambique, Mauritius, Aden, Ethiopia. And the next wave on to Birmingham, Bradford, Bristol, London and Toronto. And to Flushing, Jersey City, Chicago, San Jose, Houston and even Johnson City, Tennessee.

In their herald migration, my parents individually and then together reenacted the peregrination of an entire race. Like ontogeny repeating phylogeny—the gills and one-chamber heart of a human fetus in the first trimester reenacting man's evolution from amphibians—they presaged their own subsequent wanderings and those of their children.

DURING THE HIATUS IN my medical education, while I worked as an orderly in America and before I went to India to finish medical school, I had seen from the vantage of a hospital worker the signs of urban rot in Newark, Elizabeth, Jersey City, Trenton and New York. The (insured) middle class continued to flee farther out to the suburbs where chic, glass-fronted hospitals complete with birthing suites and nouvelle cuisine popped up on the freeway like Scandinavian furniture franchises.

Meanwhile, the once grand county hospitals were sliding inexorably, like the cities themselves, into critical states. Understaffing, underfunding, the old stories. Their patients had become the uninsured and indigent whose problems revolved around drug addiction and trauma. In the emergency rooms of these fading institutions, bodies were pressed together like so many sheep. Old people languished on stretchers shunted into hallways and corridors while beleaguered nurses attempted some form of triage.

An inevitable accompaniment to this scene of a city hospital under siege was the sight of foreign physicians. The names of these doctors—names like Srivastava, Patel, Khan, Iqbal, Hussein, Venkateswara, Menon—bore no resemblance to those of the patients being served or the physicians who supervised them.

City and county hospitals were the traditional postgraduate training grounds for foreign medical graduates: hospitals like Cook County Hospital in Chicago, Nassau County and Kings County in New York and dozens of others across the country counted on foreign interns and residents for manpower, particularly in internal medicine.

By the time I completed medical school in India and returned stateside, a few of my seniors from my medical school in India had begun internships at county hospitals across America. Through them and through their friends and their friends' friends, an employment network extended across the country. With a few phone calls, I could establish for any city which hospital to apply to, which hospital to not bother with because they never took foreign graduates, and which hospital took foreign graduates for the first year, used them for scut work, but never promoted them to the second year—the infamous "pyramid" residencies. And the network invariably provided me with the name of someone to stay with.

At hospitals that took foreign physicians the work was grueling, the conditions appalling—but only by American standards—and the supervision and teaching often minimal because of the sheer volume of work. This was particularly true in hospitals that were not university-affiliated. The scut work—wheeling the patient down to x-ray, drawing blood, starting intravenous drips, putting in Foley catheters, doing ECGs— was endless and the every-other-night-call schedule was brutal.

As I crisscrossed the country, in search of a residency slot, by way of Greyhound, sleeping on friends' couches (or on their beds if they were on call), I was amazed by the number and variety of foreign interns and residents I met in these hospitals. I overheard snatches of Urdu, Tagalog, Hindi, Tamil, Spanish, Portuguese, Farsi and Arabic. Some hospitals were largely Indian in flavor, others largely Filipino. Still others were predominantly Latin or East European.

In the cafeteria of a hospital in a less-desirable section of Los Angeles, a hospital at which I was interviewing, I took my tray over to a table where an Indian physician sat. She had the handsome Aryan features of a Parsi or a Kashmiri. I thought she might be from Bombay or Chandigarh or Delhi—the other end of the country from where my parents were born. But when she spoke I was bowled over: from her lips emerged the purest Birmingham cockney! (I recognized this accent easily: as a ten-year-old I had spent a year in Birmingham while my father was there on sabbatical.)

She told me her family had fled Uganda and settled in Britain when she was a young girl. She had never seen India, neither had her parents. Her family had been in Uganda for two generations. She had gone to medical school in Leeds and then come to the States. When I told her I was born in Ethiopia, she tried her Swahili on me and I my Amharic on her. Neither of us got very far with that and so we retreated to English.

The England she reminisced about was vastly different from my memory of it. The Asians, she said, now had pubs of their own in Asian strongholds like Wembley and Southall. These hybrid establishments served *tandoori* chicken, *pakodas* and *samoosas* to be washed down with pints of the finest British bitter. And the music and dance were likely to be "bhangara-disco"—an electronic rendering of Punjabi and Gujarati folk music. The youth, most of whom, like her, had never been to

India, had taken up the music of Lata Mangeshkar, Mukesh or Mo-
hammed Rafi—old playback singers for Hindi movies.

Before she left to return to the wards, she paged a fellow intern, a
Zachariah Mathen. From his name I knew he was a Christian-Indian
like me. Zachariah took me around the hospital and as a matter of
course offered me his apartment and car keys. "Make my home your
home! Explore the City of Angels," he said.

SOME HOSPITALS, like Coney Island Hospital in New York, sent con-
tracts to graduating medical students in India who had been recommended by their seniors. Come July, the seniors were dispatched to
Kennedy to pick up the new blood fresh off Air-India, bring them to
Coney Island and orient them. The cultural adjustment was simple: the
reassuring scents of green chili and frying *papads* wafted down the
corridor of the house-staff quarters. Indian sari stores, Indian restaurants
and Indian grocery stores abounded—some even delivered. The latest
Hindi blockbuster starring Amitabh or Dimple could be rented in
Queens on bootleg video within days of its debut in Delhi or Poona.
And the faces of the physicians on the wards were those that one might
have seen on the platform in Victoria Station, Bombay.

The few *American* interns and residents I saw in the various hospitals
I visited were graduates of the "offshore" or Caribbean schools in places
like Antigua, St. Lucia, Montserrat or Grenada. These schools existed
solely for Americans who could not make it into U.S. medical schools.

NOW THAT I HAD RETURNED to America with my medical degree, a
certain perverseness and contrariness made me want to buck this system. What was the point in coming to America to train if I wound up
in a little Bombay or a little Manila? In India I had met Rajani Chacko,
a lovely, sloe-eyed account executive working for a leading advertising
agency. After a whirlwind courtship, we were now newlyweds. I was
loath to bring her to an urban war zone, to an apartment where she
would have to be alone for long periods of time while I worked as an
intern.

Through a relative who was on the faculty, I heard of a new medical
school: East Tennessee State University. It had started a residency program in internal medicine. As residents we would rotate through the

Mountain Home Veterans Administration Medical Center (the "VA")
—a veritable town within the town of Johnson City—as well as the
adjacent Johnson City Medical Center (the "Miracle Center"), a community hospital. This rural setting in the foothills of the Smoky Mountains, in the shadow of the Appalachian Trail, seemed a beautiful place
to bring my bride.

DURING MY INTERNSHIP AND residency in Johnson City, I moonlighted
on free weekends in small emergency rooms (ERs) on the Tennessee-
Virginia border. I pulled sixty-hour shifts—Friday evening to Monday
morning—in places like Mountain City, Tazewell, Grundy, Norton,
Pound, Lebanon and the Lonesome Pine Hospital in Big Stone Gap,
Virginia. These hospitals had anywhere from twenty to forty beds,
two-bed intensive care units, and the ambience of a mom-and-pop
grocery store.

The ER nurses were on a first-name basis with every patient that
came in. The ambulance drivers rarely resorted to the "forty-three-year-
old-white-male-with-chest-pain-unrelieved-by-nitroglycerin" jargon.
One was more apt to hear on the scanner that "Louise Tipton over on
Choctaw Hollow says Old Freddy's smothering something awful and we
better get over there right away, 'cause it's worse than the last time when
he came in and Doc Patel put him on the breathing machine."

If I was lucky, no more than eighteen to thirty patients came through
the ER in twenty-four hours. The drive up through the mountains was
breathtaking, the staff exceptionally friendly, and the cafeteria food free
and plentiful.

The patients were earthy and appreciative and spoke a brand of English that made diagnosis a special challenge. Who knew that "fireballs
in the ovurus" meant uterine fibroids, or that "smiling mighty Jesus"
meant spinal meningitis? Or that "roaches in the liver" meant cirrhosis?
Soon, "high blood" (hypertension), "low blood" (anemia) and "bad
blood" (syphilis) became part of my own vocabulary as I obtained a
patient's medical history.

It was at one of these small hospitals that I met Essie, an affectionate
woman with pretty doll's eyes, a generous bosom and dimples deep
enough to get lost in. Essie worked as a lab technician. Like so many of
the other hospital staff, she was from the area and, except for a brief

sojourn in Kingsport, Tennessee, had lived her entire life there. The tiny communities nestled in the hollows and connected to each other by narrow mountain roads provided a security that made city life difficult to contemplate. Her parents and her brother and cousins all lived within a mile of each other.

"I know one day I might *have* to leave. Say if the jobs around here dry up. But I can't imagine living anywhere else."

This attitude made jobs precious. One was apt to encounter people whose first job was also their only job and they had worked at it for twenty years or more.

Of course, not everyone felt the same way. Many of the young felt confined by the little towns and had moved at least to the Tri-Cities area (Johnson City, Kingsport, Bristol) or even farther afield to Knoxville, Atlanta, Charlotte or Memphis.

Essie's brother, Gordon, was a case in point. It seemed he couldn't wait to leave their small town. She said he had moved to Kingsport as soon as he finished high school. Shortly thereafter he moved to Atlanta. Then, after a year in Atlanta, Gordon had vanished from the face of the earth.

The small hospital where I moonlighted the most had an on-call room leading off the ER corridor. There I could read, sleep, or watch TV till a patient signed in. Or I could come out to the nurses' station and shoot the breeze with the ER clerk, with the nurses, with Essie, and with "J.D."—the part-time security guard and self-styled entrepreneur.

J.D., Essie and the rest of the gang took it on themselves to not only feed me but also expand my Appalachian folk lexicon and coach me on the right way to "talk country." I was a quick study.

It became a challenge for them to find food that I would not eat. I enjoyed corn pone. I tolerated hominy grits. But I loved homemade biscuits, a great improvement on "whopping" biscuits—the frozen kind you whopped on the refrigerator door to open. I graduated to poke salad and tasted "dry-land-fish" (fried mushrooms) and ramps—an oniony tuber that you excreted in your sweat glands for weeks after. I tried and liked squirrel stew. Baked possum in a collar of sweet potatoes looked better than it tasted, while 'coon tasted better than it looked. Hog brain with scrambled eggs both looked and tasted wonderful.

In return for the incredible hospitality and the culinary treats, I would sometimes relent and crack the ER staff up with my mimicry of the regional accents of India. The nuances that differentiated a Punjabi accent from a Madrasi accent from a Gujarati accent were appreciated by the ER folk: The staff physicians in the tiny community hospitals that served the scattered mining towns of southwest Virginia, east Tennessee and Kentucky were predominantly from India or the Philippines with a smattering of Pakistanis, Koreans and Palestinians.

The few white M.D.s and D.O.s around, it seemed to me, were near retirement or else were serving out a National Health Service commitment. It was evidently difficult to entice young American medical school graduates into these isolated and often depressed rural areas where reimbursement depended heavily on the health of the coal mines and on being willing to have a large proportion of Medicaid patients in the practice.

Meanwhile, year by year, more foreign physicians, recruited by the same word-of-mouth that brings fresh blood to the newspaper kiosks, motels, gas stations, taxi fleets, restaurants and wholesale groceries of America, were completing their training in American urban war zones and moving into these rural havens.

The foreign doctors—with some glaring exceptions—were well received. They developed reputations as sound physicians. Though they were friendly, the majority chose not to integrate with the community except at a superficial level. They retained many of their foreign customs, the women wore saris, they were very protective of their children, and most of their socialization was with each other. In the corner of the kitchen or in a separate *puja* room would be a collection of Hindu icons: invariably Lakshmi (the goddess of wealth) and Ganesha. Also Muruga, Venkateswara, Sai Baba, Durga, according to taste. Once a day the incense and the oil lamp would be lit, the silver bell rung and burning camphor waved around the idols. And at least once a year the family would travel to the Hindu temple in Nashville to do a more elaborate *puja* or *mahabhishekam*.

The effect of having so many foreign doctors in one area was at times comical. I had once tried to reach Dr. Patel, a cardiologist, to see a tough old lady in the ER whose heart failure was not yielding to my diuretics and cardiotonics. I called his house and his wife told me he was at "Urology Patel's" house, and when I called there I learned he and

"Pulmonary Patel" had gone to "Gastroenterology Patel's" house. Gastroenterology Patel's teenage daughter, a first-generation Indian-American, told me in a perfect Appalachian accent that she "reckoned they're over at the Mehtas' playing rummy," which they were.

Rajani and I, perhaps because we were of a younger generation, traveled easily between these two worlds: the parochial world of Indians in America, and the secular world of east Tennessee. For the Indian parties, Rajani wore a sari and we completely immersed ourselves in a familiar and affectionate culture in which we had our definite place as the juniormost couple; but at night we could don jeans and boots and go line dancing at the Sea Horse on West Walnut or listen to blues at the Down Home.

I REMEMBER AS AN INTERN IN 1981 reading a *New England Journal of Medicine* article with the curious title "*Pneumocystis carinii* Pneumonia and Mucosal Candidiasis in Previously Healthy Homosexual Men—Evidence of a New Acquired Cellular Immunodeficiency." It described the seminal AIDS cases in Los Angeles. Companion articles described cases in New York and San Francisco. Three things about these reports stayed in my mind: gay men, immune deficiency, and death.

I knew precious little about gay culture.

In college I had picked up and parroted the snide asides and took part in the buffoonery and condescension that constituted the heterosexual response to homosexuality.

For me, reading about ritualized meeting places like bath houses and gay bars and understanding the extent of gay culture was astonishing and eye opening. It was as if a whole megalopolis had existed around me, intertwined with my city, and yet invisible to me. I was intensely curious.

I knew no *openly* gay men. I only knew the stereotype. I sensed the stereotype might be as untrue as the stereotype of the southerner, the redneck. If the southerner was a born racist and terribly intolerant, I—a brown-skinned foreigner—had never experienced this. In fact, the first time I experienced racism, felt it as a palpable presence in my daily life, was in Boston, not Tennessee.

The month the first papers on AIDS came out, the disease became a topic for late-night, idle discussion in the Mountain Home VA and

Miracle Center cafeterias. AIDS seemed so far away, so bizarre: New York and San Francisco were its epicenters. We were seeing in our lifetime, so we told ourselves, yet *another* new disease. And surely, just like Legionnaire's, Lyme disease, toxic shock—all new diseases—we felt this new disease, this mysterious immune deficiency, would soon be understood and conquered.

To say this was a time of unreal and unparalleled confidence, bordering on conceit, in the Western medical world is to understate things. Only cancer was truly feared, and even that was often curable. When the outcome of treatment was not good, it was because the host was aged, the protoplasm frail, or the patient had presented too late—never because medical science was impotent.

There seemed to be little that medicine could not do. As a lowly resident, I was inserting Swan-Ganz catheters into the vena cava and the right side of the heart. Meanwhile, the cardiologists were advancing fancier catheters through leg arteries and up the aorta, then using tiny balloons to open clogged coronary arteries or using lasers in Roto-Rooter fashion to ream out the grunge.

Surgeons, like Tom Starzl in Pittsburgh, had made kidney, liver, heart and heart-lung transplantation routine, and they were embarking on twelve- to fourteen-hour "cluster operations" where liver, pancreas, duodenum and jejunum were removed en bloc from a donor and transplanted into a patient whose belly, previously riddled with cancer, had now been eviscerated, scooped clean in preparation for this organ bouquet.

Starzl was an icon for that period in medicine, the pre-AIDS days, the frontier days of every-other-night call. My fellow interns and I thought of ourselves as the *vaqueros* of the fluorescent corridors, riding the high of sleep deprivation, dressed day or night in surgical scrubs, banks of beepers on our belts, our tongues quick with the buzz words that reduced patients to syndromes—"rule out MI," "impending DTs," "multiorgan failure." We strutted around with floppy tourniquets threaded through the buttonholes of our coats, our pockets cluttered with penlights, ECG calipers, stethoscopes, plastic shuffle cards with algorithms and recipes on them. The hemostats lost in the depths of our coat pockets were our multipurpose wrenches and found uses from roach clips to earwax dislodgers. Carried casually in sterile packaging in our top pockets were seven-gauge, seven-inch needles with twelve-inch trails of tubing. We were always ready—should we be first at a Code Blue—to slide needle under collarbone, into the great subclavian vein, and then to feed the serpent tubing down the vena cava in a cathartic ritual that established our mastery over the human body.

There seemed no reason to believe when AIDS arrived on the scene that we would not transfix it with our divining needles, lyse it with our potions, swallow it and digest it in the great vats of eighties technology.

I HAD MADE UP MY mind that I wanted a career in academic medicine. If there was glory in medicine, then I was not satisfied with the glory of saving a patient and having the family and a few others know about it. The rewards of private practice—money, autonomy, the big house, the big car, the big boat, the small plane, the bubble reputation in a provincial hospital—were not enough for me. I loved bedside medicine, the art of mining the patient's body for clues to disease. I loved introducing medical students to the thrill of the examination of the human body, guiding their hands to feel a liver, to percuss the stony dull note of fluid that had accumulated in the lung, to be with them when their eyes shone the first time they heard "tubular" breathing or "whispering pectoriloquy" and thereby diagnosed pneumonia. The acclaim of the lecture hall, the lead article in the *New England Journal of Medicine*, the invitations to be a keynote speaker at gatherings of my peers—these were the coins I wished to hoard.

My mentor in Tennessee was Steven Berk, an infectious diseases specialist fresh out of training at Boston City Hospital. Boston City Hospital was for many years the premier infectious diseases (ID) training program in the country. Steve, a quiet, unassuming and shy man, had already published several important papers prior to coming to Tennessee. His ability to see research opportunities in the wards, nursing home and domiciliaries of the VA excited me. Steve was quietly cataloguing the causes of pneumonia in the elderly, a domain in which he would become the world's expert. And I was along for the ride. I came to value a good sputum specimen that was not contaminated with saliva as much as I valued gold.

I became Steve's shadow. I worked long hours in the library looking up references, painfully composing the first draft of a manuscript that he would then take and revise and hand back to me for further work.

I took Steve's rationale for why he had gone into ID as a specialty and made it my own. Infectious diseases, he said, was the one discipline where cure was common. In the battle of man against microbe, man was winning. Astute diagnosis was rewarded by a return to perfect health. Death from infection used to be common on bone-marrow-transplant wards and on leukemia wards. Now, he pointed out, with newer, more powerful antibiotics, better diagnostic tools, and a new understanding of immunology, ID physicians were getting the upper hand.

But I also had a selfish reason for picking infectious diseases. Most medical residents flocked to cardiology or gastroenterology or pulmonary medicine—specialties rich in invasive procedures (and therefore very lucrative). Fellowships in these areas were very competitive. Unlike the internship year (where foreign graduates were in much demand and were critical to the survival of many inner-city hospitals), both foreign and American medical graduates were competing for the limited number of fellowship slots across the country.

Comparatively few people went into ID. My chances of going to a top-notch university to train were best if I opted to specialize in ID.

Steve was delighted when I told him my decision. We mapped out a strategy: I would apply for a fellowship in infectious diseases at Boston City Hospital as well as at Yale, Tufts, Stanford and San Francisco General Hospital. We hoped that Steve's strong letter of recommendation, as well as the three scientific papers I had now published, would erase my foreignness.

When, after my round of interviews, William McCabe, the Chief of Infectious Diseases at Boston City Hospital and a legend in the field, called me and offered me a position, preempting the other places, I jumped at it.

MY FIRST DAYS IN Boston were anxious and disorienting. When I was on call, I had to cover three hospitals: the Veterans Hospital in Jamaica Plain, Boston City Hospital and University Hospital, both in the South End. Each hospital had its own protocol for parking, for where the patients' charts were kept, for where you could safely leave your things without being ripped off, for the format of the consultation.

The first weekend I was on call, I was summoned to Boston City Hospital to see a gay male with fever and pneumonia.

This would be my first patient with possible AIDS, my first encounter to my knowledge with a gay patient. It was July of 1983. I had read the burgeoning literature on AIDS and told myself I should not agonize over my own safety. The virus seemed to spread in the manner of hepatitis B: by body fluids and blood. None of the doctors in San Francisco and New York who had taken care of scores of patients with AIDS had as yet contracted it. On the other hand, the incubation period and the asymptomatic phase of the disease could be very long. Still, simply examining the patient did not call for gloves or any other precaution.

I was excited and a little nervous.

Osler, the dean of American medicine who had died in the early part of this century, said that to study medicine without textbooks was to go to sea without charts. But to study medicine without patients was to not go to sea at all.

I was ready to test the waters.

I found parking near the Thorndike Building. A female physician was behind me as I walked down one of the dark, dingy tunnels that ran under Boston City Hospital and connected the different buildings. We both flattened ourselves against the wall as the clatter of an eccentric wheel and a rattly frame grew louder behind us. An electric cart brushed closer to me than I would have liked. It pulled two wagons of laundry. Only the back of the driver's Afro was visible. I could smell the ammoniacal odor of soiled linen mingling with the tunnel's faint reek of wet insulation from the pipes overhead.

We rounded a corner and came to a dead end at an incinerator. The doctor behind me laughed. She introduced herself as a new nephrology fellow. She confessed that she had been following me, hoping that I knew where I was going. As we backtracked to safety, we talked about the energy we were expending trying to look unfazed in this new and intimidating environment.

The medical wards were in the oldest section of Boston City Hospital The stairs were uneven and wire mesh extended up six floors to enclose the stairwell and keep anyone from jumping over the banister. The bottom of the stairwell was dirty, dusty, and littered with cigarette butts that had been pushed through the chicken wire from the floors above.

I found Tony Cappellucci's room. An "isolation" sticker on his door warned of the need for "blood and body fluid precautions."

The rooms in the older part of Boston City Hospital were not known for being bright and airy; this room was no exception. The drawn curtains left the room pitch dark. There were two beds in the room. I could make out that one bed was empty and a figure was curled up in the second.

When I approached, a pair of close-set eyes looked at me with suspicion from behind a *purda* of sorts: he had coiled the bed sheet around his head and across his face.

I introduced myself and Tony gradually emerged from the bedclothes, shielding his eyes as I drew back the curtain. Tony was in his twenties. He had close-cropped blond hair except at the back where he had grown it out. He was about five foot six and had the compact appearance of a gymnast. His face was pockmarked with acne and his teeth were in poor repair; I remember his nails were grubby and the room had a stifling, old-socks odor to it.

His tone was defensive and combative. He said he had been visiting Boston from New York when he fell ill. He was irritated with the treatment he was getting and commented on how much better things were at Bellevue.

"I *told* them I was gay," he said. "I was up front about it. And so I'm being treated like a leper. As if I have AIDS. I don't have AIDS, do I?"

I promised him I would try to answer that after I had a chance to go over him thoroughly. Certainly there was nothing to warrant that diagnosis thus far.

The physicians and nurses had treated him well; his present mood was a result of a trip back from radiology, which in Boston City Hospital required a journey through the tunnels. The male attendants from the transport service who took him to radiology and back had worn gloves and masks and grumbled their displeasure at being pressed into this service. As far as they were concerned he had AIDS.

Fever and a nagging cough that had gone on for three days had brought him to the hospital. His chest x-ray had been suspicious for pneumonia in the base of the left lung. His arterial blood gases showed his blood oxygen to be quite normal, a finding against his having *Pneumocystis carinii*. He had noted lymph node enlargement all over his body for a year now, for which he was being followed at Bellevue. "Before I came to Boston, I was fine," he said, as if this illness was yet more evidence of the city's shortcomings.

He told me he had contracted rectal gonorrhea twice before, as well as venereal warts and syphilis. He knew people who had died of AIDS.

I examined him carefully. There were white patches of thrush in his mouth and moderate enlargement of the lymph nodes in his armpits and groin. I could detect a few crackles in the base of his left lung. His genitalia were circumcised and normal. He had a small venereal wart around his anus that he was unaware of. I searched his skin carefully, looking for the purple, violaceous lesions of Kaposi's sarcoma. I found none. I asked him if anyone had ever told him what the two coin-shaped corrugated skin lesions were on his abdomen, exactly six inches below his nipples on either side. They were brown and barely noticeable.

"These?" he asked, scrunching his head down to peek, looking worried. "I've had them forever."

"They're accessory nipples."

"What? You're kidding!"

"They're very common. This line from your nipples down to your pelvis is the mammary line. Embryologically, mammary glands develop in mammals along this line. Almost any skin blemish you see along this line is an accessory nipple. In your case there isn't any doubt about it because they are quite symmetrical, and look: they have the shape of an areola with a tiny nipple in the center."

"Damn! Do you suppose they are sensitive?" I said I had no idea.

I took a specimen of his sputum to stain and look at under the microscope, leaving him to continue his study of his accessory nipples. The sputum showed many white blood cells in it and a predominance of purple, lancet-shaped bacteria. His pneumonia was being caused by a bacterium—the pneumococcus. The pneumococcus is the commonest cause of pneumonia in people without AIDS. Osler had spoken of it as "the captain of the men of death, the old man's friend."

I telephoned my attending physician, discussed my findings, and we agreed on what we would recommend to the house staff.

I came back to Tony's room to answer his, Do I have AIDS? question.

As I write this, it is difficult to imagine that unreal time, 1983, in the history of AIDS. Not only did we not know what caused AIDS, there was no test to say who did and who did not have the mysterious disease.

The best that doctors across the country could do was to agree on a "definition" to ensure that everyone was talking about the same entity: If one was previously healthy and, for no obvious reason, developed an infection with an organism like *Pneumocystis* or else developed Kaposi's sarcoma, one had acquired immune deficiency syndrome. AIDS.

(After HIV was discovered to be the cause of AIDS, it made sense to discard the cumbersome appellation "AIDS." We could simply say "mild," "moderate" or "severe" HIV infection. But the metaphor of AIDS is so powerful, it appears impossible to eradicate the term. Eligibility for Medicaid and Supplemental Security Income revolve around the definition.)

I was able to tell Tony that he did not have AIDS. On the chart I wrote that he did not "fulfill" the definition. His pneumonia did not look like *Pneumocystis carinii* pneumonia. He was very pleased to hear this and shook my hand vigorously.

What I didn't tell Tony was that his lymph node enlargement and the thrush in his mouth suggested that he might be infected with the agent—whatever it was—that caused AIDS. There was mounting evidence that young men like Tony who had the risk factors—in his case, unprotected anal intercourse—and who had lymph node enlargement, often evolved into full-blown AIDS. I had a feeling he knew this already.

I never saw Tony again. As I write this, I have little doubt that Tony was infected with HIV. And that he is dead now.

Tony, my first gay patient, had been quite pleasant after he got past his initial hostility and annoyance. In the ensuing two years in Boston, I saw a steady increase in the number of AIDS cases presenting to the Boston University hospitals. Not the vast numbers that were being seen in New York or San Francisco or even at the New England Deaconess Hospital where many of the gay men in Boston seemed to go. Still, we were seeing enough patients to accumulate experience with AIDS and to develop some confidence in predicting what certain symptoms meant. At Boston City Hospital, we saw mostly Haitians and intravenous drug users. At the Boston VA we saw intravenous drug users and gay men in equal proportions. At University Hospital we saw predominantly gay men but not in any significant numbers; University Hospital seemed anxious not to develop a reputation like the Deaconess that would attract droves of persons with AIDS to it.

NEAR THE END OF MY training in Boston, Steve Berk, who was now Chief of Medicine at the Mountain Home VA in Tennessee, offered me a staff position at the VA and an appointment as assistant professor at East Tennessee State University School of Medicine. About the same time I was made an offer of a junior faculty position at Boston University. The two jobs could not have been more different.

If I stayed in Boston, the pay would be no better than my fellowship stipend, and within a year I would be expected to generate most of my salary by writing and receiving grants. Basic or bench research and National Institutes of Health funding were the currency of success in Boston. Therefore I would spend ten or eleven months of the year in the labs—"protected time"—and just one or two months on the wards. Most academic departments in Boston were top-heavy with researchers. In Tennessee it would be the reverse: I would spend most of my time on the clinical wards with a small amount of protected time for research; the pay would be much better and not as tenuous.

Rajani, who had completed her M.B.A. in Tennessee, was now working with a commercial real-estate company in Boston. She enjoyed her work and I was proud of what she had accomplished in her short time in America. But she was pregnant now and was planning to quit the work force for an extended period so that she could have and enjoy our first child. We wrestled with the choices: Stay in Boston? Return to Tennessee and raise our baby in a safe, rural, pastoral setting?

Going from India to Johnson City, Tennessee, had been a bit of a culture shock for both of us: the Appalachian accents were twangier, more singsong than we could possibly have imagined. Not even reruns of *The Beverly Hillbillies* that we had watched in India prepared us for this. But that culture shock was a mere tremor compared with the shock of going from Tennessee to Boston. On a fellow's stipend in Boston, a roach-infested, third-floor walk-up in Brighton off Commonwealth Avenue was the best we could do. Break-ins were so common that every time I returned to the apartment, my gaze went quickly to the TV and stereo to see if they were still there.

Three years in Tennessee had gotten us used to making eye contact with people anywhere and automatically exchanging a "How you all doing?" or at least a nod. But in Boston, neighbors discouraged this sort of familiarity. The only time we spoke with ours was when a burglar in broad daylight knocked a hole in the neighbors' wall, reached through it to open the front door and then robbed them. The neighbors came to ask if we had seen or heard anything. We hadn't.

My academic ambitions had become less lofty. I had worked hard for two years developing an animal model of pneumonia. I had learned how to anesthetize a hamster and then slide a tiny hollow tube past the epiglottis, between the vocal cords and into the trachea—much like the intubation of a patient during a Code Blue. I would then shoot a dose of bacteria into the hamster's lung. At the end of a morning, thirty-two hamsters would be lined up flat on their backs, their paws in front of them, snoring, looking like a bunch of drunken soccer fans sleeping off a hangover. I sacrificed four hamsters a day, ground up their lungs, painstakingly counted the number of bacteria surviving and plotted a "clearance" curve for staphylococci. Each clearance experiment took one week. I did many clearance experiments. Later in my fellowship I began to work with macrophages, the lung scavenger cells, testing their ability to ingest bacteria in the test tube.

But my experimental results were slow in coming and it was a long time before I had enough data to publish a paper. And despite all my effort, I was merely scratching the surface of a biological system. Basic research had become so complex: No one cared if in a certain disease you discovered that some protein in the blood was either high or low. The question being asked was what *gene* was controlling this protein? And how quickly could you clone it? Science had gone molecular. An investment of a couple of years after fellowship training was necessary just to learn the *methodology* of molecular biology.

I accepted Steve's offer to return to Tennessee. Sorting out the real-time, real-world puzzles of living people seemed to be what I wanted.

Steve would generously provide me with a lab and a technician so I could continue my hamster research. But I was returning to Tennessee to be a teacher and a clinician, not a researcher.

The impending arrival of our first child had changed our view of life. We wanted now to settle in one place for a while. We looked forward to returning to Appalachia; we were ready for a less frenetic existence in a corner of rural America that we loved.

TOWARD THE END OF my fellowship came the exciting news that Gallo and Montagnier (or Montagnier and Gallo depending on whom you believed—this too was part of the excitement: the personalities and the rivalries) had discovered that AIDS was caused by a virus: HIV.

A test to screen blood for HIV was rapidly developed, and it was confirmed that all those who had AIDS carried the virus in their bodies.

As more people were tested there came the sad confirmation that the Tony Cappelluccis of the world—people with minor symptoms of oral thrush or lymph node enlargement—were also infected with the virus. And even worse, many persons with no symptoms who appeared to be in perfect health but were either gay or intravenous drug users showed evidence that the virus was sitting silently in their immune system, biding its time. Safe sex maxims and warnings about not sharing needles had come too late for many. The virus seemed to have saturated the population of urban gay men even as they became aware of its very existence.

Still, the mystery of *causation* had been solved.

Surely, the cure was just around the corner.

3

THE MAJOR jet service to Tri-Cities Airport, serving Johnson City, Kingsport and Bristol, was Piedmont (now USAir) coming in from either Pittsburgh or Charlotte. The flight path from Pittsburgh goes over the Blue Ridge chain of the Appalachian Mountains which run parallel to the eastern seaboard. As the plane descends, the densely forested mountains give way to hills and sloped pastures.

At five thousand feet, no geographical basis for a boundary between upper-east Tennessee and southwest Virginia is visible. Here and there a gaping gray basin, like the bite of some giant creature, serves as a memento of a stripmining operation. Through the window one sees finger lakes protruding into valleys then suddenly broadening into expanses of water in which sit spindle-shaped islands crowded with spruce and pine. In September, when the leaves turn color, these islands will appear as old-time four-riggers, their prows pointed downstream, their sails on fire.

Rajani and our baby boy, Steven, now two weeks old, were with my parents. I had come ahead to meet the movers, and once the house was ready, Rajani and Steven would join me.

Allen was at the airport to meet me.

"I sure hope you're back for good," he said as he hugged me. Allen is a short, stocky man in his fifties with powerful shoulders, straight blond hair parted neatly on the side, and long sideburns. Years of outdoor work have given the back of his hands a leathery look and his

34

face a perpetual tan. A Vantage cigarette was, as always, afire in his hand, and the outline of the pack showed through the pocket of his spotless blue shirt. Above the pocket, a white patch had his name spelled out in sewing machine script.

Allen owned South Roan Shell: three bays, nine pumps, one wrecker and one flatbed truck. When I was an intern and resident, Rajani and I had lived in an apartment building just up the hill from the station.

Allen's wife, Claudia, who was part Cherokee, had jet black hair, high cheekbones, dark features and green eyes. I used to think that except for her eyes, she looked like Rajani's sister. She had gone out of her way to be friendly and helpful to us.

Allen was unfailingly polite but a man of very few words; his usual facial expression was deadly serious. He could mull over his reply to something for so long—"turn it over and tickle it first," as Claudia would say—that she would often pipe in for him. Allen said Claudia got around so much that she kept running into herself.

Sometimes when I stopped at the station, Allen would ask me in his deadpan fashion, "Hey, Doc, you got any horny pills you can give old Claude?"

The station had a tiny room behind the cash register where boxes of fuel filters and oil filters were stacked to the ceiling. At a small table, Allen and Claudia made phone calls and gobbled down lunch. The wall in front of the table was plastered with business cards of auto parts dealers, body shops, insurers and others.

If I came by near closing time when the stream of customers was dying down and Claudia was totaling the receipts, Allen would beckon for me to come to the back room and offer me bourbon or moonshine. The moonshine came in picnic jugs and had a smooth, refined taste that was quite unexpected.

Someone once asked Allen how he and I had become such close friends.

"Well," he said, after pondering this forever. "Well, see, Doc used to come down to the station all'a'time to trade. And sometimes he'd ask me where do you get this, and I'd tell him. Or how do you do that, and I'd tell him. Or how do I get somewheres and I'd tell him how to git there. Pretty soon we got to be friends—shit, that's all I can say. Just one of those things I reckon."

I considered Allen my closest friend in Tennessee.

As we drove back from the airport, Allen talked about Claudia. They had parted ways while I was away in Boston. "I go bowling some nights. I'll see her there. Son, I just turn around and walk out. If I'm there before her and she sees me, the sonofabitch just walks out."

I was fond of Claudia and torn by this state of affairs. Allen said she was now driving a truck long-distance with her new boyfriend. In the divorce settlement, Allen had kept the station and the house but parted with the Cadillac and a large sum in cash.

The airport road wandered past Boone Dam and then over a stretch of Boone Lake, dipping down into a valley before rising to the crossroad three miles from the airport where the signs pointed east to Bristol, north to Kingsport (site of the Eastman-Kodak plant and the Holston ammunition depot), and south to Johnson City.

At the crossroads was a used-car dealer who had been there for years and who specialized in cars that could be hot-rodded or already were: '78 Camaros, '55 Chevys, '55 Fords, '67 Chevy trucks, old Packards, Mustangs of assorted years. Allen slowed down and we eyed the offerings. The Packard was a beauty, I said.

"It's nice," Allen said, "but looky here at the fender over the back tire. Shit, Doc, that's all bondo. He done just bondoed it and slapped paint over it."

(I had tried and given up on making Allen call me Abraham. He enjoyed saying, "What's up, Doc?" when I walked into the station and a bunch of people were milling around the cash register.)

I asked Allen whether he still had the '55 Chevy that had sat on blocks in the field behind his house for as long as I knew him. He had bought it wrecked years ago with the intention of restoring it.

"I sure do. Still have it. Soon as I finish building the garage in the back, I'm going to fix that Chevy right up."

If Claudia had been with us, she would have rolled her eyes at this point. Allen was tenacious and eventually would get the garage built and the Chevy restored. Two years ago he had shown me where the garage would go. Then, when I next visited, he showed me the foundation that he'd poured. "I bought me the brick and cement—got the cement real cheap. I got to get me the walls and roof put up next." His sense of time had been much too slow for Claudia; that had been part of their problem.

"But I got a car at home for you to drive. I got an '82 Monte Carlo and I put a '72 Oldsmobile 455 big block V8 in it. Son, that sonafabitch will fly!"

Route 36, the road to Johnson City, wound past fenced-in farmland with late summer tobacco already standing high in its corner allotment.

A mile down Route 36, a boxlike roadside sign always caught the eye. It sat on a low dolly, its arrow pointing to a hidden driveway. The periphery of the sign had Christmas-tree lights that whipped around like a dog chasing its tail. The lettering was black vinyl, upper case, back-lit in yellow. The words LIVE BAIT NIGHT were visible on the top line; the letters on the next line had been removed leaving only a ghost of CRAWLERS. At night, the sign would stand out; now, in the midday sun, the fluorescent light in the box may or may not have been on.

Further on, after a white-on-green Boat Ramp sign, another flashing box advertised SANDY'S MODELLING STUDIO—a furrowed gravel driveway ran up to a trailer with green paneling and no skirting and too small it would seem to hold the tanning booth, the private rooms and the hot tubs advertised.

"Check it out, Doc."

"You check it out!"

"Hell, I just might, I tell you what. I just might."

The number of massage parlors in and around the town seemed to wax and wane with the mood of the sheriff and the proximity of elections.

Closer in to town, subdivision signs carved out of wood and standing high off the ground began to appear: Boone Trail, Tamassee, Sequoyah Heights, Inglewood. Behind the traditional brick houses were newer houses with angled roofs and skylights and solar panels framed in dark and light wood.

Route 36 changed its name to Roan Street immediately after a sign that said "Johnson City, Sister City to Guaranda, Ecuador." Earth-moving machinery was clearing land for a Wal-Mart.

Roan Street was the town's main drag, running through it for four or five miles, eventually passing Allen's gas station on the south side of town. The car dealers on the north end of Roan jockeyed for attention from both sides of the road. Pennants fluttered from antennae, and the Day-Glo lettering on the windshields stretched for blocks.

Allen's eyes flicked from one side of the road to the other, the cars speaking to him, his eyes never lingering on the BMWs or Mercedeses, but seeking out a car, an American car of a decade or two ago, about which he could say, "That there is a fine auto-mobile! Get you one of those, Doc."

Seven traffic lights later we left Roan and headed down John Exum where we saw signs with arrows pointing to MOUNTAIN HOME VA and to EAST TENNESSEE STATE UNIVERSITY. A quarter-mile past the Mountain Home VA entrance was State of Franklin Road on which sat the Johnson City Medical Center—the Miracle Center.

We drove through the brick portals of the Mountain Home VA and I had an immediate sense of driving into an American past. The brick buildings with their baroque, French Renaissance architecture were built in 1901. I directed Allen past the cemetery, past the theater and the post office to the Engineering Building. The keys to my staff quarters were waiting for me.

Allen and I drove to the house: a massive, two-story, white colonial with a full basement and attic. It dated back to the early 1920s and had wooden floors, high ceilings, a grand staircase, fireplaces that came up to your head, claw-footed tubs, a beautiful porch complete with swing, and acres of meticulously maintained VA lawn stretching in front of it.

I couldn't wait for Rajani to see this. She had made me haul her *House & Garden* back issues from Tennessee to Boston and now back. Rajani had done well at her job and had earned the respect of her coworkers in the professional world. But she had always looked forward to creating a home. Here was a house she would delight in furnishing and decorating; its quaintness would appeal to her. It was more house than we had ever had. The rent was nominal. All maintenance and utilities were taken care of by "engineering"—those ubiquitous men in green uniforms who seemed to be all over the campus, mowing, trimming, painting, weeding. The disadvantage might be that you were living on the VA campus: your work and your home were in the same place. But this was no disadvantage for me: I could walk over at lunchtime and play with the baby, I could go back into the office after dinner and work.

"Son, you can throw one hellacious party here," Allen said, looking around. "Unless them neighbors over there object," he said pointing to where the hospital's Chief of Geriatrics, an Egyptian married to an Englishwoman, lived.

"Frankly, Allen," I said, "I don't give a damn."

JOHNSON CITY WAS NEW as far as cities went. Three railroads happened to cross in what became its downtown. First there was the East Tennessee & Virginia Railroad. And later came the East Tennessee & Western North Carolina Railroad. By 1900, the Carolina, Clinchfield & Ohio Railroad arrived.

The railroads undoubtedly had much to do with the placement of the "National Home for Volunteer Soldiers" or "Mountain Home" in Johnson City. And that in turn fueled the growth of a tiny teachers training college into East Tennessee State University.

The land that is east Tennessee is a long oval bowl that sits between the Clinch Mountain Range above, Lookout Mountain below, the Cumberland Mountains to the west and the Smoky Mountains to the east. The early settlers found this land around the Holston and Noli-chucky and Watagua rivers to be theirs for the taking. The Cherokee had been rendered weak by their battles with the Chickasaw and were unwilling to engage this new enemy at once.

Daniel Boone crisscrossed this area of land many a time on his way between Kentucky and North Carolina. It was on one such trip that he carved the words, "D. Boone cilled a bar," on a tree that stood till 1920. Boone carried news of this territory to North Carolina and attracted new settlers.

The "Wataguans" as the early settlers in east Tennessee were called, believed in the gun, in the Bible and in themselves. They were thrifty, hardworking, and eventually organized themselves as the Watagua Association in 1772.

But at the Mountain Home VA, there was another discrete popula-tion we saw: veterans from the mining towns of southwest Virginia and Kentucky. Many were descendants of the original mountain men, men who were said to represent the second wave of emigration from Britain. The plantation owners of the New World came to England looking for cheap labor because the slave trade from Africa had trickled to a stop and could not provide the hands needed for the complex and labor-intensive task of harvesting tobacco. The British Parliament, with a series of bills, consigned the outcasts and orphans of London and England's other big cities to the plantations of the New World. These unfortunates still *owed* the Crown for their perceived misdeeds. A seven-year period of indentured labor to the plantation owner seemed appropriate penance.

Many of the new immigrants died under the whip of the plantation overseers. And others escaped out into the hinterland, pushing into the hills and hollows of the Cumberland region, becoming mountain men. (This story is to be found in Harry M. Caudill's *Night Comes to the Cumberlands.*) They were joined later by men whose bonds had expired and who came searching for land of their own. To the great surprise of the Cherokee, these mountain men with their treasured Pennsylvania Dutch rifles fought with a savagery that matched that of their attackers, even taking scalps if the mood struck them. They had none of the scruples and qualms of the Puritan. They were hard-boiled, downtrodden people who were determined to give no ground.

The only thing they lacked for was women of their own kind. Many made do with Choctaw and Cherokee squaws whom they kidnapped or bought outright. It was this intermingling, particularly with the Cherokee along the North Carolina border, that brought the high cheekbones and the dark looks that I saw in Claudia and in her son, and in so many others in east Tennessee.

The Wataguans as well as their neighbors in the Cumberlands abhorred all forms of authority. In the American War of Independence, the Tennesseans readily formed a ragtag group of volunteers who marched off with Colonel John Sevier and engaged the disciplined, loyalist troops of Major Patrick Ferguson. These mountain men, who had honed their sharpshooting skills to an art from squirrel hunting, the men whom Major Ferguson had dismissed as mere "barbarians," picked off and decimated the King's troops and killed Major Ferguson.

In every war to come these mountaineers and their descendants rushed to serve. They were killed in droves in the Civil War. Many more signed up and died in World Wars I and II and the Korean War. In Vietnam, so I was told by a veterans group in Tennessee, a disproportionate number of these good-ole-boys from east Tennessee and southwest Virginia had died. If a point man was called for and no one volunteered, a descendant of the early mountaineer was likely to say, "What the hell," and step forward. His pride in his ancestry revolved around these qualities: skill with a rifle and a wiliness and cunning in the bush, even if it was the bush of southeast Asia. The license plate of every car in Tennessee announces this to be the Volunteer State, a term originating in the Mexican War when Tennessee overfilled the state's quota for volunteer troops.

When I justified to friends in the Northeast my decision to settle in the South, I found myself talking not about the natural beauty of the place, or its climate, or the mountains you could see in every direction, or the lakes, rivers and innumerable streams where you could fish. It was the *people* of east Tennessee and southwest Virginia that drew me.

The descendants of the early pioneers had evolved from fighting with the Indians and feuding with each other to become folk who, as they told you themselves, would give you the shirt off their back—if you were their friend. They were, like the men Sevier had led to battle at King's Mountain, still willing to die for their country, be it in Grenada or Kuwait, because "that was just the way we were raised." The people I met in Johnson City would, unlike those in a big city, trust a stranger almost to the point of stupidity.

If a redneck was, as V. S. Naipaul narrates in A *Turn in the South*, someone who wore a ball cap, cowboy boots, was late on his trailer payments, someone who would rather drink ten beers and eat corn bread than converse with you, someone who was prone to say "shit" and "son-of-a-bitch" just about anytime he could, someone who was satisfied being who he was and wouldn't care to change his world or try to improve his lot for no son-of-a-bitch, then the Johnson Citian was no redneck.

Instead, to describe them, I found myself borrowing a term they frequently used themselves: "good ole boys."

"Good ole boy" was the highest compliment they could pay each other. It was the highest compliment they could pay me. This is how Allen would introduce me to some friend or other of his at the station:

"What's up, Doc?" (No one found his Bugs Bunny routine as funny as he did.) "Don't mind me, Doc. I'm only joshing. I want you to meet Gus. Gus, this here is Doc. He's a good ole boy."

Certainly, rednecks still abounded. In the little hollows one could see the trailer with no underpinning and dogs all around it and children playing under it. *That* world was food stamps and ignorance and rotted teeth and rheumatic fever and a suspicion of all strangers.

But most people in the environs of Johnson City seemed to be gravitating to a gentrification of sorts. The flannel shirt, instead of hanging out over the jeans, was apt to be tucked in. The cowboy boots, if worn, were polished and smart. But a sports shirt with jeans and docksiders was also considered a desirable look.

The younger generation that hung around the malls and in the mall parking lots were moving away from the ball cap to long hair, earrings and headbands. This was happening twenty years after Woodstock when this look had become passé in the rest of the country.

Allen would not be caught dead in a baseball cap. There may have been a time when he wore one. But now, to dress neatly, to have a neat and orderly house, was extremely important to him. These were a measure of his evolution, a measure of his business and social success. Even if he could not read well or if the word "nigger" was much more natural to him than "black," he was well aware of the world outside through TV and through living in Johnson City.

And what he had become—someone who would give you the shirt off his back, someone who worked hard and aspired to a better life—gave him more pride and more satisfaction than if he had kicked back and waited on the food stamps and worked only when it suited him. Growing up, he had seen plenty of that.

Country people had let me readily into their world. They may have been ignorant about lands like India or Africa that were outside their world. They may have been shy and reluctant to talk, but once they did, they gave me complete access.

It was not difficult to qualify for the shirts off their backs.

ON THE WARDS OF THE Mountain Home VA, I had always been conscious of being a foreign physician taking care of American veterans. As an intern, only two of my fellow interns were Americans: one was a graduate of the University of Kentucky and the other from Emory. The rest of us were from Nigeria, India, Haiti, Pakistan, the Philippines and Palestine.

Now that I was back as a staff member, I noticed that the number of foreign residents and interns had decreased and we now had a few more Americans who had graduated from the offshore schools in the Caribbean.

The patients on the old-fashioned open wards of Mountain Home seemed not to see the paradox in this situation: American veterans in one of the oldest VA facilities in the country, receiving most of their care from foreigners, the newest immigrants.

The patients were mostly men in their fifties and sixties—World War II veterans. Many of the men had taken up smoking at the age of seven or eight, rolling their own in a state where tobacco was king. And though this habit had brought them their present problems—chronic bronchitis, emphysema, lung cancer—they still talked wistfully about smoking. Even when breathing was an effort, many continued to smoke. Each ward had a television room in which the smoke was so thick you could hardly see the television. A cigarette between one's fingers was as much a part of Tennessee life as squirrel hunting or country music.

Ward 2, the pulmonary ward, was where the effects of tobacco were most evident. When you looked down the ward, you saw a sea of chubby, moon faces staring at you from on top of bloated bodies—a side effect of the cortisone that the patients were taking to control their wheezing. And green mustaches—oxygen tubing—decorated almost every upper lip in the ward.

At the very end of the ward was a chronic ventilator unit where six ventilators did the work of breathing for six patients. Some of the men in the unit had been on the machine for years. Their day consisted of sunshine coming through the window, the TV being turned on, watching the shifts change, being bathed and fed, afternoon turning to evening, the night shift arriving, and finally the TV being turned off. It was sad.

At the emergency exit near Ward 2, it was common to see a cluster of men in brown-striped dressing gowns, their oxygen turned off and the green tubing now draped around them like a necklace, puffing on cigarettes and coughing. I was sympathetic to the dilemma of these men. They were hopelessly addicted to nicotine and to tobacco.

Both on the pulmonary ward and on the other wards, the men slipped comfortably into the barracks-style existence. If they were not too sick, they joined in the camaraderie that sprang up when thirty veterans shared quarters. They looked out for each other. The open wards, antiquated though they were, had this advantage: A person who was recovering from a bleeding ulcer would take it on himself to help feed the patient with a stroke in the next bed. If a patient had a seizure there were six to seven men to witness it, summon a nurse, and then describe accurately how the seizure had begun in the left hand and marched up to the left side of the face before becoming generalized. The families that visited always brought enough food for the patients in adjacent beds.

The occasional redneck, often young and belligerent, could disrupt things. Young veterans were typically Vietnam-era. Vietnam veterans were still few in number at the hospital; most of them were healthy and doing well in society, not at the age where they might be seen for problems like heart disease or lung disease. If they were in the hospital, it was often for alcohol abuse and its consequences, such as pancreatitis or cirrhosis. Or else for psychiatric problems. These patients were the most likely, particularly if there was a tussle over pain medication and drug-seeking behavior, to spit out a diatribe about, "Here I am, fought for my country. You foreigners just come here and make money off us. I'm going to write to my congressman. . . ."

The hospital staff—orderlies, clerks, nurses, technicians, telephone operators—who had to deal with foreign physicians every day, sometimes lost their patience. The problem was most often one of poor communication, coupled at times with an insensitivity on the part of the doctor. Most foreign doctors had come from countries where doctors were venerated, while nurses were not. Women who became nurses in India were frequently from poor circumstances and had an unfair reputation as women of little virtue. (Ironically, many nurses from India and the Philippines had immigrated to America to fill the tremendous inner-city nursing shortage of the sixties and seventies, a shortage that paralleled the physician shortage. Their circumstances were now considerably better than those of the people who had looked down on them. Some of the children of these nurses were medical students under my tutelage.)

A Dr. Aziz, who was my second-year resident when I was an intern, typified the problems that could arise. He was a short, fair-skinned man in his twenties. He had a bristling mustache, thick lips and spiky, black hair. He hailed from a village outside Karachi. Despite going to medical school in the city, he had retained all his country ways. He was more of a redneck than any redneck one could unearth in the backwoods of Tennessee.

He spoke with a thick guttural accent, pronouncing "system" as "shish-tem" and "thirty" as "durty" and "zero" as "jeero," putting the burden of figuring out what he was saying onto the nurses. He felt no compunction to speak more clearly to them or attempt the intonations that would help make himself understood.

When he ate in the cafeteria, it was with his mouth open and with loud smacking noises. Had he been approachable, someone might have instructed him on what was considered good manners in America.

I once attempted to talk to him about why he was getting into so many conflicts with the ward nurses. But since he was a resident and I an intern, he did not take this well. Instead he was defensive, and even patronizing, lecturing me on the best way to "deal with these people."

Aziz was full of himself, too taken with the fact that he was a doctor. His personality, both public and private, revolved around this fact. He was abhorred by the nurses because of his curt and chauvinistic way of dealing with them. And so when they saw him in the cafeteria placing the chicken bones in a pile on the table beside his plate, or hawking and spitting into a wastepaper basket as he walked down a corridor, it made them connect his boorishness to his foreignness—they were one and the same thing.

A nurse, stepping into a staff bathroom that Aziz had just emerged from, called after him and to everyone in earshot, "Did you never learn to raise the seat before you pee? Or at least wipe it clean? Were you brought up in a pig sty?"

I cringed when I heard that. I was not from his world, nor was I his keeper, but to the degree that he generated these negative impressions it affected all the rest of us foreigners. Perhaps I consciously overachieved, worked hard to make up for Aziz, did everything to earn for myself the appellation "good ole boy."

But Aziz was long gone now, a mere memory.

And I was back and looking to settle in Tennessee. A long voyage was over. I had finished all the training I wanted to go through. I was ready to apply my knowledge. When I was an orderly in the Battley Nursing Home in New Jersey (during the period when I was between medical schools), being paid by the hour for changing diapers and giving baths, it seemed as if my medical career had ended. That I would never be a doctor. And then, as I crossed each hurdle—getting back into medical school, becoming a doctor, then an internist, then an infectious diseases specialist—I had naively expected that each milestone would transform me, bring me happiness and peace of mind.

But happiness had come in another form: my infant son, Steven, and the way he added a new dimension to my relationship with Rajani. And instead of escalating goals, I wanted nothing more than to settle in one place and be a good physician. Stateless and roaming for so long, I wanted to put down roots. My son was American by virtue of his birth and his father would become a naturalized citizen that year. I wanted my son to have a permanent home, something I never had.

Johnson City was going to be my town. I felt at peace in this corner of east Tennessee. Finally, this was my own country.

4

AT MOUNTAIN HOME, veterans admitted to the hospital section came from as far as a hundred and fifty miles away; they came from small towns in east Tennessee, Kentucky, southwest Virginia, and even North Carolina.

Some patients, however, came from a hundred yards away: they were the veterans who lived on the grounds in the giant domiciliary buildings. These older veterans had nowhere else to live. Their life *was* the domiciliary.

Many dom residents had been at Mountain Home for years. Others migrated from one VA domiciliary to another. They arrived in the fall from St. Cloud, Minnesota, or Bedford, Massachusetts, or Butler, Pennsylvania, or Knoxville, Iowa. As winter set in, they moved west to Dublin, Georgia, then to Bonham, Texas, then to Prescott, Arizona, ending up in Palo Alto, California. Or else they moved south to Bay Pines, Florida—a popular winter stop. The end of winter saw them heading north, back to Des Moines, Iowa, or Portland, Oregon, or Montrose, New York.

Rajani and I came to know certain faces well; we spotted them as they wandered around the campus, moving from a park bench under the sycamore tree, to a park bench by the duck pond, to a park bench by the Memorial Theater, cigarettes in hand, each following his own routine. Some of the veterans befriended Steven. Others made moves on Mrs. Stokes, our widowed, elderly baby-sitter, as she pushed Steven in his stroller around the campus. The men could be worldly and charming.

I asked Eloise Stokes if she ever considered their propositions, if she ever entertained the thought of marrying again. Her deceased husband had been a veteran.

"Oh, I do think about it," said Eloise. "I do get lonely. But then I think, I don't *really* want some smelly old man crowding up my trailer for the rest of my days."

One day they would be there, a craggy, familiar face, sunning by our old oak tree, and the next day they would be gone. We would wonder if sickness had befallen them or had they moved. Then, the next spring, they would reappear to occupy their familiar places, to wave at us as we drove by or walked the baby.

Pneumonia or severe bronchitis in these domiciliary veterans could be a dangerous disease: If they were heavy smokers—and so many were—they often had marginal lung reserves. If they deteriorated, they wound up on a ventilator. And unlike a young person who could be quickly weaned off a ventilator, a veteran who required it became quickly dependent on it. As if the muscles of respiration that had worked overtime for so long had gone into retirement.

I WAS PRIMARILY A Mountain Home VA employee. In the unique VA jargon, I was "7/8 VA," my salary being seven-eighths of an FTEE, or full-time employee equivalent. The VA was also where we did most of our teaching of medical students and residents and where we carried out research. I had a lab and a technician and I continued research on the hamster model of pneumonia.

In my one-eighth "free time" I consulted at the adjacent Miracle Center—the new crop of students and house staff continued to refer to the Johnson City Medical Center in this way.

The Miracle Center had a much younger patient population and many more women than Mountain Home. The pace of medicine in this community hospital was very different: You could get almost any study from a CAT scan to an angiogram done the same day you requested it. The typewritten results were back on the chart by evening with another copy in your mailbox. At the VA it would take days or weeks to achieve the same thing; the radiology department at the VA was notoriously poor: "the armpit of Mountain Home," as the interns called it.

The consultations at the Miracle Center were also different from Mountain Home. Sally Jameson, a sixteen-year-old, newly diagnosed with leukemia and receiving chemotherapy, typified the Miracle Center experience. Every time she received chemotherapy, her white cell count would drop and make her very prone to infection.

One morning when I went to see her she was complaining of facial pain. I was fearful that this was mucormycosis—a life-threatening fungal infection of the sinuses that develops in just this setting. I saw nothing in her nose. But on her hard palate I could see a telltale black eschar; I scraped it, put it on a slide, added a drop of saline and placed a cover slip over it and took it to the lab. Under the microscope I could see the broad filaments of *Mucor*. In the absence of white cells, this fungus could march right through tissue and bone, straight up the orbit and into the skull. The disease was not amenable to any form of medical therapy. Only immediate and bold surgery to cut out every trace of the fungus, well past its advancing border, could help. The surgeons responded promptly and saved her life. Eventually her leukemia went into remission.

Heroic surgery was also called for with Jeff Viner, a former biker who had been a paraplegic for many years as a result of a motorcycle accident. He was admitted for unremitting fever from a monstrous bedsore over his tailbone. Since he felt no pain, he had neglected this sore for years, continued to sit directly on it, insisting on riding in his wheelchair and being in the upright position as much as he could. To be horizontal was a reminder of his paralysis. To be upright and on wheels, even if it was a wheelchair and not his Harley Sportster, was crucial to his psyche.

He had several episodes of septic shock as the bacteria from the pus pocket spilled into his bloodstream. It was only when the smell that emanated from this sore had driven all his friends and his girlfriend away that Jeff accepted the need to deal with it. By then the bedsore stretched across both buttocks; it had rotted through into his pelvis, it threatened the blood vessels within. There seemed to be no surgical way to approach this bedsore short of a hemicorporectomy—amputation of the lower half of his body below the belly button.

I had seen patients in Boston who had a hemicorporectomy. It was disorienting to enter their room: you felt as if someone was playing a trick with mirrors. Their body ended just below the ribs. If they wanted to go anywhere, the stump of their trunk was fitted into a prosthesis that resembled a candle-holder and then they were lifted into a wheelchair.

My respect for the surgeons at the Miracle Center went up several notches when they were able to pull off the operation. A team of orthopedists, neurosurgeons, urologists, plastic surgeons and general surgeons carried out the surgery. The orthopedists sawed through the upper lumbar vertebra, and the neurosurgeons tied off the spinal cord and dealt with the plexus of nerves that emerged from it. The urologists diverted the ureters from the bladder to an artificial bladder they created out of small bowel. This bladder opened high up under the right rib cage. The general surgeons diverted Jeff's feces into a colostomy that opened high under his left rib cage. At this point, the final cut was made and Jeff's pelvis, his genitals, his buttocks, his legs and feet were slid off the table into the receptacle below. The plastic surgeon brought the long skin flap around like a tailcoat and fashioned a stump for what remained of Jeff's body. The surgical result was excellent.

Psychologically, even though what had been cut off was paralyzed and nonfunctional, even though this operation had saved his life, it was a devastating blow to Jeff. Despite intensive preoperative counseling and therapy, it was weeks before Jeff began to talk and engage with the outside world.

One of the more challenging cases I saw was a cognitive puzzle—the internist's equivalent of a hemicorporectomy. Mrs. Virginia Longtree, a pleasant, retired school nurse, was referred to me for "FUOs"—fevers of unknown origin—along with mysterious phlebitis that had baffled her physicians.

She had me stumped. She was admitted repeatedly to the hospital, each time with high fever and a nasty cellulitis and phlebitis. Each time I saw her and failed to tie it all together, it increased my frustration. I began to consider exotic things like Familial Mediterranean Fever, a condition common in Sephardic Jews, even though Mrs. Longtree was Southern Baptist with Scotch-Irish roots.

But then, on her fourth admission, I confronted her: her blood cultures had made the diagnosis! I had found fecal, vaginal and tap-water bacteria—an almost impossible combination—in her bloodstream. There was no way this could happen unless she was doing something weird to herself. She broke down and admitted that she had been deliberately injecting her bath water into her limbs to produce factitious fever. An hour later, she became hostile, recanted her confession, cussed us all out and left the hospital abruptly. We never heard from her again. In retrospect she was typical of patients with factitious fever: they often have a medical background, the psychopathology that drives them is complex and bizarre, they bolt when confronted, and the prognosis for recovery is poor.

The third arena in which I saw patients was the University Physicians Group office, which I went to once a week. All the physicians employed by East Tennessee State University (ETSU) had at least a half-day a week clinic there. My half-day was on Wednesday afternoons and I rarely had more than one or two patients. The very nature of ID practice—at least in the pre-AIDS era—was that it was hospital-based.

The consultations in the clinic tended to be fairly routine, though colorful. I remember Tracy Oliver, a sweet, nineteen-year-old college cheerleader who, after Homecoming night, had forsworn sexual intercourse for the rest of her life: she had picked up gonorrhea, *Herpes simplex* and venereal warts all from a single sexual encounter. I tried to console her by pointing out that she was not pregnant and had not contracted either syphilis or HIV. At this she burst into tears; the thought of AIDS had not crossed her mind till I mentioned it.

I also remember the garrulous Reverend K from a very distant county who, when we finally got off the topic of the origin of my name and St. Thomas's incredible mission in south India, complained of "fire at the end of my pecker and honey-colored milk a-dripping out." I told him that I needed to step outside and get a special agar plate to culture for gonorrhea, at which point he said, "While you're at it, Doc, you might get one for my throat too."

"All right," I said. When I was at the door, he made to stop me once again, but I had caught on now.

"I know," I said. "One for your backside, right?"

"There you go!" said the Reverend K.

I also tested him for "bad blood" which by now, 1985, meant both syphilis and HIV. He was negative.

———

I WAS THE DE FACTO AIDS expert in Johnson City even though there was no AIDS to see. My role was limited to talking about AIDS.

The story of the young man who had come home from New York and died in Johnson City was not known outside the hospital. Even *in* the hospital, it was suppressed like a shameful memory.

But television, *Time, Newsweek* and the supermarket tabloids were giving prominent coverage to AIDS. Perhaps this was why the *Johnson City Press* decided to do a special on AIDS and asked if I would help. I agreed on the condition that I get to look at the final product and approve what they quoted me as saying. A pleasant young lady interviewed me. She borrowed slides and printed material for the article.

When the time came to go to press, I made several calls to see the proofs but kept being put off. Ultimately I was told that there was no time for me to see and approve my section.

I insisted. I pointed out that I had lent them a drawing I had made of the "AIDS iceberg," a drawing that depicted a giant iceberg marked off in sections. The tip of the iceberg, the part that floated above the water, represented AIDS patients. The submerged part represented people who had HIV infection but no symptoms or signs as yet. The iceberg illustrated dramatically that for every known AIDS case there were anywhere from twenty to one hundred other infected persons who had not surfaced; it showed that it was insane to react negatively to, say, a schoolchild with AIDS: If a schoolchild had AIDS, the odds were high that other children and teachers and parents in the school also had the virus.

I told the *Press* I would withdraw permission for them to use the drawing if they did not let me see the galleys. They relented.

When they had wanted my help they had been solicitous and had come to *my* office at *my* convenience. Now, on the eve of publication, I found myself walking around their building, trying to track down the galleys. But I was glad I did: they had quoted me as saying there were possibly a half to one million *AIDS* cases in the United States. I had said there were possibly that many *HIV infected* individuals in the country; they had confused the tip of the iceberg—AIDS—with the whole iceberg!

When I left the *Press* it was dark. I was parked a few blocks away. This was a rougher part of Johnson City. There were a cluster of bars here favored by our veterans. There were also a few flophouses where veterans stayed from time to time if they were suspended from the domiciliary for breaking curfew.

A lady in her fifties, with a surprisingly short skirt and a good-sized behind, strode past me, walking purposefully nowhere. She gave me a bold inquiring look. I realized she was a prostitute, albeit a very faded one. The occasional sexually transmitted diseases I saw in our veterans were linked to hookers who operated around this part of town.

The people inside the bars, unlike the ETSU hangouts, were drinking quietly and with great seriousness. Muted music came from the jukeboxes. A domiciliary resident whom I recognized sat alone, sipping on a beer.

I thought to myself: If the young man from New York with AIDS who came home and died was the *tip* of the iceberg, surely somewhere in this town there must be others walking around infected with the virus. Or did that young man really represent an aberration, a chip off the New York iceberg that had drifted south?

As I drove away, I decided I would be wary of the *Press*. They were interested in the prurient side of AIDS; the scientific facts merely gave them an opening into it.

Why did this surprise me and disappoint me? I suppose I had expected the town paper to reflect the nicer qualities of its citizens.

BOTH THE MOUNTAIN HOME VA and the Miracle Center were trying to enforce a new code of safety for the handling of blood and secretions. The dictum nationwide was that health care workers should treat *every* patient as potentially infected with HIV; that was the only way to be safe. But since no one had any real conviction that there was AIDS around, these recommendations were perceived as outlandish. I often saw nurses and lab technicians drawing blood without gloves and I would gently remind them. Some were sheepish—they had a hard time remembering. Others argued that they were actually in more danger drawing blood or starting an intravenous line *with* gloves; gloves, they claimed, reduced their sense of feel and made them prone to error.

Later that year I gave "Grand Rounds" on AIDS. Grand Rounds was a weekly formal lecture that combined all staff and students from Mountain Home and the Miracle Center. Public speaking always gives me butterflies, and my way of overcoming this is to prepare meticulously and rehearse with my slides in the empty auditorium.

The day of the Grand Rounds, the auditorium was full. I got off to a good start with a graphic collection of slides from my training days at Boston City Hospital—slides that showed how this latter-day plague was devastating inner cities, burdening the public hospitals, changing the face of internal medicine, changing the shape of the African continent.

But during the nuts-and-bolts section of the talk that dealt with diagnosis and treatment of the common opportunistic infections seen in AIDS, I sensed the audience drift away. I was reminded of talks I sat through in Boston when a visiting WHO expert from Africa or India talked about kala-azar or leprosy: it was difficult to relate to a disease you never saw.

I wound down the talk as quickly as I could. I had the eerie feeling that I had just made the prospect of AIDS in our little town more remote.

Afterward, a Mountain Home physician who had been at the VA decades before the medical school arrived came up and patted me on the shoulder. "Interesting, very interesting, Abe." He fixed a look of amusement and indulgence on me. "Just hope that your speech-making doesn't rustle any up."

OLIVIA SELLS, the director of the local Red Cross and a longtime Johnson City volunteer and activist, called on me one morning. Her blood bank was feeling the pinch of AIDS phobia; fewer people were donating blood. Of more concern, people were using a blood donation as an indirect way to get the AIDS test. So far, no one had turned up positive.

Olivia decided there was a need to disseminate information about AIDS outside the medical community of Johnson City. She had a videotape on AIDS, "Beyond Fear," produced by the Red Cross, which she had already shown to some civic groups. She was, she said, excited that we now had an "AIDS expert" in town, and would I go along with her to show this videotape and to answer questions?

Olivia was a tiny, energetic woman in her late fifties who drove a giant paneled station wagon, favored thin, brown cigarettes that she tossed after two drags, knew everybody in town, and believed "there is nothing you can't get done if you know who to bug." Half-moon glasses dangled from a chain around her neck and a giant daybook in a leather case was perpetually in her lap.

I wasn't totally convinced of the need for my presence: the videotape was self-explanatory and, besides, as I was being reminded all the time, there wasn't any AIDS around.

But I couldn't resist this lady and I was curious to see how the community would react. I went with Olivia to one screening of the videotape at the Red Cross center in Kingsport. The audience was the Red Cross staff, a few policemen and a group of morticians. When the tape was over I was asked whether there was any risk from body fluids from AIDS patients going down into the sewer system? I had no scientific answer for that. Danger to whom? To the rats? I think I said, "I don't think so." Another time Olivia and I showed the video at a meeting of the Unitarian church. This time there were no questions.

Olivia now talked about setting up dates for the two of us to be interviewed on a local radio show and on television. I didn't want to seem against anything as public-spirited as what she was suggesting. But a part of me wished to retain my anonymity in this small town, a difficult proposition even without radio or television or newspaper exposure. I was noncommittal.

I did confide to Olivia my curiosity about the gay population in Johnson City. What were its dimensions? How informed were they about AIDS? What were they doing in response to the epidemic?

"You know," Olivia said promptly, "we ought to show this video to the gay community. We ought to show it at the Connection. Thank you for reminding me! Why didn't I think of that?"

I wondered what I was getting myself into as I watched Olivia pick up her daybook, put on her glasses, and use my phone to dial the number of the young man who was the manager of the Connection, the town's gay bar.

I asked Olivia if she thought he might take this as an intrusion. Perhaps we should write a letter? "Why, Abraham," she said to me as she waited for him to come on the line, "I knew him when he was a little tyke! We don't need no *letter*."

"Honey, what are you doing about AIDS?" I heard her ask over the phone.

I felt for the man at the other end.

After a pause Olivia continued, "I think we have just the thing for you!" She promptly set up an evening date a week hence for the two of us to screen the video at the Connection and then have a question-and-answer session. She would drop posters by, she told him. "There," she said when she hung up. "It's all settled."

THE CONNECTION WAS the only bar of its kind for miles around. It had been written up, I was told, in gay magazines and travel guides; its very existence in a small town in the heart of the Bible Belt was extraordinary. The bar maintained a low profile. Oh, yes, this *was* the post-Stonewall-riots era, but gay men in the Tri-Cities and environs were still very much in the closet, unwilling to risk exposure.

Periodically, the *Johnson City Press* would report on some minor incident that reminded citizens of the existence of a gay community: an alleged advance by a gay man that had resulted in a retaliatory assault. Or vandalism on the car of a patron of the Connection.

These incidents, minor though they were, and the tone with which they were reported by the newspaper, served as a reminder to the gay community that this was not the Village, or Castro, but a place where Jerry Falwell's pronouncement that homosexuals would "one day be utterly annihilated and there will be a celebration in heaven" was taken as a self-evident truth.

The Connection was on West Walnut, a long street that ran east from ETSU all the way to South Roan, ending a few blocks from Allen's service station. The strip began with Poor Richard's Deli—a popular place for the hospital lunch crowd. Farther down were a record shop, two other delis, a pizza joint, and three barnlike dance halls that changed names and owners with regularity but were packed every night with the same young, boisterous ETSU crowd. It was at one of these places, then called the Sea Horse, that Rajani and I in our first year in Johnson City had learned to two-step and even mastered a line dance: the Cotton-Eyed Joe. Farther down West Walnut was a Giant's supermarket, the Firehouse Barbecue, the old courthouse and, finally, the Connection. It sat next to a taco shop and a fishing tackle store.

West Walnut was one of the "tree streets": Maple, Pine, Locust, Poplar, Chestnut, Holly and Magnolia. It was the only one of the tree streets that was semicommercial. The other tree streets had magnificent two- and three-story colonial houses shaded with giant overhanging arbors in keeping with their names. Many of these houses now sported bright pastel siding with Greek alphabets stenciled on the roof: they were fraternity houses. Other houses had what looked like multiple fire escapes and a profusion of mailboxes on the porch—they had been split into apartments. The few remaining original residents, true Johnson City Brahmins, complained about the parties, the late-night rebel yells, and the mufflerless cars that dragged from stop sign to stop sign at two in the morning when the bars closed. They bravely tried to carry on as usual.

The Connection was a warehouselike building, painted sky blue. It had no windows in the front. Entry was through an inconspicuous door at one corner. The gravel parking lot fronted West Walnut and afforded no privacy, and so patrons tended to park on the other tree streets and walk over. The residents of the tree streets were adept at distinguishing the cars of bar patrons and were willing to express their disapproval from time to time with brickbats thrown at a windshield or by slashing tires.

If the victim lodged a police complaint, this was duly reported in the newspaper along with the victim's name and car make and with a phrase such as "parked in the vicinity of the Connection" or similar wording that implied the victim was culpable. The newspaper's reporting was in general unimaginative; still, this was too deliberate an occurrence on their pages to be passed off as mere sloppiness.

I was jittery the evening I was to go to the Connection. It was one thing to be taking care of gay men in a clinic; it was a different matter altogether to go to a gay bar. Ours was a town where under the column "A.M. Authority" the newspaper printed a list of hospital admissions and discharges; it listed the realty transfers, the building permits and who among your neighbors had filed for bankruptcy. Under "Sessions Court" and "Charges Placed" it named those arrested the night before for driving under the influence, or public intoxication or arraigned or sentenced for any other reason; once a week, while you had your breakfast, you could scan all the filings for divorce in Washington, Carter and Unicoi counties. To be seen entering or leaving the Connection or to be there when the police had cause to visit was as embarrassing as posting a picture of yourself with your pants down onto a billboard on John Exum Parkway.

In Boston, when I first started to take care of gay men, their sexuality, their gayness, was very much on my mind and colored my dealings with them. I approached them delicately, wanting to be politically correct. I suppose I was fearful that I might inadvertently give offense by saying something crass, or otherwise reveal my ingrained societal homophobia, my lack of sophistication, my foreignness. As if to affirm this, many gay men when I first saw them, much like Tony Cappellucci in Boston, had an edge of militancy at the first encounter, almost as if they expected you to manifest disapproval or to reject them, as if they could see through your white coat and your politeness and lay bare your prejudice.

In retrospect, when I entered a clinic room to see a gay patient, I seemed to have been carrying a shield to protect myself and I cautiously operated from behind this shield. Was I subconsciously fearful of being tempted? Or was I fearful of being raped if I gave out the wrong signals?

This was, of course, altogether too absurd a posture, even if it was subconscious, to uphold for very long. And when I saw the same patient more than once, got to know him well, both patient and I ceased posturing.

As I got to know more gay men, I became curious about their life stories, keen to compare their stories with mine. There was an obvious parallel: Society considered them alien and much of their life was spent faking conformity; in my case my green card labeled me a "resident alien." New immigrants expend a great deal of effort trying to fit in: learning the language, losing the accent, picking up the rituals of Monday Night Football and Happy Hour. Gay men, in order to avoid conflict, had also become experts at blending in, camouflaging themselves, but at a great cost to their spirit. By contrast, my adaptation had been voluntary, even joyful: from the time I was born I lacked a country I could speak of as home. My survival had depended on a chameleon-like adaptability, taking on the rituals of the place I found myself to be in: Africa, India, Boston, Johnson City. I felt as if I was always reinventing myself, discovering who I was. My latest reincarnation, here in Johnson City, was my happiest so far.

Just when many gay men had decided to give up the camouflage, to come out of the closet, AIDS had arrived on the scene, resurrecting the metaphors of shame and guilt, adding greater complexity to the process of coming out. Most gay men whom I got to know in the clinic were forthcoming with their stories, as eager to tell them as I was to listen.

In the debate on whether homosexuality was a learned behavior or present at birth—nurture versus nature—I favored the latter. Nature over nurture. The recent (much ballyhooed finding) of a "gene" or at least a genetic link for homosexual behavior is consistent with the stories I've heard: So many gay men have told me how from the moment they were aware of their sexuality, they knew it was directed at men, not women. James, a person with AIDS, a man possessed of great dignity, helped me understand this.

"One of my first memories is when I was three or four. My oldest brother was a jock and when he came back from football practice, he would take off his jock strap and fling it under the bed. And while he was in the shower, I would crawl under the bed, not knowing what I was doing or why, but drawn to that jock strap. I would pick it up, find it exciting, sniff it. I was not aware of sex—that wasn't a word that had even been spoken to me. But I knew what I felt and I also knew by instinct that what I was feeling was forbidden. Later, as I grew up, I always hung around my mother and sisters. Not because I was a sissy—which I was—but because I knew I was terribly attracted to men. It was difficult being around them when I was so drawn to them. I was terrified of gym class because I thought I might get aroused and give myself away. So I stayed with the girls.

"My brothers in their preteens were terribly attracted to the girls who were our neighbors. But they were at the age when to be around the girls made them mute and flustered. So they hung around each other and did boy things, and played down their attraction. Well, I was the same way with men. And to overcome my attraction I conducted myself as a good southern girl until I left home."

"Then what happened?"

At this point James flashed me a marvelous, coquettish smile and batted his eyelids: "Why then I became a southern queen!"

I understood this awakening of sexuality, this pretrembling of a carnal life in a child. I have a memory as a five-year-old of taking a bath and imagining my kindergarten teacher taking a bath with me. I knew nothing about what this vision meant; it seemed purely cerebral and lacking a physical aspect to it. But I could imagine her sitting opposite me in the bathtub; I imagined putting soap on her body—a body whose parts I could not picture. And I knew, just as James knew, that this image was intensely private, not one that I should convey to my mother. It seemed my fantasy life as a child—the sexual part anyway—began with that building block of a woman; it was added to, it became more refined and deliberate, but the gender was firmly established before I had words for it.

I TOLD RAJANI where I was going that evening. She was taken aback. "This is above and beyond the call of duty, isn't it?" I had to agree. She went on: "This is a small town. It's dangerous."

"But you know why I'm going."

"But will anyone else if they see you there? You can easily get labeled. It's bad enough that it is a small town; we are a very visible Indian community and it's tough to miss someone like you."

"It's too late. I can't let Olivia down."

Had Rajani reacted differently, seen this as no big deal, a part of the job, I would have felt better. Her concern and worry added to my nervousness.

My only visit to a gay bar in Boston was by complete accident. Some friends were visiting Boston from Tennessee and we had gone to a restaurant for dinner and then to a couple of bars. There were four men and two women in our party. We were more than a little high and quite boisterous as we walked near the Westin Hotel and close to the Boston Library.

We passed a disco that had always been shuttered when I went by in the daytime. Now there was wonderful music coming from it, music that made me want to dance.

On impulse—it was my idea, as my friends have never ceased to remind me—we decided to go in. The two men at the door who were collecting cover charges appeared a bit flustered by our group. They hesitated. When we pushed the six-dollars-apiece cover charge into their hands they let us in.

Inside, the music shook the floor. Psychedelic lighting made it feel as if we had stepped onto another planet. Rajani was pregnant with Steven and not inclined to dance. I grabbed my friend Madhu's hand and led her to the dance floor. The rest of our group found a table near the bar.

We were dancing for several minutes. I remember I was an unin-hibited dancing machine, fueled on alcohol, flailing my arms and throwing my whole body into the music.

Madhu leaned over and yelled in my ear over the music, "Abe, this is a gay bar!"

"What?"

"I'm telling you! Look around!"

Sure enough, all the couples on the dance floor were men.

We sidled off the floor, trying to be as inconspicuous as we could, and we joined the rest of our party. They were totally unaware of what Madhu and I had discovered. When we told them, it was their turn to look around and notice the couples on the dance floor.

We left as discreetly as we could. It had been wonderful in the disco. But we were embarrassed by our mistake. And once we knew it was a gay bar, we felt that we might be annoying the regulars with our presence. Some years later, it became the in thing for heterosexuals to go to gay bars to dance. It was cool. But at the time we had no idea how we were supposed to act.

OUR VIDEOTAPE was to be shown at eight thirty in the evening. Olivia had said she would meet me at the Connection by eight ten.

I drove down West Walnut and passed the Connection. There was a beige Camaro SS, early 1970s vintage and nicely restored with chrome oversize wheels and a black interior, parked outside. I drove past and circled the block.

On my second go-round, there was still no sign of Olivia and I did not have the courage to park and go in alone. I pulled up across the street and sat in the car, looking at my watch. I was early.

I thought the occupants of the cars driving by were scrutinizing me. I stared straight ahead. My palms were sweating and I needed to pee, though I had gone just before I left home. Did every gay man go through what I was going through in order to work up the courage to walk into the Connection? What a price to pay.

When I saw a police car approach from the other direction and study me carefully, I lost my nerve and drove away. I took a long loop before heading back. My watch now showed exactly 8:10.

Olivia's station wagon was nowhere in sight. I was driving away when

I saw her in the distance heading toward me. I made a quick U-turn and tucked in behind her. She pulled up to the front of the building, waited for me to park next to her, and gave me a hearty wave. Seeing her and the way she conducted herself made me feel ashamed. "Damn it, Abe," I said to myself, "you need her attitude. So *what* if someone sees you? It's their problem." Despite these brave words, I was still very nervous when I stepped into the Connection.

We entered a large rectangular room. A fake oak bar ran down one side of the room. A dance floor occupied the center and Formica-top tables with padded red chairs were scattered all around. The place was ill-lit and musty.

Three men sat at the bar. The bartender came around from behind the counter and greeted us; he was Olivia's contact. He was a handsome, brown-haired man with a mustache. He looked like a cowboy in his denim shirt and tight jeans. That whole evening he struck me as the one person most at ease, most comfortable in this setting.

I recognized one of the men sitting at the bar. He used to work behind the counter at a 7-Eleven near my old apartment. He had curly blond hair and chubby cheeks. The only reason he stayed in my mind was that he was often surly and distracted when he worked—an unusual trait for Tennessee. He was also obese, a trait that had characterized all the 7-Eleven employees in that particular store, as if they were all from the same stock.

Now he was dressed in short-shorts, sandals and a tank top. And he had applied eye shadow and lipstick. It was an incongruous, almost pathetic image: He was not in drag—all he had done was apply the lipstick and mascara. But what struck me most was how nervous and uncomfortable he looked. My own angst seemed to pale in comparison to the tension written on his face. A cigarette went back and forth from his lips to the ashtray with scarcely a pause and his foot was nervously hammering out a measure on the bar rail. It was obvious from the way he handled his glass that he was either drunk or quickly getting there.

For interior decoration, the Connection had a smattering of travel posters placed haphazardly on the wall. It was as if the owners had provided the barest trappings of a club, and even that without much conviction.

A tiny stage stood at one end of the room, near the exit, looking like the best efforts of a church preschool. The curtains were drawn.

A flyer on the wall announced our presence and the screening of the video. Next to it was a larger notice announcing the times of the "show" for that night; "Sabra," "Chanel" and "Ursula" were to be the artistes. For a fleeting moment I wondered if the 7-Eleven man might be one of the performers.

The owner-cum-manager directed us to a windowless back room separated from the bar by a cloth curtain. We set up the video player that Olivia had brought. Problems connecting it to the TV occupied us for a good while.

Half an hour later, we were ready to roll. There must have been about fifteen people in the room by then. Olivia asked if we should start or wait a little longer.

"Might as well start," said Trevor, a short black man with a baby face. Trevor was effeminate and everything he said seemed to be an attempt to be flippant. His humor was of a self-mocking variety. "Oh, let's start. These Tennessee queens don't even wake up till midnight. And it takes them another hour to get dressed. We'd be waiting all night if we waited for them."

And so, at Trevor's prompting, we started.

People stuck their head into the room during the showing, and by the end of the tape, which was almost an hour long, the audience had grown to twenty or more. I sensed that there were others outside, listening in.

When the lights went up, an awkward silence prevailed. Trevor was nudging his companion, a white boy of similar build and youthful appearance. It would be difficult not to have noticed him—he must have slipped in when the lights went down. Trevor loudly introduced him to me as "the one and only Raleigh," and Raleigh inclined his head in acknowledgment. Raleigh was a mere wisp of a boy, looking no older than thirteen. I could see vivid, purple scar tissue above his right wrist—it was not a matter of clinical astuteness; Raleigh seemed to be flashing the scar. In the lighting of the Connection I could not tell if his hair was blond or red. The hair was gelled up into a cross between a mohawk and a pompadour. He was extremely thin and wore tight-fitting jeans with black boots and a silky chemise. Thick foundation cream had formed ridges over a cluster of pimples on his cheek and chin.

Trevor and Raleigh now whispered to each other and giggled as if they were in homeroom and sharing a desk, as if I was the substitute teacher whose attention they were trying to attract, but the only way they knew to do it was to act silly. Indeed, I found it difficult to take my eyes off this black and white pair. I didn't get the impression they were a couple; they were more like coconspirators.

At long last, a question was asked. The questioner was tall, with dark hair and an athletic build. Unlike Trevor or Raleigh, there was nothing about him that might have led me to think he was gay. He had a serious, intellectual air. Later, when Olivia and I discussed him, not knowing his name, we referred to him as "the D.A." He had watched the video quietly, bringing his own chair in from the bar to be in front of the television.

The D.A. was articulate and well informed. His speaking seemed to make Trevor temporarily give up his comic routine. I sensed that the other men in the room were pleased that the D.A. was willing to ask questions. They were anxious to hear my responses but unwilling to speak up.

From a general commiseration about the inadequate Reagan response, the prospects for a vaccine, the D.A. became more specific. Did I know the risks ("percentage-wise") for specific acts such as deep kissing or fellatio? When I extended my answer to cover "rimming," "fisting," "water sports," Trevor rolled his eyes and squirmed in the chair and acted sheepish. As if I had singled him out with these words.

The D.A. asked more questions: What about poppers? And could you get AIDS from mosquitoes?

A thin young man with blond hair, a low brow and green eyes, cleared his throat and then spoke softly: "What are *our* chances for getting AIDS here in Johnson City?" I had noticed him when he came into the room because he made his way directly to the corner and crouched down there, distancing himself from everyone else in the room. He wore a batik T-shirt and jeans. He was speaking from his crouched position, his arms hugging his knees. He was nervous, not accustomed to debate in the manner of the D.A.

"If you practice safe sex, it should be extremely low."

"Well, what if you don't—or you haven't."

Trevor giggled and nudged Raleigh, who gave a little yelp. This was good for a few laughs.

The questioner flashed Raleigh and Trevor a look of exasperation. He resented having to ask this question in front of everyone else.

"If you don't practice safe sex, then it depends on how many of your partners happen to be carrying the virus. It's a bit like Russian roulette. In a place like New York or San Francisco, most of the chambers will have bullets in them. In Johnson City . . . I don't know."

"I mean," the young man continued, ". . . let's say that you have been careful. You trusted someone. But come to find out he was carrying on with everyone. . . . And the only person you were with was him."

"And is he HIV positive?" I asked.

"Well, I don't know, see. He's left to Atlanta and all I know . . . I heard he was sick. In fact, I think he's dead."

All of a sudden, from an abstract discussion, the virus was right in our midst. The effect on Trevor and Raleigh was as if someone had poured a bucket of cold water on their heads. For a fleeting moment I glimpsed the faces behind the masks; I saw two terrified boys.

Clearly, the young man who asked me the question had not been tested; otherwise he would not have to ask.

"It depends on your partner and whether he had the virus. And how long you were together, what you did together, and so on. . . . The blood test is the *only* way to tell," I said.

I looked around. There was an eerie silence in the room. Outside we could hear the clink of bottles and furniture being dragged about. I suddenly realized that none of the men in the room had been tested! I had no way to be sure of this, but I *was* sure. Incredibly, at a time when gay men in Boston and New York and other big cities had gone to be tested in droves, these gay men in Johnson City had not. Perhaps testing was perceived as cumbersome, involving red tape. Perhaps they felt that there was no place they could be tested and be assured of confidentiality.

I now saw the room in a different light. There were higher stakes involved with this screening of the video than in any other place it had been shown. *Everyone* here was at risk for HIV infection, if he didn't have it already. *Every* life here hung on the result of a blood test, a test they had not as yet taken. Trevor manifested his anxiety with his running commentary and persistent attempts at humor. Raleigh shook his bangles and feigned indifference. The D.A. was intellectually trying to determine his odds, "percentage-wise." And the young man with the batik shirt was angry, hoping that despite the odds, despite his sick friend, he had not been infected.

When Olivia and I emerged from the back room, all the bar stools were occupied as were most of the tables; people were pouring into the bar from outside. The Connection was hazy with cigarette smoke and the rumble of seventy or so people conversing. I had relaxed during the screening of the video. Now my apprehension about who would see me here started anew. And if I did see someone from the VA or the Miracle Center, would I get a chance to explain what I was doing here? "Relax, Abe," I said to myself. "Anyone you know will be just as worried about you spotting *them* here."

A woman walked out of the rest room and proceeded to greet those at the bar. Trevor, the black youth, kissed her loudly on both cheeks and complimented her on her dress. Raleigh looked at her with what I thought was a touch of jealousy. She wore a shoulderless evening gown and white gloves. The gown glittered with sequins. Her brown hair was down to her shoulders. The hair over her forehead had been sprayed to stand straight up. She was exquisite. Trevor introduced her. "Doc, I want you to meet _____." The name I cannot recall because I was so blown away by her beauty.

"Pleased I'm sure," she said and held out her hand. Part of her allure, part of the reason my eye lingered on her, was the hint in her appearance that she was a male: the shoulders were pointed and the collarbones a tad prominent. There was a firmness in the jaw line and cheekbones that came through despite her rouge. Her elaborate eye makeup and her thespian manner gave her a larger than life quality. This was neither a man in drag, nor was it a woman. It was a spectacle, an east Tennessee queen.

Her effect on me was extraordinary: I became speechless. I looked at her with a petrified expression and she in turn cast an experienced eye over me, relishing and clearly quite used to this reaction. After she walked away, I wished I had heard her say more. I was curious about the person behind the costume.

But I was too late. The music that had been held down for our meeting, now blasted forth. There was an exodus to the dance floor. The building was rocking to the tune of "Fame: I'm going to live forever."

Olivia mouthed her goodbyes to the owner of the bar—she had another social function she had to make an appearance at. "Go ahead and stay for a while, Abraham," she said to me, as if she was reading my mind. "You may only get one chance to see this." She gave me a hug of encouragement and left.

Walking into the Connection had been the hardest part for me; now that I was here I was determined not to dash right out. I wanted to survey the land.

I found a corner table that had been vacated in the rush to the dance floor and I sat down, sliding the clutter of beer bottles to one side to make room for my elbows. The lighting had changed to black lights; a psychedelic globe reflected squares onto the dance floor. The walls of the place had simply disappeared.

Under the spotlights that illuminated the bar, there were a few scrubbed faces that I could see clearly, their expressions magnified. Their eyes roved around, looking at the dancers, swiveling to look every time the front door opened, glancing at the men who, drink in hand, circled the perimeter of the club, peering into the darkness to where I sat.

I had thought of the Connection as a sanctuary for the gay men of east Tennessee, a haven where they could come and let their hair down, put their arms around each other and enjoy complete acceptance and camaraderie. But the atmosphere of the club had none of this. Yes, this was a place where a gay person could give up the pretense of being straight, but it was hardly a *natural* setting. The garish lighting, the loud music, the people coursing around the room as if at the county fair, the peering over each other's heads, the scanning, the searching as if looking for someone you knew—it all seemed a bit desperate, anything but relaxed.

I watched the face of the 7-Eleven clerk as he downed a shot glass—he was now piss-drunk, as Allen would say. It struck me that he had escaped a certain kind of scrutiny by coming into the Connection; but now that he was here, was he really himself? Was this—the short-shorts, the eye shadow, the lipstick—who he really was? Was he not exposed to a different and perhaps more intense and competitive kind of scrutiny in here? I felt I could read his uncertainty and the thoughts that crossed his mind: *Am I dressed right? Does my face look all right? Will someone want to meet me? How do I get the approval of that good-looking gang who were carrying on in loud voices and laughing near the other end of the bar before the music began? Do I have the courage to talk to someone?* I had yet to see anyone converse with him. Meanwhile he kept downing shots, as if he had not yet found the threshold dose of alcohol to produce the disinhibition he needed.

A strobe light came on. All I could see were the truncated movements of limbs cogwheeling to the music, seventy-odd incandescent faces in ecstasy. The dancers were not dancing as couples as much as they were dancing en masse. Raleigh stood out. He was somehow the center of attention: It was his mascara that seemed to fluoresce, it was his hair that appeared on fire, and it was the bangles on his wrists held high over his head that flashed over the dancers. I looked to see if I could spot the scars running across his wrists again.

When I turned back to the bar, the 7-Eleven clerk was missing! Had he left? No, I spotted him making his way to the dance floor. He was unsteady and not well coordinated, but the group made room for him, let him in the circle and he began to shake and twist his body. For the first time that evening I saw his face wear a smile, saw it devoid of tension. Every face on the dance floor was relaxed, happy, devoid of artifice, the primitive beat of the music uniting them, making them as one. Dance was the great healer here; it was only on the dance floor that the utopian vision I had of the Connection as sanctuary came close to being true.

I left as soon as the first song-set wound down and people began to return to their tables. The night air felt cool, and only after coming out did I realize how thick the tobacco smoke had been within. Despite the mass of dancers in the bar, my car was one of just a few in the parking lot. I got in quickly and drove away.

Back home, the household was fast asleep. When I removed my jacket and brought it to my nose, it reeked of tobacco. I poured myself a stiff Scotch and stepped out onto the porch. I felt as if I had returned from a dangerous mission and had miraculously emerged unscathed.

OUR VISIT TO THE BAR resulted in a flurry of testing by the men I spoke to as well as others—partners perhaps. The young man with the batik T-shirt who had been concerned about a sick lover did not show up. Neither did Raleigh.

To my utter amazement, not one of the patrons of the Connection who obtained the test was infected with the virus!

Yet, I was certain that if this had been a random sample of gay men from a gay bar in Boston's Fenway district, or San Francisco's Castro district in the same year, 1986, a significant percentage of them—20 to 80 percent?—would be infected with the virus.

This was the tragic lesson learned when the blood test for HIV became widely available: many *urban* gay men and *urban* intravenous drug users, though quite asymptomatic, were already infected with HIV.

But not so in rural Tennessee.

Based on my small sample, the disease had not reached our gay population. And gay men were the only "high-risk" group in town, since we had almost no intravenous drug use. Clearly, I was in a unique situation. Every effort I made with gay men to disseminate information on safe sex would be worthwhile. I *had* to make sure that every gay man heard the message about safe sex, that they understood every nuance of it, that they bought into it as a way to keep themselves alive.

Of the half-million people in the country with HIV, the big reservoir of infection was in urban gay men and intravenous drug users. This was the pool from which others, my townsfolk eventually, would get infected. Data from San Francisco, New York and Vancouver suggested that even after the blood test was available, uninfected gay men were contracting the virus at rates of 5 to 20 percent per year!

After my visit to the Connection, I redoubled my health education and public speaking efforts. I felt a sense of urgency that I had lacked before. I covered at some time all the Tri-Cities and ranged up into Virginia and Kentucky. I spoke to Rotary groups, to Lions Clubs, to PTAs, to physicians at their hospital's weekly "Grand Rounds." Every opportunity to appear in print, I took.

Olivia and I appeared on a radio show. And then on a TV show—the kind of community-based talk show where the furniture was dusty and of a tasteless mustard color and where the moderator spoke in a monotone and read her questions from a clipboard. The camera often zoomed in on the wrong person—and the moderator, after nodding sagely, often repeated the same question. The tape aired on TV at the most unlikely times, such as 5 A.M. on Sunday. My message everywhere I spoke was about the "window of opportunity": safe sex education in our towns *could* keep AIDS out. Everywhere I spoke, I kept the image of the young men I had seen in the Connection in my mind. I hoped that they were listening, that in the course of flipping channels or scanning a newspaper they saw the message. I hoped their parents or siblings who might know they were gay would bring my message to their attention.

MOST STRAIGHT PEOPLE I talked to in town knew nothing about the gay community beyond the fact that they had their own bar. As a community, gays seemed to be invisible. Most gay men were still in the closet, and the community for its part pretended they did not exist. A scandal about sex between men in an ETSU library had occupied the press for a while and then died.

From time to time, scattered other incidents kept bringing awareness of a gay community back to heterosexual consciousness. A young man from a small town in Virginia drove down with a friend to the Connection in Johnson City. There he met a student from ETSU. They had met in the bar once before. They left the Connection in one car and drove to an ETSU parking lot near the football field. Later, the beam of a campus policeman's flashlight surprised them in a sexual act. They were taken to the ETSU security office where they signed a confession, were sternly warned and then released.

A few days later, to their great surprise—and contrary to what they had been led to expect from the campus police—they were served notice of their arrest. This episode is recounted in some detail by Neil Miller in *In Search of Gay America*. Miller interviewed the two young men and devoted 20 pages of his 300-page book to the happenings in east Tennessee.

Courtesy of Mr. Crockett, the district attorney, the two men were charged under Tennessee's little-known crimes against nature law:

"Crimes against nature, either with mankind or any beast, are punishable by imprisonment in the penitentiary not less than five years, not more than fifteen." Included were all acts that did not result in procreation: cunnilingus, fellatio, and anal intercourse.

It did not matter at all to David Crockett that cities like Nashville and Memphis routinely dismissed such cases as a misdemeanor; Johnson City was not Sodom or Gomorrah. The D.A. was going to make this abundantly clear by prosecuting this as a felony.

The ACLU and the National Gay and Lesbian Task Force rushed to get involved. But the two young men were terrified by the prospect of more publicity; they were unwilling to make theirs a test case by pleading innocent. Instead, they pleaded no-contest and were sentenced to five years imprisonment. The young men's defense attorney was quoted as saying it was "the most disgusting thing I have ever seen . . . a guy has sex with a fourteen-year-old girl and gets a lesser sentence." (Mercifully, when the sentence was appealed the two young men were put on probation.)

Sometime later, a dramatic murder-robbery in Rotary Park brought publicity to an area downtown that had evolved into the preferred place to cruise. The "block"—in fact, a two- or three-block area—was centered around what was then called the Mid-Town Inn.

The Mid-Town Inn had cheap rooms, hourly rates and the bonus of a closed-circuit blue movie channel. The motel attracted out-of-town salesmen looking for a little action, or locals in need of a place for a few hours. Sporadic arrests of female prostitutes near the Mid-Town Inn suggested that the action there was both gay and heterosexual. A lounge attached to the motel, despite numerous changes in name and ownership and brief periods of near respectability, was a place where the women had a reputation for being older, divorced or widowed and hot to trot. Men in search of these qualities in a woman flocked there.

The cruising round the block in cars, however, involved only gay men. Cars would drive up Roan Street, past the old Johnson City Medical Center (now a nursing home), turn on Millard where the Mid-Town Inn sat, turn on Boone, then turn on Fairview and be back on Roan.

Of course, to circle the block so obviously was to give it away. Typically, then, the players would construct a complex loop, coming up through back streets like Montgomery or Davis to pop up behind the Mid-Town Inn where a few doctors' offices—those that had not made the move to the Professional Building by the new hospital—and a few lawyers' offices, and a block of residential houses could mean one had come from any of those buildings. Then one could cut straight across Roan and head out to the Country Club, drive south for a detour of two or three miles before coming up Roan again.

Eventually one car would tuck in behind the other as it looped in and out of the back streets, the Mid-Town Inn still the heart of this fandango on wheels. Soon, there was no mistaking the intention of either party. Both cars would pull into the parking lot of White's supermarket, three blocks down the hill from the Mid-Town Inn and opposite the public library and the telephone company. The cars would come together, so that driver's-side window of one car pulled up alongside driver's-side window of the other.

Now the first words were spoken—"Are you a cop?" "No. Are you?" "No." This prerequisite exchange supposedly had the magic quality of excluding a cop who it was said could not lie and still make an arrest. From there it was off in one or two cars to someone's house—the ideal scenario—or to a parking lot, or to the park.

And it was in the Rotary Park, after just such an encounter, that a chicken hawk had lost his life in a robbery-murder by the young man he had picked up. The inquiry and the trial made the news, and then this too died.

The town returned to issues such as the price of tobacco, the Vols' winning streak, a flash flood in Unicoi and other items of news that were, be they good or bad, in their own way reassuring. The town was aware of homosexuals and AIDS, but by God, the less one thought about or discussed these things, the better.

5

ON A TUESDAY EVENING in the fall of 1986, a year after my return to Johnson City, I received a call on my answering service. "Tell him that Essie Vines from Virginia, what works in the laboratory, needs to talk to him. He'll know who I mean."

Essie picked up on the first ring. I thought I had been dialing a hospital number, but she was at home.

Yes, Essie, said. She was fine and she still worked in the little hospital in Virginia where I used to moonlight as a resident.

I told her it was a coincidence that she should call me, because she had been on my mind. I was scheduled to give a talk—an AIDS talk—in a couple of days in Norton, Virginia, only a few miles from the hospital where she worked and I had been thinking of looking her and the old gang up.

I asked about some of the people I had known: J.D. from security, Clara, the nursing supervisor. They were fine, Essie said, just fine. "I'll tell them you asked after them."

Essie was pronouncing every syllable clearly, as if only a conscious effort could keep her words from running into each other.

"What's up, Essie?"

She said she had heard that I was back in Johnson City. That I had specialized in infectious diseases. "That's how come I'm calling you. I'm all to pieces about my brother, Gordon. He just come home after living in Florida for many years. I'll be honest with you. I won't beat around the bush. Gordon has the HIV factor."

She paused here. When I said nothing, she went on:

"He's been sick a long time—I mean a long time—but he's very sick tonight." Here I heard her take a deep breath. "Would you be willing to see him?"

I told her to come right away. "Is Gordon a veteran?"

"No." Again the measured, clipped speech as if preparing for a blow: "No, he is not a veteran. Is that a problem?"

"Not at all. I was trying to decide which hospital to meet you at. Bring him to the Johnson City Medical Center—you know how to get there? The hospital next to the Mountain Home VA? Come to the emergency room and I'll meet you there."

My strongest memory of Essie was of her laughter: If you made her laugh it was as if you released the catch of a wound-up music box and a peal of notes would trill out in a crescendo fashion. She sang in the choir and had done so for years. Her broad bosom suggested that God had blessed her with not just beautiful vocal cords but lungs to match. Essie was one of those who had broadened my palate with her home-cooked meals when I had moonlighted up in Virginia.

Her work as a lab technician meant much more than a paycheck every month; it defined her and she took it very seriously. The hospital was an extension of her home. When she came to draw blood from a child in the emergency room with severe asthma, it was as if it was her child. I had seen her do her part in a Code Blue and then later brush away tears and stay upset for a long time if the Code was unsuccessful.

If there was a husband in her life, I had never heard him mentioned. Outside the hospital, Essie's life had revolved around her children and her church. She lived a few miles outside the town of Blackwood, Virginia.

I remembered her telling me once about a baby brother who after high school had left their little town for Atlanta. And then he had vanished from the face of the earth. I remembered how the tears rushed to her eyes as she told me this. Had this same brother reappeared?

RAJANI, NOW PREGNANT with our second son, was in the kitchen. I went to tell her I would be going to the hospital.

"Guess what?" I said. "My first AIDS case in Tennessee is on its way!"

She shuddered as if remembering something. Then as she returned silently to feeding Steven in his high chair, her expression changed from concern and anxiety to what I chose, at that time, to think of as inscrutability. I realize now that Rajani was scarcely inscrutable at this moment in our marriage—she was merely frightened, as any wife or mother would be, as so many were in the days when we understood so little about AIDS. For my sake, she swallowed her fear, said nothing when she realized that the sound in my voice was excitement, exhilaration. As if I had been looking forward to this. I wonder now if she was more fearful of the disease or her husband's excited reaction to its latest appearance in our lives.

In Boston, when I saw Tony Cappellucci, my first patient with probable AIDS, Rajani and I had talked about my risk—our risk. Nobody at that time knew for sure what caused the disease or exactly how it was spread. It was threatening to both of us, but I felt I had no choice in the matter and Rajani went along. I was a doctor, not without my own sense of self-importance. I was even proud that my chosen specialty, infectious diseases, found itself in the front ranks of the AIDS battle.

Later, when I had my first needlestick—a true battle wound—Rajani and I had gone the abstinence and condom route until it was clear that two successive HIV tests some months apart were negative. I was stoic and Rajani seemed to realize that I expected the same from her. It took a long time for me to realize how much fear she lived with; how it, indeed, filled her days while I was off playing hero. In those days, in this country, the fear of AIDS was palpable. I gave great thought to protecting AIDS and HIV patients from the anger of so-called healthy citizens; I empathized with victims of this disease. But I did not yet see how the disease would enter and change my life and my family's. And so that night I chose to think of Rajani as inscrutable and allowed her to face her fear in silence.

I had always believed that doctoring was a hazardous profession, even if in the immediate pre-AIDS era the risks had diminished. Septicemia, tuberculosis and yellow fever had, in the preantibiotic era and prevaccine era, taken the life of many a physician and nurse. My physician-uncle in India told me how, as a young doctor, he had gone more than once into a hushed house where an entire household had bolted, abandoning their loved one because of smallpox. The unfortunate patient, covered with pustules, lay comatose on a mat on the floor, the rice and barley water that had been left beside him now crawling with ants. My uncle had hired a ricksha, loaded the patient on it and taken him to the communicable disease hospital. In the days to come, my uncle waited for the pustules to appear on his own skin, for the rigors and chills to commence. He had been lucky.

American medicine of the 1970s and 1980s was different. The new icons included the Porsche Targa, not designed for house calls. Personal risk had all but disappeared. Professional liability had taken its place. Evening clinics were anathema. In its place were doc-in-the-box centers, emergency rooms, answering services, beepers, cross-coverage and cellular phones. Money was the obvious and very visible reward for being a physician. Lifestyle was a key factor in the decision to become a doctor and the choice of specialties. Surgery, ENT, ophthalmology, OB-GYN—all specialties with *procedures* that you could bill for—were preferable to the cognitive specialties. Doctors were reimbursed generously for doing, but not for thinking.

A few days before Essie's call, I had been asked to see a patient in the intensive care unit at the Johnson City Medical Center. He had been there for weeks and had high, spiking fevers. It took me an hour to wade through the chart and retrieve those portions of it that had been thinned and tucked away in the back of the nurses' station.

I established the sequence of events, the cascade of catastrophes, that had led to the present state: chest surgery for a malignancy, then an infected surgical wound, then renal failure, then respiratory failure, then a blood clot to the lung. And meanwhile an infected urinary tract from a bladder catheter, and an infected bloodstream due to an intravenous needle site from which pus was emerging. I examined the patient carefully and found evidence of disseminated yeast infection: a telltale white splotch in the retina. I removed the intravenous line, cut its tip off and sent it to the lab for culturing. I sought out the family in the waiting room and inquired about prior allergies to antibiotics, skin tests for tuberculosis, and other antecedent disease.

I went to the radiology department and lined up all the chest x-rays and tried to figure out if the streak in the right lung was pneumonia or was it a blood clot? Was it recent or had it been there right after surgery? I went down to the microbiology lab and reviewed all the culture reports of every specimen that had been sent down there on this patient. I made fresh smears of the sputum and urine on glass slides and stained it with Gram's stain and examined it under the microscope. I found more yeast: deep blue, balloon-shaped structures with buds coming off them.

Finally I went back to the chart and made my recommendations, which included a change of antibiotics and the addition of Amphotericin B. Amphotericin B—"Amphoterrible"—was a toxic and difficult to use agent needed to treat disseminated yeast infection. It had to be administered carefully after premedicating the patient with antihistamines and Tylenol so as to offset the chills and fever it could produce. I left detailed, step-by-step orders for its use, including a test dose following which the nurse was to measure blood pressure and observe for the onset of shock.

I suggested stopping some medications that confounded the situation and that encouraged the growth of yeast. I made recommendations for special blood cultures to try to recover the yeast from the bloodstream. Finally, I recommended a tracheostomy because it appeared the patient would be on the ventilator for a long while. I wrote all the orders on the chart with instructions on the bottom to "O.K. these orders with Dr. _____."

By the time I was done I had spent two hours on the case. My office would bill the patient for an ICU consultation: the charge was somewhere in the $150 range. If the patient was indigent or on Medicaid we would see none or little of the fee. Our University Practice Group had a large overhead, and as a result, if the patient paid, I might ultimately see between $30 to $50 for my work.

The surgeon meanwhile had telephoned in, approved my recommendations and told his chief resident to do the tracheostomy—a twenty-minute procedure—for which the surgeon would bill $500 or more. This without leaving his house. The original chest surgery had already generated thousands of dollars.

None of these discrepancies in income were lost on the medical students, many of whom were already in debt and looking to pay back huge loans and begin to reap the rewards of their years in school. Specialties with operative *procedures* were the way to go.

Even if ID made no money, even if it was the pariah of specialties by virtue of its lack of procedures, an unexpected fringe benefit had become evident with the appearance of AIDS: In those early days, dealing with AIDS made us an elite group, an unexpectedly glamorous group. Even the cardiac surgeons could not approach our kind of heroism. Yes, they dealt with death every day. But it was somebody else's death they had to worry about. Never their own.

I remember playing the role of brave soldier to the hilt when my parents came to visit me in Boston. They were concerned about AIDS, fearful that it might spill onto their son from its victims. To them AIDS was certain death, a merciless killer. AIDS was the haunting image of Rock Hudson emerging on a stretcher from a chartered Boeing 707, unsuccessful in his attempt to find an extension on life in Paris. I was, in the face of my mother's concern for me, valiant and stoic.

This quality in me—the pride of the front-rank soldier—had gradually disappeared in Boston, but I could see it was now reawakening. I was talking about AIDS on television; I was lecturing to other doctors about AIDS. I stood in front of them in the flesh as someone who had taken care of persons with AIDS and felt positively about the experience, at least in the telling.

And now, finally, as if to justify my expertise, to justify my existence, my first AIDS case was on its way down. A car was speeding to Johnson City from a little coal mining town in Virginia. The excitement in my voice had been difficult to keep out. And Rajani had recognized it for what it was.

LATER, WHEN ESSIE began to tell me Gordon's story, I learned that the day she called me, Gordon had come over to her house. It had taken a monumental effort for him to cover the fifty yards that separated his duplex from her front porch. When he stepped into Essie's house, everyone could see that something was terribly wrong. He was extremely pale and swaying precariously. Essie and her daughters, Sabatha and Joy, had rushed to him and supported him and led him into Essie's bedroom. As soon as Gordon sat down, Essie could see he was in pain.

Gordon asked the children if they would excuse Essie and him for just a minute; there was something he needed to tell their mother. Essie said time stood still for her. "I knew I was about to hear something terrible. I sat down and took a deep breath. I said to myself, 'Lord, here it comes.' "

After Essie spoke to me on the telephone, she and the children helped Gordon to Essie's car and laid an afghan over him. Essie tilted the seat back as far as it would go. Gordon asked for a cushion: he had a big sore spot at the base of his spine. He had lost so much weight, the knobby ends of the vertebra wanted to grind through the skin. Essie had Sabatha fetch a big empty Crisco can to keep between his feet if he needed to pee.

Gordon insisted they stop by the supermarket. Their mother was working a part-time job taking inventory. Gordon wanted to say good-bye to her. Essie had her mother come outside to the car, telling her only that Gordon was sick and they were going down to Johnson City to see a doctor she knew.

Her mother reached into the car and kissed Gordon and stroked his hair.

"It was the most amazing thing," Essie said to me later. "There he was, laid back in the seat, a pillow under his bottom, a pee-can between his legs, looking like he was going to die any minute, his skin as cold as a witch's tit—and Mama couldn't see that something was wrong with him. She *wouldn't* see that her baby was sick. Had *been* sick for a long time but was a whole lot sicker now. She kept asking *why* we wanted to go all the way down to Johnson City. Couldn't we just go in the morning?

"And Gordo just smiles at her, like he don't even rightly know why we're going—as if *I* put him up to it!"

I HAD LEFT WORD with the Miracle Center emergency room to call me when Essie arrived. When I reached the ER, Essie had already told the nurse about Gordon's "HIV factor."

As I walked into the ER I felt as if every eye was on me. I was sure of myself, knowledgeable about AIDS, but totally unsure of how this hospital was going to react to its second case.

One of the nurses—a veteran of the ER—entered the cubicle with me. I took this as a show of support.

I hugged Essie, who rose to her feet when she saw me. Now in her early forties, Essie had bobbed her brown hair in a pert look that highlighted her huge eyes. The eyes were full of anxiety.

Gordon was lying on the examining table, and Essie introduced us: "Gordon, this here is Dr. Verghese. Dr. Verghese, this is Gordo." I shook his hand. It felt hot and dry. The nurse stood to Gordon's left to assist me in the examination. She had brought a pair of gloves with her. Now she put them aside.

My first impression was that Gordon did not look at all like his sister. Lacking her rotund face and full lips, Gordon appeared frail and wispy—not so much a matter of his illness as a matter of genetics. As if he had come from different stock.

Gordon had an odd smile on his face. It was the first thing I noticed when we were introduced.

The smile seemed unrelated to his underlying emotional state. It flickered on and off like a faulty porch light. The smile was his first response when spoken to, as if signaling his return to the secular world from an all-consuming private reality.

Though he was emaciated, pale, and his breathing labored, he was calm and resigned—quite the opposite of Essie who was overwrought, filling the space around her with nervous energy. Her gaze went back and forth between Gordon and me.

"I tell you what," Essie said, "I'm going to wait outside."

When Essie left, I began to take Gordon's history. As I interviewed him, I instinctively sized him up, trying to pick out as many clues as possible to who he was and to his condition. The patient encounter is traditionally divided into the history and the physical. But in actual fact, the examination begins the moment patients enter the room. One is alert to whether their hands are cold or warm and sweaty (which could indicate hypothyroidism or hyperthyroidism). One notes whether they are dressed shabbily or with glaring mistakes such as mismatched socks or clothing inappropriate for the season, a sign of dementia or delirium. Do they have the normal inflections in their speech or is it a dry monotone, as in Parkinson's disease? Is their facial expression or "affect" appropriate to their emotional state? A discrepancy between the sadness the patient expresses in speech and the hearty smile on their face is a clue to schizophrenia.

To me the history and the physical are the epitome of the internist's skill, our equivalent of the surgeon's operating room. Like Sherlock Holmes—a character based on a superb clinician, Dr. Bell—the good internist should miss no clue, and should make the correct inference from the clues provided.

It was with this sort of scrutiny that I approached Gordon: He was clear-eyed and clean-shaven—he had found the energy to shave before he came to Essie's house. His light brown hair was cut in two tiers: on top, the hair was longish, slightly down over his forehead in a wet, spiky look. The roots were a darker brown shade than the tips. Below an equatorial line at the level of his ear tops the hair was cut short, ending neatly well above his collar. He had cut his hair recently but it had been three weeks or more since he colored it. He wore blue cords and a blue cotton shirt with the collar buttoned. He had clearly lost weight: his belt bunched his pants around his waist.

The carotid artery in his neck was pulsating away, and there was a slight sheen to his skin, which, just to the side of his Adam's apple and above the carotid pulse, showed a gentle undulation that was not normal: probably an enlarged lymph node. There would be more enlarged nodes in the armpit and groin.

The ER clipboard showed Gordon's weight, blood pressure and the usual soundings. His temperature was 103 degrees Fahrenheit, his pulse was rapid and his blood pressure on the low side. His breathing was rapid, about forty breaths per minute.

Peeping out of his shirt pocket was a much crumpled carbon copy of a lab slip from the Dade County Health Department which he pulled out for me: "HIV positive by ELISA." The test was dated October 1985, about the time the test first became freely available.

"When do you think you contracted the virus?"

"What do you mean?"

"Well, your test says October 1985. But did you suspect you might be infected before that? Did you have any lovers who died of AIDS?"

"I've had one—no two—lovers. Who died of AIDS. I guess I must have got the virus in '80 or '81."

"How long have you been feeling poorly?"

He laughed a short, sharp laugh. "Months—no, years." A smile remained on his face. "I was tired for so long. And losing weight. Even before I came home." Now, I was certain that Gordon was the prodigal son, once given up for lost.

"What have you been feeling since you got home?"

He smiled again. "Tired. And feverish."

"Do you have fever every day?"

"Not too bad. I stay cold all the time. I can barely shower. Or wet my head, 'cause I freeze to death. And then I'll suddenly break a sweat."

"And what else?"

"Otherwise I'm doing pretty well."

"Any shortness of breath?" He was speaking in clipped sentences because he was so short of breath. And yet he did not volunteer this symptom.

"I guess."

Gordon was being a reluctant patient. Passive, as if he recognized the fever and other symptoms, but was only marginally conscious that it was happening to him. As if he had already separated from his body in some way.

"How bad is it?"

"What?"

"The shortness of breath."

"Not too bad. Only if I try to walk or do something strenuous."

I waited.

"—and I guess it has been getting worse. The last day or two. Sometimes"—and here he flashed a conspiratorial smile again, a smile that was quite inappropriate in the context of what he was saying—"sometimes it's all I can do. To get my breath. Even as I just lay here."

When I asked him about prior medical problems he told me he had contracted syphilis two years before and taken a series of injections for it.

As we helped Gordon undress so that I could examine him, I already had strong suspicions as to what was going on. The wan face and the flickering smile aroused my suspicion that the virus had made headway in the brain: he had early HIV dementia. I looked into his pupils with my ophthalmoscope for the big white splotches that indicated cytomegalovirus infection—the commonest cause of blindness with AIDS. There were none.

In his mouth, in addition to the white plaques of *Candida*, I saw a purple spot the size of a quarter tucked next to his last molar, between cheek and gum. It was more than a discoloration. It was a boggy swelling, almost certainly a Kaposi's sarcoma lesion—"KS." I touched it with the tip of the tongue depressor. "Does that hurt?" Gordon shook his head. I decided not to mention it to him for now. Most KS lesions, particularly if there were only a few on the skin and in the mouth, tended to not cause problems. If Gordon were to die, it would probably be from a cause other than the KS. I examined the rest of his skin carefully but found no more lesions.

I percussed over his lungs. The normal *thoom-thoom* of resonance that one should hear from air vibrating in the tiny air sacs of the lung was missing in the bases of both Gordon's lungs. With my stethoscope I could hear fine Velcro-like crackling sounds in his lungs when he took a deep breath. In his armpits and groin were more lymph nodes of the same size as in his neck.

His x-ray showed a lacelike pattern in both lungs that was consistent with *Pneumocystis carinii* pneumonia. His blood exam confirmed that he was very anemic and would need a transfusion. I wrote out the orders to admit him to the hospital. I went out and spoke to Essie and we both returned to tell Gordon.

"Gordon, I think you need to be in the hospital. You have a pneumonia."

"I don't want to be in the hospital. Can't you give me some medicine and send me home?"

"It's not that simple. You need blood. You need antibiotics by vein."

He smiled and shook his head.

Essie stepped in: "Now, Gordo, you are going to do what the doctor says and there ain't no two ways about it." Her tone was gentle, but brooked no argument.

I was puzzled by Gordon's attitude. On the one hand, he seemed to have given up. Yet *he* had gone to Essie's house that night. He had told her he was sick and had let her drive him all the way down to me. But he had no real interest in why I wanted to admit him and in what might be going on with his body.

Gordon was placed on the fifth floor and assigned that first night to a nurse called Mary—a stroke of luck for both Gordon and me. Mary seemed so comfortable with Gordon and his ailment that I was in awe. It was as if she had worked in a big-city hospital and had taken care of countless HIV patients. All the nursing staff had been "in-serviced" on AIDS, but that alone could not account for her attitude.

Over the next three weeks, Mary and then Eleanor and then several other nurses on the fifth floor became friendly with Gordon. There were, I would find out later, other nurses who wanted nothing to do with him. But those who were willing closely tended Gordon as his mysterious fevers and pneumonia waxed and waned. They assigned themselves back to him every day as if he was a prize patient.

Every time I visited there was some new twist: Chinese food one night when they found out he had a passion for it; Elton John tapes and a boom box because of a song on TV that had stirred some other kind of nostalgia. Later, when Gordon was discharged, Mary and another nurse traveled up to Virginia to make a surprise visit to Gordon. While there, they helped bathe and feed him and cheered the family on in their efforts.

AS I TOLD ESSIE when she first called, I was scheduled to give a talk in Norton, Virginia, a few days after Gordon's admission to the hospital. My drive would take me near Essie's home outside of Blackwood, a few miles south of Norton. Essie, who had stayed with Gordon the first two nights before heading back for a change of clothing, suggested that I visit with her and look around the area on my way to Norton. I agreed. Gordon remained an enigma to me. Two days in the hospital and I didn't know him any better than when I first met him. Perhaps by visiting his country home, meeting his family, I might get a clearer picture of the strange man who lay quietly between the sheets of his hospital bed.

Gordon's parents had been down to see him each day, but their visits had not coincided with my rounds. Essie, who was my link to them, said my visit would be the ideal opportunity to explain to them what Gordon had. It was clear that Essie, whether because of her medical background or for reasons that I did not as yet know, had taken charge of Gordon's care.

I set out for Virginia at about ten in the morning. Summer was over and fall colors were appearing on the tips of trees. The day was warm, but I was able to manage without the air conditioner, keeping the windows down and letting the air whip through my car.

It had been a while since I had driven this route. I had forgotten how much the green, undulating pastureland just outside of Johnson City looked like Ireland. It was hypnotic; it made you want to stop and inquire about purchasing the lone house that sat on a hill and all the land around it.

The tobacco allotments in the corner of these estates stood out from the rest of the fields. The big floppy tobacco leaves looked yellow and turgid, ready to pluck. In some fields the plants had been harvested and propped up against tobacco stakes in orderly stacks that looked like miniature wigwams.

The barns of Tennessee had always fascinated me. They came in all shapes; they were as individual as people. I passed several where the corrugated tin roof had one long sloping section and a short angular section, the final size and shape of the building determined entirely, it seemed, by what was available to make the roof. Another barn was little more than a lean-to. Some were painted red with Gothic roofs and shiny silos next to them. But the majority looked abandoned and only when you drew close was it apparent that they were being put to some use. The knotty pinewood had weathered to a slate gray color and looked brittle. I imagined if I touched it, it would break off in my hand like a wafer. In place of doors on hinges there were square openings cut into the walls through which I could glimpse a wagon or the back tires of a tractor, or tobacco leaves hanging from the rafters.

As I approached Kingsport and drove past the giant Eastman-Kodak plant, the acrid scent that came from this plant reached my nose. Eastman-Kodak *was* the town of Kingsport. Perhaps that was why the town was so willing to live with this daily reminder of the plant's existence and pass it off with comments like, "It's not really that bad," and "It doesn't always reach where we live."

Now the undulating pastureland gave way to hills and deep valleys. The soil was so rich that foliage and undergrowth clogged every inch of space, blanketing the land as far as I could see like a rain forest. At the top of a hill I could see a thin clearing like a hair-parting where a power line cut through the trees.

I was passing the outskirts of Kingsport and entering Weber City: the border with Virginia. The highway gave way to Route 23, which would take me all the way to Norton and on to Kentucky if I chose. Now Route 23 ran through Weber City, parallel and very close to the railway tracks. There were traffic lights every block and my pace was reduced to a crawl. A coal train traveled slowly in the opposite direction to my car. To look at it gave me vertigo.

I passed a garden of eternal rest built on an embankment and stretching right down to the highway. The neat granite and marble headstones carried familiar Tennessee and southwest Virginia names: Tipton, Caldwell, Morris, Greer. Churches abounded in this town, crowding both sides of the road like used-car dealers. Spires rose from them like the horns of unicorns. Two of the churches were giant brick edifices with ample parking lots while others were simple rectangular buildings with aluminum siding, painted white, only the spire indicating the building's purpose.

Outside Weber City, my pace picked up. And now on my left, for the first time, was a mountain range. Its presence and proximity gave a whole different feel to my drive. The mountain was an even ridge that had few peaks; it stretched into the distance, parallel to the highway. This was the Cumberland chain. I was passing through Cumberland Gap. The side of the road here was sheer rock-face.

Now, mile after mile and I was mostly in shade. The road dipped down into valleys and then rose to cross a mountain pass. Trees with dense foliage extended to the very top of the mountain.

Every few miles a roadside market—a plain rectangular building— offered gas and sodas. I passed a few houses on the side of the highway. They were really trailers that had been bricked in and a porch added. Flower pots hanging on the porch displayed a profusion of colors. When I saw a satellite dish it was always with one of these well-tended trailers.

Occasionally, I could sight down a dirt lane leading off Route 23 and see a shack with junk cars in front and a rotting roof on top.

An hour and a half after I set out I reached the turn-off for the town of Big Stone Gap. I passed through Big Stone and came out the other end into the town of Appalachia. As you drive into the town of Appalachia, you are greeted by a giant terraced rock wall where the face of the mountain has been brutally savaged. Nothing moves on this rock face; the mines took what they needed and moved on. The main street of Appalachia had old, two- and three-story office buildings interspersed with newer bank buildings, mine offices and, of course, a few churches. Downtown was barely a block or two long and then I was out of Appalachia, driving out into country again, heading to Blackwood. A few miles down the road I came to a fork: one fork led on to Possum Trot Hollow and the coal camp of Stonega. The other fork wound farther up the mountain to Sawmill Hollow, to the coal camps of Osaka and Roda. Beyond Roda, in the distance, were the Black Mountains of Kentucky and "bloody" Harlan.

Essie's directions involved taking a left turn at a house with a lawn jockey (an "artificial nigger," as Essie termed it) in the yard and driving till I came to Preacher's Creek. The house sat ten miles from the fork and Essie was standing on her porch, waiting for me. She looked tired. She was apologetic about her humble abode, though I assured her she should not be.

The house was a one-story, square-shaped, cinder-block house. It was raised three feet off the ground so that you had to climb up six steps to get to the porch. The open porch was narrow and held a swing, the lawn mower and a dog's kennel. The house was in essence a modified shotgun house—the front door was aligned with the back door and the two rooms in between constituted the living and dining rooms. A bedroom led off from each of these rooms. Essie's parents lived across the road in a similar house; cousins and relatives were scattered up and down the hollow. Not a car passed whose occupants Essie did not know.

Essie saw me looking at the mountain that rose steeply behind the house.

"This here is what you call a hollow. Most everybody lives in a hollow—there's not too many that live *on* the mountain."

Essie's hollow had been spared the fate of many others. When underground mining had given way to strip mining, the loggers had cleared the trees and then the bulldozers went to work cutting, gouging, burrowing into the side of the mountain as they had done at the entrance to the town of Appalachia, until they found the seam. When the rains came, the first spoil bank had often collapsed and fallen on to the next spoil bank until the mountain slid into the creek, plugging it, overflowing the yards, causing slag to seep into the wells.

Essie's living and dining rooms were paneled in a dark wood. The lights were on though it was early afternoon. Above the babble of the TV, I heard the staccato eruptions of a police scanner from Essie's bedroom. Later, I heard scanner chatter in Essie's cousin's house and every other house I visited. The police, fire and ambulance squawks were like a collective subconscious that played in the minds of a whole county and kept them aware of anything that affected their neighbors.

On the living room wall, Elvis, wreathed in a golden halo, smiled from a knobby walnut frame. A chubby Gordon, whom I barely recognized, looked at me from the back row of a family photograph. On top of the TV was a framed photograph of a young girl with moon eyes, a large mouth, even teeth, huge dimples and wearing a beehive hairdo.

"That was me, believe it or not," Essie said. "Lord, I was a firecracker then!" This triggered off her laughter. Sabatha, Essie's older daughter, who was in her last year of high school, brought the frame over to me. (The children had stayed home from school to meet me and to hear word of their Uncle Gordon.) Essie was heavier now than in the photograph. I saw in Essie's daughter, Sabatha, some of the young Essie—a big-boned comeliness that would have to exercise great discipline to keep from getting stout. In the photograph, the set of Essie's chin suggested no reluctance—even then—to speak her mind. And the dimples and the smile were unchanged.

Essie told me she had beaten breast cancer. This came as a surprise to me and I found myself eyeing her bosom, wondering which side had been affected. "Like when I had that cancer," prefaced many of Essie's utterings that day. The cancer was evidence of how bad luck could strike out of the blue, and her reprieve was testament to good luck and God's grace. It was the reason for her practical disposition, her vision of the world as black-and-white, her role as a doer rather than an observer or complainer. She was, for example, a die-hard Bulldog fan, and if anyone thought she was crazy to drive all over the state—even clear up to Fairfax—for the high school football team's away games, why, that was *their* problem.

"When Gordon came home," she said, "it was like a test God was giving us. 'Here,' He said, 'let's see what you all do now.' And there wasn't two ways about it—I *knew* what I was going to do."

I asked Essie to tell me about Gordon, to help me understand who he had been. Essie had made coffee and she sat opposite me.

She was a natural storyteller—the opposite of Gordon. Talking was clearly therapeutic for her. She frequently made little detours to provide background for the main theme that she was pursuing. I had no occasion to interrupt her except to relieve myself of the coffee. Essie kept going without a pause for over two hours. Her daughters sat through most of it, listening as if to a fable they had heard many times before and never tired of. Often Essie would turn to them and say, "Isn't that right, children," and Sabatha and Joy would nod vigorously, tears coming to their eyes whenever their mother brushed away her tears. Joy was two years younger than Sabatha.

Essie was the third of four children. The first child, Robert Lee, died two days after birth of "strangulation." Essie said this word to me as if I should know exactly what it meant. Just like "HIV factor" or "*the* cancer."

After Robert Lee came Herman, a confident and happy child who was head of the household when the father was away. Then came Essie, then Gordon.

Their mother was a coal miner's daughter from up in Pikeville. Essie's father repaired diesel engines at the Bullet mines till they didn't need him anymore. He went down to Tennessee, to Knoxville, to work, driving long-distance trucks. He could have visited more often than he did. By the time their father returned for good, the children had grown up, they had bonded among themselves; they had little use for their father.

The harsh, damp surroundings of Preacher's Creek toughened the children, made them as resilient as the abandoned railway tiers that dotted the hollow, enabled them to weather the measles, the mumps, the assorted broken bones, scarlet fever and even typhoid.

All but Gordon. Gordon was a sickly child, prone to the croup, the bronchitis (for which he had been hospitalized six times between the age of four and seven) and, most important, prone to "fits," the local appellation for seizures. His mother had taken him to Richmond, to Charlottesville, and even to Emory in Atlanta in search of diagnosis and treatment of the fits. Nothing was found; she was told that Gordon would grow out of them.

More than once, Essie and Herman had huddled around Gordon in the schoolyard while he had a convulsion. They recognized the eyeball rolling and the stiffening of his arms. They cleared space for him, knowing the violent limb-thrashing and the guttural sounds would soon follow. They lashed out at any kid who wanted to make a comedy out of Gordon's misfortune. When the jerking movements stopped, they took him to the bathroom and helped him wash. A phone call brought Uncle Matthew, who ran the feed store and had a car to take him on home.

Those fits punctuated Gordon's family's memories of his childhood. Because of the fits, he was forbidden to climb, swim or play contact sports. He was too frail to survive such games anyway. Instead he became a Looney Tunes aficionado, mimicking the voices of Bugs Bunny and Elmer Fudd with uncanny accuracy, taking on the persona of one or another cartoon hero for weeks at a time.

He became a collector of boxes—those days it was tobacco tins and matchboxes but in later life it would become small brass boxes, jewelry and music boxes, boxes made of beads, or out of ivory. Exotic seashells soon sat between the boxes, in the boxes, on top of the boxes. If his siblings led an engaging and exciting outer life in the hollow, Gordon soon developed an equally colorful inner world.

In his early teens, Gordon outgrew his fits. He put on inches, developed a style, became vivacious, even dated. He began to distinguish himself from his school peers, most of whom had emerged from the black wood-frame shacks of the coal camps. After their schooling, it was clear that most would return there. But equally clear was the fact that Gordon would not. He had metamorphosed into a dazzling self-creation, aware of a world far larger than their little hollow. It was as if he came from a different planet than the others. His mind was abuzz with projects and plans. Muddy Waters and Coltrane played constantly in his room; he talked incessantly and was always happy, ready at a moment's notice to imitate his high school teachers, or the preacher at church, or the preacher's wife. The family was caught up in his excitement and it became a ritual for them all to sit on their mother's bed at night and recount the day's events, a performance for which Gordon was both ringmaster and star. To his family, Gordon's transformation was nothing short of a miracle.

"Gordon always had it in his mind that he wanted to go to the University of Virginia in Charlottesville," Essie told me. "I never heard him speak of another university. He was smart too—boy was he smart. He could draw—I'd say he should have been an artist. I think that was what God had planned for him. Sabatha, fetch the two paintings in my room to show Doc."

Sabatha returned with a framed picture in each hand. The paintings were actually pencil drawings painstakingly shaded with crayon. The first was of the head and torso of a bare-chested Frankie Vallee look-alike—a latter-day ephebe in the Chippendale mold. The lines were clean. A great deal of effort had been expended on the shiny black curls and the eyes, which were too big. The upper torso showed the deltoids carefully defined and the pectoral muscles forming interleaves with the abdominal muscles. The trapezius muscles were a trifle exaggerated, looking like webs extending from either side of his neck. Despite—or perhaps because of—the technical innocence of the drawing, it was sensual.

The second picture was of a southern belle drawn in profile. She wore a shoulderless, antebellum costume. Elaborate blond curls spilled down to her collarbones; a tear emerged from the corner of one eye. This drawing was better proportioned than the other one, but it too, despite the shading, had a one-dimensional quality. Essie and Sabatha hovered over me as I studied the paintings.

"Pa went with him for the interview for University of Virginia. It was the year Pa got back for good. It looked for sure like Gordon would get a scholarship. But then Pa says to the committee that the Vines never did take handouts and didn't need any now. Well, Gordon was admitted to 'U.Va.' but Pa never came through with the money. That just tore Gordon up."

When Essie, a year after graduating from high school, moved into an apartment in Kingsport, Gordon soon joined her. They were just an hour from Blackwood. Essie worked third shift in the ammunition factory. Gordon got a job there working first shift. They cooked together, shared a car, and on the rare occasions when their days off coincided, they partied together.

Gordon was a tidy roommate and a daring cook with the ability to take his mother's best dishes to new heights and combine them with

exotic inventions of his own. His whirlwind social life included Essie
and it seemed they were always on their way to an antique show, or back
from a county fair, or heading to a quilt display.

"I used to wonder how in the world could he be so good, so capable
of always doing something different, something unique that he had
thought up. It was a God-given talent."

In the years that followed, I heard different but strangely similar
versions of this story from families of gay men: There was always the
God-given talent that accompanied their God-given sexuality, always
the special creativity and humor. This fascinated me. Was it part of the
subconscious effort to compensate for their difference? Was the charm
and talent as biologically determined as the sexuality?

One gay man had told me how he had begun to feel tense and restless
at his family house. His parents used to hear him laughing and carrying
on on the phone with his friends; they knew he was the life of the party
when he was with his friends. "How come you can't be like that with
us?" his parents would ask. "You don't understand," he would say. His
natural state was to be happy and to laugh, but it went along with his
being gay. He found it difficult to hide his gayness and maintain his
outward fun persona. I am still haunted by this remark. I have grown to
realize through years of treating gay men how few of their families were
able to see their sons' best, most engaging selves.

I asked Essie if she met many of Gordon's friends.

"I seen some of the friends he hung out with. They'd come home
and—to be quite frank—I didn't like some of them. I told him so. I said,
'Gordon, you be careful now. You watch out.' "

"You mean they were gay men?"

"Yes. I knew then that Gordon was gay. But I didn't have any special
word for it, you understand? I didn't think too much about it, you
know? He was just Gordon; it seemed like such a miracle that he had
survived his childhood. Who could have asked for anything more?
Even now, I can't think of him as gay. Gay may have been what he did,
but it wasn't who he was. He was our Gordo before he was anything
else."

I wondered how Gordon, if he could be made to talk, would have
reacted to this statement about him: gay was what he did, but it wasn't
who he was.

Essie returned to Blackwood after a year. She married and the next year had Sabatha. Gordon remained in Kingsport. After six months he called to say he had just landed a wonderful job in Atlanta. He sounded ecstatic and already far away. Kingsport had been a huge improvement on their little hollow, but Atlanta—Atlanta was Mecca. He was off and Essie was happy for him.

Essie and her mother went once to see Gordon in Atlanta. "Gordo always knew exactly what he wanted. And I tell you what—he *found* what he wanted in Atlanta. He was the kind that would rather have waited to get *exactly* what he wanted than have something second-rate. He had talked about a cocker spaniel—a black cocker spaniel—as long as I can remember. Well, when I went to visit him in Atlanta, we open the door and out comes this beautiful cocker spaniel! Lord, it had the prettiest black fur and ears just like wings!

"He lived with this guy, John, a flight attendant for an airline—a real nice guy, we liked him just fine. They shared a beautiful townhouse, right there on a lake. For the longest time I had heard him say, 'If I ever have a place of my own, it'll be on a lake . . .' and here it was, come true.

"He had a brand new Monte Carlo. And because of John's job, he was traveling to places we never dreamed of: Mexico, Paris, New Orleans for Mardi Gras.

"Sabatha, fetch me that tutu and them tassels Gordo brought me."

I fingered the tassels and the gossamer G-string sewn into the transparent tutu. I pictured Essie in them. Essie, seeing the expression on my face, burst out laughing, which set the rest of us off. "He called me up to tell me how he and John went into a bar in New Orleans and saw this woman wearing this thing here and how she was able to set them tassels a-spinning in opposite directions. 'Essie, it's the most amazing thing I ever seen. Why, when I come home, I'm going to show you how to do it!' "

"And tell him about the box collection," Sabatha said.

"Oh, Lord, don't let's start on that!"

And Essie didn't start on that. What she wanted to tell me next was too compelling for her to digress:

"One year, Gordo didn't call on Mother's Day. You have to know Gordo, but it's something unimaginable for him. I mean, he loved his

Mama to death. Then Mama's birthday came and went with still no call. Then to beat it all, Gordo's roommate calls one day to say that he hadn't seen Gordo for weeks! Did *we* know where he was?"

Essie and her mother went hurrying down to Atlanta. "It was as if Gordon had dug a hole in the earth and pulled the lid over himself. Trudie—the cocker spaniel—he'd given to his neighbor just the week before. The Monte Carlo was parked outside the bank that financed it; the keys were in the ignition and all the papers were in the glove box."

They had nothing to go on. The police, since he was over twenty-one, could not declare him a missing person until seven years had elapsed. "All we heard were rumors."

According to the rumors, Gordon's roommate might be facing charges of sexual misconduct with a minor. Even though Gordon was not involved, it might have prompted him to flee.

The only thing Gordon had not taken care of before he ran was a diamond ring he had purchased. For the next three years Gordon's mother made the payments on the ring. According to Essie, each of the payments represented a sort of offering to the memory of her prodigal son, or perhaps an offering to a deity that might, if she kept up the payments, eventually return both the ring and the young man who wore it.

"Now, I refused to give up. I said, 'Mama, let's get us a P.I.' "

I must have looked puzzled, because Essie explained: "P.I.: private investigator! Well, Mama hemmed and hawed. And so I just went ahead and did it, though God knows I sure as hell couldn't afford it."

The P.I. from Atlanta followed Gordo's trail through North Carolina, Georgia and Alabama, to Tallahassee, Florida, where Gordon had lived with an older man and his children. When the older man had died, the children were sent to foster homes and the trail disappeared.

"If I was you," the private detective advised her, "I'd give him up for dead. That way, if he shows up . . . why, it'll be one hell of a surprise."

ON MOTHER'S DAY, exactly four years to the day of Gordon's disappearance, Essie walked into her mother's house from work to pick up her kids. Her mother was frying okra. The phone rang.

Essie heard Gordon's voice: "Hey, Essie. What you doing?"

She screamed at her mother to pick up the other phone.

Gordon said to his mother, "What you doing, Mama?"

Amidst her mother's sobs and the spluttering of oil on the stove, Essie found herself shouting, unable to stop herself, happy, but so very angry: "WHERE HAVE YOU BEEN? WHY HAVE YOU NOT CALLED ALL THESE YEARS? WHAT DID YOU THINK . . . ?"

Her mother hushed her. Gordon didn't seem to mind. He was strangely calm. Gordon's father stood near the phone, listening, tears streaming down his cheeks. He grinned from ear to ear but did not reach for the phone.

"I'm fine, Mama," Gordo said. "I'm fine, Essie."

He gave them his number and his new address. Told them his name was now Brian Clark. He asked for them to come down to Florida and see him. He told them again and again that he was fine.

They dialed his number ten times that night, assuring themselves each time he picked up that he was alive, and that he would stay till they arrived.

The next day Essie, her kids and her parents piled into Essie's car and set out for Jacksonville, Florida. The family had agreed on the way down not to pry, not to ask too many questions about the years that had been lost. Whatever had made Gordon disappear for so long was to be his business.

It seemed to me remarkable that it was always Essie who took the initiative. *Essie* and her mother had gone to Atlanta to look for him. *Essie* had hired the private investigator. They went in *Essie's* car to Jacksonville. *Essie* had brought him to see me. I asked her about this.

She looked puzzled, as if the question had never occurred to her. "I guess you could say that the family more or less looked to me to do this or that. My brother is involved with his own family. And I just did what I had to do."

I was silent, thinking how utterly outward-oriented, almost unaware of herself Essie was. It was reflected in her laughter, it was evident in the way she responded to each family crisis.

"Go on, Essie." I had interrupted her train of thought.

"In Florida, Gordon was in what you call a studio apartment. It was a new development on a waterway, beautiful—wasn't it, children? He looked older. His hairline had kind of gone back and there was gray right here, over his temples. In the neighboring flats were other young men. They were all his friends. They were all single, and they were all of them working like Gordon at Dolphin-Haven. It was kind of a restaurant chain, you see."

The family stayed a week, up late every night caucusing on Gordon's waterbed just as they had on their mother's bed in the old days. His mother kept touching him, touching his hair, his wrists, as if only the feel of his flesh could convince her he was really alive. On the drive back to Virginia their mood was celebratory: God had blessed them by bringing Gordon back to life. They had a special service at church to thank God for answering their prayers. "Let me tell you," Essie said. "I never lost faith. I prayed for him every single day."

Christmas came and the family once again—this time with Gordon's brother and his children—trooped down to Florida in two cars, each loaded with presents.

It was the first time they had celebrated Christmas outside of Virginia, outside of their little hollow. When they reached Jacksonville it was seventy degrees.

"Growing up, come Christmas, Gordo would be the one to show us how to celebrate. As if he was the only one who knew how to have fun, how to make us do Christmas *right*. He always did the tree. One year, when he was in Kingsport, Mama had done the tree. Well, when Gordon came up on Christmas Eve, he took it all down and did it all over again—he was up half the night for that. He was like that. And the tree was just perfect!"

In photographs that Essie showed me of the Jacksonville Christmas, Gordon's face is wreathed in smiles and the tree is splendid. The gifts he bought for each member of the family were exquisite—he was making up for four lost years. It was on his mother that he lavished the most elaborate present yet—his diamond ring, the one he had acquired years before in Atlanta and that she had continued to pay for.

It occurred to me that the ring technically belonged to his mother anyway. And yet, the way Essie told it, it was an act of incredible generosity that typified Gordon. If there was something selfish about the way he had cut his family out for four years, Essie could not or would not see it.

I couldn't resist asking, "Weren't you curious about what had happened all those years? Why he had never called? Why—"

"—Of *course*, I was curious. Why, I was *dying* to know. But I didn't want to press him. I knew it must have been something horrible. From what Gordon has hinted recently I think it might have had something to do with drugs. He might have got tangled in something really bad." After a pause, she added. "And you know what? Now I really don't want to know. What good would it do him? We've got a totally different problem on our hands now, don't we?"

She was nodding at me significantly and I had to reciprocate.

The spring following their visit, Gordon called his mother to tell her he was going to hairdressing school because it was something he knew he would be good at and he didn't think he could go on doing restaurant work forever. "Not that he needed to go to hairdressing school," Essie said. As long as Gordon had been around, Essie had never visited a hairdresser. He had even fixed Essie's hair for the prom, "though he was flat against my having a beehive. And I wouldn't have anything else." Essie's mother encouraged Gordon to get his hairdresser's license and lent him money for tuition.

Essie recalled the day her mother came over, clapping her hands and doing a little jig in Essie's kitchen: "Guess what, honey? Gordo's coming back home. For good!"

Essie had just returned after a double shift and had taken off her shoes and was nursing her feet. She listened numbly to what her mother was saying and watched her mother prance around the kitchen. "I had this expression on my face of happiness," Essie said. "But inside, my mind was spinning. It didn't make sense to me. Why would Gordo come back? I knew—perhaps better than anyone else in the family—just how much Gordon had wanted to escape from Blackwood. And I'd seen how comfortable he was in Jacksonville. It wasn't quite the same as in Atlanta, but it was getting there—he was even talking about moving to another apartment building where they'd let him keep a cocker spaniel. Something about this coming back wasn't right."

They all went down to the Tri-City Airport in Tennessee, to pick Gordon up. His appearance shocked them: it had been barely a year since they saw him, yet his face looked deflated, the flesh of his cheeks seemed to have collapsed onto the bone.

"I had seen more meat on a Krystal Burger than I saw on him," Essie said.

The thick bushy hair now revealed scalp and was streaked throughout with gray. He brought with him two suitcases and a steamer trunk: these were his entire worldly belongings.

In the photograph Essie showed me that was taken a week after his return, Gordon looked like a wax figure next to his rosy-cheeked sister. The smile on his face, in startling contrast to that from Christmas, was stiff and strained. It was the smile I had seen in the emergency room.

If the thought of AIDS occurred to Essie, it occurred to no one else. "I mean we had heard about AIDS—sure! But AIDS in Wise County? In this little holler? I *thought* about it and said, 'No! No way Gordo has AIDS.' "

Soon they were back to the evening ritual where they all sat on their mother's bed and chattered away, poked fun at each other, told outrageous tales, caught up on the local gossip—it made them forget how tired and thin Gordon looked.

Gordon's father, a brooding, taciturn man, now clung to the house with the same diligence with which he had avoided it when the children were growing up. He was an immovable presence during these soirees, leaning against the windowsill or sitting on the quilting chair—never on the bed—observing the rituals of play of his children, laughing at times, tears occasionally coming to his eyes. He was determined to make up for the long period that he had been away. It was to Gordon that he felt he owed the greatest debt.

If there was a discordant note to these evenings it was that Gordon, wrapped in a caftan ("he just stayed cold all the time"), leaning against the headboard, would nod off in the midst of the hilarity and hysterics. It would happen suddenly, as if a switch had been flipped: His eyelids would sag, his chin and head would follow and then, as if to erase all doubt, his breathing would become stertorous.

The family sat on the bed, studying the sleeping Gordon.

They studied the face in repose, studied it without the brave smile plastered on. Conversation ceased.

A STONE'S THROW BEHIND the family house was a duplex that Gordon's mother had inherited. She and her husband went to work fixing up half of the duplex for Gordon. They labored night and day to put in wallpaper, a new dry wall in the kitchen, a new gas range. They furnished it from their own house. They drove to Johnson City and bought a brand new waterbed from California Waterbeds for Gordon's birthday—one to match what he had both in Atlanta and then in Jacksonville. A sharp exchange between Herman—Essie's brother—and her mother over the money being lavished on the prodigal was brought to an abrupt halt by the appearance of the wan figure of Gordon standing in the doorway.

Soon, Gordon was settled in his new home. The parents' dream had come true: God had returned their lost child to them and now he and the rest of their children were living around them, gathering most nights in their house for supper.

Essie visited Gordon's flat almost every evening after work. "Once, I happened to look in his bedroom and I saw on his chest of drawers a stack of medications. They all seemed to be bowel or stomach medications. All I said to him is, 'Are you all right? Do you need a doctor or something?' He just smiled and shook his head.

"I *knew*, I just knew that Gordo wasn't right. I asked him right out: 'Gordo, are you all right?' I gave him every opportunity to tell me what was going on. But he wouldn't tell me a thing. He had closed off that side of him that used to confide in me."

Gordon began to work in a hairdressing salon in a nearby town. He seemed very content with this even if he was exhausted at the end of the day.

The owner liked Gordon, as did the high school kids who began to patronize him. Gordon was able to create trendy styles, a look more chic than even the malls in Johnson City or Knoxville were able to offer.

But Gordon was limited by fatigue. By afternoon his arms were heavy and his legs could no longer hold him up. The owner eventually had to let him go with the understanding that when Gordo felt up to it, felt up to a whole day's work, he would have a job waiting for him.

"By then it seemed like I was the only one who could see Gordon was sick. Pa saw nothing unusual in his son having to give up a job for tiredness! 'He'll be all right,' Pa would say if he said anything at all. Mama just worked harder to feed him and put some flesh on him. Lord, all of us were a-baking and a-cooking and bringing it to him, but it would just sit there until we took it back or throwed it away."

His father took to driving Gordon wherever he wanted to go: up to Wise to see his friend, Bruce, who had also recently moved back home, from Atlanta. Sometimes Gordon would want to drive up behind the house, past the brooding, ugly coal tipple, up the road to the mining camps and to the lookout point at the top that white couples had favored for years. From there Gordon could look down into three counties and two states.

Gordon would sit there for an hour or more, turning his head first this way and that, as if beyond the blue mountains he could see city lights. His father sat silent next to him. When Gordon was done looking, his father would drive him back home.

"They could not bring themselves to see what was now plain to me: Gordon was *very* sick. And I could not begin to help Gordon as long as he kept insisting he was all right. It was almost a relief when he finally told me. I used to wake up and thank God for bringing him back and then worry exactly what it was he had come back with."

The day Gordon's facade of well-being crumbled happened to be the day when her children and their devilment had so occupied Essie's mind that she had forgotten about Gordon.

Essie came home to find that Sabatha had been suspended from school—"but it wasn't my fault, Mama!" The boys in her twelfth-grade class had decided to blow up a commode. They had miscalculated on the amount of explosive needed and the bomb had blown up not just the commode but the adjacent three stalls and nearly collapsed the roof. The police had arrived in short order and hauled three boys away in handcuffs.

Sabatha's troubles had begun the next period in A.C. McCaffey's geography class. A.C. had taught geography for so many years that he had even taught Essie. He was an oddity, even for Wise County, with his toupee, his pants belted almost at the nipple, and a labored manner of speaking that took every syllable of each word and spat it out like a prune pip. Whenever he said, as he often did, "The fine bitumen and bauxite found in our very own Piston Production Plants," the front row was apt to be showered with a spray of saliva.

The blowing up of the toilet had outraged A.C. He was determined to extract a moral lesson from it, to make absolutely sure that no one thought it funny. "Now take little Ruby, here," said A.C., walking up to spectacled little Ruby Presnell who always sat in the front row and had a crush on A.C., impossible as that seemed to Sabatha. "Now if Roo-bee had been in the double-you-see, what would have happened?"

The whole class was picturing Ruby in the boys' toilet.

"Well," A.C. said after a long pause, glancing around significantly, "if Roo-bee had been in the double-you-see, there would have been no more Roo-bee!"

Sabatha, unfortunately for her, had been the first one to break, a squeak erupting from her like a warning signal, followed by a low rumble that could not be contained by her pursed lips and burst through with the whole force of her considerable chest and reverberated in the classroom and down the hall. The rest of the class—all but Ruby and A.C.—were by now also convulsed, both by what A.C. had said and by the sound of Sabatha's infectious laughter.

Even as Sabatha told the story to Essie, she and Essie and Joy were reduced to hysterics.

Essie was wondering how she could begin to discipline her daughter when she found herself reacting just like the kids?

Just then Gordon walked through the door.

One look at his face and all thoughts of telling him about A.C.'s latest uttering vanished. Gordon was paler than ever. The act of standing up was making him tremulous and she could hear the to-and-fro of his breath across the room.

From behind the brave smile, what he said was, "Essie, I'm sick. Can you help me?"

MY CONVERSATION WITH Gordon's parents did not take place till the next day. I had stayed so long at Essie's home that I had to hustle to get to Norton to give my talk. We fixed a time for me to meet with the entire family at the hospital the following evening. We gathered in a "quiet" room designed just for these kinds of conversations.

Essie, her brother, her mother, and her daughters were piled on the sofa beneath the picture windows overlooking the adjacent VA campus. Gordon's mother was thin and tall and wore glasses. When she smiled or spoke she tended to cover her mouth. She seemed still unused to her dentures.

Gordon's father, his cap glued to his head—a cap I never saw off his head—stood to the side of the sofa, leaning against the window, his hands in his pockets. Gordon's sister-in-law and cousins were seated on chairs on the other side of the sofa.

Essie had told me that I could speak freely since all assembled family members had a right to know. I pulled up a chair in front of the sofa. "Gordon has been infected with the virus that causes AIDS," I began. "It appears that he has AIDS."

Gordon's father dug his hands deeper into his pockets and examined his shoes. I waited for him to look up, but he did not. Essie sank back into the sofa, partly watching me, partly seeing what effect my words had on her family.

"I don't know how much you know about AIDS. You have perhaps read about it or seen reports of it on TV."

Essie, who would normally have responded for the family, kept quiet. She was my ally in this dialogue. When nobody answered, Essie nudged her mother as if to make her speak.

"I'd say we heard of it," Gordon's mother said.

Nothing more was forthcoming from her or anyone else.

I went on. "This virus, when it gets in the body, attacks one of the white corpuscles—called a CD4 cell, part of the immune system. Our immune system is very important to us: why, right this minute, the bacteria and fungi in this room, the mold behind those ceiling tiles, would be threatening our lives were it not for the way the immune system defends us."

All but Gordon's father looked at the ceiling and around them. Gordon's father continued to gaze at the floor.

"Think of the immune system as an orchestra; it has many instruments, each of which is specialized to do certain things and do them well. When they all work together the body can resist most infections. The CD4 cell is like the conductor of the immune orchestra. Unfortunately, it is this very cell—the conductor for the immune orchestra—that is attacked by the AIDS virus. When that happens, the orchestra is without a leader. There is total confusion, mayhem, noise, cacophony. Now the body becomes vulnerable to infections caused by the simplest organisms.

"This is what has happened to Gordon. His CD4 cells have been attacked and he has fewer and fewer CD4 cells left. His CD4 cell count is so low—six instead of over a thousand—that he has thrush or yeast infection in his mouth. In addition he has pneumonia in his lungs. The antibiotics have to fight the infections that his body cannot."

Gordon's mother was watching my lips, hanging onto my every word. When she saw that I had said my piece, she sat back in the sofa.

"Well, how in the world did he get it?" she asked.

I held my breath.

"You *know* how he got it, Mama," Essie said at once.

I sensed that Essie was irritated with the denial her parents had expressed for so long. She wanted, in her practical way, for all the cards to be on the table. She wanted the family to accept instantly—as she had—that Gordo had AIDS. She wanted them to gather together, much in the way they had done when they drove down to Jacksonville to see Gordo. She wanted no time wasted in posturing.

Essie said once again, clearly throwing down the gauntlet: "You do know how he got it, don't you, Mama?"

"Lord, lord," her mother said. "How do they get that way?"

I told them what to expect in the next few days. How I would be asking a pulmonary specialist to do a bronchoscopy to diagnose the pneumonia. We would do a spinal tap to see if Gordon had any infection in the brain. Did they have any questions?

"Well, do *you* have anything to say?" Gordon's mother asked, turning to her husband. She had taken the heat from Essie. Now she was tossing it his way.

Like a pillar of salt, he stood there, his arms folded, studying the carpet, stubbornly refusing to acknowledge that anyone had spoken or that he had heard what I knew he had heard. The tension in the room was mounting. I sensed that Essie would not have approached her father so directly.

After a long while the father lifted his head up. He headed for the door. When he reached it he turned back to address his family, ignoring me completely.

"All I know," he said, "is that the good Lord did not bring him back just to take him away. I don't believe he has this AIDS or nothing like it. He's going to get better, I just know it." He exited the room and disappeared down the hallway.

That night, I was chatting with Eleanor, Gordon's nurse. I said, "I'm amazed at how well Gordon is being treated. You know there are people throwing rocks at AIDS patients elsewhere in the country. Schoolkids are being driven out of school because they have AIDS. I had good reason to have been prepared for a more negative reaction in rural Tennessee. In this hospital."

Eleanor looked me up and down and said, "You do know that this was not our first AIDS case?"

"You mean the young man who came from New York?"

"I don't mean him," she said. Eleanor was a taciturn brunette. At first glance it was easy to misread her deadpan expression and her businesslike manner. But I had come to know, even before Gordon, that she was one of the finest nurses in the hospital, capable of going to great lengths for a patient. Eleanor sighed now, almost as if she was wondering whether to tell me or not. "Do you remember Rodney Tester—the hemophiliac who was Dr. K's patient? I bet you took care of him when you were a resident."

I recalled a tall, thin man with a shock of red curly hair and a limp. I had taken care of him several times for hemarthrosis—bleeding into a joint—following some strenuous activity. Rodney had been indomitable. He hunted and fished and whenever he sensed a bleed starting, he administered factor VIII to himself. It was only when this failed that he came in for more intensive treatment.

"Well," Eleanor continued, "I was real close to Rodney. He was the very first patient I took care of when I came out of nursing school. You know how he was. So brave. Never letting the disease get in the way of his social life. Dating, sports, you name it. And the first day I was taking care of him—this was 1980 or so—I was hunting for a vein, having no luck, and getting really agitated. I was nervous. I was thinking, what will this patient think of me? He'll wonder if I am really a trained nurse. Well, Rodney says, 'Here, let me help you.' And he helped me find the vein, he gave me a few tips. He never made me feel bad. I was so grateful.

"One time when he came in—I think it was in '84—Dr. K said something strange to all of us: 'I want you all to be careful with his blood.' That's all she said. When he was admitted, he was almost always on this floor. She said it to all his nurses: 'Careful when you draw his blood. Wear gloves. Especially when you start his IVs.' It took me a while to figure out what she was hinting at and, in any case, he wasn't in for anything to do with HIV infection. In fact, Rodney had developed another problem. He had become a drug abuser."

I remembered that even when I had been taking care of Rodney, there had been some concern about drug use. Hemophiliacs like Rodney were often in much pain from their bleeding into joints or into their muscles. Narcotics were often necessary to control this pain, and narcotic addiction was a very real hazard.

"By early 1985, I guess he already had full-blown AIDS. But what brought him to the hospital was stuff related to his hemophilia. And his drug use.

"He was weak and ill, but food services would bring him his tray and leave it near the door. There was no way that he could go and get it, so it would just sit there. And if he threw up, it wouldn't get cleaned up. People would just walk right past. Well, I knew it wasn't right. I said something. I kind of got into it with a few people.

"To me, he was an old friend. I *had* to take care of him. There was no way I was going to walk away from him. So I did. I took complete care of him and it could not have made some of the other nurses happier. What I saw in them disturbed me. I had considered them my friends, I respected them as nurses. And I saw a side of them that I would never have seen in a million years, but for AIDS."

There it was: AIDS as the litmus test for nurses and physicians, a means of identifying who would and who wouldn't. I had seen this before in Boston.

I asked Eleanor why it was that I had not heard of his case before. How everyone always mentioned the young man from New York but nobody had mentioned Rodney Tester.

"Two reasons. First, his drug problem was so bad that he was transferred at some point to a drug rehab hospital in Maryland. That's where he finally died. But also, he was in and out just before or just around the time the AIDS test was discovered. It wasn't like an official diagnosis till the end and then he wasn't here that long."

"So," I asked, "is this kind of stuff still going on now, with Gordon?"

"Hell yes! Except they know who is and who is not willing to take care of a patient like Gordon. I am willing. Mary is willing. And quite a few others. But I don't think they should take advantage of us for that reason. It's convenient for them. Because if they bitch and moan and if they don't take care of the patient right, then I feel like I have to step in. I can't let that happen."

I must have looked stunned, because Eleanor went on:

"You see, none of this gets back to you. If you hadn't asked me, you wouldn't know any of this."

My elation faded. As I left Eleanor, I could think only of Essie, her parents, and Gordon's smile.

6

WEDNESDAY AFTERNOON was my time to see private, non-VA patients in the University Physicians Group office. Not long after Gordon's admission to the hospital, I found myself in an exam room with Mrs. T, a prim and proper lady, belonging to what I thought of as the blue-hair and mink-stole society; she exuded the permanence of colonnades and war memorials. I often saw her type heading for church on Sunday mornings while I made my way to the Kiwanis Park tennis courts. Mrs. T was in her early fifties, handsome and slender; she kept her fur-collared jacket on during our interview.

I blame the Chanel No. 5 she wore for lulling me into inattention, so much so that when she pulled out the envelope whose torn end was much folded over and held with a paper clip, and when she said there was something she wanted to show me, I almost let her spill the envelope's contents onto the paper runway of the examining table before I cried:

"Hold it, ma'am! Do you mind if I peek into the envelope first?"

When I looked within, all I saw were tiny brown particles. She had referred to them as "growths." Growths that she had extracted from her pubic hair. But just as I feared, the little boogers were moving!

"Take a look, ma'am," I said. "Do you see how they are alive?"

Mrs. T turned pale. She brought her glasses up from the chain on her neck and peered into the slit of the envelope with me. Now her hand came to her mouth.

"I *thought* they were moving," she said. "But then I thought it was my glasses, or that I was dizzy or something."

"Those are lice, *crab* lice, ma'am. Do you itch?"

"I itch something awful."

Blood was now rushing to her face. I felt sorry for her embarrassment. My guess was that her husband had given it to her. I took a deep breath and asked: "Is your husband itching too?"

"I doubt it," Mrs. T said, lifting her head up, bravely looking me in the eye, a firmness and resolve coming to her face. I felt for her. "No. *I'm* the one that's itching. I'm responsible for getting it." Then, after a pause, she said, "If you would prescribe for me the appropriate treatment I would be very grateful."

There was a question I had to ask, a question that despite my several years now in infectious diseases I found myself embarrassed to ask this refined lady.

"Uh, ma'am, is it your practice to use a condom with your . . . partner?"

"Yes," she said, almost in a whisper, turning red again, her eyes examining the back of her hands. She looked up now, a little sparkle in her eye: "But it didn't help me, did it? What could I have done to prevent getting this? Worn a raincoat?" Her face broke into a wonderful smile and I had to laugh. The tension in the room was dissipated.

"Think of it this way, ma'am. The condom *did* work; it may have prevented things like gonorrhea, syphilis, AIDS."

She turned pale when I said AIDS. "Oh, Lord!"

"If you like, I can test you for those things . . . ?" She shook her head. "Then don't worry," I said. "The crab lice we shall take care of forthwith. Shall I prescribe a double dose? One for your partner?"

"That won't be necessary," she said. "As far as I'm concerned, I hope they eat him alive."

She left without having removed a stitch of clothing, without my laying a hand on her body.

When she was at the door, she asked me whether her husband could contract it or might already have contracted it from sleeping in the same bed with her.

"Is there any sexual contact between you?"

"None at all. Hasn't been for years."

"Then probably not. If he seems to start itching, then we'll need to do something about it."

I escorted Mrs. T to the door of the clinic personally; Carol, my nurse, raised her eyebrows at this special treatment. How was I to explain: This genteel southern lady had contracted a most ungenteel disease; the whole business had seemed to make her more human, exposed a vulnerability that touched me. I'm a sucker for that sort of thing.

What if her husband *had* contracted it? It would probably destroy the marriage. I remembered a drug company representative, a handsome man-about-town who contracted gonorrhea from an extramarital affair. He bought tickets for a luxury cruise—a second honeymoon he told his wife—and presented them to her over dinner and champagne. He managed to convince her to come in to a doctor's office for "shots" that they would need before the cruise. He had even found a doctor to go along with this deception. I was told this story by another pharmaceutical representative. I wondered what would have happened if the wife had a severe penicillin allergy—anaphylaxis and shock—and dropped dead in the doctor's office?

I returned to the exam room and stood the envelope open and took a photograph of it and its contents with my pocket camera before dispensing with the envelope. The photo would be a good prop in my next lecture on sexually transmitted diseases. Such oddities came our way in infectious diseases that an autofocus camera that fit into a coat pocket was well worth carrying.

Thus far I had only one other photograph of something a patient produced from her body. It was a picture of a neurotic woman from Mountain City posing next to a table with a giant Winn-Dixie paper bag on it. The contents of the bag were displayed on the table beside her: There was a Mason jar full of foamy, white secretions that she claimed came from her sinuses but that I was convinced were spit. Every day for two weeks before her appointment with me, she had pooled this expectoration into a jar, and allowed it to sit unrefrigerated. She had threatened to open the lid but I discouraged her—the ripe odor had already permeated the office building. She also had an assortment of blackheads and comedones she had pinched off her skin and placed in empty baby-food jars. And an envelope of nail clippings to show me subtle color changes in her nails that only she seemed to appreciate.

"Look! Look!" she said. "You see those blue colors sparking out of it?" I saw nothing. And the last item on the table was a pile of four spiral bound notebooks containing a blow-by-blow of her symptoms for the last year, a catalogue of every twinge and throb that you and I write off daily, as well as a meticulous log of the color, quantity, odor and other subjective aspects of her stools and urine. In the photograph, she beams at the camera, displaying these goods with pride, the expression on her face being similar to *la belle indifference* of the patient with true hysteria.

CAROL, THE NURSE who assisted me in the ID clinic, retrieved me from my daydreams. She directed me to another exam room. She handed me first one chart, "Ed Maupin," she said. Then she placed another chart on top of the first. "*And* Bobby Keller. Enjoy!"

I looked at Carol in puzzlement.

"They wanted to be seen together," Carol said. "I figured you wouldn't mind. They want to be examined and they want an AIDS test."

This was a moment, this waiting on the threshold, that I would come to know well. One stepped into a limbus of time, a labium of space. This name on a new chart was like the title of a novel that you had just bought, the jacket cover still pristine, the book new. Or else it was the title of an apocalyptic short story from an anthology of stories. The first paragraph had just grabbed you and you could not put it down.

Sometimes I would say the names out loud: *Ed Maupin, Bobby Keller; Bobby Keller, Ed Maupin; Ed and Bobby; Bobby and Ed*, rolling them around my tongue where they felt strange, sharp-edged, like freshly unwrapped candy. In time they would become the most familiar names in our clinic—Bobby in particular—like the names of ballplayers or movie stars, names one does not question. "I'm calling about Bobby Keller," I would say to a consultant, or "Bobby Keller needs to be scheduled for . . ."—always using both first and last names, the singsong way they were linked bearing a relationship to the face, to the memory of what had transpired thus far in the personal AIDS drama, the anticipation of what would come next. But in that Zen moment of standing on the threshold, the name had no such connotation; it was just a name.

Later, when Carol and I had forty or so persons with HIV that we were seeing repeatedly in our clinic, a *new* patient always created an excitement, an anticipation. Carol would go in to the room to get the blood pressure and temperature and pulse and settle them in. She would wind up tarrying there, putting them at ease and hearing the story of how this individual came to encounter the virus. And when Carol came out of the new patient's room, I would do a strange dance to avoid her: I wanted my first impression to be unsullied, I wanted it to be pure like a well-struck note—I wanted to hear every quaver and intonation. My ear must not be biased.

When I think back to some of those early patients, it is that first impression that lingers; what they wore, what words they used to tell their story, who was with them, the scent of the room, how the enlarged spleen felt rebounding off my fingers, how the smooth but distended liver slid under my hand. The writer Milan Kundera says that the first ten minutes between a man and woman are the most important in their subsequent history, a predictor of things to come. So it was with me: the first ten minutes were a determinant of how I would color that patient in my memory.

I knocked and entered. The room smelled of lavender soap. The two seated men came to their feet. The butcher-blocklike examining table with its paper runway occupied one side of the room. It left us just enough space for three chairs. I introduced myself.

Ed Maupin was in his early forties: he had gray hair, a receding chin and a short beard carefully sculpted to dip down on both cheeks in a sharp U and edged to outline his lips. His high cheekbones and Roman nose made him look rugged except for the fact that he had a tiny chin. He stood ramrod straight with his shoulders thrown back. If he had worn a robe he could have played a centurion in a biblical story. But despite this stately demeanor, his clothes were simple: his shirtsleeves were rolled up to his elbows, his shirttail not tucked into his pants; a cigarette packet was outlined in his breast pocket. He wore polyester pants with battered slip-on shoes whose heels were almost completely worn out on the outer edge so that if he took them off, they looked as if they would flop over. It was Ed who did all the talking, at least initially.

His partner, Bobby Keller, was a roly-poly man with bulging, sad, moon eyes from which tears seemed on the verge of spilling. He was bald with a high peaked crown. When I looked at Bobby he seemed to cringe.

Haltingly, Ed told me they had heard about me, seen me on TV and knew that I was an "AIDS doctor." They had come to take "that blood test. To see if we got it." They had driven down from Abingdon, Virginia, just for the test.

I told them that we could do the test for them *without* their seeing me. Then they would not have to be billed for a doctor visit. Just for the test. If, in a week, the test was positive, I would be happy to see them.

"Unless you are not feeling well right now?"

"I just stay tired, Doc," was Ed's complaint. "I want that AIDS test. But I reckon I can wait to have you check me out after we get the test."

"In that case, we'll get the blood drawn and arrange to see you in a week when we have the results."

Ed and Bobby looked at each other; the plan suited them well and they both rose as if to leave.

However, I said, since my time had already been blocked out, and since Carol was busy elsewhere, why didn't they stay a few minutes and I would draw their blood myself and that would give us a little time to get acquainted.

I went out and assembled my tubes and needles and tourniquet and returned to the room. Neither of them said a word.

I told them I had driven up to Abingdon, their hometown, a year ago to have Sunday brunch at the historical Martha Washington Inn. Ed nodded but said nothing. Bobby Keller squirmed and studied the floor.

Even more recently, I added, a group of us had been to the Barter Theatre to see a show that was definitely Broadway-bound. Before the show we had stumbled onto a new restaurant in Abingdon. The decor was nice; the food, I said, had been good. The highlight of the evening had been dessert: "Resurrection by Chocolate," an inspired creation.

Bobby, the bald one, piped in now: "I live for RBC—that's what we call it. It's the greatest."

"He does," said Ed. "He could live on chocolate alone if I let him."

Their house, Ed said, was a mile down the road from the restaurant, just outside the town, on a couple of acres with its own pond. "Pretty, if you like country."

Ed told me he was a diesel truck mechanic and worked for a trucking company in Abingdon. Bobby worked as a salesperson in an Abingdon boutique.

"We are gay, you know. That's why we wanted the test. But we sure didn't want to get it done in Abingdon."

I thought Bobby blushed when Ed volunteered this. I felt sorry that they had to drive sixty miles to a stranger's office to get tested for HIV.

I was curious about Abingdon, a town much bigger than Essie's mining town, yet not as big as Johnson City or Kingsport. Did it have a significant gay population? Did it have a meeting place equivalent to the Connection?

"Lord, no," said Ed.

"I wish!" said Bobby, showing some signs of life. They began to tell me about themselves.

Ed had been married and had fathered three children who were all grown up now. Ed was not bisexual, but gay. The marriage had been an attempt to conform but after many years his instinct for a sexual relationship with men had won out. For the last ten years Ed had lived in a steady relationship with Bobby Keller.

While Ed was manly, the strong, silent type, Bobby was extraordinarily effeminate. His voice was singsong with a trilling inflection that would have turned your head in the street if you overheard him. He tended to raise the pitch when he ended a sentence as if he was asking a question. It was a baroque touch that, together with the way he tossed his head, and the way his hands were held near his face, created the illusion that he was Salome wearing a diaphanous veil, not Bobby Keller, the salesperson.

Bobby was a natural clown. To see Bobby Keller's face, his expression halfway between confusion and confession, his Jonathan Winters–like seriousness, created an anticipation, a tension that at last you could stand no longer and you wanted to burst out laughing. His technique was the deadpan delivery. I was treated to flashes of it that morning, but there were times later when Bobby would have the waiting room—both HIV and non-HIV patients—in hysterics. On one of Bobby's repeat visits, Carol reported to me how Bobby's antics caused a lady in the waiting room to struggle up from her chair yelling, "Lord, I got to pee," then dash past Carol for the restroom, where the Lord granted her her wish.

On taking Bobby Keller's history I was shocked when he told me that he had been married and had fathered two children. I had great difficulty imagining him married.

My surprise must have shown on my face because he said, "Lord knows I *tried* to be straight. I was having sex with Ed when I was seven. But I kept telling myself it was wrong, wrong, wrong, and so I got married to make me straight. Well, all through my marriage I was tempted by men. Finally I just had to more or less admit to myself that there was no two ways about it. I was about as straight as a three-dollar bill!"

I thought of a most incongruous couple I had met at a potluck dinner a few weeks before. She was grossly and dangerously obese: at five-foot-one she weighed close to 270 pounds. She puffed when she walked and had an unhealthy, cyanotic hue to her lips. He was a wisp of a man, a matchstick next to her. His blond hair and fastidious dress were accompanied by an effeminate manner that was only a little more subdued than Bobby Keller's. What would have happened, I wondered, if he had been raised in New York City instead of rural Tennessee? Or if education or work had taken him out of the area in his youth? Would he have had the courage to come out and be gay, avoid marriage? In rural Tennessee, he probably had to stifle this secret part of himself. It was presumptuous of me to assume this, but it looked as if the man had married a needy woman whose appearance might allow him to slip by unnoticed. I wanted to ask Bobby Keller about his ex-wife. But I thought I should wait till I knew him better.

Ed and Bobby had their first sexual experience with each other when they were small boys. For the longest time they had made the assumption that they were the only two gay people in town. Their relationship had continued through both their marriages. After they both divorced and began to live together, they had made one of their first trips down to the Connection in Johnson City. There, they ran into a high school classmate, a drag queen holding court at the bar, and through her learned of a regular clique of gay men in Abingdon.

From time to time, Ed and Bobby would ride north on Interstate 81 till they came to a truck stop several hours away from their town. This spot was an important intersection where truckers heading down from the New York–Washington, D.C., area branched off in different directions. These expeditions, which always culminated in quick, anonymous sexual encounters—about eighteen in the last two years—were what now had them worried. "It was plain foolishness—we knew nothing about the men we were with. We were just crazy, is all I can say."

By probing gently, I established that most of what went on at the truck stop was oral sex. Anal receptive intercourse—the riskiest form of sexual activity for acquiring the AIDS virus—had been rare. But it had happened "ones't or twice with me and a lot more with Bobby," said Ed, looking at Bobby, who blushed deeply and whose shoulders began to shake as if suppressing an explosion within.

"How much more?" I asked.

"Just about every time with Bobby," Ed answered as Bobby studied the ceiling with mock seriousness.

At home, Bobby Keller was also largely the receptive partner. The sexual encounters they had with other men in Abingdon—mostly married men—involved mainly oral sex. They perceived their occasional partners in Abingdon as inherently safer than the men at the truck stop. At neither locale did they use a condom.

By this time I had drawn the blood, labeled the tubes, taken off my gloves, and we were just sitting around "visiting," as Carol would say. Ed and Bobby seemed more at ease than when they had first come.

I told them I was curious about the truck stop sex. This was a potentially important method by which AIDS could arrive in the small towns of Tennessee and Virginia. I had pictured AIDS spreading out in concentric waves from the epicenters of New York and San Francisco. But what if it just zoomed down the interstates instead? And why truck stops?

"You mean the pickle packers?" Bobby Keller said and giggled at his naughtiness. "The pecker picklers?" Bobby was loosening up, becoming almost chatty, riffing effortlessly off Ed who now played the straight man.

Bobby said their sexual contacts at these truck stops were often people like themselves who had driven up from an hour or two away—not truckers at all, but people from Virginia or Kentucky and even Pennsylvania. But yes, the attraction *was* the truckers. The men from the big rigs parked caterpillarlike, in parallel to the interstate, the engines purring—this was the thrill.

A few of the truckers were clearly gay, but others only wanted quick relief. And if a man could provide that, it was OK.

Bobby had almost been beaten up by a burly Texan trucker because Bobby had made the mistake of *conversing* with him after the act, offering small talk and his name and an offer for him to visit on his next trip through. Those words had broken a spell. Conversation had changed the nature of the transaction from an anonymous quickie to a social exchange.

The Texan became enraged. He needed to maintain the illusion that he was not gay. He needed to believe that he was *using* a man—a man that he had great contempt for, a man that in the height of his passion he called a "bitch"—to do what a woman wouldn't do, or couldn't do. The last thing he wanted was any attempt to get friendly. But for Ed's intervention, the Texan would have hurt Bobby badly.

Something puzzled me. Since there were women—hookers—turning tricks at these same places, why would the trucker not have gone with a woman, if that's what he wanted?

"But then he would have had to pay," said Ed.

"And Lord knows he wouldn't have liked it half as much!" said Bobby.

BOBBY AND ED LEFT my office with fistfuls of multicolored, multiflavored condoms, plenty of literature on safe sex, and little Band-Aids over the crooks of their elbows. I emphasized to them that they needed to practice safe sex at *all* times, not just in truck stops.

I wondered after they left whether there was an element of relief on their part to discover that the doctor they had come to see was a foreigner, an outsider. Their sexual proclivities, if revealed, would have made them like Martians in their community. To come to a doctor's office, even a distant doctor's office, and tell their sexual secrets to a Caucasian face that could just as well have belonged to a preacher, a judge, or some other archetypal authority figure in their town, might have been difficult. I may have been flattering myself with these thoughts, but more than once I had the sense that a patient was opening up to me for this very reason, *because* of my foreignness. The preacher with penile, rectal and pharyngeal gonorrhea was a perfect example. He didn't think I would pass judgment on him—perhaps he felt that as a foreigner I had no *right* to pass judgment on him. And so he came to see me regularly for new venereal problems that indicated to me he was not practicing safe sex; he was candid with his symptoms and very comfortable in my office. Would he have been as comfortable, as forthcoming, with the internists who practiced next door, all of whom were local boys, graduates of the University of Tennessee?

Years later, a doctor I had trained in Johnson City, a native of the area, set up his shingle in a neighboring community. I sent him one of my AIDS patients who lived in his town. My thought was that the patient could get his routine blood work and simple follow-up with this doctor without driving all the way out to see me. The doctor said to the patient, "I don't approve of your lifestyle and what it represents. It is ungodly in my view. But that doesn't mean I won't continue to take good care of you."

To which the patient replied, "Oh yes it does!"

EVERY MORNING, before starting work at the VA, I would go and check on Gordon at the Miracle Center. His fever raged on and on, but the bronchoscopy did not reveal *Pneumocystis carinii*, tuberculosis or anything else for that matter. We gave him the benefit of the doubt and treated him for *Pneumocystis*. The spinal tap showed a mild abnormality consistent with poorly treated syphilis, and we added high-dose penicillin to his regimen. In search of an undiscovered infection that was causing his fever and drenching night sweats, I did a biopsy of his bone marrow—a common place for widespread infections to reveal themselves. I had gone over the slides of the bone marrow with the pathologist, looking for signs of infection with tuberculosis or with histoplasmosis—a fungus endemic to our region. But we had seen nothing. It was frustrating.

Later, as I accumulated experience, it became clear that it was not uncommon to have fever persist for days in patients with AIDS without our being able to uncover a cause. I learned that infection with organisms like *Mycobacterium avium intracellulare* (MAI)—a tuberculosis-like organism commonly found in tap water and harmless to those of us with intact immune systems—was often preceded by prolonged fever. Yet the MAI infection was difficult to detect and easily missed by the lab unless special techniques were used. Some of these fevers were probably caused by the AIDS virus itself. The virus seemed quite capable of producing damage directly to different organ systems: AIDS dementia was an example of a condition produced directly by HIV. And Gordon's lung disease—a stiffening of his lungs and an inability of the lungs to oxygenate his blood adequately—was another condition that, in retrospect, could have been caused directly by HIV, since we had found no other opportunistic infection in his lung.

But at the time, I was convinced that Gordon had an opportunistic infection that I had somehow overlooked. Each day I would examine him from head to foot, looking carefully at his retinae, the back of his throat, examining his skin for a telltale rash. I would come out of the room and order more tests. I was fishing for a diagnosis. And each day when I picked up his chart, his fever curve would mock me. It stayed over 99° F and it swung up to 103° F with regularity.

Three weeks into Gordon's stay, when Essie's mother was taking her turn to sleep in the hospital room with him, she awoke to see Gordon sitting on the edge of his bed, the light on, and a huge smile on his face. He said to his mother that he had seen Jesus Christ, clear as day, standing in the corner of the room. Gordon seemed so alert and so convinced of what he had seen that it had scared his mother, not sure whether this meant the end, not sure whether that was really Gordon sitting on the bed or some apparition.

She called the nurse and also called Essie in Virginia. At two in the morning, Essie jumped into the car and drove down to Johnson City to be at Gordon's side.

When Essie arrived two hours later, Gordon was wide awake, animated and radiating a new optimism. He was sitting in the recliner, his dressing gown on, his legs crossed, looking better than he had ever looked in the hospital.

"Essie, just like you are standing there right now, I saw Jesus Christ."

"All right . . . ," Essie said, setting her purse down and catching her breath. It was not in her nature to be skeptical about matters of faith, religious visions. But she had enough medical experience to wonder if this was a hallucination or an illusion created by fever. "Tell me about it, Gordon."

"I woke up—I was having fever—I woke up and I saw this cloud around my bed and it felt like I couldn't breathe—I wasn't dreaming, mind you. I was wide awake. My eyes were open and I could see Mama laying there. Just then a voice spoke out from the cloud, just as clear as a bell ringing: 'Everything will be all right; it's all right, Gordon,' and a hand reached out from this cloud and I *knew* it was Jesus and He held my hand!"

Essie had been prepared to quiz Gordon on his vision, test its validity. But now she found herself dumbstruck by this account of a visit from Jesus, unable to dismiss it. She and her family had a strong faith. It was that faith, after all, that had brought Gordon, once lost, back to them. This vision could be of paramount importance. If God was trying to tell them something, the greatest sin was not to be listening, to dismiss it out of hand. Gordon had not dismissed it; it was as real as the plastic urinal that hung by its handle on his bedrail, it was as real as the television looking down on them with its blind eye from the wall.

Essie led her mother out to the hallway. "Mama, did *you* see anything?"

Essie's mother had not. Evidently, she woke after Gordon's vision was over. She sensed an aura in the room, but she experienced this aura as terror. She had been startled to see Gordon sitting bolt upright in the bed. The smile on his face had at first terrified her. As if at any moment he would leap out of the bed and come at her with a knife or his head spin around on his body. When she got over her fear, she too had been impressed with the clarity of Gordon's vision.

The women were led to two gratifying conclusions: First, that God was with Gordon and would indeed look after him. Second, that Gordon, who was brought up in the church but had wandered away spiritually, had had his faith renewed by this vision.

A few hours later, when I made rounds, I found Essie and her mother in the hallway, waiting for me. I was apprised of the new development. There I was, in the bright fluorescent light, dressed in my white coat, clutching my patient list in my hand, hustling to finish rounds at the Miracle Center before I went to the VA, and being confronted with the appearance of Jesus Christ at my patient's bedside.

"How do you all feel about it?" I asked.

Essie replied: "I'm happy for Gordon because it has obviously made a difference. Go on in and take a look-see. I think you'll be surprised."

I found Gordon sitting up on the side of the bed looking more alert and interested in his surroundings than I had ever seen him. No longer passive, he was effusive and engaging. I got a sense of his old charisma. He did not tell me directly about his vision. He told me that he felt considerably better and was determined that he should go home. When I examined him, nothing had changed except that he no longer had fever.

I looked at the fever curve. It had been up and down for days but the previous night it had come all the way down to 97 degrees Fahrenheit and stayed there. I had no assurance it would not shoot up again later that day, but I was still impressed. There were no more diagnostic tests that I could reasonably do in search of the cause of fever, short of taking a biopsy of every organ of his body. This seemed to be the right time to send him home. His fever had broken, whether by divine intervention or antibiotics. I arranged for home oxygen and a visiting nurse to administer his medications. I asked to see him in my clinic at the University Practice Group in two weeks.

I LEFT THE DOCTORS' parking lot, heading for my weekly clinic at the University Physicians Group. If I had been looking for justification for the time I spent lecturing about AIDS, preaching safe sex, I had it: I had just discharged Gordon, my first HIV patient. The results of Ed and Bobby's blood tests for HIV would be in my box when I got to clinic. And, Carol told me, there were two new patients referred to me from the health department. Their problem was in all likelihood HIV-related, since the health department usually diagnosed and treated other common sexually transmitted diseases on their own.

The University Physicians Group office was run just as any private practice office. The object was to make money, or at least stop running in the red, its history for most of its existence. Patients without private insurance or with Medicaid tended to come to our practice group. At times we found they had been sent to us by private physicians who could and would refuse to take patients that couldn't guarantee them payment. There had been tensions between the private sector and the university physicians—"town-gown conflicts"—ever since the medical school had started in this area. We were viewed as competition. My specialty was perhaps the exception; there was no infectious diseases person in the private sector.

Our practice office was just down the street from the VA. It was a dark and dingy place that we were occupying while a new building was being planned. It had a large waiting area that led to a reception window where patients registered and filled out the necessary forms. Behind that window were offices where three or more people worked full-time on processing billings and insurance forms, filing lab reports, updating charts. One or two people handled the phones, and the transcriptionist had her cubicle there as well. Behind the reception area, corridors led to two different patient areas, each with a nurses' station, offices for us to dictate in, and examining rooms.

Carol, the nurse who assisted me, worked primarily with cancer patients. She administered chemotherapy in the clinic. On Wednesday afternoons, she was assigned to assist me. I found out later that she volunteered for this assignment. Carol was in her thirties, a divorced mother of two. At five-foot-two, she was thin as a reed, with brown hair, vivid makeup, and boundless energy. She would have made Dale Carnegie proud: I never saw her with a negative thought. Sadness, yes; tears, yes. But she was determined—sometimes to the point where it was downright aggravating—to see a silver lining in every dark cloud. To be around her was to be peppered with little quotes written out on "Post-It" notes. Her coat displayed the "Smile" and "Have a Nice Day" variety of buttons that changed constantly. Invariably, there was some fattening cake or casserole that she brought in to be shared. I never saw her eat a bite of it. I think her energy and enthusiasm wore thin with some of the other nurses who would have preferred the more familiar bitch-and-moan mode. Before I got to know Carol well, I also had found the Zig Ziglarisms hard to take. Later, I realized that this was her method of survival; this was what had enabled her to get past a divorce and bring up two children—both now teenagers—on one income.

When I had tested the flurry of men who came to our clinic after my talk at the Connection, Carol had put their test results in my box with exclamation marks and happy faces: the tests had always been negative for HIV. But this time Carol had her quote for the day written out for me and clipped to Ed and Bobby's test results: *There is nothing either good or bad, but thinking makes it so. Shakespeare.*

The test results showed both Ed and Bobby had been infected with HIV.

I called them and was pleased when an answering machine came on. I left a message for them to come and see me.

I put on my white coat and went to the first exam room.

I experienced a sense of déjà vu—there were two charts outside one exam room. Could Ed and Bobby have returned that quickly? But no, these were two new names: Fred Goodson and Otis Jackson. I held the two charts in my hand and paused before the closed door, rereading the names again and again, pronouncing them carefully.

When I knocked and opened the door to the exam room, I saw two swarthy men in their late thirties, very different from Ed and Bobby, the couple from Abingdon.

The little exam room was redolent with an earthy scent—partly the poor ventilation, partly the leather bomber jacket Fred wore, partly their jeans that looked comfortable but not recently washed, and partly the odor of tobacco that clung to their clothes. They both wore heavy cowboy boots.

Fred had short dark brown hair and a beard, wire-rim glasses, and despite a jocular manner was very intense, very focused on his surroundings and on everything that was transpiring. He wore a red T-shirt under his bomber jacket.

Otis was blond, slim, his hair cut close to his skull and with an even stubble of a beard. He was soft-spoken and laid-back; he had a pronounced Tennessee drawl and was content to let Fred speak for him.

Fred and Otis, though anxious about their visit, seemed much more self-confident than the Abingdon couple. They reminded me in dress and appearance of gay men I had encountered in the AIDS clinics in Boston: a clonish, Tweedledum and Tweedledee sameness, a sense that they belonged to a gay community, that they subscribed to a defined gay aesthetic—at once together, at once defiant.

Once Fred began to speak, I was almost oblivious to Otis. Fred's speech tended to rumble within his throat and bubbled out as if under pressure. He spoke in long sentences with a suppressed chuckle or a *Harrumph!* preceding something ironic or cynical he was about to say, the punctuation between phrases consisting of *ums* or *ahs* or a guttural sound in his throat. Even as *you* talked, he made grunts of agreement. He sounded like one of my former physiology professors:

"Both of us had the antibody test, *uh*, antibody for the HIV, just the other week, and the results, unfortunately, *harrumph!* were positive both on the ELISA, and, *uhm*, positive *again*, *harrumph!* on the confirmatory western blot, and so we, *uh*, decided to seek help and, *harrumph!* here we are," etc., etc.

He pulled out two slips of paper from the health department from a manila folder he was carrying.

In that instant, the number of HIV cases in Johnson City, counting Gordon, and Ed and Bobby, had just increased to five. Seven, if you counted the two who had died before I started my practice.

"I guess there is something that we have to tell you, or perhaps you already know from the chart," said Fred, "but neither of us is insured, covered in any manner, whatsoever."

I said it made no difference to me.

I took Fred's chart first and began to take his history; inevitably, I wound up taking both their histories together.

Fred was born in Morristown, Tennessee. He had gone away to college in Florida, worked for his master's at Madison in Wisconsin. Eventually he joined his uncle's accounting business in 1983. Fred's speech reflected this education. He used high-powered words, punned frequently and had a wry sense of humor. Fred and Otis had met in Tennessee after they both returned home. They had been living together for one year.

I asked Fred why he came back. "I realized teaching college wasn't for me. I had thought it was. That was what I had done all the years of postgraduate work for. And when I started to teach, it was a disappointment. It was clearly not what I wanted to do. I started to help my uncle out while I decided on what next. And I couldn't think of a better place to live than Morristown. No traffic jams. The store clerks are actually polite. I just slipped into the accounting business."

Otis was born in Rogersville, Tennessee. After his teen years, he had left the area and traveled extensively. He was trained as a cook and most recently had lived in the Castro District of San Francisco where he worked for five years before returning to Tennessee. Otis's return, in contrast to Fred's, had the same arbitrary quality of his departure. But he came back from California in 1986, because "I guess I was tired of it, I don't know."

And tiredness was what Otis had been feeling for some time now. Eight months before he had had a severe attack of shingles. It had left him with a scar on his chest and pain that continued to the present time.

Fred, on the other hand, felt quite normal.

Fred made it a point to tell me that he did not think that Otis had necessarily infected him. Fred had had "high-risk sex" (his term, not mine) prior to that with several people who he knew had come down with AIDS. He seemed more concerned about Otis than about himself. Fred was extremely well informed about AIDS.

I went through Otis's "past history" (two episodes of rectal gonorrhea, heavy use of "poppers" in the past, herpes of the penis and anus, and most recently the shingles), and his "social history" (moderate alcohol consumption, not infrequent pot use—"whenever I can get any"—and no intravenous drug use).

When I asked Otis about whether he often had anal receptive intercourse, Fred piped up from behind me: "Uh, not often enough!"

On Otis's "Review of Systems"—a checklist of questions that cover every organ and function of the body—it was clear that Otis had been having some night sweats, some weight loss and a lot of fatigue. He had occasional bouts of diarrhea that mysteriously came and went. I had Otis undress and when I examined him I found diffuse enlargement of his lymph nodes and little else.

While I was doing Otis's rectal exam, Otis looked over to Fred and said, "I wonder if he'll still respect me in the morning?" It was only about the third complete sentence he had uttered in all his time in the room.

This was the second time in a month that I had examined a couple together in one room. In years to come, I did this often—always with gay couples, never with a heterosexual couple. Now, while Otis dressed, Fred undressed.

In contrast to Otis, Fred seemed quite well. I could find no lymph node enlargement. During his rectal exam he hummed "Moon River," while Otis rolled his eyes in mock exasperation.

I was curious about their looks. If Ed and Bobby had aspired to the clean, scrubbed choirboy looks—or, in Ed's case, as close to it as a diesel mechanic can come—then Fred and Otis seemed to be deliberately cultivating a rougher appearance with the short hair, the stubby beards, the jeans and leather jacket. Even the slight unwashed odor seemed deliberate—they were not unclean but they were not attempting to douse the man scent with antiperspirants or *eau de toilette*. As yet, I did not know them well enough to ask them about this.

I did ask them what they thought about the Connection. Fred laughed and Otis smiled.

"It's tacky," said Fred. "Really campy."

"Campy?"

"You know: lots of drag queens and 'shows' and all that. The more theatrical and dramatic elements. Not my cup of tea."

"What *is* your cup of tea?"

He laughed. "There's a leather place in Asheville that would qualify."

This made sense to me. Fred and Otis's clothes were a dressed-down version of the extreme leather look. They were not wearing chaps, or handcuffs, or chains, or nipple rings, but I could see where these accessories would fit well. In later years, when I first saw Robert Mapplethorpe's photos, they reminded me of Fred and Otis and the earthy scent I associated with them.

Fred and Otis left with follow-up appointments for a week from then, at which point all the blood tests and the chest x-rays I ordered would be back. The apprehension and tension they must have experienced while waiting for the HIV test to come back was now behind them.

Ahead of them lay a difficult road.

AFTER EACH PATIENT I examined, I would dictate my findings to be typed up later and put in the patient's clinic chart. The transcriptionist, when she saw me in the hallway, would nervously scurry away. My patients' stories, the descriptions of how they came to be infected, the details of their lives in which I took delight, were scandalizing her! "Campy," "queen," "fisting," "rimming," and "water sports" were not in the medical dictionary that sat next to her keyboard.

There was a reason for a lot of my questions: for example, there was thought to be a correlation between amyl nitrite or "popper" use and Kaposi's sarcoma (KS). There was also a correlation between KS and anal practices: some people argued that KS behaved as if it was a sexually transmitted disease. Not only was it common among gay men, *within* that group it was most common among those who engaged in oral-anal sex and anal receptive intercourse with greater frequency. To know how promiscuous they had been was not a matter of prurient interest on my part: it gave me some sense for their exposure to syphilis, *Herpes simplex*, cytomegalovirus—all infections that could linger in the body and flare up when the immune system was suppressed.

But I was also interested in the patients' stories for their own sake. I was fascinated by the voyage that had brought them to my clinic door. The anecdotes they told me lingered in my mind and became the way I identified them. Most of these stories I kept in my head. Some I recorded in a journal that I kept faithfully and that became very important to me as time went on. Occasionally, I would hear a story so outrageous that I would dictate it to be included in the chart for the sake of posterity. Here is one that I dictated and saved a copy of (this part of the dictation came under social history—after chief complaint, history of present illness, family history, past history):

". . . on Mardi Gras, the patient states he walked down Bourbon Street in New Orleans at about nine in the morning, just as people were coming out onto the terraces. He was returning from an all-night tryst. Patient states it was common once the parade started for people on the terraces to yell 'Take it off,' or 'Show us your titties,' and to throw down bead necklaces to any woman who did. But it was too early for any of that yet. When the patient reached the gay end of Bourbon Street, the terraces were filling up with gay men who were readying their champagne brunches. Someone saw the patient's lone figure walk down the street and yelled, 'Show us your dick, show us your dick!' Others on other balconies took up the chant. The patient states that he proceeded to take off his pants and T-shirt, fold them neatly and then lay naked, spread-eagled on his back in the middle of the street. And pretty soon, according to the patient, 'you could no longer see me because I was all covered with bead necklaces raining down from the balcony.' "

7

VICKIE MCCRAY was a large woman whose usual attire was
blue jeans and an oversize man's shirt. Though she might have
appeared benign in a hospital corridor, her appearance would have
been unmistakably threatening if one encountered her in a dark alley.
Thick forearms swung loosely alongside her hips. You could picture
those forearms holding two babies and a sack of groceries. Or you could
picture them locked around your head in a full nelson.

The first year I knew her, she always wore a red polka-dotted bandanna wrapped tight over her scalp and low over her forehead. As a
result, the skin over her eyebrows was bunched up, and her blue eyes
appeared deeply recessed in her skull. Her eyes were her prettiest feature.

When I saw Vickie, she was bringing her husband, Clyde, back to the
University Family Practice Center for the fourth time in six weeks, and
she had completely run out of patience. After lifting all 180 pounds of
Clyde out of the car and setting him in one of the wheelchairs at the
entrance to the center, she wheeled Clyde in past the startled recep-
tionist. Clyde was a dark, handsome man with thick bushy hair and a
bristling mustache.

"Now look, you all," she said to the doctors gathered outside the
exam rooms. "Just *look* at him! Would depression or nerves do this to
a grown man? Would it make him lose weight? Would it make him stop
talking and become like a baby? Would it make him hiccup like this for

weeks? You all *are* going to put him in the hospital. You *will* find out what's wrong with him, and there ain't two ways about it!"

Clyde sat passively in the wheelchair, looking on with little understanding. When a hiccup broke to the surface and rippled across his face, he winked at the doctors.

In the hospital, the family practice doctors ran every test in the book. A specialist was called in for each organ that showed any trace of being dysfunctional.

The CAT scan of Clyde's head showed his brain had shriveled and atrophied in a way that one would have expected to see in a seventy-year-old with Alzheimer's disease. The picture was distinctly abnormal for a thirty-five-year-old truck driver who had been well six weeks prior to the test. Dr. W, an astute neurologist, ordered the HIV test on Clyde's blood—more for completion, I suspect, than with any real belief that this was AIDS. And when this came back positive during the second week of Clyde's hospitalization, I was called in.

The doctors told Vickie that Clyde's HIV test indicated he had AIDS, and moreover, she should be tested.

After hearing the devastating news, Vickie left the hospital and drove out to their trailer. She called up Clyde's sisters and his mother and let them know. Then she went to her bedroom and loaded the gun Clyde kept in his closet. She had in mind that she would go to the hospital and kill Clyde—not out of anger, but only to put him out of his misery. She had seen him reduced mentally and physically to a shell of his former self, and now she had been told that it was only going to go downhill from that point. After she was done killing Clyde, she planned to pick up the kids—her four-year-old son and twelve-year-old daughter—go back to the trailer, shoot the kids and finally turn the gun on herself. This seemed like the most logical option given the impossible events that they would all have to face if they went on living.

She was fumbling with the gun, stuffing bullets into it, when the box fell off the bed and scattered bullets all over the floor. It was while Vickie was on her knees, picking up the bullets, that she had a vision of her children holding hands, standing by the bedrail and saying to her, "Mom, we have a right to live as well. What did *we* do to deserve this?"

At this point, Vickie dropped the gun and fell onto the bed and wept.

This is how Clyde Junior and Danielle found her when they returned from school.

WHEN I WENT TO CLYDE'S room, I found Vickie there with him. I had read through the chart and had understood the medical elements of the case. But the *story* of this couple was not in there.

I prefaced my interview by telling both Vickie and Clyde that I was going to ask personal and touchy questions that were not meant to offend, only to leave no stone unturned. Vickie was standing next to the head of the bed, her hand protectively on Clyde's shoulder. She regarded me with curiosity and suspicion: this foreign doctor, this "infection" specialist. I, in turn, was quite intimidated by her.

"Has he ever used intravenous drugs?" I asked. "No!" Vickie answered without even looking at Clyde for confirmation.

"Has he ever had sex with another man?"

"Hell, no!" said Vickie.

"Yes," said Clyde from behind her.

"WHAT?"

"Yes," Clyde said.

Vickie looked at Clyde, her jaw dropping, anger flashing in her eyes. "He don't know what he's saying! They've pumped him full of Thorazine. Don't pay him no mind. It's the Thorazine what does him that way."

"I've had sex with men," Clyde said again. "With Jewell, all the time." He clammed up after that shocker, tuning both of us out in the manner of a peevish two-year-old. He began to play with the remote, clicking through the channels until Vickie snatched it from him, at which point he pulled the sheet over his head and lay still like a mummy.

As it turned out, Clyde was telling the truth. A spark of lucidity in a brain that was otherwise hopelessly muddled had brought out this unrepressed and unabashed admission. Clyde never had a blood transfusion, he had never used intravenous drugs, and, to our knowledge, never had a prolonged relationship with an HIV-infected woman. Clyde Odum McCray had contracted the AIDS virus in the same manner as almost every other nondrug-using male in North America.

Medically, then, Clyde's bizarre symptoms—the mutism, the weight loss, the regression to second childhood—were no longer a puzzle: He had a positive antibody test for the AIDS virus, he had brain atrophy on his CAT scan, and on mental status testing he was showing a global deterioration of all his cognitive functions—this was classic AIDS dementia.

I decided not to pursue any more history. Vickie was too distraught. She was wild-eyed and mute; she relinquished her post near the head of the bed and now sat in the recliner, holding her head in her hands.

I gently pulled the sheet away from Clyde. He was petulant but allowed me to examine him. I did my own mini mental status exam, a crude version of what the psychologists had already administered. Clyde was oriented to person—he knew who Vickie was, who he was—but not to place and time. I gave him the names of three objects in the room and told him I would ask him in a few minutes to repeat them to me. Then I asked him to subtract 7 from 100. He came out with 93. I asked him to subtract 7 from 93. He could go no further. I now asked him for the names of the three objects I had mentioned earlier. He recalled only one. Yet his remote memory for events like his birthday, the town where he was born, his father's name, was intact. This is characteristic of many types of insult to the brain: recent memory is lost while remote memory is preserved; new stuff is lost before old.

I looked carefully for the lesions of Kaposi's sarcoma but did not find any. Clyde seemed to be in good physical shape in terms of muscle mass and tone. His heart and lungs were quite normal. His coordination was poor and his reflexes extremely brisk when I tapped on his tendons with my reflex hammer.

I reported to Vickie that other than his confusion, Clyde was in good shape. I elected to return later and chat with both of them some more. I felt I needed to leave the room. I gave Vickie my card and told her to call me any time. When I left, Vickie had risen to stand next to Clyde, to quiz him, to explore further his revelation to us, but Clyde had the sheet pulled over his head.

I drove over to the University Practice Clinic—I had arranged to see Ed Maupin and Bobby Keller and give them the news about their tests. They were waiting for me.

"Our test come back positive, didn't it, Doc?" Ed asked me, as soon as I walked into the room. I nodded my head. He seemed resigned to this fact. Bobby Keller began to sob, his big shoulders shaking, his face taking on an expression that could have passed for laughter but for the tears that were spilling out of his eyes.

I told them how everything now rested on their CD4 count; if it was high they could count on doing well for years perhaps. And by then, God willing, we would have some sort of treatment to offer.

"It's all up to the big man up there, ain't it, Doc?" Ed said, raising his eyes skyward.

"We need all the help we can get," I said.

I told them I needed to examine them, to see if there was any evidence the virus was doing anything more than just existing in the body.

Ed Maupin stood up at once and took his shirt off. Bobby Keller was still weeping.

Ed, with his shirt off, looked older than his forty-two years. He had no fever, and his pulse was normal. But he had striking lymph-node enlargement in his neck and armpits and also some yeast infection in his mouth. His blood pressure was raised but this was an old problem, unrelated to HIV infection. He had briefly taken blood pressure medications, but was not on any now. I found his heart to be mildly enlarged, probably a consequence of the high blood pressure. I elected not to treat the blood pressure until I had some laboratory tests back and could see what his kidney function was like. I would embark on treatment at the next visit.

I coaxed Bobby Keller onto the exam table and had him remove his shirt. The tears were pouring uncontrollably off his cheeks, falling onto his breasts. He was, in contrast to Ed, quite normal except that he was overweight. Bobby now spoke the first words since I stepped into the room, sobbing them out in a manner that tugged at my heartstrings: "You don't understand, Doc. I'm not worried about myself. I'm worried about Ed. He's been real tired and at night he sometimes breaks out into a cold sweat and cries in his sleep. Take care of him, Doc. He's my life and without him I wouldn't want to live." Ed came up to Bobby now, and Bobby laid his head on Ed's chest and wailed so loud that I was sure it could be heard all through the clinic. Carol came into the room, and reflexively stood on the other side of Bobby, rubbing his back, hugging him, until gradually his cries turned to muffled sobs.

I promised I would do my best for both of them. As soon as their CD4 count came back we would plot a strategy.

When Carol left the room, I cautioned them again about safe sex. I expected them to tell me not to worry, that sex was the last thing on their minds. Instead, Ed looked at Bobby and said, "You hear what the Doc says, Bobby?" Bobby nodded his head without much conviction.

Part of the excitement of sex for Ed and Bobby was the element of danger, the breaking of a taboo, the anonymity. It was not just chutzpah that made them go to church and greet the married men they were sleeping with and say "Hi" to the men's wives and children and slyly make a date for a half-hour later. "Safe sex" was a cerebral concept that sounded good in my office. Yet, it was not the cerebrum, but some other part of the body that took over when a good-looking man cruised them in the grocery store and beckoned for them to follow in the direction of his car. Of course, this was far from a problem confined to gay men: No cerebral abstraction involving sex—whether it was the need for contraception, proscriptions against adultery, or the need for safe sex—had ever in human history fared well in the face of raw lust.

When Ed and Bobby were finally ushered out, I checked the box where lab tests I had ordered would be kept. For the whole week after I saw Fred Goodson and Otis Jackson, I had been restless, waiting to get their CD4 count. It would tell me how they would do in the next few months and years. Were they early in their infection, or had the virus been chipping away at their immune system for some time now?

When the tests came back, Fred's count was 1,100. Over 1,000 was good; below 500 was bad. In later years, a count of 500 was the threshold at which we began AZT. Fewer than 200 CD4 cells and the patient became very prone to *Pneumocystis* and other infections. Fewer than 50 and we would begin to see *Mycobacterium avium intracellulare* (MAI) and other infections. Otis's count was 30. His immune system was faltering badly.

I called Fred and Otis on the phone. Fred picked up, for which I was pleased. I told Fred what the numbers were. I did not have to explain much to him; Fred had been boning up on AIDS. He had several excellent publications written on AIDS by gays. Fred understood the significance of Otis's CD4 count. He promised to tell Otis. They had an appointment to see me in a few weeks.

VICKIE CALLED IN THE afternoon and I drove over from the VA to the Miracle Center. Clyde was back to flipping channels on the TV. I took Vickie away to the hospital's "quiet" room—the same room where I had talked to Gordon's family. Vickie and I sat there and talked for an hour. I learned her story over the course of this and several other visits with her.

Vickie grew up in the tough Greystone housing projects outside of Johnson City. Though she had food, clothing, shelter—"I was lucky compared to Clyde"—she had to use her fists to establish an identity in the projects, to keep herself and her younger sisters from being trampled over. Her father was an alcoholic and her mother had disappeared when Vickie was seventeen. Her decision to marry Clyde had as much to do with the promise of escaping the house as it did with her attraction to this brooding, silent man.

Clyde's father, also an alcoholic, had lived out in the country, scratching out an existence by raising corn and planting a huge garden. A tough, abusive man, he thought nothing of taking the hoe handle to the side of his son's head, terrorizing him in the interest of "raising him right." Clyde's mother had worked third-shift all her life and never knew or cared to know what was going on. When she gave birth many years later to two girls, Clyde became the unpaid baby-sitter on top of all his other chores. Beneath his silence there lurked some deep scars that even Vickie never came close to finding out about. By the time he and Vickie tied the knot, Clyde had been married twice.

During the first years of their marriage, Vickie and Clyde lived in Tester Hollow, surrounded by his kith and kin. They occupied a cinder block house out in a field in the back of Clyde's mother's house. It had no heat or running water and the outhouse was a good ways away, near the well. "At night we could look out through the cracks between the cinder blocks and see the stars; we just about froze to death every winter. I cooked on a little hot plate. If I wanted to bake bread or anything like that, I had to go use my mother-in-law's oven." As a construction worker, Clyde was bringing in just enough money for them to live on.

After Danielle was born and when Vickie was pregnant with Clyde Junior she found out that Clyde was sleeping with her sister. "I almost left him, but I really couldn't go anywhere. To go back to my father's would have been terrible; he didn't want me and I didn't care to be around him. Besides, my sister—the one who slept with Clyde—was living with Pa; she never did marry. My other sisters had their hands full with their husbands and children. And I had no money to take off on my own. So I just stayed.

"A part of me felt Clyde was oversexed, you know what I mean? And I hadn't been able to give him what he needed, that was why he had slept with my sister. I fought with my sister something awful for that, but even then I didn't hate her. She was heavier than me and not pretty, and I knew her life was tough living there with Pa. She got pregnant some years later, and I had a feeling it was Clyde's but there was no way to tell. To tell you the truth, I didn't care at that point. And Clyde's attitude was kind of like that joke: 'Who're you going to believe, me or your lying eyes?' Well, I chose to believe him; it was easier.

"Clyde worked so many different jobs. But it seemed like we never was getting ahead. We lived in Tester Hollow—which I just hated—and it looked like we would be there forever. He'd been a short-order cook, a graveyard digger, a mover with a moving company, a sewer worker, a construction worker. The money was never enough, not when you had two young'uns and doctor's bills and such like. Clyde was drinking pretty heavy then—I'd say he was an alcoholic—and even the cheapest liquor warn't cheap, as much as he could put away.

"One day Clyde says to me, 'Vickie, I want to be a truck driver.' He was as serious as a heart attack. He said where he'd seen this ad on TV and it had been playing in his mind. Now his heart was all set to study truck driving. Clyde talked so little that I knew it must have been building up something fierce for him to string all them words together. He sent off for the forms and I helped him fill them out. I thought to myself that maybe this was it, maybe this would be our break.

"He studied hard and I helped him—he had dropped out at seventh grade and could hardly read, see. I had done gone on almost to finish high school. Finally, in February, he went down to Florida for a week to do the driving part of the course. Well, when he came back, it took him till May to finally get a job, but when he did I thought, praise the Lord! Our life's done turned around.

"He was hauling produce to Florida and back and I mean to say he was working *hard*. He didn't get paid unless he made those schedules and they were tough. I knew he was taking what they called 'white crosses' to stay awake, and God knows what else. That's what I thought was wrong when he started to lose weight. And when he was home, the drinking was worse.

"Then he began to hiccup. I thought it was the liquor. But then he never quit with the hiccups: he hiccuped for two weeks, night and day. It was driving me crazy. And he wasn't right otherwise. He would just sit there on the sofa and watch TV, not even know when we came and left the room—I had to remind him to go to work. He became more and more tired, lost more weight and, meanwhile, the goddamn hiccups, every twenty seconds. They finally let him go at work; I don't blame them.

"That's when I brought him to the doctors. And you know the rest."

When I left Vickie, I made an appointment for her to see me in the following Wednesday's clinic. The Family Practice Group had already drawn her blood to be tested for HIV. The result would be out in the next day or so. I thought Vickie had a good chance of not being infected. If only because Clyde was too busy sleeping around with others.

THOUGH I WAS PRIMARILY a Mountain Home VA employee, lived on the Mountain Home campus, did my research in the laboratories at the VA, my thoughts were very much on the HIV-infected persons I had seen at the Miracle Center and at the University Physicians Group office. For several weeks now—ever since Essie Vines had brought Gordon down to the emergency room—I had been going through the motions at the VA. Patients at the VA were interesting (though somewhat predictable), my research was going well, and I had my hands full with student and resident teaching.

But I couldn't stop fingering the index cards I now carried in my breast pocket: one each for Gordon, Ed and Bobby, Fred and Otis. One for Clyde McCray with Vickie's name penciled in on the seventh card, awaiting the results of her test. I put a date on Fred and Otis's cards and wrote their CD4 counts next to it. I spread the cards in my hand and wondered idly, How many cards I would be carrying next week? Next year?

THAT EVENING, after Steven and Rajani had gone to sleep, I called Essie to ask how Gordon was doing. She was pleased to hear from me. If she thought it strange that the doctor should be calling at a late hour to inquire about his patient who had been discharged some time ago, she said nothing. Besides, who was to dictate what conventions applied to AIDS? With just seven cases under my complete care—not the surrogate care of a Boston City Hospital where ten other specialists and interns and residents were seeing the same patient—I was developing a patient-physician relationship unlike anything I had known.

Essie said that Gordon's temperature had remained normal with only a few spikes ever since his discharge. As soon as they got home, Gordon had wanted to be baptized before anything else was done. He talked of nothing else for that first day. His uncle was a lay preacher. Gordon asked his uncle if he would baptize him. He agreed.

The next morning, the family took Gordon in a borrowed van to the church. The pastor had given Gordon's uncle free rein to use the place. They walked Gordon into the vestry, one of them on either side. He was extremely short of breath but they helped him up the stairs to the baptismal tank and then down the stairs into the water. The process exhausted them all. They had to carry Gordon back to the van and later lift him like a baby into the house. But it was worth it: the expression on his face was priceless; he was at peace and greatly relieved.

The baptism produced opposite effects on Gordon and his father. The father was sure that now Gordon was going to live. The father's denial had taken on new heights. He talked about perhaps starting a business with Gordon. His speech was peppered with "when Gordon gets better . . ." It was not possible to reason with him about this.

Gordon, on the other hand, Essie reported, was feeling a genuine peace, not the passivity with which he had dealt with his illness thus far. He told Essie he was ready to die, and that his Saviour was waiting for him. The Gordon who returned from Florida may have seemed like an impostor, but the impostor had been exorcised. Gordon was back. His major regret at this point was the burden he felt he was on his family.

At one point Gordon felt well enough to sit out on the porch. When Essie had returned from work, she found Gordon there in his dressing gown. When she stepped out of the car he put on his Bugs Bunny voice:

"Hello, dolling! What say you and I go rashmagooling, just you and me." Essie had laughed till she cried.

Gordon was trying to use the bathroom himself, but his legs were tiring out and sometimes he did not get there in time. They had convinced him to wear diapers at night. He was having frequent accidents, day and night.

I asked Essie how the community was reacting to this. Did anyone know?

"Oh, I think everybody knows."

"*How?*"

"*I* told them. I don't think we have anything to hide."

Essie had no time to waste on worrying about the reaction of her neighbors. If there was shame in her brother having AIDS, in his being gay, she did not feel it. If anyone else felt it, it was irrelevant. I remembered her saying when I had visited her house that "he was Gordo before he was anything else. Gay was what he did, not who he was."

"And have you had any negative reactions from anyone?"

"Not really. Some women from our church have been coming by, bringing food—not that Gordo eats anything. If there is negative reaction, they sure better not come and say anything to me."

I was sorry I asked. It was as if I was digging for dirt. But it was something I wanted to know. The reactions to AIDS elsewhere in the country had not exactly been kind and understanding.

Essie went on: "I think people are real scared of AIDS, if that's what you mean. One time I was cleaning up Gordo when Jack, my friend from work, walked in. I'll be honest with you: Jack never has married. I have heard tell that he might be gay—which don't matter to me none, cause I love him to death. Well I had Gordo rolled over in bed and you know how skinny he is now. His back is just bones, a line of little marbles running down from his neck to his butt. And his buttocks—he don't have buttocks anymore. His butt is as flat as a pancake. The skin sort of sags there like an old man's. And his anus is one big hole in the middle of all this sagging flesh, bigger than all the rest of him. Well, I turned and I seen Jack looking. He was in shock, his mouth open. I don't think it had really hit him till then how bad this disease does you. Well, I stopped what I was doing and just let him see that—I wanted him to see it. Gordo's face was turned to the wall; he didn't know Jack was watching.

"Son, he just about froze there in the doorway. I thought he might faint. When I was done with Gordo and tucked him in good, I went out to find Jack. He was sitting on the porch, a-shaking and a-quivering like he was ready to have a fit. I sat next to him, tried to tell him how this was a bad, bad disease. To make sure that he understood everything about it, that he protect himself. Well, he up and bolted from there. I don't think he can bear to look at Gordo again. And used to, he was here every day, chatting with Gordo, keeping him company—"

"—because he wants Gordo's box collection, that's why," Sabatha piped in on the phone. She must have been in the same room as Essie, overhearing her talk. She had spoken loudly, intending for me to hear.

"Now hush about them boxes," Essie said. "He said they're going to be yours and that's all there is to it."

I heard Sabatha's voice say, "But I know Jack has his eye on them. Never mind that Gordo wants me to have them."

"Hush now."

VICKIE'S BLOOD TEST came back positive. Clyde had infected her.

When Vickie found out she was positive, she told the family practice doctors that they needed to test her sister. Her sister's test came back positive—she too was infected. None of the children—neither Vickie's nor her sister's—were infected.

I had been talking to Vickie off and on by telephone. Visiting nurse services were arranged to help her care for Clyde. At home, Clyde had become a little child, just like his son, Clyde, Jr. He and Clyde, Jr., would roll around on the carpet together, would play elaborate games, lining up Junior's Big-Foot trucks and racing them over the tops of his matchbox sedans. Danielle, who was twelve years old, began to help Vickie take care of Clyde. The family roles had been exchanged: Clyde had become the baby, Junior became the brother, Danielle was the mother and Vickie had become the provider and guardian.

Vickie's sister could not be convinced to come and see me and let me evaluate her. She had allowed herself to be tested, she had found out she had the virus, and that was it.

When I talked to Vickie on the phone, I could tell that she was very stressed. She was taking Valium that I had prescribed, but she was still walking the edge of a mental breakdown. Word had got around her community that Clyde had AIDS. And that Vickie had it too. "I'm driving down the road and my neighbors look away. I stare at them, but they won't look at me. I tell you what, I am keeping a list in my mind of the people who did that. They'll get theirs one of these days."

I blocked out an hour and a half for Vickie's visit with us at the clinic. When Vickie came in, Carol, my nurse, introduced herself and ushered Vickie into a room. When Carol came out, she said, "I'm going to get a suture set; you might have to do a little sewing!"

I entered the room and saw that Carol had exposed and cleaned with peroxide an ugly V-shaped cut on the third knuckle of Vickie's right hand. The skin hung down in a flap.

"That's my cousin Grace's tooth what done that."

Carol and I waited for the explanation.

"Andrew and Grace, my cousins?"

Vickie saw that this was hardly an explanation and so she sighed and said, "You all are going to think I'm awful. But what the hell. See, there's someone what works at the Medical Center—a relative more or less, you could say—who done told a bunch of folk in Tester Hollow that Clyde and I have AIDS. You know people around here are so damn inquisitive they wouldn't hesitate to stop a funeral to ask what deceased the corpse! But whoever he *didn't* tell, Grace, my cousin, did.

"Grace and her husband, Andrew, go to this Holiness church, just a little ways from the house? I never go no more—I can't take all that babbling in tongues and holy spirit stuff; scares the shit out of me. But Clyde, now that he's sick, has been wanting to go to church. Well, my big-mouth cousin stands up in church and tells the whole goddamn church that Clyde has AIDS and would the church be willing for him to come there, cause he very much wants to."

"Did you or Clyde ask her to do that?"

"*Hell, no!* She just took it on herself to do it! And by the way, the church congregation said No! When I heard about it, I called her on the phone and said, 'You little dumbass, who told you to go talking like that? How would you feel if the shoe was on the other foot? Don't you *ever* step in my house again or I'll kick your ass till your nose bleeds.'

"Well, Andrew gets on the phone and says they would come and see their cousin any time it pleased them. I said I'd like to see him try. Can you believe it, they came right over! And when I picked up a poker and went after Andrew, buddy, he just lit out like his pants were on fire. Grace was just standing there. I got so mad just looking at her face. I dropped the poker and just let her have it with my fists. I dropped her with one shot and then I sat on her and just done give it to her, bust a few teeth I reckon."

As Vickie said this, she made the motion of cupping one fist into the palm of the other. It was a powerful little gesture; there was nothing dainty about it. Clearly she knew what she was doing.

"The only reason I stopped was because Clyde was weeping and crying from the sofa, begging for me to quit. By then I had whopped her good."

I trimmed Vickie's wound and dressed it. I decided against suturing it because these sort of closed-fist injuries commonly get infected. I made a mental note to prescribe an antibiotic for her before she left.

I began to examine Vickie with Carol in attendance. This was the first time I had needed a chaperon with an HIV patient.

I went through Vickie's social history and family history and past history, much of which I already knew. Vickie had been under treatment off and on by a local psychiatrist for "nerves." She was taking a blood pressure pill. Despite that her blood pressure was high. I looked carefully into her retinae to see if she had narrowing of the vessels or hemorrhage that might suggest the high blood pressure had been present for a long time. Her retinae looked normal.

Vickie balked when I asked her to remove the bandanna knotted over her scalp and low over her brow. I told her I needed to go over her head to foot.

Her lower lip began to tremble and tears formed in her eyes. "I'm real ashamed about this." Very reluctantly she began to unknot the bandanna, pausing once, as if she had changed her mind. I could see beneath the bandanna that she was totally bald.

Carol looked puzzled.

"I did it," Vickie said.

Vickie had picked out every hair on her scalp herself: trichotillomania, a compulsive disorder, an indication of her extreme psychological distress. Sometimes these patients would also develop trichobezoars, or large hair balls, in their stomachs from swallowing this hair. Carol and I were affected by this sight: this outwardly tough woman who had picked herself bald because of the hell she was going through, a hell that had *preceded* Clyde getting ill. We reassured her, told her we understood; I was pleased to find that she seemed in fine physical health except for the elevated blood pressure. Carol and I stood by as Vickie retied the bandanna.

When her CD4 lymphocyte count came back, it was over a thousand—just about normal. Clyde's CD4 count in the hospital had been 7!

Vickie would be with us a long time. It was unclear about Clyde.

LATE THAT NIGHT, after Steven was asleep, Rajani and I sat outside on the porch swing. The demands of one child so occupied her that we had few moments like this. She sat beside me brushing her hair which she had recently bobbed because it was easier to take care of. I mourned the loss of her long hair which I had always believed she kept for me. But I said nothing. Rajani seemed more efficient and serious now; she was a mother, less relaxed, less carefree. I told her about my day, about how preoccupied I was with my seven patients with HIV infection in our small town, how these seven people eclipsed whatever else I was doing in the medical school.

She asked me, "Why is it different here than in Boston? You saw AIDS in Boston, and I don't remember you being this involved."

"I think it's because I am their sole doctor here; there *is* no one else following them."

Out of the blue she turned to me, put down her brush and asked me, "Are you sexually attracted to the gay men?"

"WHAT?" I felt she had entirely missed the point, that she had been waiting for this moment. I couldn't believe my wife was capable of reducing my complicated feelings to something just sexual.

"I'm curious. You seem comfortable enough with them."

It was true that I had become comfortable around gay men. I was too interested in them and in their stories to be judgmental.

"In a way," I said, "these men are more representative of *men* than heterosexual men, if you know what I mean?"

Rajani looked at me warily.

"I mean to say, with gay men you are looking at men *without* the confounding influence of women to deal with. You are looking at the behavior of men left to themselves, men not conditioned by what women allow, what women find acceptable, what society thinks is normal."

"Meaning what?"

"Meaning perhaps, that some of the sexual activity of gay men, their sexual drive, the number and variety of partners, the ready possibility of anonymous sex, might represent what *all* men want, except that they can't get women to agree."

I was pleased with my little thesis. Rajani was not impressed. As she went into the house, I called after her, "By the way, the answer to your question is no."

8

THERE HAD BEEN some debate when Gordon came home as to whether his nieces and nephews should be allowed to spend time with him. The visiting nurse who had instructed Essie and her mother on the use of bleach for spills, on the need for gloves when handling secretions, was consulted and saw no reason for the children not to be there.

"Has she any experience with AIDS?" I asked Essie.

"No. I guess she just got it from books."

I was amazed by the ease with which medical services were being delivered to Gordon. A local pharmacist was providing the medications I prescribed, which he had in turn acquired from a distributor in Charlotte; the pharmacist knew the diagnosis. The nursing supervisor at the hospital, a friend of Essie's, had loaned her some oxygen equipment. This was a time when elsewhere in the country, AIDS had generated some ignoble responses from doctors and other medical personnel. But in Blackwood, none of this was in evidence.

Gordon spent great lengths of time with his nieces. He asked Sabatha to fetch his box collection from the duplex, and he would tell her the story behind each box. He took long naps. He rarely watched the TV in the room, preferring instead the company of visitors, or staring out of the window at the cars driving by or at the mountains just behind the house.

Gordon hated his diapers and he tried his best to use the bathroom himself. It embarrassed him greatly when Essie or his mother had to clean him up. Essie said to him, "Gordon, there's nothing I haven't seen. Now you lie back and hush."

Gordon's father did not participate in the cleaning up, but was ready to do anything else Gordon wanted. He spent long hours with Gordon, though they rarely had much to say to each other. "It's come twenty years too late," Gordon said to Essie about their father's attention to him.

When it came time for Gordon's follow-up appointment in the clinic, his father insisted that *he* would drive him there and back. Essie and her mother could have taken off from work, but the father wouldn't hear of it.

I WAS IN an exam room with another patient when Carol poked her head in and said that she needed me right away. She led me to the exam room where she had placed Gordon.

I was shocked at Gordon's appearance. It was not just that he had lost so much weight, or that his eyes stared out of deep hollows, or that the flesh above his temples seemed to have collapsed, sticking to his skull; Gordon was gasping for air at forty-two breaths a minute. His lips were blue. He was sweating profusely, and he had a look of fear on his face.

I asked Carol to give him oxygen and call an ambulance. We would take him over to the emergency room at the Miracle Center. I took his blood pressure; I got a systolic reading of ninety. "How long has he been this way?" I asked the father, who was standing close to Gordon, his hat firmly on his head.

"Oh, he's fine, he's fine. He just got a little winded walking from the car to the office, is all." I wanted to say that there were wheelchairs in the lobby for just that purpose. And how could the father look at Gordon and think he was fine?

"Why do you want to take him to the emergency room?" the father asked.

I asked the father to step outside with me.

"Gordon looks very sick and I'm worried that he might stop breathing any second now."

Mr. Vines had his arms crossed and was staring at the floor. His jaw was set and he plainly didn't agree with what I was saying.

In the emergency room, after some fluids and high concentrations of oxygen, Gordon began to look a little better. The expression on his face in my office had told me that he sensed impending doom. Now, this look was receding. An arterial blood oxygen measurement showed that his oxygen level was safe again, although it should have been much higher for a man his age. A portable chest x-ray taken in the emergency room showed a honeycomb pattern to both lungs. It was similar to what he had when he was in the hospital, except now it looked a little coarser, more chronic, as if the interstitium of his lungs was getting thick and fibrous from persistent inflammation.

I called Essie at work in Virginia to tell her what had happened and to find out how recent this degree of shortness of breath was. She said Gordon had not been anywhere as short of breath as I was describing. But he had been puffing ever since he left the hospital; the slightest effort took away his wind. He had been trying to go to the bathroom every other day so that he could stand in the tub while they showered him. But now he was unable to do that because the steam in the bathroom made him suffocate. Essie wondered if the oxygen tank he drove down with had become empty. Or had Gordon and his father forgotten to hook it up?

I described the x-ray to her.

"What do you think is going on in his lungs?" she asked.

I said that I didn't know. I wanted to put him in the hospital and have the pulmonary physician do another bronchoscopy and try to find out. The last bronchoscopy had not revealed *Pneumocystis*. It was my suspicion that Gordon had an inflammation of the interstitium or supporting framework of the lung, an inflammation caused by HIV itself. There were a few reports of this in the medical literature. But this was a diagnosis we could only arrive at by excluding other infectious causes of lung damage.

"I've got to warn you," Essie said, "that both Pa and Gordon are determined that he not be admitted to the hospital again."

"Why? Even if he is suffering?"

"I'm with you, Abraham. But Gordo's got it in his head that he is dying, and he wants to do so at home, not in the hospital. He's real worried about running up bills, though he won't say so. And my father feels that Gordon got worse in the hospital, and he thinks Gordon is getting better at home."

When I went back to Gordon's cubicle and suggested admission, father and son declined, just as Essie said they would. Gordon was still very short of breath, but not *in extremis* as he had been. The father couldn't wait for us to get Gordon ready to leave. Gordon wanted no medications. What was the point of their two-hour drive to see me, I wondered? We set Gordon up with fresh oxygen, took him in a wheelchair to his father's van, and sent them on their way.

I called Essie that evening to make sure they had reached home safely. They had. Essie sounded really tired. "But Gordon's breathing is definitely worse than it has been for some time."

TWO NIGHTS LATER, Gordon's mother woke up after hearing a loud thump. She had been sleeping next to Gordon. Now the bed was empty. She found him in a fetal position at the bedroom door. She lifted him back onto the bed—he weighed only eighty pounds—and he proceeded to have a seizure, reminiscent of the "fits" of his childhood. Essie was called and they took him to the local hospital.

The ER physician found that Gordon had had a stroke. He did not move the right side of his body; the right side of his face was drooping. He did not speak.

The ER doc called me. I suggested that he perform a CAT scan of the head. The hospital did not have a CAT scanner, and it would be a day before the mobile scanner that served the area came by. If Gordon was stable to be transported, I said, I would be happy to receive him in Johnson City. He said the family did not want that. In that case, I recommended they begin treatment for toxoplasmosis—the commonest cause of seizures and strokes in AIDS. Other infectious processes seemed less likely. During Gordon's previous hospitalization we had treated him presumptively and intensively for neurosyphilis based on some abnormalities in his spinal fluid. The spinal fluid, bone marrow and bronchoscopy specimens had not shown any signs of tuberculosis. Toxoplasmosis was a likely cause of his problem.

Essie came on the line. "Abraham, if you tell me that bringing him there will make a real difference, I'll bring him there myself even if I may not have a family left when I get back."

I could not say that bringing him to me would make a critical difference. We might learn exactly what Gordon's problem was. But I doubted that such knowledge would increase the quality of his life, or even extend it.

Gordon was taken home from the ER. The next day he was able to open his eyes, though nothing else moved. Essie, on her way to work in the morning would look in on him. She would wave when she left and call out, "Bye, Bugsy. 'Vive gwot to go earn me a viving." She thought Gordon smiled and tried to move his good arm to wave back.

WHEN HER MOTHER CALLED Essie at work, five days after the stroke, to say she thought Gordon was dead, Essie shouted into the phone: "Don't touch a thing! I'll be right there."

"Gordon's gone," she said to her supervisor as she hung up the phone and grabbed her jacket. She was at her mother's house within twenty minutes of the call. She found her mother sitting bent over in her armchair, wringing her hands. Essie's father stood by the west window, his cap on and his hands deep in his overalls. Essie wondered why she had risked her life in the little pickup, hurtling down the mountain road to get back to the house. Her parents wouldn't have done anything till she came anyway.

In the bedroom the curtains were drawn and the scent of menthol liniment was still strong. She pulled the covers back and watched Gordon's belly, as if, just to prove his parents wrong, he might suck in a breath. His belly was scooped out from rib cage to hips. His eyes were shut. His mouth was closed. Her brother did not move.

She peeked under the edge of his diaper as she had done that morning before going to work: he was dry. There was nothing for Essie to do but cross Gordon's arms over his chest.

She came out to the living room, picked up the slim telephone directory for Wise County, Virginia, and dialed A. J. "Doochie" Jones's funeral home. Her mother said, "Essie . . . ?" but Essie shushed her as Doochie came on the line.

"Doochie? This is Essie Vines. My brother Gordon done passed away. You knew he was sick? . . . That's right . . . for a *long* time. Now, I'm going to tell you the honest truth: Gordon had the HIV factor. That's what killed him." Here she took a deep breath to keep her words from running into each other. "Now you just tell me, yes or no. Can you take care of him?"

There was silence on the other end, and when he started with "Lord ha' mercy, Essie. I'm real sorry to hear it," she could hear the fear in his voice. She could feel her anger rising.

"Just yes or no, Doochie?"

"Now, Essie, I got to tell you, I never studied how to prepare that kind of a body . . ."

"You buried everyone else in this family that ever died. That's why I called you. Yes or no?"

"I want for us to do the service, Essie. And all the other arrangements. It's just that I got these cuts on my hands from where that formalin dries me up? And I worry, you understand?"

"I understand where ignorance could lead you to believe that," Essie said before she hung up on him.

Her parents stared at her, her mother about to say something. Essie said, "Now hush, Mama. I said I'm going to take care of this, and that's all there is to it."

She dialed George Wiseman in Norton, ten miles away. She knew George from church. What would she do if George said no?

George came on the line. She told it to him just as she had told Doochie: Gordon had died, Gordon had the HIV factor. "AIDS," she added for emphasis. Her parents winced when she said the word. In all the time Gordon had been sick, Essie had never heard her mother or her father say "AIDS" or "gay." Not once.

She told George how Doochie would do the service but was scared to prepare the body.

"—*I'll* do it," George said. She felt a huge burden lift off her shoulders. "Don't you worry none. And I'll ask if Doochie'll let me use his mortuary. He won't have to do a thing—I'll do it all myself. That'll save me from having to take the body all the way to Norton and bring it back."

"*I'll* tell Doochie," Essie said.

Essie called A. J. "Doochie" Jones and told him how it was going to be.

TWO HOURS LATER, old Doochie's black Cadillac pulled up outside the house. She saw George get out from the passenger side, calm and professional in his maroon blazer. Doochie was in shirtsleeves, fussing with the back door of the Cadillac. His hair, which he dragged from one ear to the other, had fallen away like a wing, revealing his bald scalp.

They carried the gurney into the bedroom, unfolded its legs and set it parallel to the bed. Doochie pulled on what looked to Essie like calving gloves. George, gloveless, went to the head of the bed. Doochie gingerly peeled the covers away from Gordon's feet. Essie couldn't stand it any longer.

"Doochie Jones! Just move out of the way. *I'll* help George." She pushed past him.

"Why, Essie," Doochie whined but stayed back against the wall. She and George unfolded the plastic sheet, rolled Gordon to one side and tucked it under his body. Then they rolled him the other way and pulled the sheet through. They wrapped Gordon in the sheet, then lifted Gordon onto the orange blanket that lay spread out on the gurney.

"Folks like you," Essie said to Doochie as she helped George fold the monogrammed blankets over Gordon, "is supposed to be *educated* about this sort of thing. This here is nineteen and eighty-seven. Do you think for one moment that this is the last time you're going to be called to do this?"

Doochie made no answer. He and George maneuvered the gurney out of the bedroom and into the living room. Essie's father came and put his hand on the orange mound, silent tears trickling down his cheeks.

The men waited.

After a while Essie nodded at them to go on.

Essie watched them down the porch stairs. She watched Gordon's legs disappear into the back of the Cadillac. She watched until the car turned at the end of Preacher's Creek. She felt like bawling; she wanted to scream, to fill the valley and its every hollow with the sound of the loss of her baby brother. But there was much that remained to be done. And back in the house, she could hear the awful sound her father made, a sound like the splintering of an old tree, and then a high wailing as big buckets of tears came gushing out of him.

ESSIE CALLED TO thank me for what I had done. I was tempted to go for the memorial service or the funeral. The drive did not dissuade me and I could have found someone to cover for me. I felt as though I had not done much for Gordon. As his father had pointed out, hospitalization had only resulted in Gordon's getting sicker. Perhaps to see me at the funeral would be a reminder to his parents that he had died of AIDS. I elected not to go.

A few weeks later, I called on Essie at her house.

"You know," she said, "my father still says he died of a stroke. Stroke, he understands; AIDS, he does not. And my mother is keeping it all inside. She won't even talk about it."

I asked Essie to tell me about the funeral. "Gordon had wanted a closed casket. He said, 'When my time comes, I don't want everyone gawking and staring at me to see if they can see AIDS on my body.' So that's what we had, a *closed* casket.

"I went up to his duplex the night that he died to get his white suit. He had this *bee-yu-tiful*—I mean it was gorgeous—white suit, and he had a silk tie and shirt and handkerchief all picked out. He told me where it all would be. I took the suit over to the funeral home. They were working on him till late in the night. Then the next day, I went over to Kingsport and bought two dozen yellow roses, his favorite kind. I went back to the funeral home—I wanted the roses laid on the casket with a picture of Gordon in front of them. Doochie Jones showed me which room we were in. The casket was sitting there.

"Suddenly I got to thinking: What if Gordon's really not in the casket? I've read about stuff like that happening. Or what if they didn't do him right? I said to Doochie: 'Doochie Jones, I want you to open that casket!' He said, 'Why, Essie, you said you wanted a closed casket!' I said, 'I wanted it closed for everybody else. But I want to see that he looks all right. You open it right this minute.'

"Well, he went off looking for the key. I was getting more and more nervous. He finally comes back with this big old key—I mean it was *huge*. And he puts it in the lock and opens the casket and sure enough there was Gordon. And he looked so pretty in there with his white suit. They had done him good, I had to give Doochie that. I almost wished that it had been an open casket service so they all could see how beautiful my baby brother was.

"But then I looked at his feet and he didn't have no socks on! I said, 'Doochie, hows'a'come Gordon don't have no socks on?' 'Essie, we don't usually put no socks on,' he says. I said, 'I don't want my brother

going to heaven without socks. You *get* some socks for him, right now.'
Well he goes off and gets some white socks and he comes back and he's
got them big calving gloves on again! Son, I was mad. 'Doochie Jones!
What in the world do you think you're going to catch from him now?
You done pickled his body; there ain't a bug that's going to survive that.'
He says, 'Why, Essie—' And I said, 'Don't you *why Essie* me! You take
off those gloves and *put* his socks on right now. Go on. I want to see you
do it. Git!' I stood there and *made* him put those socks on Gordon's
feet."

Essie's eyes were still flashing, her hands were on her hips, and as she
told me the story she was reliving the anger that she felt that day. Essie
held her pose for a few seconds more, and then her dimples flashed to
high beam and peals of laughter escaped from her body as she reflected
on her own audacity.

I told Essie that I would like to see where Gordon was buried. The
kids wanted to come with us but Essie discouraged them.

We drove out of Blackwood to Big Stone Gap and then out of the city
limits into the country. Maple and pine trees lined the side of the road,
forming a shady canopy. We drove past sea-green pastures with mares
and foals grazing freely. Essie pointed out a driveway that sprang on us
suddenly; the driveway led to a mansion on top of a knoll. She told me
the name of the owner: a doctor from India, who was now also a
gentleman farmer.

The road became twisty and I took the curves carefully, staying clear
of the median. The traffic coming round the curves in the opposite
direction was hidden by the overhanging foliage and the hedges that
spilled onto the shoulder. We seemed to be descending, plunging down
into a basin.

Suddenly, as we rounded another curve, the trees dropped away and
the whole world seemed to open up: I saw ahead of me a breathtaking
valley, huge in its expanse, gradually rising on all sides to towering
mountains, the shadow of one range thrown onto the other.

Essie guided me to the cemetery entrance, a discreet path off the
main road that I barely saw for the splendor around me. I stumbled out
of the car when she told me to stop. High up, at the top of the mountain
facing me, I could see the faint outline of the bridge that Essie told me
was part of the new highway to Norton, a highway that had been under

construction when I last visited. That mountain had to be Stone Mountain. And the one to my left was Little Stone Mountain—the town of Big Stone Gap sat right between the two. To my right was Powell Mountain. The cemetery sat at the very center of Powell Valley.

We trudged past neat brass plaques in the grass. When I looked ahead, I saw Sabatha and Joy: they had driven Essie's pickup through the back roads and arrived at Gordon's grave ahead of us. Essie scolded them but without any conviction.

Gordon was right next to his infant brother, Robert Lee, whose epitaph read, "Safe in the arms of Jesus."

I slowly turned my body 360 degrees, taking in the vista from Gordon's vantage point. Frothy white clouds, tinged with gray, spilled over the tops of the mountains and looked as if they would flood the valley. It was drizzling though the sun was shining. The valley was so green that it was almost too much for the eye. The mountains ringing it pressed on me as if they were God's own toes.

"It's where he wanted to be buried," Essie said, studying my face. She must have known that in all my travels, I was unlikely to have seen anything quite like this. I thought to myself that it was where I'd want to be buried.

"That's my plot," Essie said, pointing to the ground to the left of her brother's grave.

9

WEDNESDAY, JUNE 10, 1987, a few months after Gordon Vines's death.

I awoke dreaming that my beeper had sounded its two-tone signal. Its imaginary echo lingered in the room. I sat up, eyeing the silent black form on the night table The previous day its summons had been unrelenting, insistent, like a truculent child.

Rajani, now in her ninth month of pregnancy, slept propped up with four pillows. A little mound of blankets separated us, and when I pulled the covers back I found Steven, his right hand on his face, his fingers curled delicately across his cheek in a thoughtful, Nehru-like pose. My two-year-old had taken to appearing magically in our bed; we were never aware of when he came.

While the household slept, I showered and shaved. The rattle of the hot water in the pipes, the groans and sighs of the wooden floors of the old house were reassuring, as if my home were stirring with me, keeping me company. When I closed the back door behind me—never locking it—and stepped out, it was five minutes before 6 A.M. I was on my way to see Scotty Daws in the ICU at the Miracle Center, the first stop of my day.

Outside, the morning silence was broken only by the hum of the window air conditioner from our bedroom and by a bird cry that sounded like *Sweet, sweet, I'm so sweet.* A yellow warbler, I thought. I started the car and let the motor idle while I studied my pocket appointment book to remind myself of where else I had to be that day. The penciled notations under "Wednesday" were in contrast to the sparse entries on either side. Wednesday had ballooned into the rest of the workweek. My Wednesday afternoon clinic had been transformed: Instead of a faculty wife with the chronic fatigue syndrome, or a Southern Baptist missionary back from Kenya with indolent malaria, my clinic at the University Physicians Group had become an HIV clinic.

This turnabout had happened suddenly: one week, my first and second patients were both follow-ups with problems related to HIV, and my third patient was a no-show. The next week, three out of four patients had HIV-related problems—one new and two follow-ups. When the following week's clinic looked like it might shape up the same way, I joked with Carol that "pretty soon they're going to call us an AIDS clinic!"

"Honey, they've been calling us that for some time now. You just didn't know it."

" 'They,' who?"

"The front office. Everyone that works here. All the other doctors."

"And how does that make you feel?" I asked

"About what I do? I *love* what I do. There's them that don't want to be assigned to this clinic; they'd rather work on the other side. But I don't mind. And Hope doesn't mind working here if I'm tied up giving chemotherapy."

According to my appointment book, this afternoon I would see Fred and Otis (Fred had called to say he was bringing Otis in) as well as Vickie and Clyde McCray. And there was one new person with a positive test referred to me from the Public Health Clinic—a new person who in a few short weeks could become a regular.

Gordon, my first patient, had materialized in the fall of 1986. Now, the summer of 1987, and I had reached double digits.

The morning was unusually foggy and a heavy mist clung to the shrubs that ringed my house. One sweep of the wipers cleared my windshield, but all I could see of the sprawling lawns of the VA was a green fringe on either side of the asphalt. The mist gave the illusion that it hung over a body of water, a giant reservoir that had appeared overnight. A few domiciliary veterans were on the road, collars upturned, hands in their pockets, cigarettes stuck to their lips, trekking to the cafeteria. It was difficult to imagine that in a few hours the heat and humidity could climb to a level that rivaled anything I had experienced in Africa or India.

The doctors' parking lot at the Miracle Center was almost empty. A handful of dew-coated cars, the windshields dull and opaque, were scattered around the parking lot. They belonged to doctors who had spent the night in the hospital.

The side entrance to the Miracle Center led directly to the doctors' lounge, a room with tan wallpaper, orange carpets, crate-shaped orange armchairs and silky white drapes—a corporate art-deco look. The TV was on, the coffeepot full, and the tray of doughnuts covered in Saran Wrap slightly ruffled at the lower right hand corner where Dr. H, the neurosurgeon, had extracted his sweet jelly roll. My favorite doughnut, the chocolate-glazed kind, awaited me, a proper reward for being up this early. There was a move afoot to replace the doughnuts with a fruit bowl. I was dead set against it.

I poured my coffee and, doughnut in hand, moved to the workstation in the corner of the room. GOOD MORNING, the monitor read, a clock ticking away in the top right-hand corner of the screen. I punched in my code and used the pen pointer to scroll to my name and print my "list." This terminal supposedly spoke to a mainframe somewhere in California which tracked the data on all the hospitals across the country that were managed by this same corporation. I was told that I could use the computer to order tests, to schedule appointments, to check on the patient's insurance status and to perform assorted other tricks. All I ever needed from it was a patient list.

The printer came to life, spitting out four names and room numbers. Every name except that of Scotty Daws had an asterisk next to it, to indicate that I was a consultant and not the primary physician on the case. Two of the names had the word DISCHARGED in parentheses next to them. Scotty Daws's name had no asterisk. I was his primary physician.

I refilled my coffee. A woman from medical records next door poked her head into the lounge to check on the coffeepot, see that it was full—part of her duty.

"Misty out there, ain't it? How are you, Doctor Verghese?"

"Very well, thank you," I said, the coffee and the doughnuts having done much to lift my spirits. "Fog'll burn off soon."

This doctors' lounge with its coffee and chocolate-glazed doughnuts, its carpeted floors, its printer chatter, seemed to objectify the difference between the private sector and the spartan VA hospital next door. At Mountain Home, the coffee came out of a coin-operated machine; you punched the buttons for extra cream or extra sugar. What emerged tasted faintly of the beef bouillon the machine was also capable of dispensing. And there was no doctors' lounge at the VA; you met your fellow physicians at the nurses' stations.

I took the back stairs to the ICU to see Scotty Daws. Scotty had come to the emergency room three weeks before with fever, headache and stiff neck. He had complained bitterly of his symptoms in a nonstop soliloquy that, after three minutes, suggested that more than just the meninges (the lining of the brain) was inflamed; the underlying brain was surely affected. The ER physician summoned the neurologist, who did a spinal puncture. The lab called back to say that the fluid was teeming with *Cryptococcus*, an unusual fungus for an apparently healthy young man. The neurologist had gone back and readily elicited from the garrulous Scotty that he was gay, that he had been living just across the North Carolina mountains in Greensboro, and that Desmond, his lover, had recently died of AIDS. The HIV test came back positive. I was summoned, and wound up inheriting Scotty from the neurologist.

Scotty, like a myna bird, would parrot everything I said to him. It was as if I stepped into an echo chamber: Scotty took on not just my speech and tone, but that of the nurse with me, as well as the audio from the television on the wall. It was a feat that drove me batty. I thought more than once of Gordon's Looney Tune imitations.

I learned that if I shouted "Scotty!" I could stop this cycle. In the stunned silence while the feedback loop was momentarily arrested, I could ask Scotty a question about himself, and the echolalia—the parroting of what I said—did not resume. Instead, a torrent of speech would commence, a veritable word-salad that climbed up the drapes, bounced off the ceiling and circled the bed.

The content of this speech was peculiarly lucid, even though it had no discrimination or restraint. It had a tangential relationship to the question I asked: he would tell me how he was feeling and in the next breath tell me how he could make the drive from Greensboro to Johnson City in four hours flat, how his uncle had beaten the hell out of him for being a faggot, and then he would go on to a discourse about the faggots in Greensboro, their classification, the prevailing hierarchy. He would leap from there to an analysis of his excrement. Interspersed with this were loud laments over the death of Desmond. Sometimes he repeated Desmond's name over and over again and thereby soon slipped back into the echo mode.

But ten days after his admission, the myna bird had suddenly been stilled. He remained alert, the blue eyes darting around, following me, the face animated and twitchy, but no words emerged. Scotty's meningitis, which had seemed to improve, had now suddenly worsened. Perhaps the area of the brain that subserved speech had become entrapped in pus and clotted off. The silence was eerie; the room seemed to want to implode from the vacuum created.

And then one day when I walked in, I noted he was breathing very rapidly. I percussed his lung: it had lost its normal resonant tone. My stethoscope confirmed that he had developed a pneumonia in his left lung base: I heard a harsh, loud, aspirate breath sound that told me his lung had solidified.

When the pneumonia worsened, interfering with his ability to oxygenate his brain, I summoned his family. Sister and uncle arrived. His uncle—a scruffy individual whose long hair emerged out of a ball cap and who reeked of stale liquor—was indifferent. When he used the word "faggot" in front of me, I was certain that he had in fact beaten Scotty up. Scotty's sister was a heavyset woman. The leathery skin of her face, the puffy bags under her eyes, her steel-wool hair and her missing eyebrows made her look like an old lioness. I was sure she was an alcoholic. I explained to the family about the pneumonia. I felt there was a good chance I could pull him through, but he would need to be on a ventilator, at least temporarily. The uncle seemed indifferent to this idea, and the sister had no concept of what being on a ventilator meant. I went ahead and put him on one.

A cascade of catastrophes ensued: renal failure from the amphotericin B with which I was treating the *Cryptococcus*, a blood clot to his lung from his leg veins as a result of his prolonged bed rest, a severe rash from the Bactrim that I had placed him on presumptively when he developed pneumonia, an infection from the intravenous catheter that had to pass through the inflamed skin. . . . There was no way he could survive. And yet *another* event would have to occur to actually kill him. The body blows had taken their toll; a clean punch to the chin had not as yet landed.

That morning, there was "nothing" to do for Scotty, but it took me almost an hour to achieve it. It was a peculiarly distasteful task for me: much of ICU care has this futile quality, this illusion of purposefulness generated by the trappings of technology and invasive procedures. A novice in medicine sees only the drama of the pacemaker and the Swan-Ganz catheter; more years in medicine and you see how suffering is prolonged, hospital bills multiplied tenfold, the possibility of a dignified death diminished.

I examined Scotty carefully. I spread out the ICU flow sheets— modified ledger sheets—for the last twenty-four hours and looked at Scotty's fever curve, his temperature, his blood pressure, his fluid intake, his output, the lab tests that had come back, the medication that had been administered, the readings on his ventilator dials. His kidneys had shut down. I had to calculate the fluid and electrolytes he was losing through diarrhea fluid and "insensible" losses such as sweat, and then write orders for intravenous fluids to replace what he had lost and exactly what he needed for the day. Any more, and he would balloon up; too little, and his blood pressure would drop.

I made fine adjustments on the ventilator, trying every day to decrease the percentage of oxygen in the inspired air, or to decrease the number of breaths the machine gave him every minute in the hope of weaning him off the ventilator and getting him out of the ICU. If we succeeded in weaning him, I would definitely not put him on a ventilator again.

I wrote a note as well as a page full of orders for the day. The eleven-to-seven shift was signing out, "giving report" to the seven-to-three shift.

Most days I stayed clear of the ICU nurses. It was one reason why I chose this time of day to make rounds—the nurses were occupied in the change of shift. I recognized that Scotty's condition was pretty hopeless and he was now merely a nursing burden; I felt guilty each day that

Scotty survived. Scotty was not the sort of AIDS patient that I wanted to bring to the ICU; as a test case, it sent the wrong message, it played right into the hands of nurses who thought treating *any* HIV patient was futile, and could point to Scotty as an example of that futility. But it was difficult legally and ethically to simply unhook the respirator and let him die.

The nurses who took care of him, for the most part did not voice their discomfort to me. But the way they gloved, gowned, goggled and wore booties when entering his room, as if they were going to the moon, reflected their disquiet. One time I overheard them giving report: the nurse who would have been assigned to Scotty had just called in sick; the general grumbling suggested that she had done so in order to avoid this assignment. There was a fairly heated debate as to who should get him now. Could I really blame them? All *I* had to do was examine him and write orders. I didn't have to deal with the diarrhea, the skin breakdown, the incipient bedsores.

But this morning the nurse taking care of him *did* question me: "Why are we going on?"

I was taken by surprise. This nurse had previously been quite friendly to me; I had always thought her competent and caring. Now all I could see were cold green eyes behind the goggles, mask, cap and double gloves. I was standing in the room minus any special garb—none was needed. And I was being questioned by an apparition. Her tone seemed to discount any past relationship we had.

"We really aren't going on," I said. "But you know as well as I do that we can't just turn everything off now."

"I don't think we should have bothered in the first place." Her voice was cold and the anger quite naked. "He deserved what he got. It's no one's fault but his. And I don't see why *we* should have to take care of him."

There it was. Naked, ignorant and shameful prejudice that I had anticipated, had feared, but had thus far been spared, at least directly. After she said this, she turned her back on me.

I took a deep breath and tried not to let this rattle me. I reminded myself that I was only indirectly responsible for Scotty's illness, his failure to respond to therapy, his present irreversible state.

But I *was* rattled. *I* had become the target of her venom—the discussion had not really been about Scotty. It had been about me.

BY 7 A.M., when I stepped out to the Miracle Center parking lot, the fog was burning off and there were many more cars in the lot. The Miracle Center was built on the edge of a plateau which the Mountain Home VA shared with it. Now, in the distance, I could see the long uninterrupted chain of mountains to the south, beyond which was Asheville, North Carolina. Fog filled the valley in between.

I drove back to the VA, to my lab, a distance of a quarter of a mile. Betty Franzus, my research technician, was waiting for me with five cages of hamsters. The hamsters were peevish and irritable from riding the rattly elevator so early and being brought down from the dark animal facility to the fluorescent daylight of the lab. They surged from one end of the cage to the other, climbing over each other, poking their whiskers through the bar, sniffing nonstop as if to divine our intentions. I was continuing my research into pneumonia, the research that I had begun in Boston. I had modest funding from the VA Research Service, and I now had a few published papers describing this model. The hamster lung proved a good model for the human situation, and there were simple questions about pneumonia that could be answered.

With my left hand I grabbed a hamster by the loose fur behind the neck and shoulders, and bunched the fur up in my hand so the paws and legs splayed out. The hamster was now immobilized. With my right hand, I slipped the needle of a tuberculin syringe into the peritoneal cavity, injected 0.4 ml of pentobarbital and dropped the hamster back into the cage, drawing my hand away quickly to avoid getting bitten: they whirled around snapping before their feet even hit the ground. In assembly-line fashion, I injected twenty-four hamsters with pentobarbital. When I had injected the twenty-fourth hamster, the first was already snoring.

One after the other, Betty would hand me a warm, furry, snoring body from the cage she had solemnly labeled, "Preop holding." I positioned the limp hamster on my dollhouse surgical platform, propped its jaw open with a special setup of rubber bands and retainers, adjusted my headlamp, grabbed the tongue between my thumb and index finger using a piece of gauze for traction, gently pulled the tongue forward till the liplike rim of the epiglottis came into view. Delicately, I slid a curved tube into the trachea and shot down a measured dose of staphylococci.

The hamster responded with a gasp. Soon it sputtered, gave a cough, and then resumed breathing again. If after thirty seconds it did not breathe—a hamster Code Blue—I would cannulate the trachea one more time and using a small syringe—a Barbie-doll ventilator—push air in and out of the lungs till spontaneous respirations resumed.

Once I was satisfied that the dose had been delivered and the hamster was breathing, I handed it back to Betty who propped it up, its back leaning against the wall of the cage, its paws in front of its face. The cage was labeled "Recovery Room—Immediate Family Only." Betty now handed me another hamster. This clearance experiment would keep Betty busy for a week: my part was just the intubation, which Betty as yet found tricky.

I rushed from the lab to the hospital building at the other end of Dogwood Avenue. Cars were pouring into the VA now, just as the fog was lifting over Mountain Home. Two yellow school buses waited to take the domiciliary veterans on an excursion to Laurel Falls. A mini traffic jam on Dogwood Avenue finally eased and I saw the cause for it: two ducks from the duck pond had taken their own sweet time crossing the road.

I was just in time for VA morning report held in a paneled conference room dominated by a large oak table and rimmed by chairs upholstered in rich mahogany leather. The new cases admitted to all three medical wards from the previous night were presented to me by the chief resident in brief thumbnail sketches. In attendance were the three medical teams, each consisting of a senior resident, two interns, a fourth-year medical student, and two third-year medical students.

I picked one of the cases and asked to have it presented in detail, stopping along the way to quiz the students and residents on various aspects of the history and physical. We studied the x-rays and constructed a differential diagnosis on the blackboard, then formulated a diagnostic and therapeutic plan. To discuss a case extempore like this was fun and challenging: what my audience did not realize was that I was free to take the discussion into areas that suited me. Over the years

I had perfected certain elaborate proofs, rehearsed anecdotes illustrating cherished doctrines, polished bawdy stories that illustrated Occam's razor, Sutton's law and Buridan's ass, resurrected eponyms that kept alive the memory of Traube, Courvoisier, De Musset and Skoda. Of course, I repeated myself—one had to. Fortunately, residents rotated every few months and graduated every few years.

From morning report I went on to Ward 8 where I was the attending physician that month. That morning, as my team walked in and milled around the nurses' station and readied the chart rack, there was a strong odor of feces. No one mentioned it and we were in a learned discussion about the low serum sodium on Mr. McGregor, the patient in bed one, pointedly ignoring the odor, when Maggie, a buxom nurse who had worked in the VA for years, long before the medical school had arrived, looked around, sniffed twice and said in a loud voice, "Do y'all smell poop?" We looked at her and nodded reluctantly. "I sure do!" she said and marched off to establish the source.

Poop or no poop, it was a pleasant contrast from the Miracle Center to push the chart rack down the aisle between the beds, our entourage of residents, students and ward nurse moving together as a pack, being able in one sweep to see *all* our patients, wish them good morning. We began at the solitary private room at the near end of the ward, nicknamed the "Rose Room." This was where patients who were dying were moved. It was inconvenient to keep them on the general ward with the curtain always drawn around their bed. In the Rose Room, a veteran with metastatic oat-cell cancer of the lung was drawing his last few breaths. We examined him and made adjustments to his morphine dose. Somewhat subdued now, our team moved out to the open ward.

In the past two months the VA, which till then had been spared any experience with AIDS, had seen two veterans with AIDS. The first patient, Arthur Simpson, a male in his late fifties, had lived in Boston for years before he came home to Tennessee. He vigorously denied any risk factors for HIV infection—he said he was not gay, had never used intravenous drugs. He admitted only to occasional contact with prostitutes while in the service. He had come in for *Pneumocystis carinii* pneumonia. An astute medical student spotted a strange skin lesion in his armpit which, when biopsied, turned out to be a Kaposi's sarcoma lesion. In all my years in AIDS (ten at the time of this writing), I have never seen Kaposi's except in gay men. Arthur Simpson had been lost to follow-up and eventually we learned he had died at another VA facility.

The second veteran, Seth Barker, was a sullen, young black male from Knoxville. He had been on active duty and was medically retired as soon as he became ill. When he too blamed "prostitutes" as his risk factor, saying the word without any conviction, as though it were a boring but necessary password, I sensed that this was what we were destined to hear in the VA.

But this morning, on the VA wards, it was not AIDS but the usual VA fare: one of the Roach brothers in for the umpteenth time with possible angina; a Mr. Trivett with chronic lung disease who had his condition exacerbated when he tried to spray-paint a car without benefit of a mask; "John Doe," a neglected and debilitated old man with a stroke, diabetes and pneumonia who had been left at the emergency room entrance while the family went to "park the car" and were never seen again.

After rounds, I met with Doyle, a third-year medical student for whom I was adviser. Doyle was cocky, ambitious and impressionable; he was definitely leaning toward surgery as a career choice. We talked about where he would apply for residency. I encouraged him to take a few senior-year electives away from Tennessee, preferably in a giant institution in a big city. That way he could get a flavor for city medicine; it would help him decide what he ultimately wanted to do. He was keen to do an elective in Houston—a former girlfriend of his lived there and he was hopeful that he could resuscitate the relationship.

I met with Karen and Bud—the infection control nurses at the VA— and went over the latest data on hospital-acquired infection at the VA. I also drew up the agenda for the infection control committee meeting for the next week. I checked the mail and signed the paperwork that was in my VA office.

At lunchtime I snuck over to the Miracle Center again, this time to see a new consultation that my answering service had called in to me. Cindy Johnson was an unfortunate girl with cystic fibrosis who was now sixteen years of age—a long time to survive with cystic fibrosis. She had come in for a flare-up of her condition and had pneumonia. She was unlikely to survive this hospitalization, primarily because she had vetoed a ventilator—we were to do everything else. Cindy recognized that if she got onto a ventilator, she might wind up living on it; she didn't want that. I made recommendations for antibiotics and even tried something experimental: aerosolizing gentamicin through a mask to try to get high antibiotic levels into the collections of pus in her bronchi. I was deeply affected by the sight of this brave and dignified teen. She sat upright in bed, elbows resting on her bed tray, unable to lie back. Her raven hair contrasted with her blue lips, clubbed fingers and blue nail beds. Her parents and siblings had gathered around her. She was fighting for every breath, and it was inevitable that she would tire soon. Still, she was possessed of a certain calm, she was resigned to the end of her life, tired of the unending struggle it had been.

I was fifteen minutes late for the afternoon clinic at the University Physicians Group office. In between patients, I scanned lab reports from the previous week's clinic and signed the mound of forms that seemed to spill out of my box every week: applications for Social Security supplement, applications for disability, applications for handicapped parking, work releases . . .

I checked with Betty in the lab at the end of the day to see how our hamsters were doing: all had survived thus far. My beeper had gone off regularly through the day: a nurse calling to clarify an order on Scotty Daws; a patient's wife wanting to talk to me; a long-distance phone call from Boston that I had been anticipating; a surgical resident who had stuck himself with a needle. . . . The last page of the day was from my friend Earl who wanted to know if I could play tennis. I begged off—I wanted to go home.

When I finally headed home at about six thirty, I felt as if I had spent the day darting around the various campuses, circling the parking lots looking for a legal place to stick the nose of my old Datsun 280Z, scurrying in, scurrying out. As the day went on, I felt the Z's lack of an air conditioner. I had bought the car five years before from a medical student whose daddy had bought her a Porsche for graduation; the Z had been her high-school graduation present, it was almost ten years old. The air conditioner had never worked ever since I bought the car. But I was fond of it, unwilling to part company with it.

During the course of the day, I had driven past my house several times—waving once to Steven, whose face was smudged up against the playroom window—but each time I had been in too much of a rush to stop. I was home relatively early now. I just hoped that none of the patients I had seen in afternoon clinic—Otis in particular who was complaining of a headache but had no fever and seemed in no great distress—would suddenly worsen and necessitate my going out again.

AIDS, AIDS, AIDS: the word seemed to inform my every action. Like barnacles on a ship's hull, the stories of the Scottys, the Clydes and the Otises of the town clung to me. Here we were, in our corner of east Tennessee, the embodiment of small-town America, seventy-two churches watching over the flock, the perfect symmetry of the Lions and Kiwanis and Rotary clubs, with their staggered meeting dates. Our town had its minor celebrities: the TV weatherwoman who did Zak's Furniture ads on the side, the sports anchor, a white man, imitating the dress and manners of Bryant Gumbel, the young schoolteacher who had made big bucks on *Jeopardy* and put us on the map for one night. And wherever you were—be it on the high end of this matrix in a Carl Jones faux-Victorian on a double lot in Roundtree, sitting in your jacuzzi in the master bath, looking out over your Japanese garden, or else the proud possessor of a double-wide in a southside trailer park—you viewed the town with a certain satisfaction, a reassuring sense of being insulated from all the foolishness you saw on TV: subway vigilantes, mass murders, drive-by shootings, AIDS.

AIDS simply did not fit into this picture we had of our town. The TV stations and the *Johnson City Press* did a fine job of parroting what the wire services carried about AIDS. But they never succeeded in treating the deaths of Rock Hudson or Liberace as being any more significant to *our* town than famine in the Sahel or a plane crash in Thailand. You could shop in the mall, cut your hair in Parks & Belk, pick up milk in the Piggly Wiggly, bowl at Holiday Lanes, find bawdy entertainment at the Hourglass Lounge—and never know that one of my patients was seated right next to you, or serving you, or brushing past you in the parking lot, a deadly virus in his or her body that was no threat to you, but might nevertheless cause you to stand up and scream if you knew how close it was.

My problem was the opposite: I saw AIDS *everywhere* in the fabric of the town; I wanted to pick up a megaphone as I stood in a checkout line and say, "ATTENTION K-MART SHOPPERS: JOHNSON CITY IS A PART OF AMERICA AND, YES, WE DO HAVE AIDS HERE."

My ubiquitous stack of index cards floated in front of my face at night. I could rattle off precisely where each person was in the downhill trajectory that was the natural history of HIV infection. The integers and the units of measurement—"liters," "cells per cubic millimeter," "grams per deciliter"—sometimes inhabited my dreams in a peculiar "dream-work" routine, as if I was on the eve of a math exam, a Cambridge tripos, truly a nightmare for one so disinclined toward mathematics as I.

When I awoke I would make calculations: If I had twenty patients and they were the tip of the iceberg, then how many others did the town have? Two hundred? Four hundred? Could one in every five hundred persons in town be infected with the virus?

At times I was angry with the town—how could I be in this landscape of death, the unholy minister to a flock of dying people, while Johnson City went on with business as usual? While I was awake, everything I did—be it with hamsters or with humans—seemed to be a way of marking time while waiting for the next HIV case or the next opportunistic infection in my old HIV patients. Would there come a point where AIDS would grow until no one could ignore it? Where every church member, every person in the mall would have this knowledge rise to their consciousness? Where every doctor, every nurse would have the disease drop onto their plate the way it had been dropped onto mine?

As I entered my house through the kitchen, more than twelve hours after I had left it, I took a deep breath. I decided I would not think about AIDS for a while.

STEVEN CAME RACING around the corner in response to the squeak and slam of the screen door. I barely had time to rid myself of my briefcase and the mail before he came flying into my arms. My mother and father were visiting us and would stay with us till their second grandchild arrived. My mother had clearly been hard at work in the kitchen. There was the rich aroma of cardamom and ginger and green chilies; every ring on the stove held a pot. A mound of *papads* sat in a sieve on the counter. The food made me feel famished: I remembered that I had not eaten lunch and only the one chocolate-glazed doughnut had sustained me all day.

I loosened my tie and, still carrying Steven, pushed through the swinging doors into the dining room and greeted my parents. Rajani was upstairs having a bath. I poured a Scotch for myself and a sherry for my mother. I poured ginger ale into a wineglass for Steven, who preened with self-importance. We toasted each other until Steven had his fill of clinking glasses. Ever so gradually, I felt the shackles of work slip from me.

Just before dinner, as we waited for Rajani to come down from her bath, my father, mother, Steven and I went out to the front porch where Steven wanted to see the fireflies. My father asked me about work. I told him about Scotty Daws, my silent myna bird in the ICU. And about the clinic. Here I was, despite my promise to myself, talking about AIDS.

"Do you wear gloves when you touch them?" my dad asked.

"*Them?*" I was on the defensive. "No. Not unless I'm going to draw blood or do a rectal or something."

"You mean you don't wear gloves when you touch their skin?"

"No. Dad, you can't get it from touching the skin."

My mother shuddered.

"Still," my dad said. "I think you should wear gloves. Why don't you? You have a young child at home. A baby coming. Don't take chances."

I kept quiet. On several previous nights I had heard myself justify to my parents what I was doing—the AIDS work—telling them how much satisfaction I was getting from it. What I didn't mention was how stressed I felt some days, how alienated I felt from other physicians, from friends, and even from my wife. By God, if what I was doing was noble, why did it feel like something . . . something *shameful*?

I remembered Scotty Daws's nurse, the green eyes over the surgical mask. *Why are we going on?* And now my father's *Do you wear gloves when you touch them?* I seemed to be living in a separate world which those who had not been touched by the disease could not enter. I felt alone at my own table, alone and unclean, chastened by my father's attitude. I thought at that moment of the gay men I had met during the last months. I thought of how often they had felt alone at the table among family and friends.

During dinner, Steven fell asleep in his grandfather's arms and I carried him up to bed. When I returned, the others were sitting around the dining table, eating coffee cake. The chandelier was dimmed and light came from the candle-shaped fixtures on either side of the china cabinet. I had turned off the air conditioners and opened the door to the front porch to let the evening in. The chirping of the crickets came through, a reassuring sound. Through the black living room window we could see the fireflies zigzag across the lawn, and behind them, occasionally, the headlights of a car tracking through Mountain Home.

My mother was telling Rajani a tale from my childhood in Ethiopia. Some escapade of mine that with each telling seemed to be embellished. It was amazing how this yarn brought a smile to my father's face. At the time it happened, I had been punished: an ear grabbed and twisted, or a stick to the seat of my pants—I don't remember. In any case, the event was no longer mine. It had gone from fact to anecdote; it was the property of my mother.

Listening to my mother's voice, I felt as if I was on the outside, looking in: the four of us around the dining table, bathed in the soft saffron light, a family tableau, Indians in east Tennessee. The perfect family—well fed, safe from danger.

Rajani sat still, a distracted, faraway look on her face as my mother talked. My wife's expression revealed nothing. Occasionally she smiled pleasantly, laughed on cue. But it was as if she responded without truly hearing anything. Still she was beautiful in the soft light. Her beauty was what had drawn me to her when I saw her at a cousin's wedding in India. Of course I wanted to possess it, wanted it to adorn my vanity. When we met, I was on the eve of graduating from medical school in India, on the eve of coming back to the United States. I had no intention of getting married. She had finished her bachelor's degree in English literature and a postgraduate degree in mass communications and was working for a large advertising agency. She was very eligible, and her parents were looking to get her married—an arranged marriage. Despite her education, she was not a woman who would have considered rebelling against this custom.

The arranged marriage system, primitive as it sometimes sounds, is nothing more than an elaborate form of the dating system. *Good* girls, by definition, are difficult to meet because they stay at home. When they sally out, they are carefully chaperoned. I saw them around, tantalizing, but quite unapproachable. I got to chat with interesting women in the medical school or in the hospital—but it was rare that they agreed to go out. Much of that is changing, but even with the modern Indian girl, the parental voice echoes strong in her mind and keeps her from being too adventurous. So how does an Indian male meet a woman and get married if women are so cloistered? When you are ready to marry, your parents might say something to you like, "Do you know so and so's daughter? Why don't you go see her? Go for a movie or something. Get to know her. They will be expecting you." Two movies and three lunches might be the limit before you have to commit yourself. Or bail out.

Rajani had been approached in this fashion by several suitors, and the stories she told me of these meetings were comical. But I could understand how a man could become tongue-tied in her presence—it happened to me. She and I went out a few times without her parents' knowledge—a dangerous thing to ask of her, the sort of thing that could ruin a girl's reputation. I began to feel that if I wanted to be with this gorgeous and intelligent woman, if I wanted to solve the mystery of her reserve, of her imperturbability, I needed to make my move at once; otherwise she would soon be married. I had no time to waste.

I proposed on our third date, by which time I was quite infatuated with her. She accepted reluctantly; she really did not want to leave India, but of all the suitors I had proven, at the very least, the most tenacious. We went to our respective parents and suggested they arrange our marriage.

Those first years of marriage were exciting stages of discovery that perhaps Western couples go through when they are dating, well before they marry. Now, after seven years of marriage, I felt I was still getting to know her, still unraveling the Gordian knot, still unsure what was on Rajani's mind. If I tended to be the extrovert, Rajani was the opposite. She could hold a thought for months or years. She had a black-and-white sense of wrong and right, good and bad—quite the opposite of the chameleonlike instincts I had accrued from being a lifelong expatriate. What I saw as relative, she saw as absolute. If she was calm and even-tempered, my personality was much more cyclothymic, the downs in particular could be prolonged and could try the patience of anyone around me. And my practice, particularly now with AIDS, was making me more emotional, less able to hold back my feelings and less tolerant of anything I saw as hypocritical.

I often felt as if I had failed her, as if she would have preferred the privileged life she led in India—maids, chauffeurs, an exclusive and entitled circle of mannered friends, the society of tea planters, estate owners, and tea brokers that characterized the small hillside resort town she grew up in—to the rough-and-tumble existence we had led through my years of training.

With the press of time and the demands of one child and a second on the way, we rarely debated the gray zones that separated us anymore. We loved Steven; he made it even easier to sidestep these issues, delude ourselves into feeling that to be together with him was to be communicating with each other.

Forewarned with the knowledge of what Rajani approved or disapproved of, I spared myself her disapproval. I spared her any angst. My time with my wilder friends like Allen was more likely to be spent outside the house or at his house than in mine. I could sit in the back room of his gas station and shoot the breeze and taste his moonshine, and bathe in his cigarette smoke, but it was something I would never dream of asking Rajani to do. I had a cadre of friends who I knew would probably be ill at ease at our house, less inclined to be themselves. And her small circle of friends and their interests I found difficult to relate to.

My work with AIDS in the community fell into this chasm between us. AIDS was like another wild friend, a friend from a different social stratum, a friend I indulged but no longer brought to the house or even discussed with her.

RAJANI NOW HEAVED herself up from the dining table and went to the kitchen even before my mother came to the punch line of the story. From the kitchen, Rajani beckoned me.

"The baby has stopped moving," she said.

The little kicks and punches had been virtually incessant till then. Now, for twenty minutes, while we were sitting at the table, she said she had felt nothing.

I shook off the torpor of the evening. I was fully alert. Rajani was looking to *me* to see if this was something serious. *I* didn't know! New life—birth—was not my area of expertise.

I called our obstetrician, Dr. Dunkelberger. He told us to go right away to the Miracle Center so that Rajani could be hooked up to a fetal monitor. We left my stunned parents behind, the coffee cake half-eaten, my mother's anecdote still incomplete, hanging in the air. At the doorway, Rajani gave hasty instructions to my parents on what to do if Steven woke up.

By the time the fetal heart monitor was hooked up, Dr. Dunkelberger was by our side. The tracing showed that the baby was alive but its heart rate was erratic. It was in distress. A cesarean—at once!

As Dr. Dunkelberger was making preparations for the cesarean, the baby's heart rate normalized. Perhaps the cord had got kinked from the baby's wriggling into an awkward position. And perhaps, in the process of examining Rajani, Dr. Dunkelberger had managed to shift the baby into a better position. In any case, the crisis had abated for now.

Dr. Dunkelberger elected to induce labor; it would take a couple of hours. We settled back to wait for the first contraction.

L&D, Labor and Delivery, was in the bowels of the Miracle Center: there were no windows, only the contrast of fluorescent daylight in the corridors outside with the soft light from the table lamps of the birthing suite which looked like an Ethan Allen showroom. All sense of time disappeared. It was a strange feeling to be in this hospital as an observer, awaiting the birth of a child. Upstairs, a young man on a respirator had his every breath and sigh controlled by me; a young girl inhaled an antibiotic I had prescribed. Elsewhere, in other rooms, my handwriting was on many a chart. But in this room my function was simply to wait.

Rajani's contractions began. They were widely spaced. I waited at the bedside. Periodically, Dr. Dunkelberger would materialize, scan the fetal heart monitor, smile at me, say a few words of encouragement to Rajani, and then withdraw as quietly as he appeared. I was in awe of his alertness. I felt punch-drunk from lack of sleep.

Next door, the faint sounds of "Push, push, push" had given way to a "Stat" call for a pediatrician crackling on the overhead speakers and echoing in the hallway, rupturing the silence. There was the clatter of running footsteps and agitated expressions on the faces that passed our door. Running is ominous in a hospital. It can only mean trouble.

I slipped out into the hallway, curious. A medical student, looking ashen, told me that the baby in the next room had been born with exomphalos: the abdominal wall was missing and the intestinal organs were retained only by a thin membrane. If the baby survived, it faced many operations to reconstruct the abdominal wall.

I said nothing to Rajani. But my anxiety for our new baby increased.

MY BEEPER WENT OFF at two in the morning: my father was paging me. Steven had woken up and had gone to our bedroom and was terrified to find us gone. He had walked around the house looking for us. My parents had heard the pit-pat of his feet on the wooden floor below as he ran from living room to dining room to kitchen in search of us. They called to him. Much as he loved his grandparents, he was frightened and inconsolable, my father said. He had been pacified only when my father told him he was going to telephone me. I could hear him sniffling in the background. I talked to him on the phone. "Daddy, come here," he said.

"Daddy'll be right there," I said.

I sped home and found my little two-year-old in the living room—he had refused to go upstairs. He was sitting on the edge of the sofa, between his grandparents, holding back his tears with pouting lips, his eyes glued on the door. When I picked him up he put his little hands around my neck, wrapped his legs around me and cried angry tears—"how could you leave me?" he seemed to be asking. The tears diminished and finally ended with a big sigh.

I sang "Puff the Magic Dragon," his favorite sleepy-time song, and soon I could hear his breath, soft and regular against my neck, an occasional involuntary sob like a hiccup shaking his body. I took him upstairs and laid him down in our bed, his hands still locked around my neck, the fingers grasping my hair. Like a contortionist, I extricated myself from his grip, patting his bottom all the while in time to my singing. I tiptoed back out of the room, wishing the floorboards of this old house would not creak so, humming while I retreated. I held my breath on the stairs, hoping I would not hear an anguished sob that would mean I would have to start all over again.

Downstairs, I asked my parents to sleep in our bed with Steven—the simplest way to keep him from roaming. I promised to call when the baby came. I headed back for the hospital.

The night air was thick and the pollen tickled my nose. There was no mist. It was instead a still, summer night. I felt tense. I had no control of what would happen in the next few hours. I was totally at the mercy of God or nature. Would that this birth be uneventful. Given all that I had seen recently, all the suffering, all the sadness, an easy uncomplicated birth seemed almost too much to hope for. As a reflex, I prayed.

A driving blues number was playing on the radio. The song brought back memories of my first year of medical school in Ethiopia when, for a while, I had played bass guitar in a band. I didn't need the money, and I couldn't afford the time, but there had been benefits: looks of interest from the girls, the exhilaration when a number spun out perfectly. At the time, I couldn't imagine giving it up. In the haze of smoke and the press of dancers of all races and colors against the stage—this was the East Africa of the early 1970s, East Africa in the first cataclysms of a subcontinent about to fall—I had stayed close to my amp, next to the drummer, watching his bass pedal, he and I solely responsible for keeping the skeleton of the song intact. Some undefined melancholy for which I never found a reason had justified my being high every night— the beer was free, and between sets there was always a joint making the rounds. Yet, I lived for a special moment that came every night, an instant of absolute clarity, a tungsten light that washed away all the fuzziness (and stayed with me long after I left the club and was still with me in the early hours of the morning when I propped open my *Gray's Anatomy*). It came in a twelve-bar blues like the one I was listening to now. It was the number with which we closed our second and final set, a blues with a driving, funky rhythm that set heads nodding and feet tapping from its first bar. When we came around to the climactic eleventh and twelfth bars, a point in the song where the musical tension was so high that you could be tone deaf and still know that a resolution *had* to take place, we would go silent. We let the climax happen in thin air, in people's minds, punctuating just the ghost of these remaining bars with single beats from my thumb against the string. By the twelfth bar, the crowd would go wild, spilling into our song, threatening to mess us up altogether, drowning out the sound of the lead guitar, the drums and the organ kicking back in. While the strobe lights spun and the dance floor became a lunar landscape in which ghostly figures held poses, the drummer, Solomon, would look at me and I at him. Solomon would call across the void that separated us, "Steady, Abe! Steady!"

That is what I said to myself as I drove back to the Miracle Center for the fourth time in twenty-four hours, as I slammed the car door and walked across the parking lot, as I eased back into L&D in the silent hospital: "Steady, Abe, steady."

IN THE EARLY MORNING, Rajani gave birth to a baby boy. He was perfectly healthy. We called him Jacob George Verghese: his first name after Rajani's father and the middle name after my father.

I was ecstatic, jubilant. I held Rajani's hand and searched for the right words for the occasion. I said how this was a new beginning for us, how I would work hard to make things better for us as a family. She was exhausted, distracted by the baby being bundled away to the nursery. She turned to look at me; she did not respond but instead fell into a deep sleep. After a while, I left the room.

I drove back to the VA. I reached the card-key barrier that separated Mountain Home and the Miracle Center. My wife and newborn baby were on one medical campus, Steven on the other. The sun was coming up and I stopped at the threshold for a minute. I cut the engine to look at perhaps the most glorious sunrise of my thirty-two years. Thank God, everyone was safe.

10

THE WEEK FOLLOWING Jacob's birth was strangely calm.
Steven and I spent our evenings together. Suddenly he was
elder brother, no longer the baby. I was trying to wean him from his
mother, help him deal with the arrival of a baby who had consumed the
attention of his grandparents, a baby who had stolen my heart. It took
all my will and concentration to walk into the house and not let my eyes
drift from Steven. I trained myself to give him my undivided attention
for five minutes. Only then would I sidle over to the baby, letting the
infant's unfocused gaze play over me. When I reached out to put my
finger in his palm, Jacob would squeeze it.

Steven, at two years, was a quiet child, startled by sudden noises,
quick to clamp his hands over his ears, hesitant whenever he ventured
beyond the boundaries of the familiar world around him. If he felt
rejected now, betrayed, he did not express it in tantrums or by uttering
a word of protest. Instead, there was only a puzzled look. Later, a
sadness set in on his face.

Tuesday, a week after Jacob's birth, Steven, his grandfather and I
took a walk. We headed down from our house and cut across the lawn
to reach the old jail and guard house which now served as the Mountain
Home VA personnel office. There we left the manicured bluegrass and
the flower beds of flame azaleas and reached the perimeter of the
campus.

To enter this forest of maple, ash and pine was to go from light to

shade, to enter the silence of a grotto, a silence broken only by the call
of birds, each of which caused Steven to pause and look at me inquiringly, his hands raised, ready to clamp them over his ears should the
sound get louder. I told him what I knew: the raucous *thief-thief-thief*
cry was a blue jay. The whistled *ree-ree, ree-ra* could be a chickadee or
a pewee.

We halted on the thick mat of leaves and twigs, looked up, tried to
keep our feet silent as we searched out the singer. The summer foliage
was so dense we saw nothing.

On we went, behind the interns' quarters, behind the psychiatry
building. At the horseshoe pit, in a little clearing in the forest, three
males in their thirties, all smoking, were playing a desultory game.
The horseshoes seemed inordinately heavy in their hands, hanging in
the air like giant transport planes, landing with a thud and kicking up
a spray of dust. The men waved. Steven, with encouragement, waved
back. One of them made the grimacing and smacking movement of
his lips and face that is a side effect of Thorazine, an antipsychotic
medication.

We emerged from this enchanted forest behind the main hospital
building. Here, in a giant clearing, the "bed towers" was under construction next to the old hospital. I resented this project for a new
hospital, resented the trees it had cost, resented the glass, concrete and
steel scale model that stood in the director's office—try as it might, it
could not help but betray the symmetry and grace of our old brick
buildings. I could not picture myself working in a building like that.

We came here many an evening because of Steven's fascination with
the cranes. There were two of them, their cabs empty, their hooks
raised. They stood unnaturally still, like monuments; they towered over
the deep crater where the foundation was being laid; they presided over
the assembled backhoes, bulldozers, ditch-witches, portable toilets, storage trailers and flatbeds that cluttered the ground below.

The silence of this scene was powerful. I think this is what Steven
liked: the sense of machines that at any other time would be making an
infernal racket, now stilled. The only time he wanted to see them was
in the quiet of the evening. To Steven, they were like dinosaurs. His
hand clutched mine tight, in case the cranes should move. My father
and I followed Steven's example and gazed at this scene with reverence,

our heads tilted back, silent, until Steven indicated his readiness to leave.

We returned via the paved walkway. Some days we ventured down to the pond where, at this hour, solitary veterans, couples from town, whole families came to feed the ducks. But on this day we wanted a last look at the "roof birds": pigeons and mourning doves that roosted in great numbers under the eaves of the hospital as they had done on every old building on the VA campus. The pavement beneath the overhang was painted with a salt-and-pepper fringe of droppings. As you approached the hospital doors, the collective, low-pitched *coos* made it seem as if the building was grieving aloud.

The VA maintenance crew, the ubiquitous men in green, had tried all sorts of tricks to drive the birds away: noisemakers, repellents, grease. Nothing had worked. The previous week they had installed chicken wire under the eaves of the watchtower building and the domiciliary buildings. The doves had promptly moved from the domiciliaries to the hospital building. In the week to come, the hospital was slated for the chicken-wire treatment.

I wondered what would happen after that? Where would the doves go? Would they fly west to Murfreesboro where another quaint old VA of similar construction awaited them? Or would they go down to the Bay Pines VA in Florida, mimicking the migratory pattern of our domiciliary residents? Had an eccentric old domiciliary veteran brought them here to begin with, only to have their population explode, much in the manner in which the aggressive European starling had first arrived in America?

After our walk, Steven and I went to the mall to roam in the air-conditioned coolness and to pick up diapers, milk and other sundries. On the way back, we stopped at Allen's gas station where Allen raised and lowered a Camaro on the hydraulic lift, just for Steven's pleasure. Then Allen opened the soda machine and extracted a Coke from its innards for Steven. Steven was awestruck by this trick; all his Daddy had been able to do was put coins in and punch a button. What Allen did must have seemed like a cesarean.

Back at home, we checked on our "garden"—a narrow strip of earth outside the front porch that Steven and I had reclaimed from the lawn and that the groundskeepers had not as yet taken back. The tomato seeds we had planted months before were now full-grown plants. We had put stakes up to support them. Until two weeks ago, they had looked scraggly and their fruit was jaundiced and anemic. I broke down and added store-bought fertilizer to the soil. It had worked miraculously, just as the proprietary name had suggested it would. Steven plucked one ripe tomato and ran in to show the voluptuous ruby-red orb to his mother and to the new baby.

After his bath, Steven and I stepped out to the porch to look for fireflies. They were not abundant that night for some reason.

We stood on the driveway and looked at the stars. The night was so clear, the stars seemed to be within our reach. Steven said, "Oh!" as if understanding completely when I pointed out to him Orion the Hunter, then Orion's head, Orion's belt. The reverse-question-mark shape of the body of Orion had always seemed as if it was my talisman, watching over me in Boston, and now in Tennessee. Steven repeated after me, "Bellatrix" and "Betelgeuse." I had such ambitions for my son: astronomer, astrophysicist, astronaut.

THE NEXT EVENING, before Steven and I could take our walk, my beeper went off. Scotty Daws had stopped breathing. A few days before, Scotty had been taking enough breaths on his own to wean him off the ventilator. I had quickly shipped him out of the ICU and back up to the fifth floor. His sister, uncle and I agreed that we would not put him on a respirator again if his lungs failed. But now the nurse had found him without a pulse, and with gasping respirations. She had called a Code Blue, even though Scotty had been made a "No Code," a "DNR"—Do Not Resuscitate. The message on the phone was from the telephone operator at the Miracle Center informing me that "your patient is coding."

I rushed over, ran through the parking lot and took the stairs three at a time.

The assembled crew looked at me wide-eyed as I walked into Scotty's room in my street clothes and instructed everyone to stop at once. I found an army of persons dressed in yellow gowns, green caps, gloves and goggles, administering CPR. There was little room to maneuver, what with the crash cart, the ECG machine, the pharmacy cart, all assembled in his room. Half the people in the room I did not know—

they had rushed up from the operating room and elsewhere in response to the Code Blue. I was incredulous: I thought I had made it clear on the chart and to the nurses that none of this was called for with Scotty.

The respiratory therapist who had been bagging him, now lifted the rubber mask away from Scotty's nose and lips. The person who had been kneeling, administering chest compressions, now stepped off the bed. While they looked on in astonishment, I felt for a pulse, my bare fingers pressed to one side of Scotty's neck. On the other side of his neck, blood had trickled from where an overzealous intern had tried for a central venous line. There was no pulse. I pulled back his eyelids and saw that his pupils were fixed and dilated.

I saw looks exchanged by the persons in the room: *Is he crazy? No gloves?* This only goaded me on. I was irritated at this production at Scotty's bedside, the moon-suits and yet the paradoxical and absurd effort at resuscitation.

I laid my hand over Scotty's left nipple, feeling for the apex beat of his heart. I put the diaphragm of my stethoscope over his heart, my fingers cupping the head of the instrument and resting comfortably on Scotty's sweaty chest. Silence. Only the rush of blood in my own ears.

I lifted myself up, thanked everyone and stood there till they filed out. When everyone left, I asked the nurse (a face I did not recognize, perhaps that explained the Code Blue) to get me a biopsy needle and small bottles of formalin and gloves. She seemed confused, lost. She would be gone a long time.

In death, Scotty already looked *long* dead. I was conscious of a peculiar, sweet, mousy odor in the room; I had noted it on previous visits to Scotty, but now it was particularly strong. It evoked a sense of nostalgia, an olfactory déjà vu. Was it an odor I had detected at an AIDS deathbed before this?

As I looked at Scotty's face, the way the skin was stretched taut over his bones, the fat of his cheeks long gone so that what could have been a smile was instead a grimace, I felt sorry that he had suffered so long in the hospital, sorry that even in his last minutes our mindless technology had so rudely interrupted his transition, leaving him with oozing puncture wounds over his neck and a red splotch over his chest and cracked ribs from the cardiac compression.

I wished I had seen him earlier in the course of his illness, gotten to know him in the clinic, instead of first encountering him already *in extremis* in the hospital. How many other men did we have in our town with time bombs ticking in them? How many others had returned home from elsewhere and were too scared to come to me or were still in denial? How many others did not even know they were infected?

When the nurse returned, I took biopsies of Scotty's lungs, his liver and his spleen, leaving tiny, almost invisible punctate marks on his skin where the biopsy needle had gone in. The previous day, when I had talked to Scotty's sister about his inevitable death, something she was resigned to, I had asked whether she knew what Scotty's wishes were: cremation? burial? . . . autopsy? She had flatly vetoed an autopsy; she had been agreeable to the postmortem biopsies I was now performing. I labeled the little formalin bottles and sent them off to pathology. I washed my hands in Scotty's bathroom. I was curious to know what had gone on in Scotty's body other than the pathogens we already knew about: *Cryptococcus* and *Pneumocystis carinii*.

By the time I got home, Steven was already asleep. The baby was awake. When I reached for little Jacob, Rajani asked me, "Did you wash your hands?"

I washed once more.

THE NEXT DAY, Wednesday, and my clinic had only two patients, both with non-AIDS-related conditions. The first was a pretty, waiflike young lady with infection around her left breast prosthesis. Multiple courses of antibiotics prescribed by the surgeon had failed; she continued to ooze pus from the operative scar and to have pain—it had been a year since the surgery. The right prosthesis was fine. I was convinced that the left prosthesis would have to come out to cure the infection in the chest pocket in which it resided. Once the infection was totally cleared—a matter of four to eight weeks, during which she would receive intravenous antibiotics at home through a special venous catheter—she could have a new prosthesis inserted. I explained to her that the silicone prosthesis was now acting much like a splinter in the pulp of a finger, it was a foreign body: no amount of ointments or antibiotics would help until the splinter came out. She left, disappointed, having hoped for a magic drug to cure her, but promising to think about my recommendation. I dictated a diplomatic letter to the plastic surgeon who had sent her to me. I know he also wished the problem could be solved without undoing his handiwork.

The second patient was a farmer with a chronic bone infection that had followed a motor vehicle accident when he was a teen. The broken tibia had mended, but for years he had drained small amounts of pus through a sinus track that came out onto the skin just below his knee. He was in the habit of tying a bandanna over the pouting mouth of the sinus track; the bandanna concealed this proud flesh and picked up the two or three drops of pus that trickled out every day. He replaced the bandanna with a fresh one each morning—he had a large collection of bandannas.

Multiple courses of antibiotics over the years had not helped: at best, the sinus opening would close over temporarily. Then, after a few weeks or months, he would get fever and chills and bony pain, which was relieved only when a red spot blossomed again on his skin and burst, allowing the pus to come out. His incentive for coming to me now was his upcoming second marriage. When he and his future wife had reached a critical state of undress, she had been startled by the bandanna and slightly repulsed by what was underneath when she insisted on looking.

His x-rays showed fragments of dead and infected bone in a pocket deep within his tibia; the infection was surrounded by very dense but healthy bone; the little tunnel to the surface served to drain the infected cavity whenever pus built up in it. For him to have any chance at cure, it would be necessary for a surgeon to aggressively cut out all the dead bone and unroof or "saucerize" the cavity and thus drain the infection. He would be bedridden for weeks. It would be painful. And the problem was that such surgery, if it was to cure infection, might cut out so much bone that it would compromise the ability of the tibia to bear weight. Worse still, there was a good chance that infection would recur despite surgery. And as a tobacco farmer, he could ill-afford the downtime the surgery and recuperation would entail. My recommendation was to leave well enough alone; nature was providing him with good drainage of a well-localized infection, even if the means it chose was not aesthetically pleasing. I suggested we work on his fiancé, encourage her to visit me, help her come to terms with his chronic osteomyelitis and the bandannas.

In between my two patients, I saw Fred Goodson walk in and hug my nurse, Carol. I saw a nurse who worked on the other wing of the clinic make a long face at this demonstration. Fred gave this nurse a stately bow, which made her turn away, flustered. Fred had come by to pick up forms that I had signed for Otis and to visit with Carol. She had now become an integral part of AIDS care in our town. Patients came as much to see her, and be cheered by that visit, as they came to see me. When I finished with my second patient, Fred was still there, chatting with Carol. Now he came to the dictation room to visit with me for a while.

When I had first met Fred and Otis, I had been struck by their Tweedledee and Tweedledum sameness, by the Castro-clone look they seemed to be affecting. I still saw Otis this way.

But not Fred. Now, whenever I saw Fred Goodson, I thought *bear*. His thick, gray-speckled beard stretched up in a skullcap and then swept down the back of his neck to disappear into his T-shirt, showing every possibility of reaching the soles of his feet. The tangle of hairs in his nostrils, the way his neck ran into his arms without intervening shoulders, and the serenity with which his hands stayed folded over his belly were all bear. His close-set blue eyes peered out through Gandhi glasses and took sight of you down his nose, and he often cocked his head to one side or the other. It was the exact demeanor I had seen a few months before when we drove through Cades Cove in the Smoky Mountains and were scrutinized by a hulking specimen of *Ursus americanus*, standing by the side of the road.

Fred was telling me about the Tri-City AIDS Project, TAP, a community-based group in Johnson City that he had been instrumental in forming.

I was incredulous! I had been unaware of the group which was already having regular meetings.

I felt left out. How had TAP come about?

"Well, you know when Otis and I were diagnosed as having HIV infection, I began to look around for community support. The director of St. John's Church mentioned an organization that he thought he had heard about—Tennessee AIDS Project. Of course, that turned out not to be the name, but he *did* have the phone number for a woman, Elaine Shuman, who worked at the medical school. She was coordinator of a very loose group of medical students, psychologists and other professionals—they hadn't actually *met* in several months. Elaine convened the group for their first *real* meeting as a result of my call.

"We've had several meetings. The first were just feelers, you know. I keep pushing for things like bylaws, Robert's Rules of Order, and so on, and people just say, 'Oh, we don't *really* need that.' All we have in terms of a budget is about three hundred dollars. The organization office is basically Elaine Shuman's dining table. She will be leaving shortly, and in all probability, the office will move to Bettie Lee's dining room!"

Bettie Lee was Fred's sister. I had met her a few times. She was very supportive of both Fred and Otis. It didn't surprise me that she had become actively involved in the community response to this disease.

Fred went on: "There was quite a bit of awkwardness, particularly in the first few meetings. I *try* not to be too pushy; I'm not that used to working with *straight* people. We have one real firebrand in our group: Dale. Dale has experience with an AIDS support group in Knoxville. He's full of ideas and *really* motivated, really charged, which I think is great! But there's a clash of personalities between him and Elaine. She feels he is trying to come in and take over. She *really* resists. And so do some others. I think they resent him as much because, uh, because he is gay as anything else. That's irony for you: the people who try to work with AIDS still have their homophobias!

"There's lots of people in the group who are 'interested' and gave it lip service, if you know what I mean: 'Oh, we want to do this and we want to do that,' but when it comes time for them to actually *do* something, for one reason or another they don't have time."

I recalled with shame that Fred and others *had* mentioned the first few organizational meetings of what turned out to be TAP to me. I had begged off, largely because I had little faith that much would come of these meetings. My clinical load was getting so large that I felt overwhelmed by patient care; and patient care made me impatient with *all* committees. Besides, I felt the AIDS lectures I gave all over the region, and for which I was now in some demand, represented my community effort.

"The professionals want to meet during the day, and the rest of us—those who have the virus—want to meet in the evenings," Fred said. "The professionals basically want to meet during office hours and count this as part of their work—get *paid* for it, you know? Whereas for me, my livelihood depends on getting to the tobacco warehouses on time, or visiting offices in the daytime to pick up my receipts."

Fred continued: "I can't tell you how important TAP has become for me. It's made me feel that there are people interested in me. And that's what I wanted to talk to you about. Would you refer new patients to us, or patients you have that I may not know about? I really have no idea who else could use our services or benefit from the support group; we aren't at a stage where we can like, take an ad in the *Johnson City Press*. Can you picture it? *Seeking persons with AIDS to form a support group; meeting at the Unitarian Church.* We'd be firebombed or else have the KKK drop by."

I promised that I would send patients to TAP. It would ease some of the pressures on Carol and me. We were novices at trying to get patients their Social Security supplement, their Medicaid, their handicapped parking stickers, and the myriad other needs that blossomed with this kind of illness.

Fred invited me to come to the support group. Be the "facilitator" if I chose to be. I told him I was very interested in being supportive but had to beg off. I wanted to be sure to save energy to fulfill my clinical role as effectively as I could and to have something left over for family. "Time is my currency," I said to Fred.

"Mine too," he replied. We were both silent for a while. "Living in Morristown and driving down here for all these meetings, what with Otis getting sicker, it's going to be tough to make it all happen. *And* to keep up with my work. But I'm absolutely committed to the idea of TAP."

I had forgotten how Fred made his living. "You work as a book-keeper, right, Fred?"

"I'm an accountant," Fred said.

I was amused: these were two incongruous images: bear and accountant.

"I know, I guess I don't look much like an accountant. It's not a bad job. I have two real busy stretches every year: January to April—tax time—and Thanksgiving to January when the tobacco market peaks. This is a slow time for me. It's my uncle's business, you know. Yeah, he was in tobacco for years, and his business gradually evolved into a one-man accounting business: taxes, inventory, audit, payrolls and issuing checks, all for the tobacco warehouses. When I returned home to Morristown, my uncle's health was failing and so I took over the accounting business. It's still a solo affair. The Burley warehouse accounts are at the heart of my business."

I was familiar with the tobacco warehouses around the area—New Burley, New Dixie, Farmer's One and Two, Central One and Two, Grower's Warehouse, Jimmy Green's. They feature prominently in the directions you are given if you are in Greene County and ask for help. They stand like airplane hangars, but with ne'er an airfield in sight. I had been to a tobacco warehouse in Virginia once, even attended an auction. I remembered the event distinctly and could picture the warehouses Fred was now describing to me. When you walk in, the scent of tobacco floors you, brings spittle to your lips and makes your stomach call out as if in hunger. Picture opening a fresh can of Prince Albert or Copenhagen and sticking your nose into it; magnify this picture fiftyfold and you will know the sensation.

Each warehouse has an "office" in a corner with a large wood stove. It is here that the farmers wait on benches or fold-up chairs, wait for their checks. Some farmers dandy up when they come for their checks; a few others send their wives or children. But the rest are here in person, dressed in jeans, flannel shirts, denim jackets or down vests, and ball caps. A telltale bulge under their lower lip is where they have parked their dip; it gives them a serenity that by late morning borders on frank torpor. They wait and wait, stepping outside every now and then to spit, or else using a Styrofoam cup held carefully in their hands for the same purpose.

While they wait for their checks, they talk about the weather and how it was on the leaf. They talk about the price the Burley fetched at the last auction. The farmers all know each other and are linked in the same way a small rural Southern Baptist congregation might be.

A staircase leads up from the waiting room to a work area above where "the girls" sit and calculate how much each basket of tobacco brought. "The girls" are on the average over sixty years old. The heat from the wood stove rises up through the stairwell and between the gaps in the floorboard. The girls have the warmest spot in the building.

Downstairs, next to the waiting room, is an enclosed office. It is this spot that Fred or whoever does the warehouse accounts shares with the BSC men—the Burley Stabilization Corporation, the regulatory agency that monitors sales. The BSC office, as it is called, is very cold. At the expense of losing some privacy, of which there is little to begin with, one can remove some boards at the base of the wall that separates the waiting room and its wood stove from the BSC office, thus allowing heat to come through from the wood stove.

The offices occupy the smallest corner of the warehouse; the rest of it is row upon row of "baskets," each containing up to two hundred pounds of tobacco leaves wrapped into bundles. It is these baskets that the buyers from the big companies come to inspect and to grade.

There are Oldsmobile Cutlasses or Delta 88s or Chevy Impalas parked outside the Burley house. Small stickers on the bumpers indicate these belong to Hertz or Avis or National. All around the sedans are row after row of pickup trucks, some shiny and with Armor All on the tires, others with mud on the wheels and a dirty truck bed. The pickups belong to the farmers; the buyers are in the sedans.

Inside, the buyers are in suits; some wear topcoats against the cold. They have little briefcases in their hands. One can sometimes see these individuals in the Holiday Inn lounge or the Sheraton in Johnson City: shrewd-eyed city men with a matchless understanding of how to do business in rural Tennessee.

The buyer grades the tobacco prior to the auction. It is a process similar to grading tea, except nothing is put in the mouth, nothing is lit. Some buyers use a simple A,B,C rating. Others—the younger men from the big companies—use a much more elaborate system. The grading is based on color, on how dry or wet the tobacco is, on how much of each lot is available around the tristate area that season. The buyer is searching for just the right kind of tobacco to make his company's particular blend, create the distinctive company "flavor." The thick, oily pull of an extreme American cigarette like a Camel, the raw, roasted flavor of an archetypal American cigarette like Marlboro or Winston, the silky, almost sweetish taste of an English Rothman's, all result from the purchase of a particular lot of tobacco at these auctions.

Having inspected every basket and made their judgment, the buyers now wait for the auction to take place. The auctioneer begins his breathless descant. The buyer is looking at his list. He decides what he will pay. He keeps in mind how much of the season still remains. He pictures the other towns in Virginia and North Carolina that he will hit before he is done.

It was difficult to picture Fred in the midst of this activity. Such a contradictory image: Fred, sitting in the BSC office, taking the data from "the girls" and preparing the checks.

I asked Fred how Otis was doing. Did he help with Fred's business?

"Otis is just too tired these days, too tired to work. My sister set up a job for him, sitting with an elderly man at nights. He did that for a week or so but it got to be too much for him. At times he helps me picking up checks or delivering checks. It's often late evening when I get home—my home is also my office. After supper with Otis, if it's not a day when I have choir practice or something else, I *frequently* have to put in another hour or two of work in the office to stay abreast of it all.

"It doesn't help that many an evening I dash into the house, grab some dinner and head off to Johnson City. Otis doesn't care to come to TAP, nor does he appreciate that I spend so much time with TAP. Morristown is a good thirty-five-minute drive from Johnson City. When I get back, Otis is often asleep. And he might still be asleep when I leave for the warehouse early in the morning to make up for my early departure the previous day!"

Fred's description of his home situation sounded like many marriages I knew. I had to prod myself, remind myself that this was a gay couple infected with a deadly virus. Taking advantage of Fred's gregariousness, I asked him some of the questions I had been wondering about, questions about gay men.

Did he know he was gay from an early age?

He pondered this for a while, pulled on his chin hairs. "I can look back *now* and categorize feelings of difference that I felt that I can *now* label as being gay—as early as six or eight years of age. But in a way that isn't fair because I didn't really think that *at the time.* I was over-weight—in some ways even a bigger difference than being gay. You become more of an outlier in the spectrum of schoolyard society by being fat, rather than being gay. I was, uh, very intelligent and that also set me apart. All those differences kind of worked together for me. I came to view my differences as something to be proud of, not to try and change. When someone gave me a hard time—say for maxing a test—I attributed it to them. It was *their* problem.

"In high school, I discovered people with similar feelings to mine. We had no word like gay. And yet we were experimenting. We got, *harrumph!* shall I say, uh, pretty damn well advanced. Some guilt, of course. Especially the first couple of times. But then I rolled up this difference—this experimenting and liking it—with all the other things that made me different. I said to myself: *I'm* okay. *They're* different! I wasn't going to take a lot of guilt that others lay on me. Still don't."

This explained something of Fred's demeanor, the way he had shrugged off the nurse who had looked at him disapprovingly when he hugged Carol. He felt no compunction to be apologetic for his lifestyle.

Carol poked her head in and wished us goodbye. The office was closing. Fred seemed in no hurry and I was enjoying getting to know him. I brought us the last two cups of coffee in the pot.

I told Fred how I had gone through college with little or no awareness of the existence of a real gay culture. I was aware of homoerotic acts among men in the college, even aware of men who were *rumored* to be gay. But, in general, homosexuality in India was regarded as a joke of sorts, evidence of the frustration of the Indian college male who has very little contact with women. And how it was only with my return to America, and with the onset of the tragedy of AIDS, that I became truly aware of the existence of a gay culture, not just in the big cities, but even in the small towns of America. I asked him when he became aware of a gay culture.

"For me it began when I went to college at Florida Southern. I lived in a dormitory and had a straight roommate. He was very nice, but I didn't like the idea of a roommate, a straight one at least. The rest of my time there I opted for a private room. My junior year I went to Germany on an exchange program. I had picked up German so well in my freshman year that I jumped at the chance to go there. It was also a time when I lost a lot of weight. I went from 255 pounds to 180 pounds."

This was extraordinary weight loss. Now he weighed about 200 pounds. How had he lost the weight?

"My motivation was that I had read somewhere that every twenty pounds over normal that you carried on yourself was like carrying another suitcase. That kind of stuck in my head. I was going to be carrying a backpack and a few other things in Europe. I had this vision of these three additional suitcases on my body—suitcases dripping with fat. It was a grisly image, it did something to me.

"That entire time was a period of enormous change for me—college, Germany. I did some heterosexual dating. I was kind of pushed into it by friends, sort of a 'How-can-you-knock-it-till-you-try-it?' thing. I enjoyed it as far as it went. Even had, *harrumphf! sex* with a girl! No problem. But *no* thrill. *No* spark. With this one girl it got pretty serious. It in fact became a major traumatic event. She was getting demanding, wanting to make long-term plans. Rather than encourage her, I decided to tell her all, to put an end to it. I liked her very much and didn't want to mislead her. I called her on the phone. I picked a bad day to do it—turned out she had just been to the dentist and had a tooth pulled and its root extended into one of her sinuses, so she was in a pisser of a mood. But she didn't tell me that at the time.

"When I told her why it wouldn't work between us, she got so mad. She went up and down the dormitory telling everyone that would listen that I was gay. I was really embarrassed. . . . It was one of the low points in my life. . . . I felt as if the world was collapsing in on me."

Here Fred paused, and his features became wooden as he relived the moment. The clinic was silent now; most everyone else had left. He sat up in his chair as if to break the spell of the memory.

"Surprisingly, it had very little effect! Nobody seemed to worry about it. Mind you, this was, I think, just before the Stonewall riots. But people in general were cool. And the ones who shied away from me after that I figured to be the ones I didn't want to have anything to do with anyway."

I asked Fred to tell me about his emergence as an openly gay man. Did he remember when he first visited a gay bar? Was the Connection around when he was growing up?

"I knew nothing of the Connection when I was in high school. The first gay bar I went to was in Florida. The bar was called the Green Parrot. I had it pointed out to me by some friends—heterosexual friends—as we were driving by. Someone said 'That's where the faggots hang out,' and everybody said, *Oooh!* and I said to myself, *Ah-haah!* It was a long time before I actually went in there. I remember a strong sense of unease—it was a small and very dim place. I think my unease was because I had a sense I was walking into a different society. I was looking at gay society as one homogeneous group. Knowing what I know now about how layered and fragmented gay society is, it's really funny. But at the time my feelings were like, 'Wow! I'm actually here!' But I also had feelings of terror. I thought I was fresh meat walking in!

"People in the bar were very friendly. I was at one end of the long bar. Someone told me how the bartender tended to hang around the middle of the bar and that if I wanted a drink and some attention from him, then that was where to sit. Pearls of wisdom like that! I tried to be friendly, but didn't really know the signals."

Signals? What signals? Was Fred talking about the red or yellow or robin's-egg blue handkerchief in the pocket? The key chains? The short-hand signals of sexual preference that were used on Christopher Street or in the adult bookstores?

"Lord, no! I'm not talking about those kinds of signals at all. I'm talking about signals really not that different from a heterosexual bar. If you look and exchange a long glance, it indicates interest. Accepting a drink says you are open to conversation. There is also lots of hugging and touching, physical contact. That's not necessarily sexual. It's more like an affirmation. Gay men hug a lot. It's a way of saying you're OK. But the lingering nature of a touch or a slight massage with your touching hand can be a message. And it's interesting how you terminate a hug: You ever notice how a friendly hug always terminates in patting the back? That pat means 'You can let go now.' Later, I went to large gay bars in the big cities in Florida. But I was glad that I had the experience of the smaller bar. I think I would have been blown away by one of the big, huge bars."

"And is that when you came out? In the Green Parrot?"

"Not quite. I was in Karlsruhe, in Germany. It was a wonderful time in my life. And I was a novelty to them. Americans were still exotic. They weren't sick of us in Europe the way they are now. And the gay scene was very stylized. It blew me away totally. There was a strong distinction between macho men and effeminate men. Very clear-cut roles. A huge emphasis on leather. I was not into S&M, all that slave-master stuff. Didn't do anything for me. But I think Germany defined for me that it was the more masculine men that turned me on. My interest in effeminate men had been because it was easier to discern that they were gay. But it is the masculine look that turns me on. I could now see the cliques: leather, sweater, dykes, tykes, fag-hags or fruit flies—"

"Fruit flies?"

"—Women who hang out with gay men. But my most enlightening and exciting experience was in Amsterdam. I was seeing bars where I never felt I had to be furtive going in. The atmosphere of the bar spilled out into the street! I could be just as gay in the streets outside as in the bar! It was my first taste, in a sense, of gay liberation."

The atmosphere of a bar spilling out into a street. I thought of the atmosphere of the Connection, which had little, at least as far as I could tell, of this exuberant spirit of liberation. Then I remembered the dancing at the Connection and at the bar in Boston I had wandered into— the men dancing, not in couples, but together as one entity, like a family or tribe. I could understand how someone would want to be part of that feeling, especially someone who had never really belonged to any group. Someone like Gordon who had left home looking for a place to feel truly accepted without having to hide.

"So that's when you came out?" I asked Fred. "In Amsterdam?"

"No, not really. When I got to Wisconsin for my postgraduate work, I was so conditioned by what had happened in Florida—the incident with that girlfriend, my general secretiveness—and by what I had seen in Europe, that I swore in this new town I would never hide who I was. I got into gay liberation in a powerful way. There was an advertisement in the college paper: *Gay Liberation Group Meets at . . .* It was in a church somewhere. The group had been going for six months already when I got there. For its time, Madison was really advanced. This was, I think, the time just after the Stonewall riots, but I may be wrong.

"I called the contact number, and as it turned out the person who answered was someone I already knew from one of the gay bars in town! When I walked into the first meeting at the church, I already knew half the people there from the Rathskeller Student Union building where one corner had become an informal gay corner."

"When you say 'knew' them, do you mean knew them sexually?"

Fred laughed and said, "Yes, in some cases."

As Fred said this, the picture of a wheel came to my mind: In models of sexually transmitted disease, spread of infection among gay men is often depicted as a wheel. Aggressive contact tracing often establishes that there are multiple cross-links: The "index" case may have had contact with not only the next person in the chain but others farther along; a circle is formed. In a small town the circle is small; in New York City it is larger, but the circle still closes. Gaetan Dugas—identified as "Patient Zero" in Randy Shilts's *And the Band Played On*—the handsome, Air Canada flight steward, showed just how large the circle could be: At least 40 of the first 248 gay men diagnosed with AIDS in the United States had sex either with Gaetan or with someone who had. By contrast, heterosexual contact tracing resembles the spokes of a wheel: the wheel is so huge that it is practically infinite, with contacts leading linearly away from the index case. The AIDS virus took advantage of, and drew attention to, a level of sexual activity among an exclusive group of individuals in a way that no other sexually transmitted disease had done to that point.

Fred continued: "We called ourselves the Gay Liberation Front, the word 'front' designed to be offensive. And that was our mood. We had a great deal of consciousness raising. We brought in speakers. Some of the 'speakers' were really people we put on the hot seat. They had no idea what they were getting into. We had a psychiatrist who thought that he was being invited to convert us—this was a time when the American Psychiatric Association had just stopped listing homosexuality as a disease, but I think most straight psychiatrists were still into *curing* gay men. This guy got there and he didn't know what hit him. We had some of the best minds on campus in the audience, and they just about mentally *raped* him, *beat* him to a pulp, figuratively speaking; he got away with his life.

"All of us were very young, we had tremendous revolutionary spirit—public protest and so on. We formed a corporation. It mutated several times and became the forerunner to the major gay group in Madison that I think still exists to this day."

It was still not clear to me how Fred had wound up as an accountant for the Burley warehouses around Morristown.

"I was taking more and more psychology courses. To the degree that changes were happening in my psyche, I became more interested in the human aspects of science, less so in protein chemistry and DNA. I wound up with a degree in psychology.

"I returned to Tennessee. For the next five years I was a home manager at a learning center for disabled adults in Knoxville and I taught at a community college. It was a time when I stayed very active with the gay community—the Metropolitan Community Church in particular. I was a student minister, I worked on east Tennessee's first gay newspaper, *Pride Press*. I was involved with a gay discussion group for people who were coming out: There was a kid one time whose father had him locked up in the basement when he told his parents he was gay. Well, we went and got him. Others had more in the way of psychological problems than that kind of a physical problem. I helped organize a Gay Cover Group—an umbrella group to bring all the smaller groups together."

I could see now how Fred had gravitated toward TAP, why he spent his evenings running off to TAP meetings despite Otis's disapproval. He had spent a lifetime training for the role of AIDS activist in Johnson City. The stakes had never been higher; his activism now had a clear focus. It would be his therapy, it would give him long life, it would greatly better the lives of persons infected with HIV in upper east Tennessee. Otis could object all he wanted to; but he had better realize that Fred *needed* to be involved in TAP for his psychic well-being, as much as I needed to be a physician for mine.

"But why did you come back to Morristown?" I asked. "Don't you see how strange it is for someone as educated as you to return to a town of less than 40,000 people and be in an accounting business? Why not stay in Knoxville?"

Fred pondered this a while. "When I came back in 1983, I was ready for a rest. I was burned out. I had been an activist since 1973—a full-time thing. *Every* gay pride march, *every* gay this-or-that, I *had* to go. I was worn out, ready to live a calmer life. A quieter *social* life, and a quieter *political* life."

"Were you prepared to hide your sexuality?"

Fred was silent again and when he answered he sidestepped the issue of returning to the closet.

"I was so glad to be back in Morristown—no traffic, no hassles, just a simpler existence. And it was less of an effort to blend back into the shadows than to always be projecting this militant gay image and dealing with the bad stuff that inevitably came with it."

"Did your parents know you were gay by then?"

"Oh, yes! There was a week in Knoxville where I was going to be appearing on TV, Channel 2, for Gay Pride Week. I decided to tell my parents beforehand. I had this vision of my parents discovering Grandma facedown on the carpet, one hand on her chest and the other pointing to the television set! So I came down one weekend. It was when we were having family pictures taken, everyone was there: Bettie Lee, my brother-in-law. We were sitting around the living room, my father was sitting on a stool, my mother in the big armchair. And I told them."

I was curious to hear *how* he told them, what words did he use? Did he say "gay" or did he say "homosexual"?

"I may have said 'homosexual' first and then moved to the word 'gay.' I didn't want my mother to say when I said *gay*, 'Oh, that's nice, dear; I'm so glad you're happy!' I did it in my typical way, my cerebral way, if you will: I brought a lot of pamphlets and literature. I had a speech, or at least a plan of how I would word things. To my surprise everyone was calm. Bettie Lee was, of course, helping me along. My father said nothing and my mother was quietly crying."

"Did she say *why* she was crying?"

"Because she worried for my safety. She was thinking of my *physical* safety, that I could get killed in Knoxville. And she was right, of course. But to this day I am amazed and in total admiration of my family's resilience. My grandfather wrote to me and said: 'I don't understand, but will not condemn you.' You'd have to know him. He was old Morristown stock, a big landowner, he was an *extreme* conservative. And my uncle . . . it didn't bother him.

"So when I returned to Morristown for good, my family knew I was gay. I didn't flaunt it any longer. But here I was, unmarried, in my thirties. And I'm sure quite a few people either knew or speculated about my sexual leanings."

"How did you integrate?" I asked. "I know you are a regular church member; I have heard you mention choir practice on several occasions. Did you have any problems being accepted by the community?"

"Church is really important for me. Growing up, my parents thought church was important for us even if *they* didn't go themselves. I was dropped at church every Sunday, and picked up after Sunday school."

I was thinking back to my own childhood in Ethiopia. The church services of our small Christian Indian community were interminable and conducted in an ancient language, Syriac. My parents and the other Indian Christians in Ethiopia knew the liturgy by heart, it was what they had grown up with. And to stand together in an Ethiopian church that they rented, to worship together in a language that could be traced to St. Thomas and to Jerusalem, was an affirmation of who they were, a connection to a corner of India so far away from Africa.

But for us fidgety children the services were boring and sadistic—two hours of standing and listening to someone drone on in a language you do not understand is the surest way to dry up religion in a young child. When, years later, my brothers and I negotiated our own paths back to some form of religion, it was *despite* that childhood experience, not because of it.

Fred went on: "When I was in Wisconsin, I became involved in the Episcopalian Church. I liked it so well that I was confirmed. The people there tended to be intelligent, educated. I liked the doctrine of the *via media*—the concept of a middle way. I could have a relationship with God, whatever I conceived Him to be. At the same time, in the evenings, I was involved with MCC—the Metropolitan Community Church."

I had heard of MCC. It was formed by a Pentecostal minister, Troy Perry. He was thrown out of his church for being gay. After much soul-searching, he eventually founded MCC, now a huge international organization that has been admitted to the World Council of Churches. Perry had written a book, *The Lord Is My Shepherd and He Knows I Am Gay*.

"When I came back to Morristown," Fred said, "there was an MCC group in Johnson City. But it was a long drive down on Sunday evening when I preferred to be at home. So I went to the Episcopalian Church in Morristown when I first got back—after all, I *was* a confirmed Episcopalian. But I was disappointed. They were very stodgy. And for a while they didn't have a pastor. I thought of them as the 'brooches, minks and morning prayer group!' They had Communion rarely, mostly morning prayer. I missed the doctrine of Communion; it was very important to me. I didn't go back for a long while. Then the Episcopalian Church got a new priest, an older fellow but with an unshakable belief in goodness, grace and God's mercy. I went to meet him. I told him I was gay. Told him I wanted to be more of an activist, socially: outreach, helping the poor and all that. He encouraged me to get involved, but *without* telling the church members I was gay."

"Why? And did you go for it?"

"His reasoning was that if I said I was gay, people wouldn't get to know me before they voiced opposition. So that's what I did: I went to choir, deacon's committee, Church Society meetings."

"Do you think you compromised your beliefs by coming back and taking on the role you did in your town?"

"No, I feel it was more a growth process than a compromise. I met with the pastor privately once a week. Even though he did not agree with my outlooks on sexuality, he did not believe it impaired my ability to be a Christian. He *believed* in me. My perseverance and his have paid off. He turned out to be right in terms of my not bringing up my gayness right off the bat so people could make an issue of it. For example, when I first joined the choir, I think there were some men who were fearful that I would grope them! That—"

"—But how did they know you were gay if you hadn't told anyone?"

"Well, I had appeared on TV in Knoxville, on stations that are carried in Morristown. People knew. Or at least, some did. But then when I turned out to be a loyal, regular, reliable choir member *and* did not grope them, they became friends and supporters. The issue of my being gay became quite secondary. If *anyone* asks me, I will willingly tell them—that has *never* changed. And I can be *anywhere*, and if I hear someone tell a gay joke, I will tell them why it is not funny." Here Fred gave a nervous laugh. "Except perhaps in the tobacco warehouse. There I let it go."

WHEN WE STEPPED outside to our cars, ours were the only two vehicles in the parking lot. The house neighboring the clinic had giant sunflowers spilling over to the clinic parking lot. There were yellow jackets that congregated around these flowers and made parking here treacherous. My beeper had gone off twice in the last five minutes: both times the number displayed was my home number. Since I was on my way home, I did not call back.

I walked Fred to his car. "Look," Fred said, stopping and pointing. A cardinal was perched on a fence post about ten yards from us, its handsome crest clearly visible against the sky. In the shadows it looked more black than red, but its silhouette and the large conical beak were distinctive. We stood and watched it, until, feeling our gaze, it flew away.

I shook hands with Fred. He headed in the direction of Market Street to catch 11E to Morristown.

As I pulled onto Lamont Street, heading home, I realized how unburdened I felt by Scotty Daws's death. For the first time in a long time I could go home directly without going to the Miracle Center first to check on Scotty. My visits to him every morning and evening had felt like parentheses that hemmed me in, left me little room to breathe. I always felt like a prisoner in his room, standing next to his bed, up so close to his pain. I could not escape the idea of what was coming for Fred, for Vickie, for Clyde and the others. Not just death, but the path *to* death, a path that might be filled with the same suffering that I saw Scotty go through. Surely, Fred must have this same sense of something hanging over him, no matter how hard he tried to put it out of his mind. I was telling my patients that they must learn to live in the present moment, but I could not always heed my own advice.

Perhaps this was how it was destined to be, I thought as I pulled up into my driveway: long dry spells while Fred and others lived relatively healthily, then spurts of in-hospital activity.

OUR BABY-SITTER'S car was parked outside the house. Steven peered out of the dining room window. His head disappeared now, as he raced to the kitchen door so that he could greet me when I walked into the house.

Pulling in next to Mrs. Stokes's orange Dodge Dart with its vinyl top reminded me why she was here: we were invited to dinner by an Indian family. I had promised, for once, to be home early. But the conversation with Fred had kept me.

I gathered Steven up, said hello to the baby who was in Mrs. Stokes's arms, and headed up to shower and change. Rajani was in the living room, dressed in a sari, with all her jewelry on, looking gorgeous. She sat on the sofa, a magazine in her hand. She glanced up as I mumbled my apologies. She did not say a word to me, nor meet my eyes.

11

RAJANI AND I made our way to the party that was being held in the gym of a local school, the Ashley Academy. We were quite late.

The Ashley parking lot was full: a few Honda Civics, an abundance of Honda Accords, a few minivans, a few Acuras (a natural progression from an Accord), and one Mercedes-Benz were in the lot.

The Indian community in Johnson City was growing logarithmically. The new complement of interns and residents always included three or more Indians, most of them married, some with children. They were the friends, relatives or classmates of those who had gone through the ETSU residency program, people who now put them up, lent them the rule book to study for the Tennessee driving license exam, shepherded them to the Highway Patrol office to take the test, cosigned their loan for the Honda Civic, helped them find an apartment, instructed them on whether the vegetables were fresher at Kroger's or Winn Dixies, and introduced them to the old-timers of Johnson City, like Rajani and myself.

Once the newcomers were settled, they expressed their gratitude by inviting their mentors and their mentors' friends over for a grand dinner. The mentors, once newcomers themselves, now had moved one step closer to the inner stratum of the social circle. At its center were a patriarchal group of families who had been there before the medical school and before liquor-by-the-drink had come to town. They had been there when North Roan Street was the edge of town; they were there before the mall, the banks, the car dealers, and the little strip malls with their necklace of colorful awnings had arrived on North Roan. Like a water beetle, the new development on North Roan had sucked the life out of downtown, leaving only a carcass. The old-timers told us how beautiful and quaint downtown had been: the Majestic Theater, the Fountain Plaza. . . . Now it was an empty shell of a business area with a few boutiques displaying slope-shouldered mannequins in faded and dusty fashions from the fifties.

Texas Instruments and Eastman-Kodak also brought in a regular crop of engineers of Indian origin. These "techie" types, when I saw them at a party, always struck me as unused to the bright glare of the outside world, staring out at it ferretlike. After four years of cracking books in the library of some state university (those at Amherst and Buffalo were especially popular) and skewing the grade curve in a manner to make things impossible for their American student peers (who still held dear the three Fs of college life—fraternities, football, and frolicking with the opposite sex), they appeared quite lost.

Meanwhile, more foreign doctors were setting up practice in the smallest towns of rural Tennessee, southwest Virginia, and Kentucky, after completing their training in an urban residency. They made expeditions to our provincial metropolises of Johnson City, Kingsport and Bristol—the Tri-Cities—to do their shopping, to look up families that were friends of friends of friends, and to gradually become regulars at any of the major functions, such as Dipavali or Indian Independence Day, that justified an excursion of such length.

New York City and Chicago had long gotten used to the sight of Indians manning newspaper kiosks, driving cabs, running gas stations, working as staff nurses or doctors in the metropolitan hospitals, and even trying their hand at the pretzel and hot dog concessions. And now, the glittery variety shops that were once the province of the Lebanese, the Yemenis, and the Jews had competition from Indians. Indians had learned the art of cramming the window displays with autofocus cameras, palm-sized cameras, video cameras, 8-mm cine cameras, hand-held televisions, car televisions, stereos, VCRs, CDs, radios, two-in-one boom boxes, three-in-ones, four-in-ones, five-in-ones, computers, calculators, pens, time managers, wristwatches, pen-size dictaphones, strobe lights, binoculars, telephoto lenses, tripods, telescopes, and lava lamps. This phantasmagoria was peppered with SALE! SALE! banners and little fold-up cards sat below each item with the "price" prominently displayed in fluorescent green, yellow and red, below the crossed-out "retail" price. It was as difficult for a grown man to walk past such a store as it was to whisk a child through Toys "R" Us without stopping. And once you were caught by this display, transfixed by the stare of the one hundred lenses, captured by the four video cameras that now projected your image onto every TV screen in that window—shopper transformed into variety store star—you became like a deer trapped in a hunter's flashlight.

The dark-skinned man at the door, with hair curling out of his shirt collar and peeping out at his wrists, watched you, smiled easily, nodded to his assistant who mysteriously appeared with the *one* item that had tugged at you. As he ushered you into the interior of the shop, where incense burned at the foot of idols of Lakshmi and Ganesh, he reminded you how indispensable a pair of binoculars with power-zoom was to a citizen of the world.

These visible Indians in the big city were but a fraction of the total number of Indians who lived there, worked quietly as accountants, engineers, Port Authority workers, students, computer programmers, immigration officials . . .

In a town our size, without the very visible trades of taxi drivers or newspaper *wallahs* to use as a yardstick, it was tricky to establish exactly how many Indians there were. My friend Brij, a traveling Hong-Kong-suit salesman (the kind who will set up his tie and shirt displays on the ground floor of an Embassy Suites for a day, run advertisements in the local paper, then take orders for custom-tailored suits which are stitched in Hong-Kong, by Indians, and mailed back in a week), describes his foolproof method of gauging the local Indian population and finding an Indian restaurant in a strange city:

"You look in white pages under B for 'Bombay Palace' or T for 'Taj Mahal' or I for 'India House.' These are equivalent of Asia Palace, Bamboo House, China Garden, or House of Hunan in the Chinese restaurant business. If there are no listings under those names, take my word there are probably no Indian restaurants in town. Failing this, you simply look up number of Patels in white pages and multiply by 60; that will tell you size of Indian community *not* counting wives, children and in-laws. Take my word: less than ten Patels means no Indian restaurant. If more than ten, you call, say you are from India, ask them where to go to eat."

"But, Brij," I asked. "Why don't you just look under 'Restaurants' in the Yellow Pages?"

"*Aare*, that's no fun, *yar!*"

Even if it was not readily measured, Indianization, the entrepreneurial spirit of the variety store, was trickling out to the hinterland. The sari shops, the video stores, and the spice shops in New York, Atlanta, and Chicago were now into mail order. Indian culture was following on the heels of the Coca-Cola truck, going wherever it went, probing deep into rural America. A Gujarati couple from Charlotte sent flyers out in the mail to announce the days they would be in Johnson City. The flyer listed their complete itinerary which, much like the itinerary of a country singer, began in Charlotte and took them up to Boone, North Carolina; Johnson City, Tennessee; Bristol, Virginia, and Bristol, Tennessee; Wise, Virginia, and then back home.

In Johnson City, they parked their van at the former Mid-Town Inn, with the blessing of the new Indian owners. Along the insides of their Ford van they had rigged up crude shelves. The floor of the van was loaded with giant sacks of basmathi rice, raw rice, rice flour, lentils and a balancing pan to weigh out the rice. In the recesses of the van were bottles of Ambedkar mango and lime pickles and *papads*. They carried the complete product line of the Surati Sweet Mart, a company with offices in Toronto, Ontario, and River Rouge, Michigan. Surati Sweet Mart produced a line of packaged and canned goods that included *badam puree, barfi, badampak, bundi ladu, farsi puree, gulab jambu, ghari, jalebi, khaman, khajli, kachori, mesub, mohan thal, penda, surti bhusu, chevdo, sev* and *gathiya.*

The wife, a formidable lady with a giant diamond in her nose, thick gold bangles on her wrists and a no-nonsense air about her, sat on the lip of the cargo space, further jeopardizing the van's suspension. Her hand rested possessively on the weighing machine. If you requested an item other than rice or flour or lentils, she yelled the order to her husband, a thin individual who never emerged from the recess of the van, but stayed crouched in the back. You only saw his gangly arms handing out items to his wife. Her size precluded her fulfilling this task.

The parking lot was full of doctors and engineers. I spoke no Hindi and the Gujarati couple spoke no Tamil or Malayalam, so when it came my turn, we carried out our transactions there in the former Mid-Town Inn parking lot in English:

"Three packets of *papads*—"

"Plain or chili?"

"Chili. And two kilos of basmathi rice—"

"I give you discount on five kilos."

A NEW FAD HAD swept the Johnson City Indian community. Instead of inviting people to each other's houses for dinner, families were renting out the gym of the Ashley Academy, a private school, to host dinner for sixty to a hundred people. In one fell swoop, a family could reciprocate for every dinner they had been invited to over the previous year. In doing so they also racked up the certainty of invitations for the rest of the year, a year that could be spent at leisure until they were in the debit column again.

As more families followed this trend, the dinners took on a surreal quality: the same gym, the same crowd, almost the same food—only the host changed.

Rajani and I stepped inside the gym. The women had, as usual, gravitated to one side, the men to the other, and children were playing noisily in the middle. There was a constant din in the room from all the voices.

I moved around the room greeting people I had seen just two weeks ago in the same gym.

This party, like every other such party, was "dry"—no alcohol was served. This was in itself curious, as I had never known any of these hosts to decline my scotch or gin or rum at our house. Of course, a "dry" dinner could be thought of as being more traditional, like in the old country. But here in this prep school gym, children running around with ninja figures and robot transformers in their hands, the most fluent east Tennessee patois rolling off the tongues of toddlers and teens alike, it was difficult to invoke the old country, difficult to ascribe the "dry" dinners to anything but an unbecoming miserliness.

I looked around the room and saw Rajani with a group of fifteen women, all of them, including Rajani, wearing colorful saris, or *salwar-*

kamiz, all of them sitting on the gym benches and chatting. The different states of India that were revealed in subtle aspects of dress and jewelry included Maharashtra, Andhra Pradesh, Uttar Pradesh, Punjab, Tamil Nadu, Kerala, Orissa; there were an equal number of unique dialects. English was the only language common to all. Rajani was laughing and enjoying herself in a way that I hadn't seen for a long time. Another group of women with a few men were helping the hostess bring the food (prepared at home over the past few days) in the giant cooking pots to the row of tables strung end to end to make a buffet table.

The teenage girls buzzed and whispered together, staying in their one geographic spot all night. The teenage boys stood sullen together, on the men's side of the room. They looked displeased at being made to come to these functions.

Among the men, the pecking order at these functions was clear: doctors ruled over engineers, who lorded it over everyone else. The motel owner's status depended on how successful he was as an entrepreneur. But then financial success was really at the root of the hierarchy among the doctors: surgeons—particularly thoracic surgeons—were treated as the maharajahs, everyone rising when this persona entered the room. Plastic surgery and urology were a notch below thoracic surgery. (And even if the urologist made more money, there was something just a little unclean about the idea of urology—it had tinges of untouchability, what with working with urine and all that.) Then followed the cardiologists and the gastroenterologists and the other *procedural* medical specialists. Needless to say, on this ranking, being an infectious diseases specialist was equivalent to being a bathroom sweeper.

To have made the choice of the specialty of infectious diseases was, in this circle, considered akin to buying at full price a motel that any Patel could have told you was going belly-up and that you could have bought for a *bhajan* at foreclosure.

Tonight, as always, I was the recipient of much advice. Most of it was on how to make money, since I clearly wasn't making any. In the competition to build a larger and fancier house, I was not even in the race: I was *renting* from the VA—a heinous crime from the perspective of an Indian community that saw land acquisition as a primal necessity. ("But what about my oak trees?" I wanted to say. "What about the bed of red salvia I have in front? What about the yellow and red roses? What about my tomatoes?" I knew the answer: it would be "What about equity?")

I acted as if money meant less to me than it did to them, a childish reflex. This was, of course, not true: I valued money and would not have minded a ton of it. But I didn't feel I had to do something different in medicine *just* for that reason. I was every bit as well trained, just as talented I like to think, as the doctors who made twenty times what I made. The monetary disparity was not due to their skill or their intrinsic worth (even though at times I think they succumbed to this delusion); it was due to a payment system that placed greater value on procedural specialties than on those without them.

"Ah, but in *Sweden*," I would say when I grew tired of being needled about my specialty, "thoracic surgeons and infectious diseases specialists get the same salary. And you know what, if the *Democrats* win the next election . . ."

This was guaranteed to produce a loud outcry that I delighted in. There were no stauncher Republicans than the Indian doctors of east Tennessee.

I tired of this after a while, tired of the talk of stock options and mutual funds and the benefits of incorporating. I drifted over to the teenage boys. To them I was a hero of sorts. Not only did I *not* drive a Honda Accord, not only had I *never* owned a new car, I even owned a motorcycle and rode it when the weather permitted. I took them for rides, not necessarily with their parents' knowledge. And on top of that, I took care of AIDS patients! Whatever it was their daddies did, there was no personal danger. In truth, there was no personal danger in what I did, but that evening I did not fight the St. George-the-dragon-slayer metaphor.

With a little encouragement, I found myself waxing eloquent about AIDS care, telling them how it enriched my life, changed its direction. Some of the teenage girls shuffled over. I marshaled a passionate argument against Reagan, deliberately planting a seed of dissension in their family. I told them a risqué joke: how the urologist who removed Reagan's prostate was asked later by Reagan if all was well, would the plumbing now work well? "Everything is perfect. Your bladder is fine. Your penis is one-hundred percent. You can go out and fuck the country for another four years!" The loud laughter drew looks from the parents.

As I talked to the teenagers, I was conscious that my words created a reality far superior to the actual reality of what I did. But the teens were chiming in now: They had such pure ideas of justice, of right and wrong, of what they would do if they were in control. I loved it! If their parents were the ultimate pragmatists, these kids were beautiful idealists.

When the summons for dinner came, and the line started to form to walk past the table and pick up the pooris, the channa, the rice, the vegetable curry, the pickle, the yogurt and the sweet, our little group broke up. Children went first. I picked up my paper plate and stood with the ranks of the men. By long-standing Ashley Academy Indian dinner tradition—a token concession to years of oppression—the men would serve themselves *after* the women.

An hour or two later, I was ready to leave. I thanked our host. Looking for Rajani, I approached the side of the room where the women were sitting. A father stopped me, his expression half-serious, half-joking. He said he was mortified to hear his daughter say to him a few minutes ago that when she finished medical school (and these kids were *all* going into medical school, even the ten-year-olds) she thought she would become an AIDS specialist.

I shook his hand and offered him my warmest congratulations and turned away. Ahead of me I could see Rajani, still laughing, at the center of a circle of women. She seemed perfectly at home. I didn't want to take her away.

12

A FEW WEEKS LATER, I went to see Vickie McCray and Clyde
at their home in Tester Hollow, a mile or two out of town.

I had just seen a patient at Northside Hospital. Northside was built by
one of the medical groups in town. It was much smaller than the
Miracle Center, laid out ranch-style, with three wings fanning out from
a lobby. I tried not to encourage consultations at Northside because it
meant yet another place to dart to during my lunch break or after my
hours at the VA. But since I was now on the north edge of town and had
time to spare, I gave Vickie a call.

To get to Vickie's house, you head north on North Roan, past the
Holiday Inn, the Sheraton, the International House of Pancakes, and
Putt-Putt Golf until you come to where North Roan forks into two. The
left fork is the Kingsport Highway leading to the airport and then on to
Kingsport. The right fork is 11E to Bristol.

At this Y junction, on the Bristol side, there used to be a bar called
Cowboys. It had been a country-western place whose parking lot was
filled with pickups; the gals and guys coming and going wore cowboy
hats, a look quite out of place for east Tennessee, more suited to
Nashville or Austin. The building itself was a large ranch house with
light cedar paneling. Cowboys had closed, and in its place was a bar
called New Beginnings. New Beginnings was Johnson City's new gay
bar; the Connection had moved to this bigger, more visible locale, and
had in the process taken on a new name. I had been meaning to work

up the courage to visit someday, perhaps asking Olivia Sells, my Red Cross friend, to come along for company.

North Roan is segmented by traffic lights that can make a midday drive a frustrating stop-and-go exercise. But a mile on the Bristol Highway, and you are free of lights. The strip malls, car dealers, and gas stations, which till then have been neck and neck, now give way to businesses with a little yard around them, space between them for a shed or a prefab storage barn.

The highway here is raised. The turn-offs from the shoulder of the road lead steeply down into country. Driving by, you see only the rooftops of the small enterprises on either side of the road, the billboards strapped to the chimneys that identify the businesses as "Country Florists," or "Lawn Ornaments," or "Tennessee Headstones."

Vickie had given me good directions. Nevertheless, I drove right past my landmark, an antique store which looked to me like an ordinary house with junk piled on the front porch. The shop had no rooftop billboard, only a dark-cedar slab nailed to the railing on which the word ANTIQUES was painted in black letters.

The turn-off from the highway ran behind the antique store, crossed over a creek and then went plunging down, down, deep into a valley. I was on Tester Hollow Road. On either side was a steep embankment coated with a blanket of pine needles and maple and poplar leaves. The newly fallen leaves were saffron and ocher in color, their outlines preserved, as if someone had set them down carefully by their intact stems to form a mosaic around the bases of the trees. And the trees that soared up from this earth-coat were on fire: wild maples, pine and sycamore, tall and still full of leaf with colors from crimson to gold with every shade in between. They formed a canopy over the road, diffracting the light, making me feel as if I were driving into a Cezanne painting.

I traveled a mile down Tester Hollow Road, followed it as it twisted and curved with no shoulder on either side. In places the foliage was so thick and so little light came in that I could see fern and moss growing on the fallen trunks of trees. I came to a crossroad: McCray Road.

It was strange to see Vickie's surname on a road sign. It didn't seem to go with what I knew of her financial circumstance. The only people I knew who had things named after them in Johnson City *were* the city. Like the Gumps of "Gump Addition," a subdivision where some of the most stately homes of Johnson City were situated. But here, in Tester Hollow, in this junglelike setting, the names of the McCrays, as well as their kinfolk, the Millers, the Testers and the Grangers, were immortalized. They may not have succeeded in raising themselves completely out of poverty, but they had ensured themselves one kind of immortality.

I came onto Vickie's trailer just as soon as I turned off Tester Hollow Road and into McCray Road. It sat fifty yards back from the road, up on the gradient, with the trees and the wild grass reclaiming the earth behind the trailer and rising steeply behind it. There was just enough room in the clearing in front of the trailer to park two cars. The sheet metal of the trailer reflected my blue Datsun Z and Vickie's bile-green Torino. She referred to her car as a "junker": she told me it was in such poor shape that she carried parts in the back seat.

The trailer was a sixty-by-twelve. Its metal roof was rounded in the manner of a railway carriage. The oil furnace was strapped to one end of the trailer like a backpack. The other end of the trailer abutted on a tiny two-room shack with a red roof and white window frames. The trailer had been parked to make a "T" with the shack.

A crude latticework provided a skirting for the trailer. The skirting was missing big pieces here and there, and I could see the welded metal tongue by which the trailer had been hauled up there. The wheels had been removed and the trailer rested on a stack of cinder blocks. Pipes led from under the belly of the trailer into the sewer.

There were no other dwellings to be seen anywhere around. Later that day, Vickie would drive me farther into Tester Hollow, show me how McCray Road looped around in a full circle and how there were in fact other houses and trailers and shacks around, but each with plenty of brush and forest separating it from its nearest neighbor. A quarter mile up the street from Vickie's house, on an unpaved trail that led steeply down from the main road, were the houses of Clyde's cousins and his mother.

Vickie's trailer may have been small and nothing to write home about, but, by God, they had their privacy and a gorgeous setting.

I negotiated the cinder-block steps to the small porch and entered the house. Vickie gave me a warm hug. She was wearing her bandanna and there were deep rings around her eyes. She told me that Clyde had slept little the previous night and that he was now fast asleep. The children were at school; it was a little after one o'clock in the afternoon. She led me into the house.

The kitchen was to the left, really just a part of the living room and separated from it by a counter. To the right was a hallway. The floor was red linoleum. Everywhere I looked was dark paneling.

"You ever been in a trailer before?" Vickie asked.

"I have, but I wouldn't mind the tour."

I had once gone with Allen to visit a friend of his who was ill and Allen had wanted me to "check him over." The man lived in a trailer in Erwin. When I went to use the bathroom, I saw a monster river rock parked on top of the commode lid. The man explained that sewer rats had been climbing up the pipes and coming out of the commode. Though it hadn't happened to him, it had happened to others in the trailer park. One such sewer rat, "the size of a grandfather skunk," had, he claimed, "bitten a chunk out of this ol' feller's balls, and another done took a piece of this old lady's ass." The river rock was there to make sure no rat came in and settled in the dead space of the trailer, either under the stove or in the ceiling. Despite his reassurance, I found myself quite disinclined to pee at his house, and confident I could hold my water till we got to the forest outside.

"Clyde's sleeping so let's leave that end of the house for last," Vickie said.

Vickie led me down the hallway to the right. A teeny-tiny bedroom opened off the hallway. The hallway then ended in a bigger bedroom. A half-bath sat between the two bedrooms.

"This is Danielle's room," Vickie said as we walked into the big bedroom. She went to the window and began cranking a lever. "These are jalousie windows—they crank out. I tell Danielle to keep them closed because I do believe that magnolia tree outside is what makes her wheeze. Every time I close it, she opens it."

There was a dresser in the bedroom that was built into the wall with a large mirror and a picture of Michael Jackson above it. Vickie showed me how the built-in closets on either side of the dresser had sliding doors that when they slid back covered the dresser and mirror. The space-efficient designs of the trailer were impressive.

There were floor vents in each room.

"That's where the heat comes in. It can get as cold as a headstone in here, come January. Particularly 'cause we ain't insulated the bottom of the trailer too well. But I tell you what, you stand over one of these vents in your nightgown in winter and it'll warm you right up, son; puff you up like a hot-air balloon."

We walked back to the kitchen and toward the other end of the trailer. There was a utility room where the washer and dryer were. A back door next to the utility room was the trailer's other exit.

"You seen that shack outside? Well, Danielle was born in it. Can you believe we used to live in that till we got us this trailer? We use it to store stuff now."

Past the utility room was a master bath. The trailer ended in the master bedroom where Clyde lay on the bed, curled up like a baby, his arms tucked between his thighs, snoring loudly. Also between his thighs was the remote control for the TV; the TV was on, and it filled the room with the dialogue of a midday soap opera.

When Clyde was in the hospital we ruled out syphilis and other treatable infections of the brain. His childlike behavior, the complete disappearance of his previous personality, the prolonged hiccups, and the motor slowing and apathy were all the result of HIV directly affecting the cells of the cortex. As yet, we had nothing with which to treat the HIV. Vickie had decided to take him home. A visiting nurse came by daily to assist Vickie.

When Vickie first brought Clyde home he was both bedridden and demented. He recognized only his immediate family. Even that was inconsistent: he addressed his cousin once as if he were the preacher. Sometimes he looked at Vickie with puzzlement, until she told him who she was.

Now we both stood looking at the sleeping Clyde. Vickie had told me over the phone that Clyde showed little interest in the outside world. His sole passion was television; it absorbed him and he would never let it be turned off, day or night. Vickie told me he could become agitated if he was taken too far from it.

I was fascinated by this: modern television, it seemed to me, robbed the mind—a *healthy* mind—of its need to explore the recesses of its subconscious. The fabric of dreams such as love, murder, war, incest, betrayal, riches, now played on the screen incessantly, removing all mystery, leaving the mind with little to imagine, no uncharted areas of fancy that had not been reduced to a miniseries or a sitcom. But in Clyde's case, he used the television concretely. It *was* his mind. Its buzz and hum and incessant flashing images and commentary filled the void behind his eyes and the silence in his head. To turn it off was to turn him off.

At first, Vickie had used a condom catheter to catch his urine in a bag tied to the bed. Clyde was able to tell her when he wanted to have a bowel movement. She would help him up and they would hook the urine bag to the walker. With Vickie walking behind him, Clyde would lean heavily on the walker and they would negotiate the narrow doorway and turn into the master bathroom.

Vickie told me that one day, after she had helped him to the bathroom, she was sitting in the living room, waiting for him to call her and tell her he was done. When she looked up, she saw him standing in the kitchen doorway, without the walker, looking wobbly. She jumped up to hold him, but he told her to back away and he made his way unsteadily to the couch. Vickie said she had cried to see this small victory.

From that day on, Clyde had gotten back to his feet more and more, taking to bed only if he was tired. His motor skills had returned even if his intellectual skills had not. Clyde had improved enough to wander off down the road to his mother's house or to his cousin's house. Vickie, who was still working a full shift at Pet Dairy, would return to find him gone and would have to call around to see where he was. At times he landed in downtown: he had simply wandered out of the hollow, hitched a ride with a stranger, and headed to his favorite watering hole.

He had begun to resent Vickie's controlling him, much like a child might resent it. When she went to his mother's house or his cousin's house to pick him up, he would sulk and sometimes refuse to leave.

It was difficult for me to look at the sleeping Clyde and picture him walking about Tester Hollow, hitching rides to town.

We tiptoed out of the bedroom and went out and sat on the porch, our feet resting on the cinder-block stairs. Vickie brought us both coffee. Vickie lit a cigarette. It was perfect weather; the sun did not shine right on the house and it was cool in the hollow. On the other side of the road, I saw a trail winding up the slope between the trees. I could picture Clyde, Jr., and Danielle playing up there, or Clyde heading up there to hunt squirrel or possum.

Neither Vickie nor I were inclined to say much. We both sat with our elbows resting on our knees, staring out. I glanced at Vickie; I was struck again by her eyes: beautiful blue eyes that were now looking at the land around her and at the sky, taking it all in as if seeing it for the first time. The wound on her hand from where she had punched her cousin had healed. I could not help smiling at the thought of her busting her cousin in the chops. Vickie saw my expression and turned and asked, "What?" drawing out the first two letters until the word sounded like *Whooo-at?*

"Nothing," I said.

"Like hell, nothing," she said, and we both laughed.

I felt the trailer shake beneath us and I looked inquiringly at Vickie. "Hell, that's just Clyde turning in bed. You can feel a tick burp in here. It don't take much to shake the trailer." She smiled. "One time Clyde and I were doing our thing back there, you kno'what I mean? And the headboard of that bed was slapping the wall, just a-slapping it, and Clyde moaning like a bellyached hawg. He had a gun rack above the bed where he kept an old squirrel rifle and a hunting bow with razor-head arrows in a quiver. Well, that gun rack fell right onto the bed, and one of them arrows gave him a nick, right on his butt. Scared the hell out of him, and he yelled, I won't tell you what. And I thought he done come so big he had a heart attack. And the kids came running in screaming, thinking I killed him. There was so much noise you couldn't hear your ears. Thank God the rifle didn't go off."

It took me a while to stop laughing. "How are things with you and him, Vickie? Are you angry with Clyde?"

The smile vanished and Vickie stared into the distance. She took a pull on her cigarette, making the tip glow a long time; it was forever before the smoke came pouring out of her nose and mouth as she sighed and said, "Yes and no." She tilted her chin up and blew the rest of the smoke out. "I know I *ought* to be angry for what he done to me, to the family. But I just can't *get* angry. There he is," she said, pointing back to the house with her cigarette, "like a child. When Junior comes back from school, Clyde'll be rolling with Junior on the carpet, playing with Junior's toys, looking up at me with those puppy-dog eyes. And how he got AIDS is from being a child, from not knowing better. I mean he has always been kind of a child—it's what I loved about him when I married him.

"I know he'd been married before. Still, I felt I was marrying a child. Though, I tell you what, he showed me some bed stuff that warn't no child's play. He knew all that stuff. Oh, he learned me that good. Those first few years we had no money and all we did was go to bed and get it going just about any chance we had!"

There was a broad smile on Vickie's face and she blushed.

"But to answer your question, ever since I found out he has AIDS, I've been feeling too sorry for him to be angry with him. *No one* deserves to be sick lik'at," she said pointing back again. "*No one* deserves to lose their mind lik'at."

A car squealed round the curve: a Camaro with all the paint gone and the dull coppery metal showing through. It had oversize black tires, shining with Armor All, and elaborate, sparkling, custom hubs. A brief glimpse of the driver conveyed an impression of youth, of scruffy long hair, grubby hands on the wheel. The interior of the car was as bad as the body. It was extraordinary to see this fastidiousness with wheels while ignoring the rest of the car.

"Know him?" I asked Vickie.

"Hell yes. A Granger boy. Know everyone that come by here, just about."

We watched the car till it vanished out of sight. We could hear it for another minute or two and then it was gone.

Vickie was the first to break the silence.

"A couple of days ago, I lost it with Clyde. I was at the stove fixing oatmeal when he pipes up from the dining table: 'Why, hell, I think I might just go around and give this to as many people as I can. Seeing as someone done gave it to me'—he has moments like that when he speaks just as clear as you please, just like the old Clyde. I was so shocked! I thought I would hit the floor right there. Well, I just lit into him. I had the oatmeal in my hand and it wouldn't have taken much for me to fling it on him. I said: 'You've already done put the death sentence on two people. Don't you even dare think about it, or I'll kill you myself, you son-of-a-bitch.' Son, he never has talked that way again, and I don't think he will."

"Tell me about Jewell," I said.

Jewell was the name that Clyde had come up with in the hospital when I asked if he had sex with men. It was possible that Jewell gave the HIV infection to Clyde, or vice versa. Jewell was not someone I knew; he did not come to our HIV clinic. Not yet. He was out there, possibly in the same shape as Clyde.

"Jewell is a family friend of Clyde's folks. You might say he'd taken an interest in Clyde from the time Clyde was twelve years old. When I got married to Clyde, he was introduced to me as a close and dear friend."

Another car went roaring by.

"What can I say about Jewell? He was just a good ole boy—know what I mean? Like, he wears overalls and is bald and don't put on no airs." Here Vickie chuckled. "Between you and me, he's ugly as sin, but that's neither here nor there. One thing about old Jewell, though, is that he always drives a beautiful blue Oldsmobile, a Delta 88. Trades it in *every* year for a new one. Seems like he always has money—he owns land and an apartment building. There's been money in his family from way back. He helped us out with money many a time.

"Every now and then old Jewell would come by and he and Clyde would take off: they'd tell me something about needing to fix a socket or a leak at Jewell's place or something else they had to do. And they'd be gone thirty minutes or so. I never did pay it no mind, till later." Here Vickie turned and put her hand on my forearm: "Why, Jewell even grabbed at *me* a few times!"

"What kind of work does he do?" I asked.

"I don't think Jewell works. He just has money, know what I mean? Land, property. When Clyde come out with Jewell's name there in the hospital it set me thinking. I had heard rumors about Jewell. See, Jewell was never gay acting or nothing—if you get my meaning. I never *believed* the rumors. I never for a moment thought that *Clyde* had anything to do with that sort of stuff."

Vickie stubbed the cigarette on the step and flicked it away into the driveway. I could see a number of stubs, some with dark brown filters, some filterless, in the gravel of the driveway, all within the same radius from the stone steps. She reached for her cigarette purse. It was leather with a side holster into which her lighter fit neatly.

"I know I shouldn't be smoking. I switched to these ultralights? And, shit, I have to smoke ten of these to get the same buzz I used to get off one of my Pall Malls."

She offered me a cigarette and I accepted. The filter had small perforations in a circle about half an inch from its end. When I drew on it, I felt as if nothing came into my mouth, as if the shaft was broken and there was an air leak. But what little I did get into my lungs was enough to send my head spinning. Vickie looked at me curiously.

"You gone be all right?"

"Go on, Vickie."

"When Jewell came to visit Clyde in the hospital," she said, "it happened that Clyde had gone down for that CAT scan. There I was alone in the room with Jewell." Vickie's face became cold and hard as she relived this. She used the measured tones she must have used then. And when she spoke now it was with a classic east Tennessee mannerism: reaching for a higher diction and with a much clearer enunciation of each word than one would use when one was not angry:

"I said to him, I says: 'Jewell, you are aware, are you not, of the condition what Clyde has got.' He says, 'Yes, Vickie, I am. And I've been waiting for you to say something.' He seemed calm as anything, I could not believe it. I says, 'Well, I have something that I need to ask you. I heard you were gay. Have you or have you not had anything to do with Clyde?' He said, 'I have, Vickie. I have for years.' Just like that! No shame, no covering up. All I could bring myself to say was, 'Then, Jewell, I reckon you ought to be tested for AIDS yo'self.' He just looks me straight in the eye and says, 'Vickie, I don't want to know. I don't want to know,' he says."

I tried to put myself in Vickie's shoes. How does one react to a spouse whose sexual betrayal has involved both sexes? A spouse who brings home a deadly virus? And what do you say when you confront the person who had led your spouse astray, perhaps led him astray when he was still a child, in all probability abused him?

Sitting there on Vickie's stoop, looking down at the trees and treetops of Tester Hollow, seeing the young man in the Camaro roar by, I had a sense that all these elements—betrayal, sexual abuse, bisexuality—were much more common than anyone realized. Not just in this hollow, but in every hollow and even in the stately sub-divisions. HIV infection had merely brought all this to the forefront, had exposed the acts of deceit and betrayal of trust that happened every day.

"I was angry with Jewell," Vickie said, as if reading my mind. "I was furious. And you know me," she said, making a little flexing movement of her fingers, cupping one fist into the palm of the other, "I could have strangled him if I put my mind to it. But what was the point? It wasn't like Clyde was innocent. And I don't think Jewell *meant* for this to happen. Lord knows he helped us so much over the years—money, food, clothes for the kids. I have to say that he loves Clyde and he loves me and he loves Danielle and Junior."

I was incredulous: we were talking about a probable pedophile, a man I would not want anywhere *near* my kids.

"Does Jewell have a family?" I asked.

"Oh yes! He was married for years."

This was a picture of Jewell I found difficult to form in my mind.

"He and Clyde were in the same lodge. Last week Jewell made the lodge come up with a pledge to help me out. Jewell even gave me three hundred dollars of his own money after that for my expenses. And, believe it or not, I know I can count on Jewell in a way that I can't count on my family."

CLYDE WAS STILL sleeping when I left to go back to the VA. Vickie took me for a quick drive through the hollow.

Before I left, I told Vickie about TAP and about the support group meetings organized by Fred Goodson, "the bear." I suggested that she and Clyde go to a meeting. I wasn't sure how much Clyde would get out of it, but I wondered if Vickie would not be helped by seeing that there were others with the disease. "You want me to sit and talk with a bunch of queers?"

"Try it. This disease is too much to carry alone."

"Why, hell, everyone in this hollow knows. I wish they didn't, but they do. I ain't carrying it alone."

I pictured her life in this isolated hollow where people avoided her gaze, where she and Clyde and even the children were probably social pariahs, the untouchables of the hollow.

The support group was perhaps the one place in Johnson City where she could be sure that she would not be condemned.

"Promise me you'll think about it."

"I will." ,

I left her standing in her doorway, a cigarette in one hand, waving at me with the other. I drove up out of the hollow, back into Johnson City.

13

BOBBY KELLER called me in the office as I was about to leave for home. He sounded shrill and alarmed.

"Doc? Ed is *very* sick! He is *very, very* short of breath and running a fever. A hundred and three. Dr. Verghese, he's turning blue on me."

"Bobby, call the emergency ambulance service—tell them to bring you to the Johnson City Medical Center."

Ed Maupin, the diesel mechanic, had had a CD4 count of 30 the previous week when I had seen him in clinic; Bobby Keller's was 500. At that visit, Ed's oral thrush had cleared up but he was still feeling tired and had been missing work. When I had examined Ed, the lymph nodes in his neck, which had been as big as goose eggs, had suddenly shrunk: I had thought to myself that this was either a good sign or a very bad sign; his immune system had either given up the fight or successfully neutralized the virus. The latter was unlikely.

Bobby, at that visit, had looked well and continued to work in the fashion store. I hoped now that Bobby's description of the gravity of the situation was just histrionics.

I was at the Miracle Center well ahead of the ambulance. Soon it came roaring in, all its lights flashing. When the back door opened, I peeked in: Ed's eyes were rolled back in his head, and he was covered with a fine sheen of sweat. Despite the oxygen mask that the ambulance crew had on, his skin was the color of lead. His chest was making vigorous but ineffective excursions.

Bobby, who had ridden in the front, was scarcely able to stand up. His face was tremulous; he was on the verge of fainting.

"Don't put him on no machines, whatever you do," Bobby begged me. "Please, no machines."

"Why?"

"Because that's what he told me. He doesn't want it."

"When did he tell you? Just now?"

"No. A long time ago."

"Did he put it in writing? Does he have a living will?"

"No . . ."

In the emergency room, I stabilized Ed as best I could without intubating him. I took his oxygen mask off momentarily and looked at his mouth. His mucous membranes were loaded with yeast again—it had blossomed in just a week. But I was examining his mouth to try to decide how difficult it would be to intubate him. His short, receding lower jaw, which the beard concealed well, could make this a tricky intubation. I asked him to say "aaah." He tried to comply: his uvula and tonsils just barely came into view, another sign that he would be a tough intubation.

Ideally, an anesthetist would have been the best person to perform intubation. But I didn't want to call an anesthetist who, given the patient, might or might not be willing to do this procedure. Time was running out.

Ed was moaning and muttering incomprehensibly; his brain was clearly not getting enough oxygen. His blood pressure was 70 millimeters of mercury systolic over 50 diastolic. This was extremely low for him, because he had baseline hypertension. His cold, clammy extremities told me that the circulation to his arms and legs had shut down in an effort to shunt blood to the brain; even so, what blood got to the brain was not carrying enough oxygen. Ed's chest sounded dull in the bases when I percussed it; on listening with my stethoscope, he was wet and gurgly. The reason he was not oxygenating his blood was clear: his lungs were filled with inflammatory fluid. I ordered a stat chest x-ray and arterial blood gases. I had only a few minutes before I had to either breathe for him, or let him go. I needed more guidance from Bobby as to Ed's wishes.

I had an excellent nurse assisting me; she had already started an IV and brought the "crash cart." The respiratory therapist was administering oxygen and had an Ambu bag ready. I asked them to get goggles and masks in addition to their gloves, and to get a gown, mask and gloves ready for me. They were to put theirs on and wait for me. The curtains were pulled and Ed's presence was largely unnoticed in the bustle of the ER. An orthopedist was putting a cast on an individual in the next room, and patients were waiting in the other cubicles.

I came out to the waiting room, but Bobby was not there!

I hurried outside.

Bobby and three other men and one woman were near the ambulance entrance, smoking. The men bore a striking resemblance to Ed Maupin—the same sharp features, the slightly receding chin. One of them, the oldest, wore a green work uniform. I recognized his face as a familiar one, someone who worked in an auto parts store where I had ordered a replacement bumper for the rusted one that had fallen off my Z. Bobby Keller, still trembling, introduced me to Ed's brothers, all younger than Ed. The woman was the wife of one of the brothers.

"Bobby," I asked, "can I tell them what's going on?"

"Tell them everything," Bobby said, the tears pouring down uncontrollably, his body shaking with sobs.

I addressed the brothers: "Ed is very sick. A few months ago we found out he has AIDS." (There was no point in trying to make the distinction between HIV infection and AIDS. If Ed had not had AIDS when I saw him in the clinic, he most certainly did now.) "Now he has a bad pneumonia from the AIDS. I need to put him on a breathing machine in the next few minutes or he will die. I have a feeling that the pneumonia he has can be treated. If we put him on the breathing machine, it won't be forever. We have a good chance of getting him off. But Bobby tells me that Ed has expressed a desire not to be put on the machine."

The assembled family turned to Bobby who nodded vigorously: "He did! Said he never wanted to be on no machines."

The family was clear-eyed, trying to stay calm. They pulled hard at their cigarettes. The smoke rose quietly around their weathered faces. They looked like a Norman Rockwell portrait—small-town America's citizens in their work-clothes in a hospital parking lot, facing a family crisis. But this situation was one that Norman Rockwell hadn't attempted, one he had never dreamed of. I felt they were fond of their oldest brother, though perhaps disapproving of his relationship with Bobby. Yet judging by how they had all been standing around Bobby when I walked out, I didn't think they had any strong dislike for Bobby—it was almost impossible to dislike him. They had had many years to get used to the idea of Bobby and Ed, the couple, and it was only the idea, I sensed, that they had somehow not accepted.

"We need to discuss this," the older brother said.

"We have no time, I need to go right back in," I said.

They moved a few feet away from Bobby and me. I asked Bobby, "Do you have power-of-attorney or anything like that to make decisions for Ed?" Bobby shook his head.

We looked over to where the family was caucusing. The oldest brother was doing all the talking. They came back.

"We want for you to do everything you can. Put him on the breathing machine, if you have to."

At this a little wail came out of Bobby Keller and then degenerated into sobs. I put my hand on Bobby's shoulder. He shook his head back and forth, back and forth. He wanted to say something but could not find a voice.

The oldest brother spoke again. His tone was matter-of-fact and determined:

"*We* are his family. *We* are legally responsible for him. We want you to do *everything* for him."

We are his family. I watched Bobby's face crumble as he suddenly became a mere observer with no legal right to determine the fate of the man he had loved since he was seven years old. He was finally, despite the years that had passed and whatever acceptance he and Ed found together, an outsider.

I took him aside and said, "Bobby, I have to go on. There is no way for me not to at this point. There's a really good chance that I can rescue Ed from the pneumonia. If I thought it would only make Ed suffer, I wouldn't do it. If this is *Pneumocystis*, it should respond to treatment."

Bobby kept sobbing, shaking his head as I talked, fat tears rolling off his eyes onto the ground, onto his chest. He felt he was betraying Ed. He could not deliver on his promise.

I had no time to pacify Bobby or try to convince him. I rushed back in. Ed looked worse. As I went through the ritual of gowning and masking (it was reassuring to have rituals to fall back on, a ritual for every crisis), it struck me that the entire situation had been in my power to dictate. All I had to do was to come out and say that the pneumonia did not look good, that it looked like the end. *I* mentioned the respirator, *I* offered it as an option. I could have just kept quiet. I had, when it came down to the final moment, given Ed's brothers the power of family. Not Bobby.

But there was no time to look back now.

I LEANED DOWN TO Ed's ear and explained what I was about to do. He showed no sign of understanding. He was expending tremendous amounts of energy to breathe.

I stood behind Ed with the endotracheal tube in my right hand and the laryngoscope in the other. I put Xylocaine jelly on the tip of the endotracheal tube. We lowered the head of the stretcher, extended Ed's head over the edge.

I had the nurse now give Ed an intravenous bolus of 20 milligrams of Valium. An anesthetist might have used a curarelike paralyzing agent. In a few seconds, Ed's breathing ceased altogether.

The respiratory therapist gave him a few brisk breaths of oxygen from the squeeze bag and stepped away. I inserted the laryngoscope blade into his mouth and heaved up on the tongue. I could not see the vocal cords and could only barely see the epiglottis. I pushed the tube past the epiglottis, giving the tube some torque, hoping to steer it into the voice box and down the trachea. It went in too easily and I knew I had missed.

I pulled out and we bagged him with the squeeze bag again. I was talking to myself: *Come on, Abe; hamsters are ten times as difficult as this, and you have intubated 260 hamsters at last count.* Another voice in my head replied: *This ain't no hamster.*

Ed was a deeper shade of blue now. If I didn't do it in the next try, we were going to have to call an anesthetist. Or call a Code Blue. The second time and I still did not see the vocal cords. But this time I felt the tube grate against the tracheal rings, just as with my hamsters. I listened over first one side of the chest and then the other while the respiratory therapist pumped air into the tube. I could hear good breath sounds on both sides; we had secured an airway and the tube was sitting in perfect position, just above the carina, where the trachea divides into the left and right bronchi.

It had been a while since I had intubated anyone myself; usually there were layers of interns and residents and students who fought for and did all the procedures. I was pleased with our success. The nurse patted me on the back.

"Did you know," I asked her, in the glow of my postprocedural success, "that intubation was invented by a physician named O'Dwyer as a lifesaving measure in diphtheria? It's therefore an infectious diseases procedure!"

"Yeah, right," she said, unimpressed. "I'll keep that in mind. Next time we have a trauma case that needs intubation we'll call in an infectious diseases consult."

I WENT UPSTAIRS WITH Ed to the intensive care unit. Now I wrote orders for the settings on the ventilator that would optimally oxygenate Ed's lungs. I put him on a 100 percent inspired oxygen concentration (in contrast to the 21 percent oxygen concentration we normally breathe) and dialed in the rate and the volume of each breath the ventilator would deliver. I wrote an order to have an arterial blood oxygen measurement made in half an hour to allow me to cut back on the oxygen if at all possible; pure oxygen in high concentrations is damaging in and of itself. I wrote orders for intravenous fluids and for laboratory tests. I felt better about Ed in the ICU than I had with Scotty Daws. I had inherited Scotty Daws and in retrospect it had been a no-win situation. Ed was the best sort of patient to bring to the ICU. Someone who I thought would perhaps walk out of there.

Pneumocystis pneumonia is easy to diagnose if you get a good specimen of sputum. Secretions obtained by washing out a segment of lung during bronchoscopy—so-called bronchoalveolar lavage or BAL—are ideal, but even an ordinary sputum, as long as it is not grossly contaminated with saliva, can serve almost as well.

Since Ed had a tube going down into his trachea, breathing for him, it was simple enough to squirt some saline down it and then suck it back out with a catheter.

I carried the specimen down to the lab, made some smears of it on glass slides, then looked at them under the microscope after staining them for bacteria and TB. I saw only an outpouring of inflammatory cells and little else. To see *Pneumocystis carinii* requires a special stain called a silver stain. It would take a day for the pathology department to complete the stain and give me the definitive word on what it showed. The fact that I saw nothing but pus cells on my simple stains—no TB, no bacteria—suggested that this was *Pneumocystis*. I began Ed on trimethoprim-sulfamethoxazole, or Bactrim, the drug of choice for this organism.

The only cases of *Pneumocystis* pneumonia I had ever seen were in persons with AIDS. This was unique to my generation of infectious diseases physicians: We had all come of age in the era of AIDS.

But *Pneumocystis* had a long history before AIDS made it a household word. Epidemics of *Pneumocystis* swept through Europe in the 1940s. They occurred primarily in premature infants in orphanages, in the setting of overcrowding and malnutrition.

After the war years, the organism began to manifest only in select patients with immune-compromising conditions such as leukemia or after long-term cortisone administration. St. Jude Children's Hospital in Memphis, at the other end of the state from us, had accrued tremendous experience with this disease by virtue of their patient population—children with leukemias.

How are we to view this organism? As an invader from outside? Or an opportunist from within? To give a rat *Pneumocystis* pneumonia, all you have to do is give the rat cortisone—a potent suppressor of the immune system—and the rat then *spontaneously* develops *Pneumocystis* infection. By contrast, Betty and I had to pour staphylococci in massive doses down the hamster trachea to produce infection with staphylococci. The rat experiment suggests that *Pneumocystis* is present in low numbers in the lung at all times. The *Pneumocystis* that at this moment was filling up Ed's lungs lives in my lungs and in yours. The constant vigilance of the immune system keeps it in check. Immune suppression by steroids or, as in Ed's case, AIDS results in unchecked multiplication of this organism.

I SOUGHT OUT Bobby Keller in the ICU waiting room. His eyes were red and puffy from crying. I tried to explain what I had done so far. Bobby listened perfunctorily to what I had to say about *Pneumocystis* and the amount of oxygen Ed required. It was clear he felt Ed's time had come and that we had gone beyond a threshold of intervention that Ed had not wanted to cross.

WHEN I GOT HOME it was after midnight. Steven was in our bed. Rather than disturb them, I went to Steven's room and crawled into his bed.

It felt as if my head had just touched the pillow when my beeper went off. It was from the ICU at the Miracle Center. An intern was calling to say that Ed's heart had gone into a malignant and chaotic rhythm. A Code Blue was in progress.

"What time is it?" I asked.

"Four thirty in the morning," he said.

"How long has the code been going on?"

"Five minutes. And there has been no sign of his heartbeat coming back."

"Keep going, I'll be right there. Ask the nurses to call in his lover and the family and have them wait in the quiet room."

In the ICU, a furious Code Blue was in progress. All the bustle and activity *around* Ed was in contrast to the activity *in* Ed's body: there was no heartbeat, and only the forceful chest compression by the intern was sending blood around. I reviewed the code chart—everything I would have done had been tried: calcium, epinephrine, bicarbonate. I waved everyone off, thanked them, and we pulled out the tube from Ed's trachea. Ed now looked peaceful, asleep.

In a few minutes there was no one in the room but an ICU nurse and myself. She was a night nurse I had seen around, but never worked with. She was picking up the debris from the code. She was dressed for a shuttle mission—gloves, gown, mask, goggles. This was not inappropriate, as during the Code Blue there was potential for splashing.

I said to her, by way of small talk, "I'm surprised that his heart should have quit so quickly. I really thought I could cure the pneumonia, wean him off the respirator, get a few more meaningful months or even years of life for him."

She stopped what she was doing, looked at me and said, affecting nonchalance: "Well, they're *all* going to die, aren't they? There's not much point to this."

She left the room before I could think of an appropriate reply.

I was furious.

I wanted to ask her what the "point" was in the ninety-year-old patients that they played with in the unit for days until they were brain dead, all the while running up a huge bill that we, the taxpayers, would pay? Right at that moment there was a patient in the ICU whom we were sending up for dialysis three times a week when there was no hope of any other organ in the body recovering.

I wanted to ask her if *she* was in the same boat, would she like an extra year of life, or would she opt to leave the world right away? And for that matter, weren't we ALL going to die one day? Did she think her job was to solely take care of immortals?

I calmed myself. "Pick and choose your battles, Abe," I said to myself. In a way she had been baiting me; anything I said back to her would have been a self-fulfilling prophecy for her. It would prove my lack of objectivity. Besides, I *had* failed in this instance. Ed's corpse was proof of my failure.

When I stepped out of the room, I saw her with some other nurses at the nurses' station. She had surely finished telling them about our little encounter. I bade them all good night.

BOBBY KELLER AND the Maupin family were in the quiet room. It was very difficult for me to go in there and tell them Ed had died. Bobby cried. His sobs were big and wrenching. Ed's brothers covered their eyes or turned their heads away from me. The eldest came over and shook my hand and thanked me. Bobby came out with, "Praise the Lord, his suffering is over," and walked alone toward the door.

The next day the pathology report of the bronchial washing from Ed's lung came back. The specimen had been loaded with the saucer-shaped, dark-staining *Pneumocystis*. At this point, of course, it hardly mattered. Ed was dead.

I thought of funerals I had been to in Johnson City where the grieving widow was escorted to the memorial service by friends and family. Tears and hugs, happy memories, casseroles and condolences. Who would comfort Bobby Keller, I wondered.

14

IN THE WEEKS AFTER ED DIED, my life changed. Not in its circumstances but in its shades and colors. Now it seemed as if everything I witnessed was imbued with this sense of loss. I was a doctor, a scientist, trained in professional detachment, but all the usual postures seemed satirical in the face of AIDS. I felt these deaths. I was filled with a longing for home (whatever I conceived that to be) so strong that I sometimes wondered if I myself was dying and this feeling was foreboding, the bittersweet messenger.

One Friday evening during this period I drove from the mall to downtown, heading to Cates Music Center on West Walnut. I was looking for guitar strings. The piano-and-organ store in the mall didn't carry any.

I negotiated my way to Cates: down Knob Creek, past Kiwanis Park, up Lamont, skirting the front of Mountain Home, then down Lamont past the Oak Hill Cemetery, emerging in downtown near the Diamond Cabs sign, pausing dutifully at the many railway crossings. Like a Seeing Eye dog, my Z knew the one-way streets and the dead ends; it left its master to his thoughts. Nothing on the radio had appealed to me and I drove in silence.

The sagging wall on the side of the Majestic Theater on East Main Street caught my eye. The theater went belly-up years ago, but in its time it was the jewel of downtown, just a few yards away from Fountain Square and the railway station. On that patched-up wall, old brick and new brick formed an abstract pattern, an inadvertent chiaroscuro. I had seen the pattern for years, noted it, but it had never been more than that—a pattern. But that night the unwitting design became a symbol for me of my years in this town, of how *I* had changed. It spoke to me. It was much like the painting my mother has hanging in her dining room: an oil painting of an African woman with a baby strapped to her back; the painting affects me every time I visit my parents, every time I see this relic of my childhood hanging in yet *another* continent, yet *another* house. That painting is the one thing I want to inherit from my parents.

I suppose this is when you know that a town has become *your* town: where others see brick, a broken window, a boarded up storefront, you feel either moved to tears or to joy. The map of the town becomes the map of your memories, the grid on which you play out your obsessions, on which you mark your great loves and your enmities; its geography becomes your destiny.

That night, and for every night I lived in Johnson City, the town became the geography in which my dreams were set. Oh sure, I still dreamed I was in Africa, facing an anatomy exam, or in India, riding my trusted Jawa motorcycle through the streets of Madras. But even these dreams were framed by and happened within the larger dream of Mountain Home, the town within the town of Johnson City.

Some nights, in that fugue state between dreaming and wakefulness, I would float down from my bedroom, drawn to the VA hospital, up the stairs to my old Ward 8, my sentimental favorite. The ward had its own scent—not the medicinal smell of Lysol and carbolic acid. It was a warm and familiar scent that lingered in the curtains between the beds, a scent that even the freshly washed green-striped dressing gowns and pajamas carried back from the laundry, a scent that even when temporarily tarnished by the smell of booze and blood, poop and pus, was still the dominant smell of the ward.

I floated past the nurses' station where the regulation federal calendar sat next to a picture of Reagan, and where the credenza that held the charts was full. I went on into the ward, down the aisle between the beds, the lights turned off now, the ward silent like a giant baby, only the snores and coughs and expectorations of old men to be heard. I was now near the smoking room at the end of the hall, a room yellowed with nicotine, the scent of many decades of tobacco having penetrated the brickwork, only to emerge richer and more refined.

I loved the old men; I loved their sounds; I loved the way they let us take care of them and the way they and their wives bonded to us, seeking us out on every visit. And when finally oat-cell cancer of the lung or a fatal variceal bleed claimed them, I would hear from the wives for years: cards on Memorial Day, a surprise visit to my office with a present of a giant hug and homemade corn bread.

I hovered near the ceiling in my astral voyage, watching over this pastoral scene, as if my vigil were protective. I watched the tiptoe of the nurses armed with flashlights as they went to and fro to get a late-night admission settled in without disturbing his neighbors. They released the curtain from the rubber thong that held it to the wall and drew it around the bed. They put on the night light. They summoned the on-call intern, and, after he came, they would traipse back and forth again down the ward to start the IV and administer the other medications, while all around the patient the veterans who could sleep slept.

In the early morning the veterans would wake to find the newcomer in their midst. I stayed to watch this ritual: they would introduce themselves by name, then by disease, then by company and recitation of their army service, finally by their hometowns: Limestone, Knoxville, Oak Ridge or any one of the towns in a hundred and fifty mile radius from Johnson City. By first light they were all family.

And this was the time when I headed back to my home, to my sleeping body.

I cannot tell you whether my dreams were a true reflection of the spirit of Johnson City or whether they more accurately reflected my intense need at this time for home and community. I cannot tell you whether Johnson City had truly made a place for me, a brown-skinned man, among its own or whether I, like some of my patients, was forever outside its real heart. I can only say that in these strange times when it seemed death was everywhere, I thought of this place as a kind of safe haven, and when I dreamed of falling, as I often did, there were gentle hands waiting to break my fall.

15

ONE EVENING during the late summer of 1987, I was strolling up and down the front porch with Jacob in my arms. He was wearing only a diaper; I held him facing me, so that his feet were curled up against my chest, his body resting on my forearms and his head in my cupped hands. His eyes focused on my mouth, watching in disbelief, as I sang "Teach Your Children." His tiny hands with the gold bangles Rajani had put on them were dancing around his face. He showed no signs of sleep. Rajani had gone for her evening walk and I was holding down the fort.

Steven came out and clambered to the porch rail, his attention riveted on the lawn, a Mason jar clutched between his hands. His head swiveled this way and that as he tried to spot the fireflies flaming against the dark lawn and the sunset's last light.

"Ping! Ping!" he called, in time with the soft flash of one firefly. "Ping, ping." When the telephone trilled within the house, I thought for a moment that the noise was coming from Steven. I resented the sound of the telephone, resented its intrusion on an evening that belonged to my family. I hoped that it was not for me.

DR. SARAH PRESNELL was a general internist near Pikeville, Kentucky. She sounded tired. I had never met Sarah, but I had spoken to her on the phone more than once to discuss a patient of hers with a knotty infectious disease problem. Twice I had admitted Sarah's patients to work up an FUO: fever of unknown origin. One old man with fever and recurrent phlebitis had an occult cancer of the pancreas show up at exploratory laparotomy, an operation we undertook when all other tests had failed. The other patient, a man in his forties who worked in a doctor's office, had fever that I could never find the cause of. The fever diminished in the hospital and did not recur when he went home. I wondered about self-induced fever but could never prove it.

Sarah had always impressed me with her soft-spokenness, her precise diction and her wry sense of humor. The case summaries she sent with her patients were lucid and clear and her diagnostic workups thorough. I guessed we were the same age and had gone through training in the same era.

"I'm sorry to bother you at home, Abraham. I have a sad, sad situation here. A couple I know, the Johnsons, are both infected with HIV. They are pillars of our community; nobody but me—and now you— knows they are infected."

I was not sure what Sarah was after. Did she want advice over the phone? Was she asking me to see the patients in my clinic?

"He contracted HIV by a blood transfusion when he underwent emergency coronary artery bypass surgery at Duke University Medical Center. He had a massive heart attack and was airlifted to Duke. The surgery was complicated by enormous bleeding. He recovered from surgery but had lymphadenopathy and weight loss and vague fevers. I was racking my brains, trying to figure out what he had. I finally ordered an HIV test and it came back positive; it's the first case I have ever seen. I tested his wife, and she is positive as well."

"When did he have his bypass?"

"A few weeks before the blood test came out. A few weeks before they were screening all blood for HIV. Such bad luck."

Will Johnson must have become infected just prior to March of 1985 when the blood test first became available. He was now in his second year of infection.

"They are such a wonderful couple. You can't imagine: incredible human beings. It's breaking my heart to go through this with them." Sarah was more emotional than I had ever known her to be, and I sensed that there were tears she was holding back as she talked.

"And before I tell you anything else, I have to tell you that their *primary* concern is confidentiality. It's the reason that I can't admit him and treat him here. I'm quite willing to, but *everybody* knows him here. *Everybody*. It would knock this town for a loop. Even his son and daughter don't know what he has. I can't send him to the University of Kentucky. I think at one time he was even on the board of directors there; he never misses a home basketball game. He chairs one of their foundations. I have even been going to his house to draw blood; I keep his medical records at my house under lock and key.

"He has told everyone that he has a form of lymph cancer. He is such a charismatic, convincing person that no one questions him. You'll see when you meet him."

"When are you sending him over?" I asked. I hoped it would not be till the morning.

"Tonight, if it's OK with you. For the last week he has been complaining of severe difficulty swallowing. He's not able to swallow a drop of water."

Steven was signaling to me excitedly that he had caught a firefly in his jar. I gave him the thumbs-up sign.

Sarah went on: "But I have to tell you something else. Years ago he set up the health insurance for his own firm. When he is admitted, he doesn't want AIDS listed as the diagnosis. Otherwise, in no time everyone at his company will know. You'll have to list something else. Can you do that?"

I grunted in agreement.

Sarah went on: "I've been scheduling him at the end of the day because his visits take so long. I've just finished seeing him. It's not that he's long-winded. He's just a meticulous observer of every minute symptom. He wants to participate completely in each decision we make. He wants to be in control. It's his nature. That's not a problem with me because I like him, and I'm drawn to him—particularly now. I give them all the time they need. I'm telling you all this to prepare you."

I was faintly irritated: all these proscriptions before I even saw the patient.

"How soon can you send them?"

"They have their bags packed and the car tanked up. He's waiting for me to call him and tell him. He told me it will take him two hours and twenty minutes to drive down."

"Send him on to the Miracle Center."

"Where?"

"I'm sorry: the Johnson City Medical Center. It's an inside joke."

I HELPED RAJANI coax Steven into the house and upstairs for his bath. She accepted without comment that I had to go back to the hospital. Steven sat at one end of the tub while his baby brother looked on from a port-a-seat that Rajani had parked in the bathroom. Steven's brown body was iridescent with water and his little shoulders were so perfect.

I wanted to freeze this scene, seal the sounds of the water splashing and Steven's yips and yells; I wanted to bottle the puppylike scent of Steven's hair, never let my little boy and his baby brother grow up. Now that Steven was mobile and free to roam, I worried about him, worried that he might hurt himself as he probed the world around him, pushing gravity and his body to the limit.

At some peril, I leaned into the tub and kissed Steven good-night: there was firefly glow on his hair and his hands were sticky. I knelt to kiss Jacob, saw him blink as my dark head loomed over him, felt his petal-soft cheek against my lips, smelled the milk on his breath.

I DECIDED I WOULD walk to the Miracle Center. The dogwood trees near the Intermediate Care Building were in bloom; the petals all looked faintly gray. In the moonlight I could not tell the pink-petaled Cherokee Chief from the White Cloud variety. I picked up the ticklish, ripe scent that told me the pine trees and perhaps the redbud or magnolias on the campus were flowering. By morning a fine yellow coat of pollen would be visible on the hood of our cars.

The two-story domiciliary buildings, symmetrically placed, barracks-style, on either side of the road—eight of them altogether—shone like images on a daguerreotype. Along the upstairs balconies of each building, I saw the glow of cigarettes, the faint outlines of figures looking down on me. When these buildings were first built at the turn of the century, each had a special function: one was for "restive" TB cases, another for "cripples," another for "nervous" disorders. Each time I walked by, I tried to picture which was which. I tried to feel the anima that each building gave out. From which building had the coughs emanated all night: short, sharp coughs like nails rattling in a paper bag?

And which of these buildings had held captive the men who talked to themselves, who tried to escape from imagined voices from which there was no relief in those pre-Thorazine days?

I walked parallel to the north fence that separated the Mountain Home campus from a string of Johnson City row houses. An old veteran once told me that in the days when the campus was an Old Soldiers' Home, "women of a certain kind" from Johnson City would line up against this fence on the first of each month, the day the checks came in. That image lingered in my mind whenever I walked here.

The VA police pulled up alongside me in their squad car. They doubled as a transport service, driving the staff to the outlying buildings, particularly if the weather was poor. A pretty ward secretary was riding in the back seat; I had known her from the time I was an intern. Over the years, she had told me the saga of her love life: a divorce, remarriage and very recently another divorce. It was she who called out now, "Hey, Abraham! Need a ride?"

"Thanks, but no. I'm going to the Miracle Center. I'll walk."

"Well," she said pouting, "I reckon some people's too good to be riding with us!" All of them had cigarettes going and streams of smoke slipped out of the windows.

"Now you know that isn't true," I said. "I'd ride with you anytime. But it looks like you got two good men with you already." The policeman in the passenger seat winked at me.

"Tell her, Doc. She don't know *how* good."

"Shoot, they can't handle me. I need me a real man!"

She waved as they pulled away. She turned once and smiled at me through the rear window.

Every time my path crossed hers, we bantered like this, sparred with each other, the sexual innuendo not far below the surface. It had become our ritual, a ritual now several years old that was never acted on. Was she *really* coming on to me? What if I ever *did* make a move, what if I took her up on one of her invitations? Would I find that I had made a horrible faux pas? But meanwhile, this tension, this never knowing, was titillating in itself.

Was it this complicated between men? Would two men in the same situation, feeling the same attraction, have danced around each other like this? Or would they have made their meaning crystal clear, perhaps consummated the relationship promptly? Why was it that *anonymous* sex, not just casual sex, rarely happened between men and women, only between men? Was it because the *woman* was the gatekeeper? Because *she* was less inclined to anonymous or casual sex? But a man, whether gay or straight, given his druthers, was quite capable of anonymous sex, could find it thrilling. I had never known a bar or club in any country that I had lived in where I could go and be *sure* of a sexual encounter with a woman—not without a monetary transaction. Did the prolific sexual activity of a gay bathhouse in its heyday, the anonymous sex, the multiple partners, the group sex, simply represent what *all* men were capable of if they had willing partners? Was this what a man would do if the gatekeeper were removed?

A cab drove past me and the driver waved. I recognized him as a cabby who often drove me to the airport. It was the first of the month, and all that day and late into the night an armada of Diamond Cabs would shuttle past our quarters, carting the domiciliary veterans to downtown Johnson City. There, in the cluster of bars that propped up the pawn shops, the shoe shops, the used-furniture stores, the flophouses and the liquor stores, another generation of veterans spent their pension and disability checks. And, there in downtown, they sought female company. Most of the time they had to pay for it.

Ahead of me now, the Miracle Center was flood-lit and pushed up at the sky like a giant lingam. Its smooth, concrete, multistory, multipronged silhouette was so different in mood and feel from the VA. The fringe of city land around it had been blacktopped into parking lots. The building, adorned as it was with a weather vane, satellite dish, and helipad, seemed to stand as a rebuke to my timeless Mountain Home.

I WOULD NORMALLY have waited in the doctors' lounge for the admission office to page me. But this evening I walked over to tell them Will Johnson was coming. I wanted to check on the status of rooms and ask that they hold one for him on 5500 wing. I wanted to minimize any paper obstacles to his admission.

As I walked in, I saw a well-dressed man, gaunt under his fedora, approach the admission counter. He was in his early fifties, wearing a light overcoat, which he was now taking off with his wife's help. Beneath it he wore a jacket and tie. The tie was much like what my father would wear: dark and unmemorable; men of that generation do not use ties to make statements. When he took off his hat, I saw he had a buzz cut, his sideburns shaved almost above his ears, the flesh at his temples looking red and angry. He was slightly stooped over, fatigue more than age. He took one last step to reach the counter.

The woman with him was the same age and was wearing a tweed suit with leather pumps. Her hair was gray, curly, and down to her shoulders; a pale, almost invisible lipstick was the only makeup she wore. She draped his jacket over her arm. She stood close behind him, both feet together, her shoulders back, her head held firm, an unaffected elegance in her manner. Only her chalky white knuckles, wrapped around the handle of a Gladstone, as if its contents were too precious to put it down, betrayed her anxiety. She now stepped closer to her husband, as if they were physically connected and the cord between them had been stretched.

He was not as yet aware of me, though she had glanced at me and smiled. I was not wearing my white coat.

He braced one hand against the counter, the other reaching for his wallet. He took a deep breath as if steeling himself for the laborious process of registering and proving he had insurance.

How difficult it must have been to pack that bag. Did they pack for a day or for a few weeks? As they pulled out of their driveway and made the long lonely drive to Johnson City, what falsehood did they invent for their grown son and daughter, for their grandchildren? How much dread must have filled their hearts when they entered the grand lobby of the Miracle Center, a hospital so different from their familiar little community hospital where, but for the disease they had, they could have been received like royalty?

I heard him tell the admission clerk that I was his doctor; I heard him pronounce my name carefully. The way they stood there, husband in front of wife, dwarfed by the high ceiling and the imposing foyer, they looked quite forlorn and forsaken, having only each other. It was a heart-wrenching sight. I stepped forward quickly.

Will Johnson turned to me. He seemed to instantly know I was the doctor he had come to see. He grasped my hand in both his. I was looking for signs of surprise or disappointment: Was he expecting a foreign doctor, was he prepared for my relative youth? Since Dr. Sarah

Presnell had never set eyes on me, she couldn't have told him very much about me, except that she trusted me with his secret. Will Johnson had blue eyes, spaced closely together, and now he fixed them on me and said he was delighted to see me. These words were not merely a figure of speech: his face broke into a warm smile. Crinkles formed all around his eyes and the strain and worry I had seen in his expression dissipated. A gap between his two upper incisors gave him a Huckleberry Finn impishness.

While still holding my hand, he turned, drawing me to him, and said proudly, as if he had just discovered me, "Bess, *this* is Dr. Verghese!" She shook my hand, the natural smile on her lips now deepening. I decided that in her youth she had been a very beautiful woman.

Less than thirty seconds had elapsed since I set eyes on them. And whatever preconceived notions I might have had about this patrician couple, whatever grudge I was nursing about the interruption to my evening and the caveats and admonitions that Sarah had given me, disappeared. I was drawn to the Johnsons in their plight, touched by the sight of them in the bright lights of the Miracle Center admission office, determined already to do everything in my power to ease their distress.

I asked the admission clerk to assign them a room on 5500. I told her she could come up later and fill out the forms she needed.

I took the bag from Mrs. Johnson's hand and she surrendered it to me willingly. I led them to the staff elevator. Will Johnson held the back of my arm, walking slowly, leaning on me from time to time, while Mrs. Johnson walked on his other side. As we made our way down the corridor, I felt as if these were *my* parents or a favorite uncle and aunt who were sick and needed my help.

"How was your ride down?"

He contemplated the question seriously. I was merely making small talk, trying to break the ice. But he addressed the question as if it was the most important thing he had ever been asked. "It's a ride that Bess and I have always enjoyed, coming down to Johnson City. But it was difficult tonight, given the reason for the journey."

We made our way to 5500. I saw Mary, one of the nurses who had taken such good care of Gordon, come down the hall to meet us; I was sure the Johnsons would be well taken care of tonight. I introduced Mary and then left them in the room to get settled and to allow the admission clerk, who had dogged our tracks and now hovered in the doorway, to get her paperwork done.

Half an hour later, when I returned to do my history and physical, Will Johnson had changed into his own pajamas and a comfortable red robe. He was in bed with the head of his bed up. Mrs. Johnson was sitting patiently in the recliner, which she had pulled close to the bed. The TV was not on. It struck me that unlike Clyde, and very much like my parents, the thought of turning the TV on did not occur to the Johnsons. Every other hospital room I walked into, one of the first things I had to do was turn the TV off so as to pursue a conversation. In all the time I spent with the Johnsons, I never saw the TV on. Now, as I walked in, both of them broke into smiles, as if seeing a long-lost son.

Will Johnson patted a spot on the mattress indicating I should sit by him. He held my hand and inquired about me. Where was I from? Yes, of course, they were familiar with doctors from India. But how, if I was from India, did I have a name like Abraham? When I told them I was a Christian, told them the story of St. Thomas and his landing on the coast of India in Kerala, the Johnsons turned to each other and exchanged looks as if to say: Look how God works!

"Abraham," Will said, "I want to tell you everything that has happened to us, the living hell we have been through."

IN MARCH OF 1984, Will Johnson lost his good friend Chuck Hoover to a heart attack. The funeral for Chuck was in Bluepark, Virginia. It was a dank winter morning. When Will Johnson stepped out of the church with the other mourners, the cold seemed to penetrate through the layers of his clothing. The retinue of cars, their headlights on high beam, snaked down to the cemetery. Will Johnson had controlled his emotions in the church. But now, riding alone in his pickup truck, he wept over the loss of his best friend.

Chuck Hoover had been a mining engineer just like Will. One of the first jobs Chuck ever did was an underground mining survey for Will Johnson. That had been the beginning of a long professional and personal association. Chuck's firm had grown to be one of the largest engineering firms in Kentucky, while Will had seen his own firm grow from a single-owner-operated mine to a management company: Johnson Mining Consultants. They served five major mines in the surrounding area as well as a host of smaller mines. He and Chuck sat on many state and federal boards.

"Abraham, have you ever visited one of these mining towns in the Cumberlands?" Will Johnson leaned forward in bed to pose this question to me. It was surprising to me that as gaunt and tired as he looked, his speech was animated and his eyes glowed like a visionary.

"I've been close by," I said, picturing Essie's house outside of Blackwood, Virginia.

"You've seen the dingy row houses crowding the mountain roads? You know how they're always subject to flooding? You know how miserable it can get? Well, a year before Chuck's death, he and I had talked about building a *planned* coal community—a first in the country!" Here he smiled and paused, to let it sink in.

"This is what Chuck and I had in mind: Instead of the big coal trucks thundering through town, dropping coal debris as they go up and down the mountain, why not let the miners enjoy the same peace and quiet that the more affluent in a community seek? Why not let them have the spectacular views, beautiful parks, the opportunity to live in a community whose construction enunciates dignity? Abraham, who knows to what heights people can rise if given the best living circumstances instead of a hellhole built on a slag heap? I believe that geography is destiny, and Chuck and I had in mind a new kind of geography, a different destiny for the people of our county."

Here Will Johnson was, having traveled over two hours to see me, and instead of talking about his symptoms, we were talking about a project that in the telling made him young again, a project that seemed to take away his stoop, take away the worry lines from his face. I listened carefully, determined to let him have his say.

Chuck Hoover and Will Johnson had staked their own money and borrowed heavily. The community would be called "Wilkishire," a striking contrast, I thought, from appellations like Stonega or Osaka or Roda—the camps near Essie's house—or even cruder ones like "Hunk Town" or "Nigger Town."

Will Johnson now described the layout for me in detail, making little trails on the bedsheet with his index finger and pushing the sheet into a small mound in places to simulate the mountain. He went on for five minutes and then stopped abruptly:

"But when Chuck died, I knew 'Wilkishire' was doomed. It would never come about. The financing had been tenuous and tricky and had depended on Chuck's being around. Work had already started when Chuck died."

At Chuck's funeral, after the graveside service, after the last prayer and as the crowd slowly dispersed, Will Johnson climbed up the slope to where he had parked his Chevy pickup truck.

As he stepped into the truck, he began to experience massive chest pains.

A few minutes after burying his friend, a second after starting the truck and shifting out of park, William Johnson's heart stopped.

When his brain failed to receive oxygen, it protested: an explosive seizure focus formed in his cortex. It raced through his brain, sending his limbs and trunk flailing violently and repetitively. His now practically dead body was snapped back and forth in the confines of the driver's seat. The force of these convulsions snapped two vertebrae in his back, a fact that would be discovered only many months later. There were even bruises on his feet.

During one of these convulsions, Will Johnson's chest smashed the steering wheel with enough force to jump-start his heart. (Will smiled mischievously as he told me this and leaned forward to say: "That was God waking me up only to put me down.")

The other funeral attendees rushed to the truck. Chuck Hoover's wife, a nurse, pushed through to Will Johnson and saw that he was *in extremis*, that he needed to be in a hospital as soon as possible.

The hearse, now empty, seemed the logical means by which to take Will Johnson to the hospital in Bluepark. But the driver of the hearse balked—he was in the business of transporting the dead, not the near dead. When he mumbled something about liability, Will's friend Matthew Elliot, who had played offensive lineman at the University of Kentucky, grabbed him by the collar and convinced him that he was liable to lose his life if he didn't get moving. And so Will Johnson arrived at the Bluepark emergency room in a speeding hearse, Matthew Elliot riding shotgun next to the driver.

In the ER it quickly became apparent that Will Johnson's seizure was secondary to a heart attack. (Will now showed me a copy of the ECG—he pulled it out from a thick folder. He did not hand me the whole folder; I was going to hear the story—medical and otherwise—chronologically and at his own pace.) When I saw the ECG, I was amazed that Will Johnson had survived. The ECG showed the telltale signs of acute ischemic damage to the heart: instead of the up-and-down deflection representing the normal electrical activity of the ventricle, this segment was now bowed—"coving"—in a classic pattern of injury. The heart attack involved the entire anterior wall of the heart, crippling the left ventricle, the heart's main pumping chamber. It was the worst kind of heart attack.

Hour to hour, Will Johnson's condition deteriorated. His blood pressure was low and it was easy for me to imagine why: so little muscle of the left ventricle survived that the heart was functioning inefficiently as a pump. Blood was backing up behind the failing pump and accumulating in Will Johnson's lungs, causing him to be short of breath. The increased work of breathing, in turn, put more demands on his heart.

"Did you have any warning of heart disease in the years prior to that?" I asked.

"I used to smoke." He gave me a sheepish grin. "And six months before my heart attack, a routine stress test by my doctor in Pikeville suggested I had ischemia. I never touched a cigarette since. I was referred to the cardiology division at Duke University Medical Center; they did a thallium stress test. They told me that my heart was perfectly normal, that I could go run a marathon. They said the rudimentary stress test done in my community hospital must have been erroneous."

Will had clearly had a false-negative thallium stress test. Short of a catheterization with injection of dye into the coronary arteries, no test was infallible in determining the presence of coronary artery disease.

The doctors at Bluepark decided that since Will already had a chart in existence at Duke, this was the place to try to transport him.

"As luck—if you can call it that—would have it, Duke had just begun an emergency helicopter service to transport patients in my situation. The helicopter was summoned to Bluepark."

Mrs. Johnson spoke up now: "You can't imagine how bitterly cold it was the night they flew Will out. There were snow flurries in the mountains and the wind in the hollows was shrieking something awful."

A catheterization of his heart at Duke University, shortly after Will arrived, showed narrowing of short segments of the coronary arteries. Will was lucky: It would be feasible to surgically reroute blood around the obstructions using pieces of a leg vein. Perhaps this would allow the heart muscle to receive more blood and once again function efficiently as a pump.

In the early morning, a big black man came into the room to shave Will Johnson's body from neck to foot. Will Johnson chuckled as he related this: "In the months to come, this shaving of my body was huge in my memory, perhaps because I remember nothing of the operation. It recurs to me in nightmares. In one dream, the doctors told me that the surgery would be fine but the body shave was going to be touch-and-go!" He laughed with delight, as if this image was hugely funny, and he turned to look at his wife. She reached for his hand.

"The surgery began at about four in the afternoon. When they were done they kept me in recovery because I was still bleeding. They poured blood into me. At one point they told Bess that they might have to go in again and open me up, stop the bleeding. I got a lot of blood, a lot of blood, didn't I, Bess?"

Mrs. Johnson nodded and said, "My daughter Lee Ann and I would go in and stand around the bed whenever they would let us in. We were staring at him lying there with all these tubes and things in him and blood pouring into him. This intern—this black intern whom I can never forget—was so kind and attentive to us all night. At the end of the night, he held my hand and said, 'It's all right now. Looks like he's okay and they won't need to open him up again. The bleeding is finally quitting.' "

Mrs. Johnson paused, and stared at the bedsheet, as if trying to remember exactly what transpired next. "Then the intern says to me: 'He's gotten a lot of blood, lots and lots of blood. If he doesn't recover fully, or afterward if strange things happen, please remember what I just told you. He's gotten a lot of blood. Tell that to any doctor that he goes to see.' "

WILL JOHNSON survived his surgery. He went to his brother's place on Kiawah Island on the South Carolina coast to recover. His recuperation was slow and difficult. His back had never stopped hurting.

On a follow-up visit with the surgical team, he complained bitterly about his back pain, but it did not seem to register. Their only interest was in Will's chest, and checking that the sternum, which they had split to get to the heart and which they had then wired together at the end of the operation, was healing well.

"They told me I needed to pick up the pace of my rehabilitation. I felt as if I was being chastised for complaining of the back pain. As I said to Bess later, the after-sales service was poor."

It was left to a chiropractor in Kentucky, many months later, to take x-rays and diagnose the fractured vertebrae in his back. The fractures were a consequence of the seizure Will suffered in his truck after Chuck Hoover's funeral.

Exactly four weeks after his surgery, Will Johnson experienced the sudden onset of fever, severe sore throat, and lymph node enlargement in his neck and armpits. He had such tremendous fatigue that the act of bringing a coffee cup to his lips seemed almost beyond him. At night he had sweats that drenched the sheets and required them to be changed once or twice. This dramatic illness lasted a few days, and although the fever and night sweats gradually subsided, the malaise and fatigue did not.

A doctor in Charleston was unable to put a finger on his symptoms—his surgical wounds were healing well. Mrs. Johnson dutifully told him about the blood transfusions and the intern's warning. The doctor listened but said nothing. He wrote it off as a "viral" illness, a diagnosis that in retrospect was quite correct.

Many months later when Will Johnson returned to Kentucky, he sought out a physician who could follow him for his heart problems. He had heard good things about a new young doctor near Pikeville, Sarah Presnell. The fact that she worshipped at his church, that she and her husband were new and active members, was a definite plus.

Will now handed me Sarah's summary of her involvement with him. He continued to speak as I scanned Sarah's notes. She had sent away for his medical records from Duke. Will Johnson described to her in detail the viral or "mono"-like illness which still lingered many months after its acute manifestations had subsided.

Then, a year later, on a routine follow-up visit, Sarah was alarmed to discover that he still had abnormally enlarged lymph nodes in his neck. One in particular was so grossly enlarged that it was visible across the room. There were also enlarged nodes in his armpits and groin. Sarah's first thought was that Will Johnson had a lymphoma—a cancer of the lymph nodes—or else a leukemia. She felt carefully for the spleen, which is commonly enlarged in these disorders. Will's was not enlarged.

Sarah elected to put him in the hospital to initiate the workup of his puzzling symptoms and signs. His heart seemed fine. But a CAT scan of his abdomen and chest revealed that he had enlarged nodes straddling his abdominal aorta.

She went back over the medical records from Duke. Will Johnson had received a huge number of blood and plasma infusions during his stay at Duke.

A warning bell began to sound in Sarah's brain. Could Will have contracted HIV from the transfusions? She recognized that the "viral" illness Will Johnson had developed four weeks after the transfusion was consistent with reports describing the first stage of HIV infection. She ordered the HIV test.

To me, this was a remarkably astute observation, considering how new these reports of "primary HIV infection" were and considering that Sarah was not someone who dealt with AIDS every day.

The first report of this "HIV-mononucleosis" had come from Sydney, Australia, just that year. It happened like this: A group of researchers were following a large cohort of gay Australian men as part of an ongoing study of hepatitis that had begun years before AIDS. One patient in their study had contracted *Herpes simplex* infection of the rectum, a painful and debilitating condition that rendered him sexually abstinent for a month. Then, after he was completely recovered, the patient had anal receptive intercourse with another male who was also part of the Sydney study. In retrospect, from blood samples that had been stored and that were tested later when the HIV test was available, it was clear this new partner harbored HIV. A little over a week after this sexual contact, the first man developed an illness much like infectious mononucleosis: rash, fever, sore throat, headache, swollen nodes. Blood drawn before, during and after this illness and tested later for HIV showed that he was not infected before this sexual encounter, but the virus appeared immediately afterward. Other medical reports confirmed that almost 50 percent of patients when they first acquire HIV have a "mono"-like illness. Fred Goodson could recall such an illness; so could Otis Jackson, Bobby Keller and several others.

The blood test Sarah ordered on Mr. Johnson came back in a week.

"It was Friday when Sarah called. We were at the supper table with plans to see the Pikeville-Hazard football game. We went to her office. She was alone. I was really apprehensive. She told us what was wrong. We all cried. She said she had tried and failed to reach the minister at the church where we all worship; she wanted his advice and assistance. I was glad she didn't get him. It wouldn't be fair for him to know unless my son and his wife, who are very close to the minister, were also to know.

"Sarah was very emotional when she told us. She has been our support and given tender care ever since. She even comes to the house to draw blood samples. She got a sample of Bess's blood right away and then called us back down in about a week with the news Bess had it too. My heart broke then. My grief that my Bess had been infected with this virus from hell knows no bounds."

There were tears in both their eyes now. He squeezed his wife's hand and kissed it. I was fighting back tears.

"Duke didn't warn us I was at risk. If they had, Bess wouldn't be infected now. They saved my life and I am grateful. And even if they *told* me they were giving me AIDS infected blood, I would have said, 'Go ahead!' But they should have *warned* me about the possibility, helped me to avoid infecting Bess."

Will Johnson was barely controlling the anger in his voice. He took a deep breath to compose himself. Bess Johnson rose from the recliner to hug him, to sit beside him and to wipe away his tears. The mattress was sagging under the weight of the three of us.

"I had been infected in March of 1985. They began screening blood only a few months after that. The blood they gave me was not screened.

Although they knew, or should have known, they didn't tell me I was at risk for AIDS. So I infected *my* Bess and we knew nothing about it until eighteen months later."

I was trying to think objectively about Duke University's role in this regard. He was talking about the year 1985: the connection between AIDS and blood transfusions was known for at least three years by then—even longer in academic centers. This was a time, even in Tennessee, when people were so aware of the risk of blood transfusions that they had stopped *donating* blood, mistakenly equating any contact with the blood transfusion system as putting them at risk. This was one reason why Olivia Sells of the Red Cross had recruited me to speak about AIDS, to clear up that sort of misunderstanding.

Prior to the blood test for HIV, the Centers for Disease Control (CDC) had pushed for testing for antibodies to hepatitis B as a means of indirectly screening for HIV infection: Many donors who had HIV—drug addicts and gay men in particular—often also had antibodies to the hepatitis B virus since the hepatitis B virus was spread in ways similar to HIV. The CDC had evidence that in the absence of a direct test for AIDS, such a "surrogate" marker could crudely screen blood. One of the most tragic tales recounted in Randy Shilts's *And the Band Played On* is the procrastination, delay and rationalization by leaders of national blood banking institutions and the FDA who were unwilling to institute screening for hepatitis B as a surrogate marker for HIV. It would cost blood banks vast sums of money to institute these tests. At an epic meeting on January 4, 1983, at the CDC, the president of the New York Blood Center is quoted as saying, "Don't overstate the facts. There are at most three cases of AIDS from blood donation and the evidence in two of these cases is very soft. And there are only a handful of cases among hemophiliacs." Equally vocal in their opposition were gay groups who argued that such testing would stigmatize gay men. It became a cliché for blood bankers to say the chance of getting HIV from a transfusion was one in a million.

By early 1985, the year that Will was infected, there were over one hundred cases of unequivocal blood transfusion–related AIDS and perhaps hundreds more who were still asymptomatic. Still, except for a few places like Stanford, blood banks had not put into place the hepatitis B screening the CDC had recommended in 1983.

Undoubtedly the blood bank at Duke, like every other blood bank in the country, had discussions about AIDS risk and was aware of the potential for this agent to enter their system. A patient like Will, with his huge transfusion requirement, was particularly at risk. Perhaps, as often happens in big institutions, of the many people involved in his care, each assumed that someone else would warn him. The cryptic comment by the black intern had been the closest thing to a warning. There was no legal obligation to inform patients. The way to view what happened to Will Johnson is as a failure, not of Duke, but of society as a whole.

An hour had passed. I wanted to get on to work up Will's present problem and start therapy and make him comfortable. His main complaint now was difficulty and pain in swallowing—dysphagia. To swallow anything hurt him in his chest and upper abdomen. The pain probably came from the lower end of his esophagus.

I stood up and began to examine Will. I found a few white plaques of *Candida*, thrush, stuck to the mucous membrane of his mouth. Perhaps candidal infection of his esophagus was responsible for his pain. Another common cause of dysphagia in immunocompromised patients like Will was *Herpes simplex* infection, but I saw no herpetic lesions in his mouth or on his lips.

With his pajama top off, he looked like an Auschwitz survivor; the buzz cut added to that appearance. There were big lymph nodes in his neck and armpits and groin, but according to him, they were nowhere as big as they had been. His chest scar was well healed, and when I tried to "rock" the sternum it was solid. The apex of his heart was palpable in the space between the fourth and fifth ribs, and it gently lifted my finger up and down. The heart sounds were normal. The scars on his leg where the saphenous veins had been harvested for the bypass grafts were well healed.

I elected to begin Will Johnson on amphotericin B, the powerful but toxic drug that was effective against *Candida*; it was given intravenously. (The late Scotty Daws, who had received amphotericin for weeks for his cryptococcal meningitis, had referred to it as "Shake 'n' Bake," because of the chills and fever it produced.) I would also use intravenous acyclovir that first night, a drug for *Herpes simplex*. I wrote an order asking a colleague in gastroenterology to see Will the next morning.

I WALKED BACK to Mountain Home. Outside, the weather had changed. The stars were blacked out by clouds; I could see flashes of lightning far away and I could smell the rain in the air. I thought of calling the VA police to ask for a ride home, but then decided against it.

The wind was whipping through the trees, and I was leaning into it, my head down and my arms wrapped around myself, feeling dust and grit sting my cheeks.

I was deeply affected by the story of the Johnsons, very sympathetic to them. Why? Was it easier for me to sympathize and identify with this beautiful couple because they were *not* gay, *not* intravenous drug users? Because they reminded me of my parents? Will Johnson had at one point used the words "innocent victim" when describing his and his wife's situation. I had wanted to interrupt him and say that *all* victims of this virus were innocent.

Yet I hadn't said it, partly because I didn't want to engage in that sort of a debate with him. It would have been unnecessary and even churlish to have done so. But in addition, I said nothing because for the briefest moment I had accepted what he said *as if he were stating a well-known fact*!

I liked to think of myself as nonjudgmental; I thought I didn't discriminate in my services: a gay man with AIDS or a drug abuser could expect to be treated the same way as I would treat anyone else. But did I have a blind spot? After all, how many other patients had I personally escorted up to their hospital rooms? When had I ever carried luggage for patients, spent hours of my evening listening to them and settling them in, allowing them to dictate the pace of the interview, leaving only when I thought they would not mind my departure?

And if I had a blind spot, a class prejudice, was it perhaps because I too, subconsciously, subscribed to the concept of their "innocence"? The word "innocent," used in this context, implied, of course, that everyone else out there with HIV who did not get it by a blood transfusion was "guilty."

At the root of this metaphor of guilt is the fact that, in North America, males with HIV outnumber females, almost ten to one. Anal intercourse is an efficient means of transmitting the virus—more efficient than vaginal intercourse, perhaps because with anal intercourse there is always some microscopic trauma to the rectal mucous membrane. And in all sexual acts, whether gay or straight, it is the male that is always *injecting* semen, injecting a secretion into a partner, whether a woman or another man. For these reasons, gay men had been disproportionately affected by the virus. "AIDS" in a man had come to mean "gay" until proven otherwise.

Oh yes, there were the other *H*s: hemophiliac, Haitian, heroin, heterosexual. But the big *H* stood for homosexual.

To a heterosexual world—perhaps a slightly *envious* heterosexual world—it was possible to point at sexual behavior in some gay men (its variety, the anonymity, the frequency) and at promiscuity in general, and link it with the deadly virus as cause and effect. Almost as if, *without* gay men, there would be no AIDS. And it was easy to view intravenous drug addicts as pernicious disseminators and recipients of a deadly virus; this was not a great leap from the Hollywood depiction of them as thieving, lying, murdering individuals who were a drag on society.

Of course, the virus, unlike human beings, lacked all class prejudice. The proof of this was Africa, where HIV behaved like gonorrhea or syphilis: men and women were affected in equal numbers. In Africa, *other* sexually transmitted diseases which cause open ulcers on the genitals were common and seemed to thereby facilitate the transmission of HIV. Another widely touted reason for the democratic spread of the virus in Africa was that friable scar tissue from female circumcision made vaginal intercourse somewhat traumatic, prone to cause microscopic bleeding, made it akin to anal intercourse. Since these "facts" about HIV in Africa were standard fare in any journalist's update on AIDS, it had become possible for middle America to believe—if only subconsciously—that since Africans practiced female circumcision, copulated indiscriminately, and suffered chronically from other sexually transmitted infections, they too were in some way "guilty," just like gay men.

It is interesting to me that many gay men infected with HIV can use the metaphors of innocence and guilt just as the Johnsons did. A friend by the name of James, whose quiet dignity I have come to admire, said to me, "I have nobody to blame. It's my behavior that did this, that made me get the virus. I'm not saying that I *deserved* this, but I am saying that I have no one to blame but myself. I *never* used a condom, never thought of it. In the heyday of being gay in a big city—the bathhouses, Fire Island and all that—I had more sex than ten heterosexuals would have had in a lifetime. I don't believe it's a punishment from God or any of that kind of crap, but it clearly was a *consequence* of a certain lifestyle. Just being gay, just being attracted to men, *isn't* the issue. For most of us, being gay also meant sex, sex, sex. As if to make up for all the years we hid, and pretended, and listened to queer jokes. I mean we fucked like crazy! And now here we are."

And then, as if feeling the need to qualify what he had just said, James had looked around at the bare study in my house where I write and said defiantly, "Mind you, I won't take anything back. As much suffering as I have gone through—my lover's death in Charlotte, my illness—I would not take any of it back. Most gay men have traveled to several countries, have seen the best shows, movies, plays, have taken an interest in art, in their clothes, in the way their house is decorated, have experienced more of this world than any heterosexual. To me, a heterosexual male is a slob. If he gets divorced the walls of his house will stay as bare as when he first moved in, and it will be dirty, dirty, dirty. If he gets married, that's it—he has no desire to improve himself past that. His idea of a good time is to get a six-pack and park his truck on the side of the road with his buddy and drink. He might beat his wife, be mean to his kids and ultimately die where he was born having seen nothing, done nothing. But, by God, the one thing he knows is how he feels about queers! When he sees a queer he can look down on him, feel contempt, beat up a queer because it's justified."

I thought of myself as completely different from, say, the televangelists, who had exploited this theme of guilt and innocence for all it was worth. Jimmy Swaggart and Jim Bakker had been obsessed with sex, preaching incessantly about its evils, bringing in examples of pornography from school libraries and from magazine stands so as to show their congregation the evils out there. After their downfall, it was clear their polemic was a classic example of what Freud called "reaction formation": deep sexual urges in the subconscious mind had resulted in the conscious mind overreacting in the opposite direction. Ultimately, the subconscious broke through: both these men of the cloth were betrayed by sexual desires that could not be suppressed.

Was something like this happening to me? Was my egalitarianism nothing but a cover-up for a deeply rooted prejudice? Was my outward proletarianism, my disdain for what I saw as the avarice of modern medicine, my compassion for gay men and for the underdog in general, merely a posture? If so, this posture was costly: It was responsible for the increasing sense of isolation I felt from my community, even from my own wife. By taking up the cause of AIDS, I had become tainted, the associations of this word had tarnished me, I often felt as "guilty" as the kind of people I cared for. Perhaps *this* was why I was so drawn to the Johnsons, the "innocents": they were an affirmation of *my* self-worth, of *my* innocence.

A hundred yards from the house, the skies opened up. I was soaked. Once inside, I stripped off my wet clothes. The ink in my pocket diary was smudging in places. I peeked into Steven's room, studied his face in sleep and wondered if he was dreaming of fireflies. And in our bedroom, baby Jacob lay next to his mother, both having fallen asleep after a breast-feed, milk still on his lips and hanging off his chin.

Rajani awoke. She came out of the bed and offered to fix me something to eat. I put on my pajamas and joined her in the kitchen. We sat across from each other and I told her the story of the Johnsons. It was a gripping story, one she could obviously relate to. A husband infected "innocently" who then infects his wife. I was describing our very own nightmare. But she had little to say. I had been taught professional detachment; she, like many doctors' spouses, had mastered it.

"You know," Rajani began, " Mrs. D_____ spoke to me the other day." (This was the wife of a doctor friend of ours, a pulmonary physician.) "She says that every time her husband gets a consult with your name on it, he dreads it because he might have to do a bronchoscopy on an AIDS patient."

"Really? But it doesn't stop him from doing it. He comes right away and does a beautiful job," I said.

"Still, he is scared," Rajani said.

"We are all scared. But we have to do it."

"I wish this disease was gone, that you were not so close to it. It's kind of become who you are and what you do."

"I wish it was gone too."

"But it's not going to," she said. "Is it?"

16

BY THE NEXT MORNING Will Johnson felt no better. A mouthful of water caused the abrupt onset of searing, lingering pain behind his breastbone. He had a temperature of 102 degrees Fahrenheit and had received one dose of amphotericin and three doses of acyclovir: the former for *Candida* and the latter for herpes.

The gastroenterologist, one of several in town, was a very competent individual, an excellent diagnostician. But even as I discussed the case over the phone with her, I could tell she did not relish this consultation. Nevertheless, she went down Will's esophagus with her endoscope and saw several discrete ulcers at the lower end. They did not appear characteristic of either herpes or *Candida*, nor of cytomegalovirus (CMV), another cause of esophageal ulceration. She took biopsies.

That evening when I went to see the Johnsons, I asked Will how the day had gone.

"It was very strange, Abraham. The procedure was all right. But I could tell the doctor was uncomfortable. On the one hand, she felt sorry for me, felt inclined to be nice to me. On the other hand, she seemed kind of grumpy with me, a little short, as if at one level this AIDS was *my* fault, *my* doing, even though she knows the facts. I could see her emotions going back and forth, back and forth. I must say, I haven't experienced anything like that from the nurses or anyone else in this hospital thus far."

After the procedure, the gastroenterologist did not come by to see the Johnsons again. I called her on the phone to let her know how Will was doing, to discuss Will's continuing symptoms. She made recommendations, but she never came by, a fact that was not lost on the Johnsons. The gastroenterologist was knowledgeable about the latest reports on esophageal disease in AIDS, her advice was helpful. But whatever assistance she gave to the Johnsons and to me was negated by her failure to visit again. From then on I tried to direct most of my consultations to other gastroenterologists in town. They seemed to have no qualms about dealing with HIV-infected persons and they provided excellent care.

The biopsies of the ulcers in the esophagus were not revealing. In later years there would emerge a body of knowledge about these mysterious ulcers: they are aphthous ulcers—canker sores—except that they are much bigger and much more severe than the usual canker sores seen in the mouth. Some of them respond to steroids. But at the time when I was taking care of Will, such knowledge did not exist. I treated Will Johnson with antacids and with viscous Xylocaine, a local anesthetic to ease the pain. I decided to continue the antifungal and antiherpetic medications for a full ten-day course.

THAT AFTERNOON I went over to the University Clinic at lunchtime to meet B.J. Hilton's father and to check my mail.

B.J. worked as a manager at a well-known restaurant near the mall. He was, according to Carol, the handsomest man the front-office staff at our clinic had ever seen. She told me that at his first visit, they were all swooning over him. He wore his blond hair in a ponytail; he had the long limbs and muscular physique of a ballet dancer. Had you seen him on the street, you might have wondered if God was fair in blessing one person with all these attributes. He came to me when he found out he was HIV positive. He was asymptomatic with a CD4 count near a thousand.

B.J. told me on his first visit that there was no possible way he could tell anyone but his mother about his infection. His father and his brothers would never understand.

Imagine my surprise, then, when his father called and asked to see me. I telephoned B.J. at once at the restaurant where he worked. He said he had just had a wonderful heart-to-heart with his father and that I should feel free to talk to him.

B.J.'s father was a large balding man who showed up in a safari shirt and slacks. If B.J. possessed a ballet dancer's body, his father was more in the linebacker mode, a linebacker who had gone to fat. He told me how sad he was at the news that his son had HIV. And yet, he was glad that his son had come out and told him. He said, "For the first time in ten years, I hugged my son and told him how much I loved him. I would not want him to get sick without knowing that." He reached for a handkerchief and dabbed the corners of his eyes.

I told him as much about HIV infection as I thought he could digest; I told him what B.J. could expect in years to come. He seemed reluctant to leave. I asked him if this was the first he knew his son was gay.

"No, I suppose I've known for some time now. One time he got in trouble with the law. I had to go bail him out. It had to do with something in the bathroom at J.C. Penney." At this point his face hardened and he looked at me and said, "All I can tell you is it was something disgusting. Just plain disgusting."

I could imagine what it might have been and how painful it was for the father to picture it.

"Plain disgusting. I mean, I more or less knew then but I just turned away from him. Well, even before that, growing up, he was always . . . different. And maybe I was hard on him, tried to get him to do the things his brothers were doing, but it never worked. He had his own friends, his own interests—still does."

He stared away now and was silent before he looked back at me, the tears pouring down his cheeks, the hankie quite ineffective. "Isn't it a shame for it to take a disease like this for me to be close to my boy again? The little baby boy that I carried and loved—he was the youngest— somehow got away from me. Now we're back loving again, but he's going to die, isn't he? That's the bottom line, isn't it?"

I hedged. But yes, it was the bottom line. Every study at that time, during the seventh year of the epidemic, suggested that most infected patients gradually declined.

Mr. Hilton finally left my office. I found myself thinking about him and B.J. all day, trying to picture them both twenty years ago. I could identify with B.J. and his father, identify with them as a son and as the father of two little boys. I knew exactly what Mr. Hilton meant when he talked about the little baby boy that he carried in his arms who had grown up and gotten away from him. It was happening to me: Even as I cradled Jacob in my arms, Steven, who it seemed only yesterday had been an infant, was now a little boy, exploring the world around our house. My time with my sons was filled with this sense of urgency—that I could not waste a moment and that it was crucial to record it all on film, in case the memory failed. It was difficult to picture my little cherubs one day reaching their teens, one day developing the secondary sexual characteristics that presaged their becoming men: the voice breaking, the appearance of pubic hair, the phallus enlarging. I remembered a moment in my childhood, when I was about eleven: I was secretly reading *Lolita* in my room—I was a voracious reader. Suddenly, over the edge of the book, I became aware of a foot: it was an adult foot, a large foot with well-formed nails. The big toe was dominant and had character, the other toes looked like they knew what they were doing. There was a deep plantar arch and the tendons on the forefoot stood out like cables under the skin. It dawned on me that this was *my* foot. Though I was going through other shocking and exciting changes— helped in no small measure by the book I was reading—it was the sight of that foot that let me know, as surely as anything before or since, that manhood had arrived. It was for this reason that Jacob's baby feet were the part of his body I adored the most: those rocker-bottom-shaped plantar pads and the way the toes looked like little buds were the essence of what made him a baby. Already Steven's feet had formed an arch and his toes had begun to resemble his mother's.

I took a deep breath and dictated a note in B.J.'s chart recording this visit, documenting that B.J. had given me permission to chat freely with his father.

I checked my mail: a sweet card from Mrs. T, signed with only her initials, and with *Personal* marked on the envelope. *Thank you so much for the way you dealt with my situation. Both the lice and the louse are gone.*

Habit being so strong with me, I peered into the envelope and even shook it out over the sink.

EVER SINCE their arrival two nights before, Bess Johnson had spent all her time in the hospital with her husband. His swallowing and his pain were *maybe* better, certainly no worse. We waited for the pathology department to be done with the more exotic stains and cultures we had ordered on the biopsies, though I knew they were going to be unrevealing. Meanwhile, I put a venous catheter under Will's collarbone, into his subclavian vein and on into the superior vena cava. Through this we were feeding him hyperalimentation fluid; the bottle looked as if it held milkshake. It contained all his nutritional requirements in a readily assimilable form. We were bypassing his gut and trying to put some weight back on him. I had talked to the Johnsons about the need for me to examine Bess and establish what, if anything, the virus was doing in her body. She protested, but Will and I insisted, and I made an appointment for her in my Wednesday afternoon clinic.

I had one patient scheduled before Mrs. Johnson. This was the first *male* patient for whom Carol suggested I needed a chaperon. "Absurd!" I said, until I marched in and saw who it was.

It was none other than Raleigh, the young man who had been at the Connection when Olivia and I screened the video. He had sat next to Trevor, a black male of about the same age, and the two of them had carried on like schoolgirls. My eyes went to Raleigh's wrist, looking for the vivid purple scar that I had seen there. But the shirt he wore today had ruffled Victorian cuffs that hid his wrists. When, after our appearance at the Connection, a cluster of men had come to my office for testing, Raleigh had been conspicuous by his absence.

"Remember me?" he asked, giving me an impish smile.

"I certainly do," I said, shaking his hand.

"I was already HIV-positive when you came to the Connection. But I didn't want to say anything."

In the setting of the exam room, in the absence of Trevor, Raleigh was a little subdued, a little more serious. But it still appeared to be an effort for him. If he could not be the clown—I think Carol's presence had something to do with that—he settled for a parody of a southern belle. He was missing only a parasol and a bonnet. If he wanted to pass through the world and our clinic unobtrusively, not draw attention and persecution, he was not dressed for the part. In the fluorescent light of the clinic, he appeared thirteen, not twenty-one as the chart stated. Since I last saw him, he had shaved the sides of his scalp, giving him the appearance of a plucked chicken. The hair on the crown of his head was cut close and dyed blond. He wore clear nail polish, a musky perfume, a silver brooch on his collar and tight jeans that appeared to have shrunk onto him and fused with his pelvis. He carried an alligator-skin clutch bag with a side pocket from which his cigarette case and lighter protruded. He had covered his acne with a thick layer of foundation that gave his face the look of a minstrel.

During the course of our interview, Raleigh adopted several different demeanors, as if he was trying each one out for size: For a while he was seductive and determined to titter his way through his visit; then suddenly he would regress to the child, tempting the motherly instincts in Carol.

"See, I was abused as a child," was the sentence Raleigh began with. It was as if he felt his affect and his sexual preference needed some explanation. I didn't doubt that Raleigh could have been abused as a child. But from what other patients told me, often *they* were the ones who as children had sought out sex with adults. Yes, it was abuse, because of their age; and the role of the adult was unforgivable. But very often there was no coercion, no threats. They had slipped into a precocious ritual that did generate guilt but gave them lots of pleasure.

Raleigh continued, "I smoked cigarettes and pot from the age of eight; my parents thought it was cute to get me high. I used uppers and downers from the age of ten and I have been an alcoholic since I was twelve." There was a practiced quality to this recitation of his. Carol was shocked, on the verge of tears. For some reason, I resisted his tale. I was not willing to be sympathetic because I felt he was trying to draw sympathy out of me.

I asked about his sexual history. "Men were having sex with me from the time I could first remember being on earth." The self-pity had slipped out of his voice and a note of pride had crept in. He was about to give us numbers but then—perhaps because of Carol—thought the better of it. "I grew to like sex with men. I grew to not like *myself* for having sex with men, but I liked the sex all right. I got into trouble a lot when I was young because I didn't know how to stop."

The story he told us was of myriad sexual encounters with men, many of which had the same reckless and abusive quality as his drug use. It was clear that he posed a risk of exposure and embarrassment to these men; his dress and manner were not conducive to a long-term clandestine relationship. One such episode with a married man had resulted in the wife calling the police, the married man going to jail and Raleigh being sent to a residential psychiatric facility. It was the first of many hospital admissions for maladjustment, for drug abuse, for depression. Twice he had slashed his wrists. He had run away to Atlanta numerous times—the city had a mysterious hold on him—but had never been able to sustain himself there. "I tried to work as a hustler outside one of the gay porn movie theaters in Atlanta. I figured, if men wanted to do it with me, I might as well get paid for it. And I wanted so much to stay on in Atlanta."

"So what happened?"

"Believe it or not, I had a hard time!"

"Why?"

"Well, the typical hustler is more macho, I guess. And I am what I am," Raleigh said, extending his arms and thrusting his chest out, as though displaying his couture. "And what the men who pick up hustlers are looking for is someone who looks straight. And I just couldn't make it. I would get picked up in bars and get thrown out the next morning like garbage. I wanted a long-term relationship, but I could never get it."

I asked Raleigh about the suicide attempts.

"Well, the first time I did it to spite the man I was with. I wasn't serious. And the next time was after I had visited the Connection. I was having the time of my life, everyone was talking to me, joshing with me. And then as the bar was closing, I was alone. I was pretty drunk, but I heard this one guy say behind my back, 'What a queen! I wonder what he dresses up like during the day.' " Here Raleigh again made his I-am-what-I-am gesture. "He was talking about me as if I wasn't a real person, as if this was not me. I just lost it, I went home and tried to end it."

Raleigh now lived in a tenuous relationship with his grandmother; his mother had rejected him well before the HIV problem arose. His father had disappeared.

My exam (with Carol in attendance) was largely unremarkable. When he took off his shirt and pants, I was amazed at how narrow his shoulders and hips were. As if his growth had been stunted in child-hood. His CD4 count (which had been done before he came to see me) was over 400.

I recited my litany of dos and don'ts for Raleigh, but he had by now let go of his serious side and had climbed back into his shell and put the mask of the jester back on. He had briefly let us in, but now he slammed the door. I could imagine that a psychologist working with him would be constantly struggling to get him to be serious. Raleigh let a giggle burst forth when I mentioned easing up on smoking. The serious ex-pression on my face and on Carol's only made us seem more comical to him.

"Well, Raleigh, in that case *try* to ease up on the smoking, *try* to ease up on the drinking. You are doing really well from the point of view of HIV infection."

Raleigh smiled sweetly at me, but said nothing.

"Come back and see me in the office in four months and I'll check you over again. . . ."

To what end? Clearly not to *do* anything as much as to confirm that nothing was a-doing in him. This impotence with AIDS was getting to me.

On to the next room.

IT WAS STRANGE to see Bess Johnson apart from her husband, away from his room, in the role of patient. Whenever I walked into their room they were holding hands quietly, or else she was reading to him. Sometimes he read something out of the newspaper to her. I was envious of their love affair. Mary, the night nurse, had stopped me in the hallway and asked, "Have you seen how they look into each other's eyes? God, I'd die for a man to love me like that!"

And even as Mrs. Johnson sat in the clinic, it was tempting to talk about Will instead of about her. Will's illness, his wasting, was so profound, and yet his personality so vital that he was the focus of our attention. I could not recall Bess initiating a discussion in his room; she sometimes added a comment to whatever we were talking about. In Will's hospital room, Bess's concentration on him was so complete that after a while she became invisible; she became an extension of Will.

"I made a drive back home to check the mail and get some fresh clothes," Bess said now. "You must have wondered if I possessed anything but that one dress I was wearing!"

I assured her that I had thought no such thing. She wore a plaid skirt with a light blue cardigan over her blouse. A tiny gold crucifix was visible at her neck.

"I appreciate your taking the time to see me; I know you are busy," she said. I realized Mrs. Johnson must have seen Raleigh out in the waiting room, must have recognized that he, like her, was there to see me.

I said, "You know I feel like I've known both of you for a long, long time. And I do know an awful lot about Mr. Johnson—at least medically. But I know almost nothing about you, about where you're from originally, and how you met Mr. Johnson." She was bashful, smiling, as if I had stumbled onto the veil she used to make herself invisible. I felt a twinge of embarrassment, as if I was fishing for details that were none of my business. I continued, "And I don't know how you're dealing with all this, with all the stress. In short, I feel guilty for neglecting you in my concern for Mr. Johnson."

With any other hospitalized patient, the spouse might have come out to the corridor and had a private conversation with me from time to time, to ask how things were really going. But I had never had such a chat with Mrs. Johnson, because for her to do that would have meant her leaving his side.

"Oh, you haven't neglected me. And Will and I feel blessed that you are taking care of him. And about me . . . well, there's not much to tell really. I have been a housewife most of my life—by choice, you understand. I enjoyed my role as the wife of Will Johnson, as a mother to my children, as a grandmother. After we married, I never wanted anything else. These were supposed to be our glory years, Will would have retired soon. . . ." Here she trailed off, the fixed smile on her face hiding the pain of the unfinished sentence.

"Where did you meet? Are you both from the same town?"

"We met in my first year of college, when both of us had come home for the holidays and we were at a social at a friend's house."

"Where did you go to college?"

"I went to the University of Virginia in Charlottesville. I graduated magna cum laude in English literature. I went on to do a master's."

I had thought of Mrs. Johnson as educated, but I didn't think of her as a scholar, particularly since she had just finished telling me how she had enjoyed being housewife, mother, grandmother. She must have seen the surprise on my face because she said, "Yes, English literature! My thesis was on Blake's *Songs of Experience*. He is still my favorite. I was accepted into a Ph.D. program at Yale based on that thesis, but I chose not to go. Years later, when my daughter and son grew up and went to junior high, I began to teach English literature and creative writing at the community college. I only stopped when Will had the heart attack."

So self-effacing was her personality that I wondered if I would ever have learned about her education had I not asked directly.

"And do you read a lot now?"

"It's about all I do. We don't care for television. I'm a member of two book clubs, and Will and I often take turns reading a book out loud to each other. We have done that for years. He loves biographies and I love the nineteenth-century English novelists. Now the reading is a lot more precious to us. As a matter of fact, we decided to try Thomas Mann's *Magic Mountain* right now. I had read it before, but it reads like a different book now."

Carol now entered the room and I began my examination of Bess Johnson. She was a fit fifty-five-year-old. Her passion for walking, a sensible diet and the fact that she had never smoked showed in her muscle tone and in her complexion. I did not detect any signs of lymphadenopathy, nor any yeast in her mouth. Vaginal yeast infection is common in women with HIV infection, but she was untroubled by this. In short, but for Dr. Sarah Presnell's word that Bess's test was positive, it was impossible to imagine that she had HIV infection.

I stepped out of the room to allow her to dress. When I returned she was seated quietly on the stool, her hands folded on her lap, patient, as if she could have sat there for an hour or two without any effort. I told her I found her to be entirely well. That we would get blood work, but that I was hopeful the virus would not trouble her greatly for a long time to come. I asked her if she had any questions.

"I want you to be candid about Will's chances." I sensed that this was one of the few times during his illness where she had acted apart from him, where the information I gave her she might not share with him.

"Well," I said, "I'm puzzled by the ulcers in his esophagus. They fit nothing that has been described in the medical literature. His weight loss and his low CD4 count—it's only ninety—suggest that he is farther along the spectrum of HIV infection toward AIDS."

"Is it AIDS?"

"Technically, no. Because he hasn't had one of the 'AIDS-defining' infections like *Pneumocystis*. But from a practical point of view, his CD4 count is in that range. Yet if we can get him over this, he could go on for a long time living very well."

"Can you tell me how long? Is that a fair question?"

"I really don't know. He isn't getting any worse and that's reassuring. I am hoping he will have two good years, but we might not be that fortunate."

She smiled as if to thank me, and now sat quietly again. She had no further questions. I was loath to let her leave; I didn't think we would get many chances to talk without Will being present. I felt as if there was unfinished business, and only politeness kept her from coming out with it.

As a means of prolonging the conversation, I told Bess how everyone who worked with Will and with her was full of admiration for how brave they were in the face of this cruel disease, how it was inspiring to all of us who saw them.

To my surprise, her face fell, her shoulders sagged and she burst into tears. I was unprepared for this, uncertain of what to do. I held a box of tissues out to her and placed one hand on her shoulder.

"I'm sorry," she said. "I don't know what happened. And I don't want to waste your time."

"*I'm* sorry. I didn't mean to upset you. I have no one else to see and we have all the time in the world."

She opened up now, as if she *needed* to tell her side of the story, as if her staying in the background and letting Will do the steering had resulted in something building up inside of her.

She said, "I only wish you had known Will *before* this whole terrible thing. He was the strongest and most caring of men. It breaks my heart to see him weaken. After his heart attack, when they flew him to Duke, my daughter and I drove down. We found Will parked in a stretcher in the hallway by the emergency room. And when I saw him lying there, so helpless, made to look tiny by that giant institution and the hustle and bustle around him, I felt something snap in me. I dragged myself around the corner and sagged into a chair, crossed my arms in front of my chest like this and wept. And that was about the last time I let myself do that around him."

She was weeping quietly now. She folded each tissue into a square and used first one side then the other to dab her eyes.

"Do you know what he wanted when he got back to his room after the cardiac catheterization? He wanted to call a board meeting! The cardiologists had told him that it looked as if surgery was the next option. Will wanted to call a board meeting! Not of his firm—but of all the doctors. He said, 'Let's get all the M.D.'s. Get them all here—cardiology and the surgery people—and we'll run a board meeting. We'll have an agenda: Will's Health. We'll hear all the opinions, hear all the options, go through a stepwise, logical process, hear the motions, take a vote if needed.' My daughter and I looked at him as if he was crazy. He said, 'Sure! We don't need to be M.D.'s to make an informed decision. Just need data. And good advice. And we'll make the right decision.' "

I was laughing, listening to this. In an institution the size of Duke University Medical Center—a medical-industrial complex—it would be a logistical feat to get everyone involved into the same room for a "board meeting." The more critically ill a patient was, the more likely he or she was to concede their autonomy and go along with the doctors' decision, even if the decision was perfunctorily presented as a choice. But not Will Johnson.

"So did they have a board meeting?"

She shook her head.

"The surgical team on duty for that day walked into the room late that evening—not for a board meeting, but because they had been consulted by the cardiologists. They had seen the film that recorded Will's cardiac catheterization; they had discussed it with the cardiologists. I remember Will struggled to sit up. He informed them that he would like to call a meeting of his doctors. A meeting for them to present their data to him and to decide on the best course. There was a silence and then a doctor said, 'You are going to have open-heart surgery in the next twenty-four hours if you want to live. Our staff is accomplished; we know what we are doing. We've made the decision for you.' When they left the room, Will just sank back into the pillows. He was totally deflated. I don't think he had ever in his life been in a situation in which he had been this helpless."

"But he agreed to go through with it?"

"Well, he had no choice. It was either that or leave. One of the things that gave us faith was that we had heard that the surgeon on duty for that day was an outspoken Christian. That he had been saved. I reasoned with Will that what the team was going to do for him was something they did several times a day. It was life-or-death for us, but routine for them. Perhaps it was too much to expect the kind of *personal* attention he needed, attention that he was used to getting in his business world. Will complained that he felt like a piece of lumber stacked up outside the sawmill. But the surgeon for the day was an outspoken Christian."

I was intrigued by this characterization of the surgeon. I asked Bess Johnson what it meant to her that the surgeon was an "outspoken Christian."

She answered without any hesitation: "It means that he is an *instrument* of God. Even though he has prestige and money, that is not his motive, merely a reward."

"Did the team anticipate trouble during Will's surgery?"

"I don't think so. We were led to believe that even though Will's heart was in precarious condition, they did this all the time. The helicopter was flying in broken hearts every day. It was going to be fairly routine . . . but I can tell you, there wasn't a family in the cardiac surgery waiting room for whom this was routine. We prayed a lot. We sat and sat and sat, waiting. We had no idea at any point whether Will was already in surgery, or was he parked in a corridor, waiting just as we were? There were stretchers rolling in and out of the operating room. When a stretcher came out it was surrounded by a ring of people, each person in charge of one tube or bottle or something. As soon as a stretcher rolled out, everybody would stand up and look. The family that recognized their loved one would hurry out and get a ten-second glimpse of the patient before the stretcher rolled into the recovery room and the door closed.

"While we were there, someone died. We saw the nurse shepherd the family into a prayer room, and pretty soon the chaplain was paged and he came and broke the news. You could hear the wailing behind the door. And you know everyone else in the waiting room was praying, 'Thank you, God, that it was not ours.' There was another family from Kentucky there, waiting on their father. We were drawn to them: it's amazing how perfect strangers can feel like kin because you share an experience. I still correspond with that woman, though now I'm easing off because I can't tell her what's *really* happening to us. Some nights I wonder if what's happening to me is also happening to her. Did her husband get the same blood? Does she have the virus, and is she writing these polite but untrue letters to me?

"Finally, at about eleven in the night, Will was wheeled out. There was blood *everywhere*. In the ten seconds we had a glimpse of him, it looked as if there were tubes growing out of his body. There was a tube coming out from under his breastbone—*pouring* blood. I mean the blood was dripping into a bottle as if a faucet was open. Another from each side of his chest. A tube was in his mouth breathing for him. A tube was in his bladder, another was in his nose. The people wheeling him looked very tense. I was shocked at his appearance."

Mrs. Johnson's face had become quite pale as she relived this event.

"Every hour they would let my daughter and me in there to be with him for exactly two minutes. You could tell it was a real burden on the staff. They were bustling around, fiddling with this tube and that tube and loading medications in syringes and suctioning the tube in his throat. Then when we came in they would stop, lean against the wall and wait for us to be done. I remember blood, blood, blood: there was blood collecting in the bottles on the floor by his bed, and meanwhile, blood was pouring in from bags running into his veins.

"We held his hands. We read to him passages for that day from the *Diary of Private Prayer*.

"We had yet to hear from the surgeons. Every now and then I spotted them coming out of the operating room and going into the recovery room; I guess they were in between operations. A black surgical intern, part of the surgical crew, was so helpful. He told us what little we knew: the operation had been difficult and Will was bleeding.

"At about one o'clock in the morning, a surgeon came to the visitors' room—we were the only ones there—and told us that there had been a tremendous amount of bleeding and that the bleeding still had not ceased. They were going to have to go back into Will's chest, take him back to the operating room and find the bleeders.

"I couldn't imagine it. There was Will with stitches up and down his chest and along his legs. Tubes coming out from everywhere. The surgeons had been up for about twenty hours—they must have been bone-tired, you could see it in their faces. I just *knew* that if they took him back in, he would not survive. It was just like when the helicopter landed in the middle of the night in Bluepark with the wind howling and the snow blowing. I wanted to say, 'No. Don't take him.'

"But I said nothing. My daughter and I held hands and prayed that they would not have to take him back, prayed that God would make his blood start to clot, stop bleeding.

"At about three in the morning, we spotted the black intern walking down the hall, walking away from us. We ran after him. He said he was heading home. And I was thinking to myself, 'How can you possibly go home when Will is still in there?' But I didn't say anything because he looked so tired. He was resting against the wall as he talked to us. He said, 'It's all right now. Looks like he's OK and they won't need to open him up again. The bleeding is finally quitting.' I was so happy I started to weep: it had been hours and hours of waiting, wondering what was happening to Will: Was he back on the table? Were they cutting into him again? When I heard the words 'it's all right' I just felt something break loose in me. I felt like I had been holding my breath from early morning and I could finally let it out."

Mrs. Johnson was quiet now, as if replaying this memory for the millionth time, trying to extract another ounce of meaning from it.

"At the time, those were the most wonderful words a human being could have said to me: *It's all right now, looks like he's OK, he's quit bleeding.*"

She looked at me now, her face full of wonder. "So when he *then* said, 'He's gotten a lot of blood, lots and lots of blood. *If he doesn't recover fully, or afterward if strange things happen, please remember what I just told you,*' it didn't really register. It didn't register until the night Sarah called us into her office and told us that Will was infected. I punish myself every time I think of this, punish myself for not paying attention. I will never forgive myself for being so passive. Not so much because it might have prevented *my* being infected, but because I could have perhaps helped them diagnose what was wrong with Will a long time before, when he was having that strange 'mono'-like illness, when he had the bizarre weight loss, when he had all those strange skin rashes."

She was now weeping again. Her face was drawn into a grimace. Between sobs she said, "Will has never said one word to me about this. And yet, I just know if *he* had been in my situation, he would have pushed the intern to explain what he meant, he would not have been content to hear something and not understand it. I failed him. I *assumed* whatever it was I had to remember would be repeated to me again later."

I tried to reassure Mrs. Johnson that she had not failed him, that no one could have made much of the intern's cryptic remark, particularly in that setting, that both she and her daughter *had* mentioned it to the doctor in Charleston when Will had the "mono"-like illness. But she was inconsolable. She was still crying when she left my office. Through my office window I saw her enter her car and sit there. She was so still that I was tempted to go down and check on her. After a long while, she started the car and headed back in the direction of the Miracle Center.

CAROL PAGED ME EARLY the next morning. Raleigh had taken an overdose of sleeping pills the evening after I saw him.

"How is he?" I asked.

"He's fine," Carol said. "He's sitting here in the office. Do you think you can see him?"

I rushed over to find Raleigh now dressed in Robin Hood boots with skin-tight purple slacks, a chiffony shirt with a frilled collar. The heavy application of mascara around his eyes matched his present mood: solemn, somber, tragic—but every bit as unreal as before.

He said he had fought with his grandmother the previous evening, had been rejected by a former lover and then had the door slammed in his face by his mother's new boyfriend. *Nobody* wanted to hear about his HIV status. As an attention-getting device, HIV had no effect.

And so he had overdosed and had his stomach pumped out in his local hospital, a ritual that both he and the hospital had been through before. I was his last physician of record. The emergency room had arranged to have him in my office in the morning.

Now the hurt, angry and scared little boy was easy to spot behind the mawkish facade. Carol and I made calls and got Raleigh admitted to a halfway house where he could stay temporarily. I called Fred Goodson and had him come see Raleigh and bring him into their newly formed support group. Though we had given Raleigh information about TAP and the support group, it had probably been too much to expect him to follow up on his own. In putting Raleigh under Fred's care, I had as secure a feeling as if I had put him in professional therapy. Joyce, my secretary at the VA, explored a job-training possibility for Raleigh.

What had happened to Raleigh was a forceful reminder to me that there was a lot I could do, a lot I *had* to do, for our patients even if we had no therapy for HIV. I could no longer sit and be the consultant and pontificate over the progression (or lack thereof) of the disease; I was providing *primary* care, total care for this group of patients, whether I liked it or not.

Unexplained fever in a transplant patient, fever in a missionary returned from South America, a bizarre rash in a leukemic—these were the summonses to intellectual adventure, brain teasers. But now, in our AIDS clinic, there were many, many visits—just like Raleigh's last visit—where *nothing* at all happened. The virus was there, but it lay dormant. There *was* no diagnostic puzzle.

I was, as never before in my career, intensely aware of the patient-physician relationship. It sat there as a tangible entity. I could palpate it on the first visit and feel it grow thereafter. In the one-shot encounter of the in-hospital consultation, everything was stacked in my favor: I walked in with advance billing as "the specialist called in for fever," I established rapport, got the facts from patient and chart, sniffed out clues, examined body fluids, made recommendations—sometimes with dramatic impact on the patient—and sallied out. Raleigh's suicide attempt shook me: I was seeing him for a deadly viral infection for which I had no treatment, and yet here he had almost died before the virus could get him. I had failed to appreciate what he was going through and perhaps underestimated the comfort I could have brought him in spheres of his life unrelated to the virus. In the absence of a magic potion to cure AIDS, my job was to minister to the patient's soul, his psyche, pay attention to his family and his social situation. I would have to make more home visits, make more attempts to understand the person I saw in the clinic, be sure I understood the family dynamics by meeting all its members. Some of this I was already doing as a matter of interest. I would now have to do it out of necessity.

But I would pay a price for this. My training had not really prepared me to be this kind of doctor. We were trained in hospitals, not in patients' homes; we were biased toward technological interventions in the form of drugs and needles; words like the "soul," the "spirit," were considered dirty words. There was no or little payment for the non-technological kind of medicine: hand-holding, family visits, home visits had no billing codes; bronchoscopies, colonoscopies and PAP smears did. For me to practice the folksy kind of medicine that was required would not only cost me monetarily, it came at the expense of time with my family and time for myself.

As if to drive home my isolation and the peculiar medical practice I had created for myself, I saw Doyle, the medical student for whom I served as adviser. He was my last appointment for the day. When we had last sat down, I had suggested he go to a big city to take an elective, to get a feel for what big city medicine was like. He had gone to a big city, but instead of going to the university hospital and medical school, he had chosen to take an elective with a group of three private cardiothoracic surgeons. The men were, according to Doyle, superb technicians, trained by Cooley and other pioneers in the area. They hardly needed a bedside manner: the metaphor of what they did—cracking the chest, stopping the heart, rerouting the plumbing—said everything; it even subserved speech.

Doyle, the medical student, said, "I never saw a single patient awake. And the only operation I saw was Cabbage!" (Coronary Artery Bypass Graft).

"Cabbage after Cabbage after Cabbage. We would be cruising down the highway, me sitting in Dr. S_____'s Ferrari, on our way from Holy Oaks to High Plains Medical and Dr. S_____ would call ahead on his car phone, and by the time we got to the OR and were scrubbed and ready, the patient was asleep, his chest painted and ready to go. Dr.

S_____ would start to crack the chest while I and the physician assistant—who has been with him for sixteen years, and could probably do the whole thing himself—would *scramble* to harvest the veins from each leg. And it was all we could do to get the veins out before he was ready to use them—he was so quick. His partner Dr. B_____ who had finished at another table would join us, and pretty soon Dr. S_____ would leave to go on to the next table while Dr. B_____ bypassed the last artery and me and the PA closed up. Dr. B_____ started a third case, while the third partner Dr. V_____ joined Dr. S_____. And at some point I would be in Dr. B_____'s Mercedes, and he would be calling ahead to Dillard Hospital and the next set of patients was being put to sleep and pretty soon Doctors S_____ and V_____ would show up there."

I asked Doyle about postop care. I pictured rounds at the bedside in the ICU under the banks of monitors and with printouts from the arterial and venous catheters. I pictured exciting discussion of hemodynamics.

"They had these preprinted postop order sheets which covered every exigency. Broad parameters were defined: if the patient's heart rate or temperature or blood pressure was to fall out of that range, then the nurse was to call. If the cardiac output measured by Swan-Ganz catheters fell below this many liters, they were to use dopamine. They were to keep the patient tanked up but the lungs dry by keeping the pulmonary capillary wedge pressure at so many millimeters; any higher than that and they give Lasix, less than that, give saline. For a major problem, the nurse called the physician's assistant who had seen it all. Just for the sake of form, he might call in the cardiologist—never the surgeon. You know there's this phalanx of cardiologists who feed the patients into the surgeons' mill and then take care of the patients for years to come."

I asked again: "So what about postop care, Doyle?" I was thinking of Will Johnson and his Cabbage operation.

"It was kind of like a howdy-doody rounds. We'd circle round the intensive care units, our team of about fifteen people, and the patients would still be out of it from the surgery and would be on a ventilator and with chest tubes coming out of their front and sides. And then we'd prod them—literally prod them to see if they stirred—glance at the numbers on the monitor, the doctor would sign the physician assistant's note, and then the whole team would troop on."

"So how did you like it, Doyle?"

"Are you kidding? I *loved* it!"

God help us!

For Raleigh, for the Johnsons, for all my patients in the HIV clinic, I would have to do a lot more than prod them with a ruler.

17

SEVEN YEARS INTO THE EPIDEMIC, four years after the
virus that causes AIDS was discovered, two years after I saw my first
HIV-infected patient in Johnson City, and I still had no treatment to
offer. Hand-holding, counseling, moral support, platitudes, bromides,
prognostications, homilies. But I had nothing in the way of a remedy.

When an opportunistic infection developed, I reacted: I scrambled to
nail down the cause of the fever, the basis for the opacity on the chest
x-ray, the reason for the seizures or the cluster of sores that had sprung
up around the chest like an encircling belt.

At a Parks and Recreation tennis tournament that week, I had come
up against a powerful kid, hitting with two fists on both sides and
wielding a fat graphite racket that strongly resembled a sledgehammer.
He had me on a long string, had me scrambling from side to side on the
baseline. It was all I could do to get my racket on the ball, keep the ball
in play, get it over the net, make him hit it one more time. But
eventually I would send up a floater or a short ball on which he closed
in, set himself, and then punished me by pounding it into a corner,
sending the chain-link fence into song and ending the point. Without
a new offensive weapon of my own, the next point and the next point
and the next would go the same way. This was how I felt off the tennis
court, in the AIDS arena—I was badly in need of a new weapon.

My townsfolk who had the virus in their bodies were, with the exception of Fred, a reticent, almost fatalistic, lot in comparison to their

counterparts in New York City or San Francisco. Everywhere but in our town, people infected with the virus were chasing down alternative therapies. ACT UP was rattling the gates of the complacent National Institutes of Health, activists were chaining themselves to the portals of the Food and Drug Administration, a thousand shrill voices were refusing to let them carry on with business as usual.

I had assumed that the customs and conventions of monolithic institutions like the NIH, FDA and CDC were carved in stone, handed down from God, not amenable to change. But gay men in the form of ACT UP had done what cancer patients, diabetics, lung disease patients, heart disease patients had never done: they questioned authority and brought about change.

But in our town we simply watched the television spectacle of mass arrests, heard the fiery speeches, saw the five-second newsflash of a bridge being blocked by activists.

My patients, by contrast, were in hiding. They were not inclined to a public demonstration of any sort, scared lest the tragedy of their HIV infection be compounded by their neighbors' knowledge of it. My patients relied on *me* to tell them if a cure was coming, relied on me to tell them that they should be frustrated and angry with the fickleness of Reagan's commitment to AIDS, relied on me to draw the parallel between Nero and Reagan, between the burning of Rome and the continued lack of a firm governmental response to AIDS.

I was their surrogate activist, their link to the larger consciousness of AIDS. They visited regularly, they were punctual like churchgoers, they accepted my prescriptions for "Stress-Tabs-with-Zinc," they swallowed the antidepressants or the appetite stimulants I prescribed, and they went on. Their battle lay largely on the home front: keeping up the appearance of health and hiding the secret of AIDS.

Meanwhile, the five medical journals I subscribed to and the ten other "junk journals" that arrived unsolicited were clogged with papers about AIDS: new manifestations of AIDS, bizarre new twists to existing syndromes like AIDS dementia, colorful and unexpected side effects of the therapy we used for opportunistic infections.

And each journal had the story of the rising numbers, the changing epidemiology: more babies with AIDS, more women with AIDS, many more blood transfusion cases now revealed, more minorities, more intravenous drug users, and more countries with AIDS. I thought of these reports as dispatches from the front reaching me in my war room where I sipped bourbon to calm my nerves. The army was advancing, and every second stolen from the war made me feel guilty.

So far, no one had described the rural experience with AIDS I was seeing: a quietly burgeoning clinic, an intimate primary-care kind of clinic, a clinic with strong resemblances to a secret society with me at its head and the various novitiates and initiates dispersed among the townsfolk, disguised as bakers, shoe repairmen, housewives, priests, waiters, blacksmiths and publicans. We exchanged our looks, our secret signals, in restaurants, in bowling alleys, at chamber music recitals.

What my journals did *not* report was what therapies were currently being tested, and whether any had shown promising results. The journals were, like the NIH and FDA, bound by tradition: they reported only completed research, not work in progress.

And when a study was finally complete enough to meet the rigorous peer review of a journal, it was as a rule preceded by announcements on CBS and CNN and in the *Johnson City Press*. I would spend an embarrassing day fending off Fred and others who called, saying "I don't know," until the journal finally arrived in the mail. When the *Johnson City Press* called to get my reaction to this or that news report on new therapy, I managed never to be in.

WHILE WILL JOHNSON was still in the hospital, I made a quick trip to Los Angeles for a national infectious diseases meeting. I met Stuart Levitz, my friend and former tennis buddy from Boston. One afternoon, we managed to sneak out of the meeting early to play tennis.

Stuart had stayed on at Boston University and University Hospital as a faculty member in infectious diseases. I was surprised to find that I was following a greater number of patients with HIV—close on fifty—than were most of my counterparts in Boston. Yes, the big city hospitals were following hundreds of patients. But since infectious diseases faculty like Stuart had with them a flock of interns, students, residents and fellows, they never personally assumed care for anyone, except perhaps one or two patients in their private clinics.

Meanwhile, at Boston City Hospital across the street, the hematology-oncology division seemed to have taken over much of the AIDS outpatient care with only a few infectious diseases people working with them. But the infectious diseases division was looking to get back in the game: what had previously been a tiresome and taxing burden was now clearly an exciting research opportunity.

In the academic centers of America, the big boys of infectious diseases were divvying up the grant money that was now finally pouring into AIDS from the NIH and elsewhere—money that had come late and was still not enough, but at least it was coming. The money was resulting in career changes, creating institutes of retrovirology overnight, providing salary support for a host of ancillary personnel, creating a major expansion in academic infectious diseases. The solitary physicians who had been providing yeoman service for AIDS with little help, and at the expense of all their other projects, were now finding themselves flush with resources: nurses, social workers, office space, salaries to recruit more physicians.

That evening in L.A., I took part in a panel discussion on pneumonia. At the dinner that followed the meeting, I was seated next to a well-known infectious diseases persona, a chief of infectious diseases at a big city hospital. Every time I saw him he was impeccably dressed: the latest Italian suits, silk ties and thousand-dollar shoes. It was said that no pharmaceutical company would dare launch a new antibiotic compound in North America without getting his endorsement. During my residency and fellowship, I became well versed in his papers and textbook chapters; upon meeting him, I found much to admire in his intellect, his speaking ability, his interpersonal skills and his industry. I was (and still am) slightly in awe of him. Now he was telling several of us of a major grant for AIDS care that his division had received. I was curious to know exactly how he managed to run such a huge AIDS clinic in a big city? What were the logistics? I knew that he was rarely in his office because he was so often on the road, almost an itinerant lecturer. Money for labs, technicians, centrifuges and incubators did not translate into patient care. Who sees the patients? I asked. He lowered his voice and looking around conspiratorially said: "What you have to do is hire 'drones' to do the day-to-day clinical work. You can't possibly be running down from your office to see every clinic patient who shows up on a nonclinic day with high fever or seizures. Your faculty will just burn out. You won't be able to keep them. It's impossible!"

He must have seen the shock on my face because he clammed up and changed the subject. I spared him embarrassment by not pressing him on who these "drones" were. I could well imagine: Indians, Pakistanis, Koreans, Filipinos, Middle Easterners—all doctors with visa problems and the need to remain in a "training" situation till they could make the switch from a J1 visa to an immigrant visa.

In Johnson City, I was providing *all* the care for my fifty patients. I was my own drone. And I was getting very tired. And sometimes very angry.

I CAUGHT the red-eye from Los Angeles and arrived in Johnson City on a Wednesday morning. That afternoon in clinic I saw a new patient, Petie Granger.

Petie Granger had been living in Baltimore for two years, working as a buyer for a clothing company. Six weeks before I saw him, he called his parents to say he had pneumonia that was not getting better. His father and mother raced up to Baltimore, found him very ill in his apartment, and rushed him to a local hospital. He was diagnosed as having *Pneumocystis carinii* pneumonia. His parents held vigil at his bedside, dealt with the certainty now that their son was gay and had AIDS. They nursed him in the hospital round the clock. Petie wanted to move back to Tennessee.

His father and brothers rented a U-Haul and emptied everything from his carefully furnished apartment close to the Chesapeake Bay. As soon as Petie was discharged, his mother took him directly from his hospital bed to a makeshift bed she fashioned in the back of her Ford LTD Wagon, drove him back to the family house in Tennessee, and moved him back into his old room.

In a week, when Petie could walk again, Mrs. Granger went with Petie to her personal doctor. He had taken care of Mrs. Granger for many years in their town; he was a man in whom she had great faith. As will happen in a small town, she was on a first-name basis with the office staff and considered them her friends. She was sure her doctor would take care of Petie or at least serve as the ringmaster and orchestrate his care.

But the doctor sat against the wall in the examining room, putting as much distance as he could between Petie and himself, appearing to try not to breathe if he could possibly help it. Suddenly, the years of their relationship as patient and physician, the Virginia smoked ham she sent over every Christmas, none of this seemed to exist. He told her stiffly that he had no experience with this disease. He offered no suggestions as to who else they could see. Conversation came to a standstill until Mrs. Granger understood that she was expected to leave. The office staff had vanished. All the doors of the doctor's office had been left conveniently open for them so that neither Mrs. Granger nor Petie would need to touch a doorknob on the way out.

After that they kept looking for a physician, going systematically through the Yellow Pages in their town and neighboring towns, candidly explaining what it was Petie had. They could not get an appointment.

Meanwhile, Petie had developed a perianal abscess that had become acutely inflamed. His father took him to see a surgeon, a man who had treated the father for two hernias and an ulcer operation and whom the father considered a friend, a fellow lodge member.

"They treated Petie like dirt, and made me feel like dirt for being with Petie," the father related to me.

The surgeon, a little more venturesome than the internist, did examine Petie perfunctorily: he had Petie spread his buttock cheeks while he peeked. Still, he apparently felt no need to use his gloved hand to palpate the area, though he wore the gloves throughout the interview. Instead, he prescribed antibiotics and referred Petie to another internist in a town fifty-five miles from Petie's hometown. But he also had a reason why Petie could not be seen.

When I finally saw Petie and his mother in my office, seventy-five miles from their home, there was an expression of fear on their faces, as though they expected to be kicked out any minute. They had reached the point where they had contemplated moving back to Baltimore with Petie so as to get *some* kind of care. It took several visits before they began to believe that they had a *right* to medical care. The family had been made to feel like pariahs because of the disease that affected their son.

I gave Petie and his mother the one thing the family wanted most: a promise to take care of him in the months to come, no matter what happened. The fact that I had no therapy directed against HIV to offer him was almost unimportant.

BUT IT WAS IMPORTANT to me. I was tired of being a watchdog for the town, seeing the disease trickle in. And despite my medical journals, I was in an informational black hole in Johnson City.

I missed out on the scuttlebutt about who was doing what in AIDS research, the kind of thing that you could pick up every week in a city like Boston with three medical schools and over ten major teaching hospitals and many combined conferences and exchange of speakers. In 1985, when I was a fellow in infectious diseases in Boston, I heard Max Essex from the Harvard School of Public Health lecture to a small group of us at Boston City Hospital and state unequivocally that he was sure a retrovirus would turn out to be the cause of AIDS. This was before Gallo and Montagnier proved that to be the case.

I took my cue from my patient, Fred Goodson. I began to subscribe to publications like the PWA (Persons with AIDS) Health Group Newsletter, AIDS Treatment News and the GMHC (Gay Men's Health Crisis) Newsletter of Experimental Therapies.

Vitamin C—doses up to 70 grams per day!—was one therapy being advocated. As many of the initial proponents of this treatment died, so did its popularity. But I added reasonable doses of vitamin C to what I recommended on the first visit. It gave me satisfaction to write a prescription for something—anything.

Then there was DNCB, a benzene-derived chemical which when placed on the skin could induce a response of the cell-mediated or CD4-lymphocyte-mediated wing of the immune system. A dermatologist in San Francisco had reported promising results with DNCB: the CD4 count had shown a small blip in an upward direction. The chemical was available in photo supply shops, and pretty soon guerrilla clinics were preparing and administering this drug to gay men. These were forerunners of the buyers' clubs that would undercut regional pharmacies. DNCB was also the first illicit drug to make it to Johnson City. Both Fred and, later, Otis showed me the dark patches on their skin where they had tried DNCB. When clinical centers began testing Isoprinosine and ribavirin—two new antiviral drugs—a black market in these drugs began, the drugs being smuggled in from Mexico. But the clinical trials concluded that the drugs were of no use.

Among the many drugs being tested against the virus in test tubes and in small open-labeled trials, one called AZT was getting a lot of press. In the preceding year—September of 1986—a placebo-controlled trial of this drug, a study involving many different universities in the United States, had been stopped prematurely. The agency that monitored the study found that after six weeks on the drug, persons getting placebo were dying of opportunistic infections at a much higher rate when compared with those getting AZT. The trial was halted because it was considered unethical to go on giving people placebo. The results of the trial had not as yet been published, but even so, in January 1987, an FDA advisory panel recommended to the FDA that the drug be approved for marketing for use only by HIV-infected persons who fulfilled the definition of AIDS. The Burroughs-Wellcome Company, just down the pike from us in Research Triangle Park, estimated that even if the drug was approved, it might be May before they had enough drug to supply patients who qualified to receive it.

After so many false hopes, I tried to remain skeptical. But it did seem at last that there was a treatment out there that held promise.

Duke University was one of the centers that had participated in the initial AZT trial. It was reportedly also involved in the next phase of the AZT trials: seeing if the drug would work in persons who did not yet have full-blown AIDS but instead were relatively asymptomatic though with CD4 counts less than 500. Duke was only five hours away, a neighbor of Burroughs-Wellcome.

I was most concerned about Otis Jackson, Fred's partner. Where Fred had much energy and had become an activist, Otis seemed to be fading. Each time I saw him he appeared a little more passive, a little flatter in his affect, almost as if the disease was happening to someone else and not to him. When they came to visit, Fred had to prompt Otis to tell me about the night sweats, the weight loss. And when he still did not mention them, Fred would sigh, then pull out a paper, and recite for me his observations of the last few weeks: fever, diminished appetite, strange dreams from which Otis woke up having drenched the sheets. I thought it was urgent that Otis get on a trial.

I called Fred's house but got no reply. I sat down with Carol and we made up a roster of patients we would call. Over the next two weeks I would set up appointments to see every patient I was following and suggest they consider going to Duke to see if they could be enrolled in an AZT trial. If they had full-blown AIDS they would immediately qualify for the drug. If they did not, they still might qualify. I would make appointments for them and put together a copy of their medical records. It was a bittersweet moment for Carol and me.

LATER THAT DAY, I ran into Bettie Lee, Fred's sister, who had come to see my secretary Joyce to drop off more TAP brochures. She told me that Fred had gone down to Knoxville with Otis to see friends. I told her about AZT and Duke University and how I felt Fred and Otis ought to try to get on a clinical trial.

"God! Fred is going to love it! When Fred and Otis found out they were infected—just before they came to see you—the *first* thing out of Fred's mouth was that he was going to beat it. I remember he was talking a mile a minute, it was really bizarre. He just went on and on: He was going to find out everything there was to know about it, find out every treatment that was being tried. *By* God, he was going to beat it, and on and on . . . Maybe this is it."

"And what did Otis say when he found out?"

"Otis just looked at Fred. He never said a word. Otis had this hang-dog expression on his face, kind of like he knew it was all over. He wasn't even sad. Just subdued, without any hope. A condemned man."

This was the first time I had been alone with Bettie Lee. When she and Fred were together it was easy to see they were brother and sister. Bettie Lee was heavyset, with dark hair parted in the middle, a slight lisp, and a beautiful, musical voice. Her manner and dress—loose tie-dye shirts or batik smocks, sandals, a paucity of makeup—made her look like a sixties flower child. Her AIDS activism lacked the militant, confrontational edge that Fred's could take. Her style was more earthy, more gentle, but every bit as committed as Fred's. She tended to make things happen by cajoling and persuasion, whereas Fred might have invoked *Robert's Rules of Order*. The content of her speech had the occasional allusions to Nietzsche and Kierkegaard—she had a degree in psychology—but these names tended to be invoked with wonder, as part of a reflective statement, not as part of a high-toned rhetoric. I was intrigued at how devoted she and Fred were to each other and yet how different they were in personality. I asked her about Fred as a child; I asked her when she first knew he was gay.

"The first time I knew Fred was gay? I was sixteen and a girlfriend came to me and told me that Fred was gay—he was twenty-two at the time. I sort of went 'Ah-hah!' to myself. *That's* why he didn't do anything with June and Sarah and anyone else. And after that, once I knew, we became closer. I guess I let him know that I knew. It was a time when everyone was smoking pot and so we'd go and do it together."

"What stopped you from being condemning of that lifestyle?"

"My father has always been really open. We had this huge house that his father had left him—the family was real old Morristown stock. He really believed people were different and there was no need for everyone to subscribe to the same doctrines. My father had black friends from way back. And when there were a group of Cuban doctors at the Greene Valley Development Center—still are—he was always having them over for dinner and cookouts. Our house was the house where all the teenagers gathered because my parents were 'cool.' So, I guess when I found out about Fred, I was cool. Which is not to say that my parents, when he told them, were cool. But they learned to accept it."

I asked Bettie Lee at what point she had become aware of AIDS.

"I guess it was 1983, when he moved back for good to Morristown and began with the accounting business. I got to spend a lot more time with him. I was married and divorced by then—got married in high school—and I lived in Johnson City. I think it was when Rock Hudson died that I *really* became aware of it. . . . Now that I think of it, Fred had mentioned 'gay cancer' before that. Said it in his usual, semicynical way—you know how he is. I didn't know if he was joking or what. I asked him if he was concerned—he said no, it's just in the big cities.

"But there is one incident I always hark back to: it was in 1983, me and my girlfriend met up with Fred and one of his friends in Kitty Hawk, on the Outer Banks—North Carolina. You been there? Well, anyway, Fred and his friend met us there after they had visited New York City. And I remember them laughing and mentioning the bathhouses, and I was thinking to myself—why would they want to do that?

Go to New York City? Undoubtedly have anonymous sex. Isn't it dangerous?"

Bettie Lee paused as if something was occurring to her.

"You know this was a time of lots of excesses. I mean alcohol, drugs, partying—not just sex. And as I think about it, it was there, at Kitty Hawk, on the Outer Banks, that he brought up gay cancer! And I always look back at that trip to New York as where he got it.

"He told me right after he got his test. Came to our house. By then I was married again. Fred and Otis had been living together for about a year by then. They both came up to the house, sat around my kitchen table, just up and told me: 'We tested positive for the AIDS virus!' I was so shocked! Total disbelief! Didn't know what was going to happen next. And how could it happen here? Not *here*, in east Tennessee!

"I remember I kept trying to find someplace to put the blame. I blamed Otis, to tell you the truth. After all, Fred had been back for some time now. It was *Otis* who had been living in San Francisco and had just moved back. This is horrible—but I even wondered whether Otis had come back from San Francisco *because* he was sick! Could he have been looking for a relationship where someone would take care of him? When I was more rational, I blamed Fred's trip to New York just before he came to Kitty Hawk."

"Did you worry about your risk?"

"That really wasn't on my mind at the time. And when Fred told me about his test, he also pretty much told me all that he knew about the disease—and he knew a lot. Told me that I wasn't at risk, told me how it was spread. But he wanted me to go and get tested. Even that, I think, was not so much for me, but for him to use; to be able to say later, 'Look, I've been close to my sister and nothing has ever happened to her.' I got tested and was negative and I've never tested again—don't think I need to.

"But I remember one time, when Otis was ill, bringing Otis's clothes home to wash and suddenly starting to think if this was smart. My son, Bill, was a year old. But I got over it just by talking myself through it.

"I've never been one to drink after someone, you know, out of their cup. Just plain unhygienic. The first time Fred and I shared a Coke or else shared a cigarette, it was a little spooky. Since then I've done that with Fred several times, even though I wouldn't normally. I do it *just* to make a point with people we are around, particularly at TAP."

I SAT DOWN WITH Fred and Otis in the clinic the next day.

"Look," I said, "for the first time there is a drug out there for HIV that shows promise. But it may be a long time before it makes its way to my hands, and even when I am allowed to prescribe it, it will probably be restricted to those with full-blown AIDS and neither of you would qualify. If I were you, and if I were pulling out all stops in trying to fight this, I would go to Duke and see if I could be enrolled in their AZT studies on early HIV infection. I will be happy to give you a letter and forward all the records they need."

Fred stood up ready to leave almost as soon as the words left my mouth. As if he was going to drive straight to Durham. Otis slouched on the stool and asked, "Well, how do we know if this drug doesn't wind up hurting me?" and a number of other "What if?" questions. When Otis walked out, it was with drooping shoulders, as if he didn't need this hassle. As if I had given him bad news.

Fred came by the next day to pick up his and Otis's records. I sensed from Fred's mood that Otis remained reluctant, fatalistic. I asked about Otis.

"Otis is Otis. You know how he is."

"That's the point. I don't really know Otis too well. I've never seen him alone and he's never ever had much to say."

Fred's manner softened. I think he felt he needed to explain Otis to me, or at least explain why Otis was his partner.

"Otis is different. He's tricky to understand, but don't hold it against him. See, Otis is real country, not as sophisticated as he appears. He left home years ago. I think his leaving was precipitated by his family finding some letters between him and a male lover. All hell broke loose with that. His whole residence in California, in the Castro, was all about estrangement from his family. He lived there for seven years—1978 to 1985. Otis, like many gay men, has inherited such a burden of guilt that it tends to make him pessimistic, negative—almost as if he's more comfortable with bad stuff happening to him than good stuff."

I couldn't help reflecting that Otis had been in the Castro—1978 to 1985—at the height of the silent spread of the virus through the gay community there. Otis had probably celebrated Gay Pride Week, been on the same dance floor with Gaetan Dugas—*Patient Zero*. It was not beyond the realm of the possible to imagine that Otis had slept with the Air Canada flight steward, or slept with someone who had slept with Gaetan, or . . .

"Did you meet him in San Francisco?"

"Oh no. I had been there, even spent a month there, and we've talked about how we must have crossed paths. But no, I met him back here. I'm not sure exactly what Otis was up to in the Castro. I know he got shingles when he was there. And I think what precipitated his leaving was that a relationship ended and left him without a place to stay. So back he came to east Tennessee. And when he first came back, though he never told me any of this, he was down with severe shingles for six months. It came again and again on his chest. We met in 1986 through a friend. By then he was healthy again. In fact the first time we met, we, *harrumph*, hit it off quite well, I must say. . . . For a while we dated, then we finally moved in together."

"Did you practice safe sex when you met?"

"We both *ignored* safe sex. We were both in denial. Otis didn't tell me he'd been sick. But then, *I* didn't tell him I had been to bathhouses in New York or Atlanta. I didn't have to tell him—he probably assumed it about me just as I assumed it about him."

Fred paused here and his voice became very soft: "That was one of the major reasons for my joining TAP, for my spending time I don't have working with TAP. I want us to hold ourselves out as examples if necessary. Before I was diagnosed, I felt immune; my denial was very strong. You can talk yourself into anything in the interest of sexual release."

MEANWHILE, back in the hospital, Will Johnson was marginally better. He still had pain when he swallowed. But his fever was gone and he had regained five pounds.

I was spending a long time in his room each day—it was almost impossible to be in and out in less than an hour. I took to visiting him in the evening when I had finished seeing all my other patients.

Each time I walked in he perked up, made room for me on his bed and asked me to tell him how my day had gone. He focused his attention on what I was saying as if it was the most important thing in the world. I found myself describing to him my problems: the pull between the VA and this private consultative practice at the Miracle Center. The long hours. The effort to publish and to bring in grant money to keep my technician and lab going. The young family I had at home. My presence in his room was part of the stress on my marriage: AIDS had become a mistress that took me away from home and that I could not introduce in conversation when I *was* at home.

At times Will drew parallels between things I told him about my job and its politics and "the firm" as he referred to his company. I had the uncanny feeling during my visits with him that *he* was ministering to *me*. He had come to understand my sense of impotence when it came to his symptoms; he knew there was little more I could do. And yet, even though I thought his lack of a clinical response indicated imminent death, he was certain that he still had a long time.

This was the great mystery to me: Here was a man infected with a deadly virus, a virus that his wife had now contracted, a man living in pain with death staring at him, a man hiding the enormous secret of his infection from his children and his social circle, and yet he had more equanimity than I had, more courage and self-assurance than I—a younger, uninfected professional—could muster. It was this that kept me in his room so long: I wanted to explore and understand the roots of his character, the wellspring of his integrity. Here was a man and a marriage that I would shamelessly copy if I only knew its ingredients.

He made a cryptic comment to me when I asked him if he didn't mind us doing a few more tests; could he bear our medical inquisitiveness a little longer? "Any man that can survive the Rat Line at VMI can handle anything in life." When I looked puzzled he said:

"Virginia Military Institute. It is the West Point of the South. Only better. When you land up there that first year you are a 'Rat.' You walk around with your chin tucked into your chest like this, you cut square corners, and you sit and eat staring straight ahead at full attention. And any time a senior sees you walking the Rat Line he can stop you and ask you to recite from the Rat Bible. It's living hell."

Square corners? Rat Bible? Rat Line? He had lost me.

"The Rat line is literally a line that all Rats have to walk on whenever they are moving around the barracks. And when you come to a corner you make a ninety-degree turn—a square corner. And the Rat Bible is a book that the Rat has to memorize: it's ninety pages long and seniors stop you twenty times a day and ask you things like, 'Who were the ten cadets killed in the Battle of New Market?' or 'Describe the inscription on the parapet' or 'Who are the ten members of the Honor Court?' or 'What's Natural Bridge worth?' "

Will Johnson had a glint in his eye and he leaned forward and said, "Try that question, Abraham: What's Natural Bridge worth?"

I knew Natural Bridge was one of the wonders of the world located somewhere in Virginia. But what was it worth? "It's priceless," I said.

"Nice try, but if you were a Rat you would be doing fifty push-ups now because you hadn't read the Rat Bible! The correct answer is, *Natural Bridge is well worth a visit by every cadet, sir!*"

He laughed delightedly. For a moment AIDS and esophageal disease were forgotten.

"It's on page 40 of the Rat Bible: 215 feet high, 100 feet wide, and spans a depth of 90 feet. Well worth a visit."

On Bess's next trip back to the house to check on mail she packed Will's VMI yearbook and some photograph albums. As soon as I walked into the room, Will patted the mattress next to him and pulled out his yearbook. VMI was in scenic Lexington, Virginia, in the foothills of the Blue Ridge Mountains. The institute was steeped in Confederate history—one early, somewhat eccentric, professor of physics was none other than Stonewall Jackson. In the coming year, VMI would celebrate its two hundred and fiftieth anniversary.

Will Johnson watched me with twinkling eyes as I turned the pages and saw the towering barracks made of light-brown stone with turrets on the top. The barracks dominated the campus. There were other photographs showing magnificent archways and long corridors—plenty of square corners. There were lush green parade grounds reminiscent of Mountain Home. And the glitter of parade uniforms that seemed to owe something in the gray tones to the Confederate uniform. I lingered over one photograph: An upper classman had his nose pushed against a Rat's face and appeared to be screaming at him; there was mortal terror in the Rat's eyes, as if in the next second he would faint or cry. I looked up at Will and he nodded at me, as if to say, yes, it was every bit as bad as that.

From the yearbook it was clear that Will Johnson had been an out-standing cadet: He rose to be the commander of one of the four com-panies that made up VMI; he was one of the ten members of the honor court. I was beginning to understand something about the construction of his character.

"The Rat year was the worst time in my life; but my four years there were also the best time of my life. It gave me a standard for how I was to conduct myself. It mattered nothing at all who you were when you came there. My daddy was a coal miner. Others had fathers who were senators. But every outward thing that defined you was stripped away and you had to find inner strength. Words like honor, honesty, self-discipline—these can mean nothing in the outside world, but they take on a new meaning there. And I have no firmer friends in the world than my Brother Rats. I kid you not, they would die for me."

"Have you told any of them?" I had broken the spell. It was a line we had not as yet crossed, the issue of secrecy.

He shook his head.

I plunged ahead. I said, "It's such a lonely business to carry this burden alone. Your children would help, your Brother Rats can help. Your church members will stand by you."

Will Johnson shook his head and smiled indulgently. "If anyone in our community knows, then the next time Bess and I go to church there will be no one there. It will be an empty church."

For once I thought he was wrong. I told him about Gordon, and how Essie and her family had the support of just about everyone in their church. How the community had rallied around the family, how Gor-don had been baptized in the church, cared for by neighbors and friends, how the whole community had shown up for the funeral of this prodigal. Will smiled: it was a nice tale but he was quite unconvinced.

"I worry about Bess," he said. "After I die, I don't want her to face the stigma of AIDS. We have no idea how our children will react to this. We have every reason to think they will support us, but we don't know that for *sure*. How will our daughter's husband feel about us being with their children, our grandchildren? We know—we researched this very carefully—that we are no risk to the children. But why take the chance that they may not see it this way?"

I looked at Bess. There were tears streaming down her cheeks as Will talked candidly about his death. Was the decision to keep this secret to themselves something that Will Johnson had unilaterally decided and that she had gone along with? Had he sought her counsel? Or had he talked her into his vision of how things should be?

"See, Abraham, I also have to worry about the firm, the possible ramifications of this on my partners, the unreasoned responses of people who hear about our plight."

At one level I was disappointed. If they were "innocent" victims, the sort that I and everyone I knew could easily identify with, then their testimony could be so powerful, so valuable in dispelling certain myths about AIDS. *They* believed the ugly metaphors of AIDS: AIDS = gay, AIDS = sin. *They* could not get past what it seemed to imply about lifestyle and morality. The metaphor was to them larger than their standing in church and community. But I felt that they far outclassed the metaphor; who they were could never be tainted by a virus. It was a curious paradox in Will Johnson that he did not see this; it was a blind spot in his view of the world.

I was in a minority, however. Dr. Sarah Presnell advocated secrecy. The few people they took into their confidence advised secrecy.

To the degree that Will and Bess needed all their mental and physical strengths to combat this disease, it seemed a shame for them to expend such prodigious amounts of energy in keeping up the veneer of secrecy. How much more painful it was to bear this all alone. How much effort was involved in making their way, just the two of them, to this faraway hospital, having only each other for comfort and support.

He seemed to be reading my mind. "Abraham, I don't think you understand. We are *not* alone. The one unshakable presence in our life is Christ. I personally think this thing, this virus, is from hell, from the devil himself. It is not from God. Nor do I believe God 'let it happen.' See, Bess told me about the strange-looking individual who preceded her into your office the day she came to see you."

Bess blushed; I knew Will was referring to Raleigh.

"I would never understand an individual like that. But I would never, ever condemn him either. I don't think any human being deserves this curse, and it is certainly not *from* God. My God is not a vengeful God. I surely don't understand the why of AIDS, but I'm convinced this is an evil onslaught from hell—a test, if you will—and I'm determined with the help and strength of Jesus Christ, I will pass this test. It matters not so much what happens to us as how we deal with it. And we'll never be given to endure more than we can bear."

I had the sense that this last phrase was something he had repeated many times before, it was his creed. He said it almost as he would say a mantra or a prayer.

"When we were driving back from Sarah's office and she had given us the terrible news—and by the way, we went on to see the high school football game we set out to see that evening; we had made an instant decision that we would conduct our outward lives as if nothing had changed—the *first* thing that came to my mind was Jesus Christ. He died an agonizing and disgraceful death in the eyes of the people around Him and He didn't deserve it. He had healed people with leprosy—the AIDS of His time. I knew that He'd know what I'd be going through all the way. From that night on and every night since, most of my prayers have been to Him. He has always answered and has comforted me. There have been several times when He's interceded and helped me. His mercy is great."

I was staring at him, speechless. Perhaps *this* was the element that distinguished us, made my life so different from his. My faith was vague, and not mediated by church or sect. In whatever way I saw God, I rarely saw him in the concrete terms that Will was describing: a protector, an immediate presence.

"I'm determined to fight this thing with all I have and by Christ's constant help. Meanwhile I'll make what contribution I can as a husband, father and grandfather. And for the firm. As long as I can think and move and breathe."

He chuckled here, and shifted position in the bed. "Oh, it will get me eventually, but only after a fight. I'll never give in or quit. Never, never, never."

Bess was weeping silently; she had moved from the recliner to sit next to him, on the other side of the bed from me, to kiss his hand. He held her but he continued, dry-eyed:

"I've grown closer to God and learned much about living each day at a time." He was looking into Bess's eyes but speaking to me. "Bess and I have grown closer to each other. She is the most magnificent woman I know. She has been the same all the time, smiling, supportive, cheerful, loving, uncomplaining. No one can ever imagine the greatness of this woman. She's in my life by the grace and through the love of God Himself. She's been dealt a bad hand but she is making her life a triumph over it."

Bess was overcome now, sobbing heartrending sobs. Will and I were crying, too. We sat like that on the bed, the three of us, holding hands.

When Bess left for the bathroom to compose herself, Will leaned forward and put his hand on my shoulder as if I were his son. He drew me to him and said to me softly, "You know I've lost all libido. I have become impotent. What once was an act of love, of joy, an act of life, has become an act of death for me. It holds nothing other than horror for me." He shuddered and looked out of the window.

A SHORT TIME LATER I stumbled out of their room, hoping no one would see my red eyes. I took the back stairwell down to the parking lot.

I drove back to Mountain Home but I was not ready to go home as yet. I parked near the bandstand. Long-distance truckers will often, on their return, sleep at the truck depot and only then shower and go home. I felt the same way: I wanted to sort out my emotions, expunge the anguish that sat heavily in me, weep for the Johnsons and all the rest of us caught up in this viral visitation from hell. When I eventually entered the house and picked up Steven and Jacob, I wanted to be able to give them the same all-consuming attention that Will Johnson gave me in his room.

In my car I had a pair of tennis shoes and shorts. I changed in the cockpit of the Datsun Z, an exercise in itself. I have never been much of a jogger—once a week is all I can stand. The thing that motivated me was the beauty of the jogging trail that circled the VA. That and the desire to optimize my tennis game, make up with quickness and finesse what I lacked in raw power.

I stretched against a lamppost next to the bandstand. It was not yet dusk but the lamp was on. The lamppost was dull green. From a thick base it tapered upward and then blossomed into an old-fashioned carriage lamp with opaque glass shutters and a metal crown. At one time this had been a gas lamp. When the first generator arrived at Mountain Home, the lamp was carefully converted to hold an electric bulb

I climbed onto the bandstand. From here one could appreciate how

Mountain Home had once been a plateau of fallow farmland surrounded by a thick forest of pine and maple with a mountain stream
coursing through it. The monotony of the land was broken up by
shallow ravines, scattered woods, small rounded peaks, rock formations.
The Great Smoky Mountains were a perfect backdrop for it all. The
architect's challenge had been to take this land and design clusters of
buildings on it of different functions but all of which were to be one
homogeneous organism that in turn was a part of the landscape, barely
disturbing it, only enhancing it. I couldn't imagine anything other than
the French Renaissance buildings of Mountain Home being on this
land; they appeared to have grown out of the land just as the magnolias
and the oak trees had.

The flag fluttered on the flagpole above me. The vast lawn over
which the bandstand looked could accommodate five softball teams and
any number of Frisbee players. It was a tempting place to fly a kite. But
a steady wind which came up from the pond and swept up to the
hospital meant a high kite mortality. I was always climbing the giant oak
tree in front of my house to retrieve other people's kites that had strayed.
Steven and I had thus built a small kite collection in our basement. We
fixed the kites up, doctored them with our colors to conceal their
origins, and went to my choice spot on a little rise by the back gate, the
perfect place to launch a kite and have it soar safely over Mountain
Home.

I jogged down to the duck pond and started my circuit there. A few
old veterans had their lines in the water. Sometimes I wondered whether
there was a hook, let alone bait, at the end of the line. They did not
appear to have the energy to wrestle a fish to land. The ducks were
having a quiet convention on the bank. They were an aggressive lot and
sometimes a goose would come after you if you jogged too close. Once
or twice a year I would see two or three magnificent Canada geese
swimming in the pond, having picked Mountain Home for a refueling
stop. The next time I came by they would be gone, having resumed
their long voyage.

I ran parallel to the railway track on the edge of the property. A
lumber yard in the adjacent property gave off the smell of fresh oak and
sawdust. I turned up, past the cranes and the new hospital construction

and into the forest, coming out near the main gate and the cemetery. The cemetery had old gravestones of Spanish-American War Veterans in a circle known as the "silent circle." All the newer tombstones were laid flat into the ground, slightly recessed so that the big mower could run over them without damaging them and still keep the lawn perfectly groomed.

I turned at the Mountain Home post office and went down a long hill, the squirrels looking at me, annoyed, as I made crashing sounds on the dry leaves underfoot. I was now at the back gate to the Miracle Center, and I ran the long half-mile stretch of wire fence that separated the Miracle Center from Mountain Home.

I made a square corner at the southern boundary of the VA and ran parallel to the railway track. Soon I was back at the bandstand. The flower beds around the bandstand were a red, white and blue display of cannas in the center with sage, dusty miller and ageratum around the edges.

I watched the sun go down. I felt more at peace with myself. The bell rang in the clock tower of the domiciliary canteen. From all over the darkening campus, veterans rose from benches, rose from the lawns, rose from their balcony chairs, rose from the duck pond packing away their rods, and heeded the call to supper.

THE NEXT DAY, Will had a surprise for me. And I had one for him.

"Abraham, last night I had a vision of Jesus Christ." He searched my face carefully for skepticism, disbelief, but I did not react. "I had a vision of the devil emerging from the television—the set was off. I called out to Jesus. I was scared. And I saw the devil driven away, and the next thing I know, I felt Jesus come out of this cloud near the foot of my bed and take me by the hand and assure me that He would be fighting for me."

I was speechless. This was the second time a vision of Jesus had occurred in the hospital. I tried to recollect whether Gordon had seen Jesus in the same room.

"I think I'm ready to go home, Abraham."

I was pleased to let Will go home. We had little more to offer him. The mysterious ulcers in his esophagus seemed to trouble him less, though they were still there.

I asked him now how he felt about Duke, about the possibility of being enrolled in an AZT trial there.

He pondered the question for no less than a full minute before he answered.

"I have a hang-up about Duke. You know I wrote to them when I learned they discharged me with an undiagnosed broken back? They didn't answer my letter. If I look at my experience with them," and now he held out the fingers of his hand, "one, the 'normal' cardiac checkup when my stress test at home was abnormal; two, giving me blood transfusions but not warning me that as much blood as I received I might have been at risk for AIDS so at least I could have spared Bess; three, missing the broken back—there is a consistent pattern of poor professional care in my opinion. One of my biggest challenges has been to handle my rage. But I *must* control my rage. And I have succeeded in this fairly well, too. I would do myself considerable damage if I went on a rampage against them—in court or elsewhere—just to punish."

At one level I felt sorry for Duke; most of us at one time or other had trained in large referral centers like Duke. We had referred in our notes to rural physicians who sent patients to us as "LMDs": local medical doctors. Now I was an LMD and from my vantage point I could see how a large institution like that could appear impersonal and uncaring.

"I don't need the money, Abraham. I feel also from the spiritual standpoint I have to find a way to forgive the culprits. Besides, I don't wish to spend the rest of my life in court seeking a judgment I might well not live to receive."

I suggested to Mr. Johnson that we had a duty to let Duke know what had happened. It was possible that they had other patients who had been transfused that they needed to track down. I looked at Bess; we were both thinking about the family from Kentucky that she had befriended and that she had briefly corresponded with.

I said, "Perhaps they will feel obliged to try to give you priority into an AZT trial. Even though Mrs. Johnson is asymptomatic, she too might be a candidate for experimental therapy."

After a long pause during which he put his hands behind his head and stared out of the window, he said, "Abraham, *you* write to them. I don't want to deal directly with them. And if they want to treat me, let me know."

With that, one of the most remarkable couples I had ever met left for home after a two-week hospital stay that was unremarkable but for a weight gain of seven pounds and a vision of Christ.

I WROTE TO Duke University outlining the relevant facts:

". . . Sometime during his hospital stay, immediately postsurgery, he received several blood transfusions and within four to five weeks developed a syndrome consistent with acute HIV infection and subsequently has developed lymphadenopathy that is consistent with the AIDS-related complex. In addition it appears his wife has become an asymptomatic carrier. There is no reason to believe that Mr. Johnson acquired this infection in any other way than by the blood transfusion during the course of his hospitalization at Duke University Medical Center.

"He has asked me to write this letter to you because he and I both feel it is important that you are aware of this tragic occurrence. If it is possible to trace the blood transfusions that were suspect and perhaps see if other individuals have been infected and perhaps are unaware of it, this also may be very important. Despite this tragedy, Mr. Johnson bears no rancor against Duke or the physicians taking care of him. He has been able to forgive and to accept his illness. His purpose in having me write is, first, because he and I both feel that if there are any new modalities of therapy that might be tested at a large university center like Duke, perhaps Mr. Johnson should be one of the first to be allowed to receive such therapy. . . ."

The response was prompt and concerned. I had letters from the cardiac surgeons and the cardiologist. It appeared that Will Johnson had a bleeding disorder; this was why he had required so much blood. I had a phone call from the Chief of Infectious Diseases at Duke University, David Durack, who was a respected expert on AIDS. He expressed his dismay at what had occurred and asked that the Johnsons be scheduled to come to the Duke HIV clinic as soon as possible. He personally would see them.

If by some chance Will had returned to Duke when he had the "viral" illness a few weeks after his surgery, and if he had been referred to Durack, in all likelihood his illness would have been diagnosed for what it was.

I conveyed the news to the Johnsons back in their home in Kentucky. From that point on, they were once again under the care of Duke, though I had frequent bulletins about them.

IN JULY OF 1987, the AZT study was finally published in the *New England Journal of Medicine*. The study findings were dramatic: 145 subjects received AZT and 137 received placebo. When the study was terminated, 19 persons had died in the placebo group and only 1 in the study group. Opportunistic infections developed in twice as many patients receiving placebo as those receiving AZT. A rise in CD4 cells was seen in the AZT group.

Here at last was the breakthrough we had waited for! There were limitations to AZT availability: It was restricted to persons who fulfilled the definition of AIDS; about half the patients who were eligible did not tolerate the drug in the doses suggested; it would cost a patient $8,000 to $10,000 a year; it was still cumbersome to procure. It was no cure, but it was the only show in town.

Along with this breakthrough there appeared a number of other new innovations: It was possible now to prevent *Pneumocystis carinii* pneumonia either by administering an aerosol of pentamidine every two weeks or by giving the patient oral Bactrim every day. The studies to prove this were not yet out, but it had become common practice in AIDS clinics all over the country. And a drug called ganciclovir was now available to treat the dreaded onset of blindness in AIDS caused by CMV retinitis. Our ability to treat *Candida* infections was improving with the use of ketoconazole; a drug called fluconazole, which was effective against *Cryptococcus* (the kind of meningitis that Scotty Daws had), promised to be available shortly.

I felt suddenly empowered. Not only did I have a drug for my full-blown AIDS patients, I had a feeling that soon AZT would be indicated for asymptomatic individuals and might prolong life. There appeared to be other antiviral agents on the horizon.

My read of the tea leaves was that we had turned a corner in AIDS: we might now convert it from a fatal disease to a chronic disease, a chronic disease to which the patient would eventually succumb but in the interim might live a useful and productive life.

18

IN THE FALL, the mountains of Tennessee glowed like molten lava in every direction. Pine needles crackled underfoot and stuck to the carpet in our house, bringing their scent within. Every day a cluster of leaves collected in the niche between the windshield and the bonnet of my car. The leaves were so brittle that they snapped and popped in my fingers when I tried to lift them out intact.

At Mountain Home, the lawns were covered with a fiery carpet of leaves. They were plastered against the wire fence, caught like fish in a net, until the VA groundskeepers came and picked the fence clean.

The giant oak tree near the old skating pond stood unshakable. Every year it grew more familiar. When I went jogging, I began at this oak tree, stretching my calf muscles while leaning against it. Where once low branches had extended out, there were now big hollows. If no one was around, I wrapped my arms around its trunk and hugged it like an old friend, breathed in its fragrance, felt the reassuring scrape of bark against my skin. With the flesh of my arms joined to the tree, my feet between its knobby roots, I felt connected to Mountain Home, to my adopted country, to the earth. I wanted to stop time.

But despite its placid veneer, the VA was abuzz with change. Rumor had it that we were slated not only for the construction of "bed towers" but also for the construction of a new nursing home and domiciliary. Change had also come about in the form of new faculty recruits. Two of my former fellow residents had returned to Mountain Home as junior faculty after completing fellowships in hematology and oncology. We who had stalked these hallways at all hours, dressed in scrub suits, now watched others ruling the hospital during the night's quiet hours. In the corridors we exchanged secret smiles, thought about how once we had plotted revolution, had considered blowing up the radiology department to inject some life into that sluggish section.

Every subspecialty division was adding new members. Steve and I were recruiting for an additional infectious diseases faculty member. We found Felix Sarubbi, an academician who had been on the faculty at the University of North Carolina at Chapel Hill before joining the Asheville VA. He was well published—a true scholar—and was well known in academic infectious diseases circles.

Fil plunged right into the business of infectious disease consultation at the VA and Miracle Center. For a while, my workload was divided in half: Fil rounded at the Miracle Center and saw consults there for a week while I covered the VA. The next week we reversed roles. Fil scheduled a half-day clinic of his own at the University Practice Group and began not only to see new HIV-infected persons, but also to get to know some of my old patients in follow-up.

I could not imagine such luxury. There was one week when I played tennis every day, clocking out of the VA at 4 P.M. like everyone else.

But the workload was decreased for only a short while. Soon we were seeing twice the number of consults from the Miracle Center; there was a perception that since there were two of us we could handle more. There were more calls from Northside Hospital. And HIV patients were now coming from far and wide; we each saw at least one or two new patients a week. Now that we were using AZT, with its propensity to cause anemia, we had to follow blood counts closely. As a result, we saw our patients at more frequent intervals than before AZT.

ON A THURSDAY MORNING, October 1987, my beeper went off at 6 A.M. The answering service informed me that Dr. J, a dentist, wanted me to call him at home. I had never heard of Dr. J. He was from a nearby town.

He apologized profusely for disturbing me so early and he sounded distraught. His voice was high-pitched and faint, and I could hear the country in his accent lurking under a thin layer of gentrification.

He told me he had performed a difficult extraction the previous afternoon. That night, he had discovered that the patient was HIV positive. The patient, Ethan Nidiffer, was under my care.

The tooth had been a deeply embedded molar. He had to cut the gum to expose the tooth. Then he had chipped at bone. The tooth had not wanted to come out. He finally had to split it into four pieces and lever it out. "There was blood everywhere, blood on my hands . . ."

"Were you wearing gloves?"

"Gloves, yes. But nothing else. I mean I never thought—"

"Were you wearing goggles, a mask?"

"I had my glasses on. No mask. . . . There was blood everywhere. Blood on my glasses. It must have fallen on my skin . . ." Here his voice broke. "Dr. Verghese, I'm so scared. I feel like my life is over. Do you think I will get AIDS?"

"No, no, no. You should be fine—"

"—Are you sure? I haven't slept all night." He was crying now. "My wife and I . . . we have small children. . . . I'm thinking of giving up dentistry altogether. . . . I'd just as soon raise cattle or move away. . . . If the Lord spares me, I swear I'll be a farmer or something else, but not dentistry. . . ."

His diction had slipped way back toward east Tennessee. I spent a long time reassuring him: he hadn't cut himself, he had no open wounds, he was wearing glasses—he had little to fear. I was a little embarrassed and taken aback by his emotional outburst. I gently asked him if he did not use gloves and goggles on *all* patients? Was he not aware of the need for barrier precautions?

"Well, who would have thought in Tennessee. I mean I know when you spoke to us . . ."

I had given a talk at the Sheraton, three weeks before, to the county dental society. Dr. J had evidently been there. The topic was AIDS and the talk was extremely well attended. The question-and-answer session went on for half an hour. I had spelled it out then, emphasized the "AIDS iceberg": there were many more HIV-infected persons than most of them realized; they needed to treat *everyone* they saw as if he were infected. From some of their questions I could tell that they were not using barrier precautions on every patient. (Will Johnson told me he had stopped going to his regular dentist, an old family friend, because despite telling the dentist he had hepatitis B, he could not seem to get him to use gloves.)

The dentists in town either did not believe there was as much HIV as I was telling them, or were relying on their ability to sniff "them" out from among their other patients; prune "them" from their patient rosters.

I asked Dr. J how he found out the patient had HIV. Obviously the patient had not volunteered this information before the procedure.

"Dr. Verghese, you promise you won't be mad if I tell you? The person who told me was only trying to help. I don't want him to get into trouble. . . ."

I insisted he tell me. My tone was commanding. If he wanted me to commiserate with him, have me reassure him and cite statistics for him, he better tell me.

"It was the pharmacist from Z_____ Drugs. Ethan Nidiffer went there to fill a prescription for penicillin. The pharmacist called me at home and asked me if I knew I had just operated on an AIDS person. I know you're going to be upset with the pharmacist, but if he hadn't told me, I wouldn't have known. Ethan Nidiffer is one of your patients, isn't he?"

"If he was, I could not possibly tell you. I would be violating his confidentiality. I would be doing what the pharmacist did. I do think it was highly inappropriate, *highly* inappropriate and unprofessional of the pharmacist to call you and tell you."

"But shouldn't the patient have told me? What about *my* risk?"

"The patient certainly should have—I'm not for a moment supporting what the patient did. Had I known, I would have insisted he tell you. And if this is a patient of mine, you can be sure I will speak to him. And I feel for you, I hate that this had to happen to you. I'm glad that from your description of events it doesn't sound to me like you are at risk. But it's important that you use precautions as if every single person you bring an instrument to is potentially infected with the virus."

"If I ever operate again."

I concentrated now on calming Dr. J down. We went over carefully the transmission of the virus. I pointed out to him that there were reports of at least five hundred health care workers with needlesticks from AIDS patients and only one or two had contracted the virus in this way. Dr. J's exposure, at worst, constituted a "splash" and was of ex-tremely low risk. We went over universal precautions, and it was clear Dr. J had only been giving universal precautions lip service. "I just couldn't imagine in this town . . ." he kept repeating.

We were on the phone for another twenty minutes. I was angry with the pharmacist, annoyed with the mewling tone of the dentist, and irritated with Ethan Nidiffer.

I arranged for Dr. J to get the HIV test done and to repeat it again in six weeks and six months. When I hung up, he seemed calmer than when we had first talked.

Ethan Nidiffer, the dentist's patient, was, in his own words, an "over-the-hill Tennessee queen." He was in his late sixties, and if you saw him on the street you would have thought of him as someone's uncle or grandfather. He had silvery hair combed straight back, walked with a stoop, and had severe emphysema, which made him pause in mid-sentence to get a breath. Polyester pants with front slit pockets and western shirts with a polyester blazer were his regular dress. He looked very much like a veteran, which he was, though since he had private insurance he never went to the VA for care. The skin on the back of his hands and on his face was shiny and very thin; it was also as fragile as tissue paper from years of taking cortisone for his emphysema. An inhaler rattled in his pocket alongside his car keys. He had stopped smoking and quit the heavy drinking in the past few years, but despite that was in a delicate state. To have found out he was HIV positive was a cruel blow so late in his life. When I first saw him, I was much more concerned about his emphysema than about his HIV infection.

Ethan was bitter about the HIV. He had not been very promiscuous, at least by his own account. He had held a steady job in town for thirty-odd years and had taken an early retirement because of his lung problems. He was in the closet and, though unmarried, had never given anyone cause to do more than speculate that he was gay.

His sexual activity of choice had consisted of performing oral sex on others. Now he rarely left his house. He claimed that for years there were at least four married men who stopped by his house every week for him to perform this service. I had once asked him, "What do *you* get out of it? Do you come yourself?" He shook his head and smiled: "No, but you wouldn't understand, Doc." He said he could count on the fingers of one hand the number of times he had engaged in rectal intercourse. But his luck had been bad because one of those "fingers" gave him HIV infection.

I had sent him to Duke to see if he would be eligible for the AZT trials on early HIV infection. Duke entered him into a randomized, placebo-controlled trial. I was to do some of his follow-up blood work in my office and send it on to them. When I saw him a month after the enrollment, it was clear to me that he was getting placebo. AZT induces a very characteristic change in the size of the red blood cell that is apparent in one of the indices measured on a routine blood count.

A part of me was sorely tempted to tell him he was on placebo and for him not to bother going to Duke. The five-hour drives across the mountain were torture for him; in summer, it was hell to breathe in Durham whether you had lung disease or not, so oppressive and humid was the air. Ethan struggled for days after each visit. Yet he went religiously every couple of weeks until he himself was sure he was getting placebo, at which point he dropped out.

Ethan had managed to keep the fact of his HIV infection hidden. I doubt that my office staff for one moment thought of him as an HIV-infected patient, but for the fact that he was seeing me. There was a bluff, good-ole-boy, old-fashioned heartiness in his manner, in the way he greeted the nurses, flirted with them. There was no trace of effeminacy, only a hint of punctiliousness in his mien that was quite allowable in a confirmed bachelor. When we were in the exam room alone, he was looser, his conversation more risqué, and his manner intimate and confiding. Above all, Ethan Nidiffer abhorred the loud "flaming queens." That adjective popped up often in his conversation. He himself was an "old queen," or a "Tennessee queen," but never a *flaming* queen. He was the only patient I had met who was critical of ACT UP and felt the cause was already lost since the public had come to associate homosexuality with the loud angry images of ACT UP protesters or members of Queer Nation.

"How can they possibly respect us if we don't conduct ourselves in a manner that they can identify with?"

Since Ethan was still in the closet, what other choice did the "public" have but to go by those who *were* willing to speak out?

As we got to know each other better, it became clear that Ethan understood that his two secrets would eventually come out; that, in fact, his neighbors and his sisters had a pretty good idea about why he was unmarried so long, and why the majority of his visitors were younger males.

I decided to call Ethan. It took several rings before Ethan came to the phone. His voice was muffled and I could hear him panting from the effort.

I had no plan of what I was to say to Ethan. What was I calling for? To chastise him? I told him what had transpired.

"I know. The dentist already called me. He was mad at me."

"I think you should have told him."

"Well, I asked him when he called. I said, 'If I had told you, would you have done the operation?' He didn't say nothing. He kept quiet."

"I *am* sorry the pharmacist betrayed your confidence, acted in such an unprofessional manner, I—"

"Well, don't worry, Doc. He's just a snake, is all there is to it. And, Doc, *I'm* not going to worry about any of that. I dialed eight dentists in three counties. I called till my fingers were just tired of dialing. I gave them a false name, I said I was HIV and needed a tooth pulled—the tooth was killing me, honest to God—and not a one of them would do it, and they wouldn't give me a name of someone who would."

"Didn't you have a regular dentist? All these years—"

"Well, let me tell you about my regular dentist! A few months ago I got a letter from his office saying he would not be able to see me any longer and asking if I wanted my records forwarded to a particular dentist."

"Why?"

"Tell *me*, Doc! You figure it out. I guess he's known me for years, had his suspicions and figured the way he would protect himself is get all the nellies out of his practice!"

"So how did you pick Dr. J?"

"Well, I just got tired of calling and calling and telling the truth. I just picked one—any one. To tell you the truth I don't know how come I picked him. Why, every one of them has a big-old ad in the Yellow Pages like a goddamn used-car dealer: WE WELCOME NEW PATIENTS or

SPECIALIZE IN NERVOUS PATIENTS or LATEST TECHNOLOGY or stuff like that. I figured that was me. I was nervous, new, and in need of the latest technology!"

What could I say? I could certainly see his point of view.

I TRIED TO DECIDE whether I should call the pharmacist and tell him off for what was a clear violation of ethics. Z Drugs was a new store, struggling to survive at a time when all around them the large drugstore chains were cutting prices and offering more sophisticated services such as home intravenous therapy and home health care. The one time I had gone to fill a prescription for myself at that pharmacy, the proprietor had been very solicitous, almost fawning. He was six foot six and towered over me. As opposed to the genuine warmth a Tennessean can project by being himself, the pharmacist's sugar-coating, his dated used-car-dealer sweetness rang hollow. On the other hand, he had at least been a face and a name I could deal with on a personal level, unlike the large chains. He asked me to never hesitate to call him, he showed me how every patient's record was on computer, how his was in fact a modern operation. He gave me a huge discount on my prescription. I called in prescriptions to his store whenever the patient expressed no preference and lived in that general area.

When AZT came along, I called him and several other pharmacists and asked if they would stock the drug. They jumped at the opportunity: the average patient would spend $8,000 to $10,000 on AZT every year.

I heard complaints from several AIDS patients who said they were made to feel uneasy in the store. After they dropped their prescriptions off and sat down to wait, there would be pin-drop silence behind the counter. There was not a doubt in the patient's mind that the pharmacist had conveyed the nature of the prescription to the other employees behind the counter. Eventually the patient's name would be called and he would step up to the counter, where every eye would watch him as he paid for the drug and then marched bravely down the aisle and out of the store. Otis had overheard a remark from one of the women in the store about "God's revenge." He vowed never to return.

I kept sending patients to that pharmacy primarily because the arrangement was already in place and, so far, the pharmacist himself had been professional, even if his staff may not have been. But this incident with the dentist and Ethan was the last straw. I would not send any more patients to him. But I decided I would not call him and chastise him. The damage was done.

As I mulled over these thoughts, the phone rang. It was my friendly pharmacist. His tone was not that friendly anymore.

"I heard from Dr. J that you weren't happy with what I did. I thought I would call you and see if you wanted to speak to me."

"I wasn't planning to call you. But now that you have called me, yes, I thought it was quite unprofessional of you to call the dentist on my patient. It does not inspire confidence—"

He interrupted me. His tone was defiant: He said he felt an obligation to warn the dentist, to "take care of my doctors," as he put it. He saw it as his civic responsibility. He didn't see anything wrong with what he had done.

I let him go on. It was clear to me that he knew he had overstepped his boundary, been unprofessional, but he was not about to admit it. Instead he was going to hide behind the shield of civic responsibility, of duty to God and country.

I waited till he was done. I asked him, "Didn't you think of the possibility of calling *me* first? After all, it was my patient. If you were going to get involved, why not call me and let me deal with it, instead of taking it on yourself to break the patient's confidentiality?"

There was a silence. "Well, I guess I could have done that."

"Am I to assume now that you will take it on yourself to call any other doctor who happens to be seeing the thirty-odd patients who fill AZT at your store? So that you can tell the doctor the patient has AIDS?"

He had no reply.

"You see, I'm afraid I can't in good faith send you my patients because I don't think I can be sure of your not betraying their confidence."

Now he dropped all pretense. The obsequious, fawning tone that he usually used with me was completely gone and in its place was this snapping, testy tone that revealed him for what he was: a weasel in sheep's clothing. His voice was dripping with hate: "Well, I don't want your business either. It doesn't matter to me one bit. And I don't want any of your patients. I'll just take care of *my* doctors. Suits me fine."

He hung up on me.

The words "foreign doctor" rang in my ears, even though he had not said them. My intuition was so strong that I could not write my discomfort off to paranoia. I caught the undertone, and all day the memory kept me uneasy.

Sometimes it was possible to have the illusion that I was so much a part of the town, so well integrated, that I even looked like the townsfolk. But at times like this, I walked around gingerly, seeking my footing with great caution.

Sometimes I felt that I was accepted only as long as they needed me, as long as I could be of service to them. I had fought the clannishness of the Indian community, felt embarrassed by their refusal to integrate. But now I wondered, did they understand something I did not?

But even within the Indian community, the issue of belonging was not so simple. The north Indians were starting to have their own gatherings; the same was true of the south Indians. The Sikhs, in keeping with tumultuous events in India, no longer felt themselves in the mainstream Indian community; their poorly concealed delight in Indira Gandhi's death did not sit well with the rest of the Indians. The Pakistanis, who till then had fit under the general rubric of "Indian," now increasingly met by themselves. And to all these groups, I was an outsider of sorts: an Indian born in Africa. Was there ever going to be a place in this world for me to call my own?

That evening, I told Rajani the story of the dentist and my subsequent words with the pharmacist. She could see I was agitated.

"He didn't actually *say* 'foreigner,' right? You just felt like he said it."

"No, he didn't *say* it. But, yes, I feel as if he said it."

Rajani could not see the point of my uneasiness. Her sympathies were with the dentist. And she was tired of losing my time and attention. She had once said to me, after seeing me come home yet again at an odd hour after answering a summons from the Miracle Center, "You have a choice, you know. You don't *have* to do the AIDS stuff; if you were full-time at the VA you would have more regular hours, you would have no involvement with the Miracle Center. You could just opt to be full-time VA."

"But it's not like cardiology or hematology," I had said. "There is no one out there doing infectious diseases. If I didn't do it, if Fil didn't do it, then there would be no one for these patients."

"It would work out. The point is you have a choice. You're choosing to do what you are doing, so you can't complain about the hours."

My conversation with the pharmacist and the reporting of it to Rajani seemed to exaggerate my feeling of alienation. And my alienation had so much to do with the fact that I was taking care of persons with AIDS. I wondered if subconsciously Rajani viewed me the same way the pharmacist viewed me: tainted by the people I took care of.

That evening, my motorcycle mechanic friend, Darryl, dropped by. Over the years, Darryl and I had worked out a barter system: he took care of my motorcycle and I helped with his kids' medical needs. Now, as a sacrifice for being a father, I had sold the motorcycle. Rajani had argued that it was dangerous and hardly fitting for a father of two kids and I had very reluctantly agreed. Still, Darryl came by from time to time, and I often went by his shop to admire a Norton or an old Indian that he was restoring.

Darryl and I started in the living room with a beer, and when he wanted to smoke, we moved out to the porch—Rajani could not abide the smell of cigarettes in the house. On the porch we had another beer. Steven stayed with us until Rajani summoned him up to bed. I debated telling Darryl the story of the pharmacist, but decided against it. I could not gauge how Darryl would respond: I could not handle a crack about "homos" or a response other than the one I had. Instead, we talked motorcycles and then marriage—specifically Darryl's marriage, which was not going well. While he talked, Darryl pulled out a reefer. Its acrid smell was nostalgic, but the memories it brought back were all of more alienation: Ethiopia in the throes of a war, India on the eve of my departure for America.

When Darryl finally left, I stumbled upstairs, red-eyed, my mind racing, my discomfort having only increased. Rajani handed me the kids who were too excited to sleep. She said, "You put them to bed then." I didn't think she took kindly to Darryl and perhaps she had smelled the reefer.

I studied the map on Steven's wall as I carried the baby. Idaho. Montana. Iowa. South Dakota. Texas. Was there some place in this country where I could walk around anonymously, where I could blend in completely with a community, be undistinguished by appearance, accent or speech?

Still carrying the baby and telling Steven to wait, I went down to the basement and pulled out my guitar, which I had not touched in over a year. I came back to the kids' room and Jacob allowed me to put him in his crib. I began to sing to the two of them. I sang song after song, with barely a pause.

It seemed like hours later that I looked up to see Steven and the baby both fast asleep. And staring at me from the doorway across the room was my beautiful wife, a puzzled look on her face. I didn't know how long she had been there watching me.

Rajani loved me, wanted to help me, wanted to make my life easier, wanted our marriage to work. But looking at me as I sat there bleary-eyed, thumping out tunes, singing like a college kid, the floor that separated us was like an abyss that could not be bridged. As she walked away, I found myself crying, but without the heart to call out to her because I didn't know what to say. I didn't think words could fix us. Our lives had changed. I was going to have to find some compromise.

19

FEBRUARY 1988.
     It was dark when I left the house, dark when I came back, dark and cold when I was called out to see a patient after hours. My tennis buddy, Earl, would telephone every evening. We would commiserate over the weather, gauge our chances for the next few weeks and lament the inactivity, the damage done to strokes we had honed to near perfection through spring, summer and fall. If the temperature approached fifty, we would attempt to play. Never mind that the balls barely bounced in the cold, never mind that our joints creaked like rusty barn doors. Tennis was essential, especially in the Tennessee winter where everyone seemed sicker and older, where all battles seemed harder to fight.
     On a Sunday night we had a mini ice storm. It froze the bare limbs and shoots of the trees in a crystalline mesh. Near midnight, as I drove home from the Miracle Center, the raindrops stuck and then smeared on my windshield when I turned on my wipers.
     And then I was suddenly skating, the normally nimble and sure-footed Z doing an elaborate figure eight on Dogwood Avenue, my steering wheel as useless as a severed rudder. The engine stalled, flooded and would not start. I abandoned my car, crawled to where road and pavement ended and lawn began, and walked home trying to stay on grass, feeling the ice crunch beneath my feet.
     By the next morning, the ice was gone from the road. The car started

on the first turn of the key. But that night, it snowed again and I dreamed of blood. I was in a white coat, white-coated students and residents gathered around me. We were a circle in the snow. My hands applied pressure to a wound on a faceless patient; blood was trickling over my fingers, into the cuticle, into the little hangnails. I watched with alarm as blood seeped over the callus on the side of my right thumb, a callus from tennis, a callus that in winter grew dry and chapped and would fissure every time I played. In my dream, I struggled to be nonchalant as the house staff watched me. I carried on with my little lecture on cellulitis and its common causes. I did not recoil from the wound nor did I wash my hands. Instead, I finished dressing the patient's wound, my pride and the stupidest form of courage supplanting common sense. I made light conversation with the students. They looked at my hands. I dismissed them and hurried to the sink to wash. Deep inside, I knew I was infected. I could picture the virus tagging onto my CD4 cells. I heard the nurses whisper: "*He's got it now.*"

I awoke in a black depression, a sense that all was lost. It took several seconds of looking around the room, of feeling Steven next to me, seeing the naked bough of the oak tree coated with snow and framed in the bedroom window, before I realized that this was a dream.

WINTER SHOWED IN the faces of my patients. When Vickie McCray came by my office at the VA to pick up a prescription for Clyde, her mood was black. It seemed like a lifetime ago that we had sat on the stoop of her trailer and felt the sun on our skin. She wore a down vest that made her shoulders look huge. I made her sit. I brought a cup of coffee for her: black with four spoons of sugar.

I had started Clyde on high-dose AZT—there was some evidence that this might work for AIDS dementia. However, the improvement he made predated the AZT; I credited Vickie's nursing with much of that. I asked Vickie how he was doing, how he was tolerating the AZT.

She said Clyde had started to tinker with his car, an old clunker that had started life as a Ford Fairlane but now had a Chevy engine, a Bonneville's front seat, and a radio from a Toyota pickup. I had seen it parked well behind the trailer when I came to visit. Vickie said, "He parks it out of view because he has this silly notion that someone might try to steal it, though Lord knows why anybody would want it." Clyde had a special place in his heart for the car. And now he would work on it or just sit in it before retreating into the house to rest.

Vickie said that one morning she heard the engine come to life. "I couldn't believe it. I looked out of the window and there was Clyde smiling at me. He pulled the car around the trailer and off he went. He must have charged the battery or got one off his cousin. I don't believe he was ever happier than when he was on the road. Happiest day of his life was when he got his big-rig license. Looking back, though, that's exactly when he was starting to get sick."

"Is he safe to be driving?"

"No! My mother-in-law called me yesterday. 'Vickie,' she says. 'I seen Clyde driving around. Either something is wrong with the car or something is wrong with him, 'cause he ain't driving right.' So yesterday evening I said, 'Clyde, drive me to the store.' He came right off the sofa—he'll go anywhere if it means driving the car. Well, I sat next to him, and my daughter Danielle was in the back. You know how you have to pull across the Bristol Highway from our road to point you back to town? Well, he misjudged the distance of the cars coming at him. I thought for sure we'd be kilt, but Clyde didn't even know it and we squeaked by. Then after that he kept going over the white line and over the yellow line, like he was drunk or something but I knew he wasn't. I said, 'Clyde, you ain't driving straight.' He said, 'Vickie, it's the car. The front end is loose is what it is.' Well, coming back from the store I told him I was going to drive. And he was right, the front end *was* a little loose. You had to concentrate and keep turning on the wheel to keep the car in a straight line. But *I* could do it. And *he* couldn't. When we got back, I told him he could not drive anymore. He's real mad with me. Says I'm being hateful to him. I done taken the keys away."

I asked after Vickie's sister. She had tested positive for HIV but she had adamantly declined to come to the clinic and be examined. I asked Vickie if Clyde was aware that he had infected her sister? Had that fact sunk into his brain?

"Oh, I'd say he knows. Hell, *I* told him more than once. Matter of fact, when he first started to drive, first thing he done is go over there. I asked my sister the other day, I said, 'Has Clyde been by?' She said he had. She said he was banging on the door, he was after something, but she wouldn't open. I asked her, 'What did he say? What was he after?'

She said, 'He wanted sex, but I wouldn't let him in nohow.' Clyde said to her, 'I have the virus and you have it, so it's OK.' "

"OK what?" I asked.

"OK to have sex I guess!"

There was hurt in Vickie's eyes and her chin quivered once after she told me this. "Can you believe him?"

"Did you say anything to Clyde about it?"

"Hell, yes! I confronted him. I said, 'Clyde, did you go to my sister's? Did you do such and such and such?' He said, 'Yes.' Just like that: 'Yes.' I'm telling you, he's like a little kid! He don't understand nothing about right or wrong."

UP UNTIL THIS POINT, most of the HIV patients, who slipped in and out of my office as discreetly as they could, had no awareness of the others in town who had the virus. They might have spotted each other in my waiting room, made informed guesses, but that was it. By February of 1988, however, TAP—the Tri-City AIDS Project—was holding regular meetings and many of my patients were attending. They spoke to me about it often.

Bobby Keller, after his period of mourning over Ed, was back in full form, a one-man blitzkrieg of outrageous repartee. He seemed determined to find the irony in every situation, sound out every double entendre, every pun, find the mot juste for each occasion. He was a compulsive performer. He could make us laugh, but then he seemed desperate to keep us laughing, to remain in the spotlight. The jokes continued in rapid-fire succession until, inevitably, they lost their power and grew hollow. Sometimes Bobby got scolded for talking too much and his cheerfulness dissolved quickly into tears.

Ethan Nidiffer despised Bobby Keller and Raleigh; they were the epitome of the "flaming queens" he so detested. Ethan had gone very reluctantly to his first meeting, and when Bobby Keller had attempted to make him the butt of a joke, Ethan had cut him down and Bobby's chin had started quivering. Ethan may have been long in the tooth, betrayed by a pharmacist, denied by his dentist, breathless from emphysema, but he could still act the part of the disapproving father with some expertise. He seemed to feel it his role to settle things down, keep the kids in line.

Raleigh, however, was not to be kept in line by anyone, particularly anyone who tried to assume a patriarchal position. "Are we to assume that you're just a visitor here?" he asked Ethan at one point. "That you don't have the virus? I'm *over* you and that attitude. I've got one good nerve left. *Don't* play with me."

Ethan mellowed. As the months passed, he became a sort of straight man to Bobby, subtly turning his sidekick's less successful cracks into crowd-pleasers with his dry deadpan retorts. When Raleigh rode in with his "don't fuck with me" attitude and extra long Virginia Slims menthols, the threesome became a force of mutual protection.

Otis Jackson—Fred Goodson's lover and companion—resisted the whole idea of support group and the fellowship to be found there. Otis sat distant, surly and removed. Thanks to his years in San Francisco, he favored the Castro look: close-cropped hair, jeans, black lace-up work-boots and a white T-shirt. He dressed carefully for the meetings, proudly, as if flying the colors. Otis watched jealously as his lover, Fred Goodson, presided over the support group. When Raleigh cast a flirtatious glance in Otis's direction, Otis ignored him.

Fred, the bear, brought a taste of big-city activism to the meetings. He was a pro with a political agenda and not much patience for small talk. Like no one else, he understood the dynamics of support groups and could see the patterns beneath the seemingly random back-and-forth that went on. He laughed at the jokes but had a sixth sense for when a one-liner was concealing something bigger, more heartfelt. Fred was about "being real." He refused to accept aimless chatter and had no time for politeness. It was Fred who made Bobby Keller stop joking and really talk about how much he missed Ed. He made each person speak about how they broke the news of their HIV to the person closest to them. He was the first to talk openly about how often during the day his thoughts turned to dying. Left to their own devices, good country boys like Bobby and Raleigh could spend the day talking about everything but what they had in common. Fred never let the conversation drift too far away. He always made a beeline for what wasn't being said.

There were tensions: Petie Granger (the young man whose parents had experienced rejection at the hands of their family doctor and surgeon) tried to browbeat the group into adopting his upbeat, optimistic attitude. He was settled at home in the very same bedroom he had grown up in and was back eating his mother's cooking. He had regained not only the weight he lost but also his voice. He could go on and on, often prefacing his remarks with "back in Baltimore" and pouncing on anyone who, in his perception, was whining about life's misfortunes. He had said "accentuate the positive" so many times that Ethan Nidiffer finally told him that if he repeated that one more time he personally would get up and slap Petie silly, to which Petie had rolled his eyes and said, "Promises, promises . . ."

VICKIE MCCRAY missed the first couple of sessions. "Clyde wasn't feeling well," she said. "But we went two weeks after Christmas—it was the first week in January, I believe. I asked Clyde if he wanted to go and he says 'Sure.' Of course, Clyde would go to a nude picnic in a field of fire ants if'n anyone invited him. *Anything*, rather than sit at home—that's just the way he is. He was getting bored in the trailer, wanted to be out on the road.

"The meeting was in that church meeting room right next to ETSU. I was nervous as hell. I kept thinking, am I going to run into someone I know getting in and out of this place? And what in the hell am I going to say? We parked the car—I drove—and Clyde and I stood out on the porch watching guys go in. Clyde looks around and says, 'This must be it,' and just marches in. I was shocked at his boldness! But I went on in with him. There was a big old Christmas tree in one corner and a bunch of chairs in the middle in a circle. Everybody, me included, was standing outside this circle of chairs, all of us smoking like sieves. I mean to tell you, we were sucking on them cigarettes as if it was the only thing keeping us alive.

"Bobby Keller was in one corner, licking his tongue and rolling them big eyes and making faces and chatting up Petie Granger—see I didn't know who anybody was at the time. Bobby was all dressed in leather—I mean he even had on a leather hat and a leather bracelet with metal thingies sticking out of it. See, I didn't realize that he had done that as kind of a joke—Petie had dared him to do it, or something like that. I just took one look at Bobby and, I tell you what, it scared me to death. I was ready to run out of there as fast as a scalded dog except I knew I'd have a time getting Clyde out of there. To look at Bobby Keller frightened me. I was watching him, but not watching him, know what I mean? And I was listening to him and Petie go on about the Christmas parties they had been to and what they wore.

"Picture this: I was the only woman in there. I looked around and I was saying to myself, 'My God, Vickie, what in the world are you doing here with a bunch of queers?' I wasn't even sure that Clyde and I were at the right place. Then one guy walks in—Jacko—only I didn't know him at the time [Jacko was a patient of mine who had Kaposi's sarcoma], and his face has these god-awful things on them, like lilacs growing out of his face. He was about the only one that looked sick—he warn't thin; it was just these . . . *things* on his face. Then Ethan Nidiffer came in and he just looked real serious and he talked with Clyde and they were next to me, chatting, and it got me to wondering did Clyde maybe know this guy? What in the world was Clyde saying to this guy who looked kind of like an ex-president of the United States or a senator or something. Then Raleigh comes in—my God, Dr. Verghese. I took one look at him and said to myself, 'What in the hell is *that*?'

"Fred got us all to sit down and I still hadn't decided if I wanted to leave or stay. People were settling down. Then they did what they do every time there is a new person: they went round the room and asked each person to say a little bit about themselves. Well, I don't even know what I said—I think I said my name, is about it. But when it comes to Clyde he just says—as normal as you please—that he is Clyde McCray, that he was my husband, and that he contracted AIDS from his male lover. Embarrassed the hell out of me!

"Pretty soon they were having a discussion and, to tell you the truth, I wasn't even there. I couldn't even tell you what was said. I felt as if I was standing back there and watching, as if this really was not happening, it was a dream. I was in the wrong place at the wrong time. I had been sent to hell and I had been sent to hell with these people.

"We've been back every week since, and I must tell you, it's different. I know Bobby Keller now, I know he's harmless, a clown. He has never worn that leather suit since. And Bettie Lee—Fred's sister—has started a caregivers support group meeting across the hall: it's me, Bettie Lee and some of the mothers and sisters of the men. These days I start off sitting in the support group—'cause I am infected after all—and then after about half an hour I go over to the caregivers side."

"So is support group helpful to you?"

Vickie gave me a sheepish smile. "It's been helpful. To be around Bettie Lee is great. And I never thought I'd say this—I'd have died if you told me I would do this—but I have come to really know some of the men and they are just as sweet and caring as you please. For a while there, it felt as if Clyde and I were the only two in the whole world—and my sister—who had this thing.

"And Clyde is having a good old time at support group, mostly bitching about me: how I don't give him money and how I took all his money, and on and on. The group has kind of figured out that Clyde is not quite there. He'll make sense for a while, then he'll say something come out of left field, the same weird things he does at home. After the last meeting, old Bobby Keller come up to me and said, 'Vickie, you be real glad you were over in the other room, 'cause Clyde went on about you. If I didn't know he had the virus, I swear I would have bust him one for what he said.' Bobby's just a big teddy bear. He couldn't bust anybody if he wanted to. But he was dead serious for a change. You'd have to know him." She shook her head quietly as if marveling at the things she had come to see and experience in the last two years.

I didn't tell Vickie that I did know Bobby Keller and everyone else she had mentioned. She went on.

"It's something I've been meaning to tell you about Clyde, Dr. Verghese: he's been cussing something awful. Every other word of his is the G.D.M.F. word. He says it to anybody. I mean, poor Danielle, if she walks in front of the TV and plonks herself on the carpet, he'll cuss her for having her leg in the way. She'll go crying to her room."

"What do you do when he does that?" I asked.

"I go to Danielle and tell her that he isn't in his right mind. 'Danielle,' I say, 'did he ever do this before? Before this virus got around to his head? No? Well, you see, it's not him. It's the virus what's doing it to him.' Then I make her come out and I confront Clyde. I say, 'Clyde, you're not going to sit and cuss your daughter like that. She *is* your daughter and you *will* say sorry to her!' Well then he puts on this real pitiful expression on his face and says, 'I'm sorry, Danielle.' Like a child. But five minutes later he can do it all over again. Say the G.D.M.F. thing."

————

MY DUTIES AT THE VA had taken on a new twist: Brian Smith, one of the two pulmonary physicians at the VA, had decided to leave. Brian performed all bronchoscopies (the examination of the inside of the bronchial tree with a flexible fiberoptic instrument) at the VA. And a good many bronchoscopies were needed every month because of the huge burden of lung cancer. Brian had been teaching me to perform bronchoscopy for a reason not related to lung cancer: to obtain samples of secretions from deep within the lung in patients with pneumonia. Now, with Brian's leaving, I was called on to do bronchoscopy for the many lung cancer workups generated by each ward. At least until a pulmonary physician could be recruited.

Over a hundred persons with lung cancer were cared for each year at our VA. It seemed to me that, unlike AIDS, there was no shame in cancer, not lung cancer, not in Tennessee. The patients were in a curious way prepared for it. Anand, my oncologist friend, who was overwhelmed and perhaps slightly disillusioned by the amount of lung cancer seen at the VA, said to me: "It's a bloody badge of honor. I happen to be here some Sundays and I'll see whole families, several generations, around the patient's bed, with the patient in the center, on the bed, kind of in the role of hero. You fought for your country, you smoked tobacco that the army gave you—the same tobacco that your father grew at home, that you helped harvest and put on stakes and hung up to dry, the same tobacco that John Wayne and Bogart smoked. Then you got lung cancer years later—it's a goddamn *war* wound."

I had already seen two patients on other wards and scheduled them for bronchoscopies when I went to Ward 8. The third patient was not in his bed. I walked to the back of the ward, to the smoking room, where a number of patients were watching *Wheel of Fortune*. I had always thought the walls of the smoking room were painted yellow; however, whenever the maintenance men came to take the clocks down to reset them for daylight saving time, I would see a perfect pink circle left behind, a tribute to the original color of the wall. I was greeted with a "Who do you need, Doc?" by the man nearest the archway. When I said, "Jimmy Roach," a tall, gangly man with dark hair stood up and came toward me. "Don't worry, J.R.," someone yelled after him, "we'll keep Vanna warm for you."

J.R. and I walked down the ward until we came to his bed.

His neighbor in the next bed was a scrunched-up old man who appeared to have had a stroke. A woman, the patient's wife, I supposed, was sitting next to him, and she looked at us through lenses as thick as soda bottles. She was spoon-feeding him ice cream, and either because one side of his face was palsied or because her aim was poor, much of the ice cream was coming out the side of his mouth, and a big glob of it hung precariously on the tip of his chin. Neither of them seemed aware of this, and she kept pushing more ice cream into his mouth.

I drew the curtain around J.R.'s bed and pulled up a chair and sat in front of him. "Where are you from?" I asked J.R.

"Over near Middlesboro, Kentucky. Know where that is, Doc?"

"Sure. Right next to Tazewell, Tennessee, right?" I had moonlighted in Tazewell, about an hour-and-a-half drive from Johnson City.

"You know your chest x-ray showed a small growth on your lung. The reason I am here is your team of physicians wanted me to see if I could do a bronchoscopy—that is go down into your lungs through your nose with this lighted tube—and get a piece of the tissue in that growth."

Even as I recited this, I was alarmed by something I had heard: J.R.'s voice was raspy and hoarse. The vocal cords are innervated by the recurrent laryngeal nerves which run through the chest to reach the cords. J.R.'s hoarseness suggested the cancer had spread in his chest to entrap one of these nerves. I examined J.R. for lymph nodes in his neck. I felt a rock-hard mass in his neck, just where his sternomastoid muscle joined his collarbone. This was almost certainly a malignant node, the cancer having spread to the neck. I called the intern, had him feel it with me. He was sheepish. I suggested a much more direct way to make the diagnosis: we would aspirate the node with a fine needle and get an exact tissue diagnosis. Even now I was sure the node in the neck together with the hoarseness meant the cancer was inoperable.

I explained to J.R. that instead of the bronchoscopy we would biopsy the lymph node in his neck. He fingered the node with his fingers. He looked straight at me, and asked without any fear:

"You reckon it's cancer, don't you, Doc?"

"It's possible that's what it is, J.R. Let's hope it turns out to be something else."

"But right now it's looking like cancer?"

"It's very possible."

"Well," he said with a wry smile, "if that's what it is, that's what it is." He stuck his hand out at me. "I appreciate you coming by, Doc, I really do."

I promised to return.

As I wrote out my consultation, I saw him head off to the smoking room, his hand reaching for the Marlboros in his dressing gown. A chorus of male voices greeted him. He fired up his cigarette and took his place next to his mates and watched Vanna spin the wheel again.

Yes, I thought. Death is not new to me or to any doctor. But nowadays, you get cancer and you die with honor, often after having lived an almost full life span. With HIV infection, you have to fight to salvage your honor, and for the most part you die young. But at least with HIV you buy some time—five to seven years even after the diagnosis. I had a feeling that not just J.R. but the other two patients I had scheduled for bronchoscopy would turn out not to be candidates for curative surgery and would die within six months. As I made my way to clinic, the prospect of seeing HIV patients that afternoon seemed positively uplifting after a whole morning spent with lung cancer.

20

AFTER CLINIC, I was still thinking of the metaphors of disease—honor versus shame—as I looked over the ultrasound of a patient's abdomen with a radiologist. As we put the films up on the screen, I told the radiologist—one of a group of four congenial radiologists who covered the Miracle Center—that the patient had AIDS. I described the location of his pain over the gallbladder area. We were at the very back of the radiology suites in a plush office. Pictures of the radiologist's family and his mentors from his training days covered the walls. The lights were dimmed the better to see the view boxes. The sumptuous leather chair he sat in probably cost more than my Z. This radiologist was the consummate jester, quick-witted, a good ole boy who immediately put you into a good-ole-boy mode and sucked you into his banter.

"Homosexual?" he asked, pointing at the film. I nodded.

"It figures," he said, shaking his head, as if there was some clue to sexuality in the black-and-white image. "Well," he said, his tone now changing, his face taking on a somber expression as if he was viewing the films of a condemned criminal, "there are no stones there. The gallbladder wall might be just a bit thick. Nothing else I can tell you." He turned to me. "No telling what can be going on. Sucker could have anything including the kitchen sink, right?"

I said nothing.

"It's just too bad, too bad—"

I felt a moral statement coming. "I wonder," I said, "whether he could have acalculous cholecystitis? [An inflamed gallbladder *without* stones.] There are reports now of this happening in AIDS. *Cryptosporidium* [a protozoan parasite that causes diarrhea] is thought to produce this, though this will be my first case. We do know he has *Cryptosporidium* in his bowel causing diarrhea."

"Is that right?" The radiologist turned back to the films, his thought train interrupted. He pursed his lips. "Never heard of that bug. Could be, could be. God almighty, what can they expect? Like I said, that wall is a little thickened, maybe some edema there." He stared a little longer. "But nothing to write home about." He took the films down and handed them to me. "Pheweee! Well, good luck! Son, I sure wouldn't want to be in your shoes."

I left the elegant radiology suites and took the back stairs up to my patient's room.

What would it be like to be in a radiologist's shoes? To spend most of my day dealing with *images* of people: plain black-and-white x-ray images, or speckled images caused by sound waves bouncing off organs, or images caused by dyes outlining arteries and veins, or contrast medium filling loops of bowel, or images reconstructed by computers into cross sections of the body—all without speaking to a patient. The only time a radiologist put his or her hand on a patient was to stick a needle into an artery so as to inject dye for an angiogram, or sometimes to compress a stomach with a lead-lined gloved hand, watching under the fluoroscope as barium negotiated the gastric outlet.

The "what if?" question occurred to me often now. What if I was a cardiothoracic surgeon? What if my income was three million a year? What if I was a radiologist with music piped into my office and a stack of images to move from my "in" file to my "out" file, and the certainty of a tee time of 3:45 every afternoon at the country club? I would want the leather chair, of course; the expense was justified. What if I was a pathologist? How would it be to stare at tissue taken from a patient, never seeing the whole patient unless on the autopsy table? Or an ophthalmologist, interested only in the eyes? On the playing field of medicine, with all its established positions and specialized players, I felt increasingly like the man from the moon, the man playing left-out. Nobody dwelled on what it was like to be in my shoes; they were merely thankful that they were not.

This was a new situation for me. I had always felt I was an important cog in the medical machine. An underpaid cog, perhaps, but still part of the team. The exile I felt had less to do with being an AIDS doc than with the fact that most of my patients were homosexuals.

A few weeks earlier, a Mrs. Lillian Paez, a well-connected socialite, had called me through an intermediary and asked if she could chat with me. Not at the clinic, but either at her house or at my VA office. I picked my office. She came in the early evening when most people had left.

I watched through a window as she parked her Lincoln Town Car and then crossed the street to my office. She was wearing a suit that I doubted even Parks-Belk in town carried. There were diamonds in her ears. Her necklace had marks of age, but the pearls it was made of were unmistakably real. "*Genuine* pearls," the voice of Vickie McCray whispered in my ears.

Mrs. Paez wanted to talk to me about her son. He lived in San Diego. "Let me be frank," she said, fingering the pearls. "My son has AIDS. My son is dying slowly but he is still working. Eventually, I hope to bring him back here when he can no longer manage over there. I love him dearly. But both he and I don't want anyone to know about AIDS. Cancer or lymphoma is what we will tell people. When my son dies, I want people to remember his life, his kindness, his personality. If they know he has AIDS, to them it will just be another faggot dying. I don't want my son remembered that way: as a faggot."

With her first few words I had been primed to resist this lady, argue with her, be the proletarian doctor and deny her any special treatment—why was her son different? But to see tears in her eyes, to find a rush of hot tears in my own eyes as I imagined my own mother in this predicament, took away all my resistance.

I cited some examples for her. People who had made the transition back successfully. Who had not hidden what they had.

She interrupted me: "I sit at dinners where they talk about faggots. Can you imagine how that makes me feel? I want to say to them: 'Do you know you are talking about my son? Do you know this could be your son and you just don't know it?' I know that it won't change anything. His own father has no idea he is gay, or at least won't acknowledge it. He doesn't know his son is sick."

"Won't he know when your son comes back?"

"We are divorced, so he isn't around. I imagine when the time comes he will have to know. To him it will be yet another reason why I failed him. He always accused me of babying my son. This will be his ammunition."

How could I argue with her? She was right about homophobia. My patient did not exist as a person in the radiology department: He was a cluster of echoes recorded on smoky paper, he was a gallbladder, and finally he was a homosexual who quite possibly had a bug "from the kitchen sink" in his belly. In the hospital it was almost as if he had no existence beyond his label of "homosexual." The "AIDS" was an afterthought. If he had hobbies, aspirations, foibles and eccentricities, a special talent, these had been discarded in the lobby. Unless they hid their homosexuality, like Mrs. Paez's son, there was the danger that when they died they would be remembered for being faggots, something less than human.

Mrs. Paez left my office with my promise to help her son when he came home, help him die at home when it came to that. As I watched her cross the street, I tried to imagine her entering a TAP meeting, tried to imagine her "being real" as Fred would say. I could not. But nor could I imagine my own mother (if life had been different and she found herself like Mrs. Paez in this situation) walking into that meeting.

THERE WERE FOUR surgical groups at the Miracle Center, a total of twelve surgeons. I had asked Sue McCoy, my surgical counterpart with the University Practice Group, to see Cameron Tolliver, the patient whose ultrasound I had gone over with the radiologist. Sue was in her forties, had gone to medical school and to a surgical residency fairly late in life, after a previous career as a researcher. She had a quiet, unassuming manner. We had worked together on several committees and I thought of her as a careful and thorough physician.

At one time or another, all the surgeons in town had asked me to see their patients. In turn, I referred my paying non-HIV patients to them for hernia repairs, gallbladder removal, or placement of a Hickman catheter into a vein for prolonged antibiotic administration. I tried to distribute these consultations evenly.

But now, when any of my HIV-infected patients required surgery, I was faced with a dilemma: Which surgeon should I ask? A surgeon operating on one of my patients was at greater risk of getting infected through a cut or needlestick than I was from simply examining patients. I had tried to be fair about it: I tried to spread my consultations around, trying not to go back to the same surgeon too often.

Most of the surgeons were older than I, not people that I knew well. There were a few who were my contemporaries. I approached one of these younger surgeons a few weeks earlier when Otis Jackson had needed a Hickman catheter. To my surprise, the surgeon balked, said he would get back to me. And to my greater surprise, his partner, a crusty old-time surgeon whom I had hesitated to ask, counseled his junior partner to put in the catheter, otherwise he would do it himself.

Every surgeon I had approached had promptly come to see the patient and did whatever was needed. However they may have felt about being consulted, or about the patient's lifestyle, they were extremely professional. They seemed less troubled by the risk than I had imagined. Perhaps they sensed my discomfort in having to subject them to risk.

For my part, I always offered to scrub with them for the surgery, hold a retractor. This was largely a symbolic gesture: Most pundits recommended that only experienced surgical personnel be in the theater when operating on HIV-infected patients, thereby reducing the chances for accidental needlesticks or cuts during surgery.

Sue McCoy, I knew, had been examining Cameron twice a day, trying to decide whether surgery was urgently indicated.

I entered Cameron Tolliver's room. It was permeated with a now familiar scent. It was a fruity odor with a visceral aftertaste that reminded me of a freshly opened cadaver. Cameron lay looking up at the ceiling, his knees pulled up. The sheets around him were soaked and redolent with the same odor. The television was turned off. He was unnaturally still, as if the bed was booby-trapped and the slightest twitch from him could send body parts helter-skelter over the Johnson City landscape. The only part of his body that moved was his eyes. They tracked me from the door to the right side of his bed. He was breathing with rapid shallow breaths, each punctuated with a soft grunt.

"I want to kick and thrash from this pain," he whispered, pausing after every other word. "But any time I move, any movement just makes that pain worse."

The pain for which I admitted him, pain over the gallbladder area, had initially subsided on antibiotics. Now, after twenty-four hours, the pain was back. His temperature had gone up during the night to 102° Fahrenheit. His white blood cell count had climbed from 7,000 the day he came in to 12,000. His pulse rate was now 112 beats per minute, and it had hit 160 beats per minute at the height of his fever. His blood pressure stayed steady.

Cameron's mouth was dry from his rapid shallow breathing. But the turgor of his skin when I picked it up and let it go was excellent—he was not dehydrated. His urine output on each eight-hour shift had averaged over a liter, good evidence that he was well hydrated.

I laid the diaphragm of my stethoscope gently on all four quadrants of the abdomen, listening at each site for twenty seconds. There was almost complete silence, only the *whoosh* of blood rushing through my ears. The normal bowel sounds were gone and replaced by high-pitched and infrequent tinkling sounds. The loops of bowel had ceased their normal peristalsis so as to wall off the inflammatory process, keep it from spreading.

I rubbed my hands together to warm them. I gently brought the palm of my right hand down over his lower abdomen, beginning palpation away from where he complained of pain. I could feel no mass. The spleen was not palpable. But he was still tender in the area near his gallbladder. When I pushed down and then rapidly lifted my hand away, the ripple it sent through his abdomen caused him to wince—he still had "rebound" tenderness.

There comes a point at which you *have* to open up an abdomen—do a laparotomy—so as not to miss a potential surgical catastrophe. A surgeon who finds something wrong in the abdomen only 60 percent of the time is being too adventurous, opening bellies that he or she should probably wait on. On the other hand, a surgeon whose batting average is 100 percent is being too cautious, waiting till it would be obvious even to a layman that an abdominal catastrophe is occurring. To wait that long is to allow common conditions like appendicitis to become very advanced and complicated by rupture and abscess formation.

I stepped outside and paged Sue McCoy. She turned out to be just down the hall. We conferred. She said she had been trying to find me. She too had decided a few minutes ago that we could wait no longer. Cameron needed to go down to the operating room. We both went in to tell Cameron.

When, later, I made the offer to scrub in at surgery, Sue said, "Good, see you down there!"

I dashed home for a quick bite and a few minutes with the kids. I told Rajani where I was going. My tone was matter-of-fact. I told her the truth: I was scared but I felt obliged to be there for my patient. But her discomfort at what I was doing was mounting; she wanted to talk to me. Only the fact that I had to rush back to surgery postponed our conversation.

A half hour later I was scrubbed and gowned, standing on the left side of Cameron, my hands clasped together in papal fashion, trying to stay out of the way until needed. The operating room nurses, notorious for being a tough breed, had been very solicitous, helping me with shoe covers, talking me through the ritual of hand scrubbing which I had forgotten, reminding me to scrub for a full five minutes, to only let water run down from my hands to the elbow and not the other way around, to come into the OR with my arms raised. Within the OR, the nurse handed me a sterile towel to wipe my hands and then helped me with gown and gloves. Sue and a young surgical resident slit the abdomen down its center, parting the rectus muscle and exposing the glistening peritoneal membrane which, when opened, revealed the shiny yellow fat globules of the omentum and beneath it loops of bowel. They had opted for a midline vertical incision rather than one under the right rib cage, because we were not sure the gallbladder was the seat of the problem; the midline incision allowed better access to other organs.

The incision was lengthened, retractors placed. Dark red drops of blood pouted at the tip of arteries that had been sealed with bursts from the electrocautery. The smell of burned flesh rose to my nostrils. The gold fat globules in the subcutaneous tissue formed a bright wreath around the incision which had now been pulled into a wide oval. The liver presided majestically over the upper abdomen, its crimson-cardinal edge like an arched curtain over the organs below. Beneath its undersurface, just peeking out, was the dark green gallbladder. Sue put her hand in and felt the gallbladder, massaged it between her thumb and fingers the way you would feel a coin purse. The purse was empty: there were no stones in it and none in the duct that led from it into the duodenum.

She stepped back and told me to feel around, and I inserted my hand into Cameron's belly. My yellow gloved hand, now streaked with blood, looked as if it belonged to someone else as I felt the gallbladder, ran my fingers across the smooth liver. She nodded at me to go on and so I felt the spleen, felt the loops of bowel and the strong thump of the aorta behind. There was blood on my hands, blood all around. As internists, how often our hands probe the surface of a belly, imagining what is below, stumbling on the surface like a skiff over the ocean beneath which all sorts of treasures lurk. I stepped back reluctantly.

Now Sue systematically examined the rest of the abdomen, palpating the spleen, the liver, feeding the small bowel loop by loop through her fingers in search of any abnormality, feeling the cecum and the appendix and the colon.

"There is nothing I can see wrong. No mesenteric lymph nodes. The appendix looks okay. The gallbladder looks sort of okay."

They irrigated the abdomen and now started a second careful examination of every inch of bowel, of all the organs.

Sue looked at me. "Well, at least there is no bowel perforation or strangulation. I'm going to go ahead and take out the appendix and gallbladder."

She removed the appendix swiftly and surely, tying a purse-string knot at the base of the cecum that allowed the stump to pucker in and be buried. Then she packed the bowel to one side, changed places with the resident, allowing him to remove the gallbladder from its bed. She hooked an L-shaped retractor under the liver and lifted up the free edge of the liver and handed the retractor to me, indicating with her hand over mine how much tension I was to apply. Then Sue and the resident dissected the gallbladder free of the undersurface of the liver. He tied off the artery to the gallbladder, tied off the cystic duct and then delivered the gallbladder into a kidney basin.

While the resident closed up, Sue and I slit the gallbladder open at a side table. The bile within was dark green, almost black. We looked for stones on its bile-stained insides; there were none.

I stripped off my bloody gloves. There were some streaks of blood on my gown. I remembered my final year of training in India, my surgical rotation: We "junior house-surgeons" did the sebaceous cyst removals, the circumcisions and occasionally the hernias and hydroceles. The surgical postgraduates fought over the stomach ulcers, the thyroids, the cancerous breasts. On my last day on the general surgery ward, I was rewarded for good work by being allowed to do a gastrojejunostomy: hooking up stomach to jejunum and bypassing an ulcer in the duodenum. A surgical postgraduate on the other side of the table had walked me through it. I remember stepping away three hours later, blood on my gloves, blood on my gown, a postcoital kind of weariness and euphoria washing over me, understanding the opium that drove people to become surgeons. It did not sway me—I was certain I wanted to be an internist.

I changed back into street clothes in the men's locker room. When I came out, Sue was in the surgical lounge where she was dictating her notes.

I waited to chat with Sue.

When she was done dictating, we talked about plans for Cameron's care. We agreed that she would take care of him on the surgical service for twenty-four hours. At that point, if all was well, I would take over.

"Thanks for scrubbing with us," she said to me. "It was kind of reassuring to have you there. I mean, despite everything the CDC says, if you listen to that Lorraine Day woman long enough, you get very scared. To see you there made me feel better." (Lorraine Day was the orthopedic surgeon who at one time worked at San Francisco General; she preached that the government was hiding AIDS facts, that the virus was much more infectious than anyone realized, that for all you knew you could get it in a salad bar if a gay cook had prepared the food and accidentally bled into it . . .)

I was flattered, pleased that my being there had been helpful.

I asked Sue how she felt about my consulting her. I said, "I feel guilty for asking you—or anyone, for that matter—to subject themselves to the risk of surgery. But I want you to know that I am not singling you out. I am using the other surgeons as well."

"I know you are, Abe, and I appreciate it. To tell you the truth, I am *very*, *very* frightened every time I have to operate on these patients."

I must have looked skeptical. Sue had certainly not seemed frightened in the operating theater. In fact, she had made it seem routine. To the point where the resident, forgetting himself, had wanted to do more and more and eventually he had done it all.

"I don't dwell on it," she continued. "I just do it. But now that you're asking me, it makes me *very*, *very* frightened."

I understood, of course. In my heart I was still frightened of contagion. I thought of the possibility at times when I played with the boys or touched Rajani.

"Is Cameron the first HIV patient you have operated on?" I asked.

"Cameron is probably the biggest or longest operation I've done on an HIV patient. But you know I trained in Camden, New Jersey. And between 1982 and 1983, we did a bunch of biopsies of lymph nodes that came back 'reactive adenopathy.' I'm sure they were all HIV cases. Not to mention all the trauma we took care of."

"Did you know that at the time? That those lymph nodes might be HIV- related?"

"I don't think we knew for sure—I don't think I was fully aware of AIDS till 1984 or so. We were very careful, but still . . . like I said, I don't like to dwell on it."

She turned back to her dictation and I left.

By the next morning, Cameron's acute pain had subsided, though he was still sore from the operative wound. Even though the gallbladder had looked normal to the naked eye, the pathologist reported that it was inflamed and infiltrated with white blood cells. Cameron did have acalculous cholecystitis.

21

NORMAN SANGER, my only patient with hemophilia and AIDS, could remember many nights in his childhood when he lay awake in pain. A knee or an elbow would start to swell from bleeding within the joint capsule. "I didn't want to wake my parents up, I wanted them to get a good night's sleep—so many, many nights they had sat on the edge of my bed with me, holding ice packs to my knee or thigh, measuring the circumference of my leg every hour, holding me when I cried in pain, watching the clock to see if they could dose me again with a painkiller. I *hated* to wake them, I hated the dutiful way they would get up out of bed, put on the lights and come to me, not complaining, not grudging the sleep lost. And then in the morning, with no sleep at all, they would still go to work and—if I was in the hospital by then—come and sit up with me one more night. So rather than wake them, I would grit my teeth and wait for morning. I'd play this one hymn over and over again on my toy record player: it was 'Joy Comes in the Morning.' I can't hear that hymn anymore without my teeth gritting and without feeling pain in my limbs. 'Joy Comes in the Morning.' "

Norman Sanger was diagnosed with hemophilia shortly after his birth. By nine years of age, the arthritis from the repeated bleeds into his joints gave Norman a stiff, robotlike gait. Those were the days before factor VIII concentrate. Treatment of hemophilia consisted of admitting the child to the hospital for every major bleed and infusing large volumes of fresh plasma until the child had enough factor VIII circulating for the bleeding to finally stop. By the age of nine, Norman had visited the hospital more times than most children had visited an ice cream parlor. By then he was also aware that if his parents made do with the same old car for years, if they dressed modestly and took no vacations, if they worked weekends in addition to their regular work, if they had elected to have only one child, it was because they were committing every penny that came in to keeping their only son alive.

I suppose every doctor at some point sees himself or herself reflected in the patient seated opposite, every doctor begins to ask what blind luck has resulted in being the *listener* and not the reciter of the horrid tale being told, what would it be like to be the patient? It was easy for me to identify with Norman; he was my age, he was male and he was heterosexual. What linked us now was that he had AIDS and I treated AIDS.

I would anticipate his visits, look forward to drawing him out. In learning about him it seemed I was learning about myself.

"I felt I was a heavy burden on my parents," Norman told me. "My father was a coach for a high school and also taught math; my mother worked in a school cafeteria. I always felt as if my bleeds happened at the worst possible times. And my parents were always good-natured about it—as if they had fully expected to have a hemophiliac son and saw no tragedy in it. They would stop what they were doing and bring me to the hospital.

"When the team my father coached was playing, or even if it was a softball meet at church, I used to have a chair to sit on and watch. I could see how much fun my father was having with the other kids, and it made me wonder if he didn't want that from me. . . ."

If my own childhood was a rich imagined one, full of imagined victories and disasters, when I listened to Norman I felt as if he never had a childhood. As a small tot he had already developed such adult feelings, experienced the kind of medical adversity most of us will never see in a lifetime. Norman showed me his high school yearbook one time: In a group photo where the other kids were in jeans and T-shirts, Norman was in a blazer and slacks with a bow tie. He was smaller than everyone else in his class, but he appeared older, more worldly. A photograph of him alone appeared later; he was editor of the school paper, and from his pose, again with the bow tie, it appeared he took this so very seriously.

His great passion was the Dodgers. As a child, unable to compete in contact sports, he had instead mastered the statistics of baseball. He could rattle off batting averages and winning percentages in a manner that dazzled his classmates, whose talents were confined to hitting or catching the ball. "One of the joys of growing out of childhood was the realization that most of my friends from high school were now mere spectators when it came to sports, just like I had been for all that time. And I had years of spectating experience over them. I felt like things had evened up!"

In his early teens he witnessed the miracle of the commercial production of factor VIII in a concentrate. The painful, large-volume and time-consuming infusions of plasma that had to be administered in the hospital were now replaced by a single infusion of factor VIII that could be given at home. Hemophiliacs like Norman were suddenly empowered: they could often tell when a bleed was beginning and could abort it with a quick infusion at home.

Norman, who had been raised in California, finished high school and chose a tiny community college in Kentucky. He was offered a full scholarship. He wound up staying in the area, living in a town of 9,000. He now held an excellent job as personnel manager for a large coal mine not far from the college he graduated from. I often wondered what would make a California boy, a well-educated one, stay in that small community. Perhaps with his learning, he found an acceptance, a respect and status that would have been lacking in L.A. or San Francisco. The townsfolk were simple, unquestioning, and very willing to enfold him into the tiny community, give him a place on the town council, welcome him into their church. Another reason Norman stayed in Kentucky was the excellent hemophilia care the state offered: every few months, a team of hematologists, dentists, physical therapists, orthopedic surgeons and social workers would hold a hemophilia camp close to his town. All the hemophiliacs in the surrounding counties would be seen, their needs for factor VIII assessed, their dental needs taken care of by dentists experienced with free-bleeders. Those who might be candidates for joint reconstruction or replacement were assessed and given appointments in Louisville or Lexington.

Just when it looked like Norman was getting the upper hand, looking to live an almost normal life, there came the news that factor VIII—the miracle potion that had liberated him—might have also poisoned him with the agent of AIDS. The mission of the hemophilia camps suddenly changed: they now seemed to revolve around AIDS rather than hemophilia. The leading cause of death in hemophiliacs was not bleeding but AIDS. The children and adults that Norman had come to know from all his visits to camp now showed the ravages of AIDS on top of their stigmata of hemophilia. With each camp, a few old friends, a few familiar faces were missing, and a few more had developed the wasting, the sallow complexion, the brittle hair. In the time period of 1982 to 1985, before the HIV test was developed, Norman became more and more aware that he might be infected. He carried on with his work and decided not to worry about something that was beyond his control. Besides, around that time, a romance was brewing in his life, a romance that in its ardor seemed quite capable of eclipsing AIDS and hemophilia.

Claire lived in an apartment just down the street from the mine. From his office window, Norman used to see her set out for her job in the Piggly Wiggly every day, leading her little son across the street to her neighbors who looked after him till she got back. He noticed everything about them: the way she said goodbye to her son, the way the little boy pouted, the way she drew away from her boy so reluctantly, the way he rushed back to her arms at the end of the day. Norman was filled with the sense that the little boy and the woman needed him in order to be complete, that they were a step away from the poorhouse, from debtors' prison. He felt as if he had been waiting in this hollow for them to come along.

A mutual friend introduced them and Norman courted Claire carefully and properly. If Norman was well read, well traveled and an intellectual, Claire was a simple girl who had known only hard times. She had survived the death of a husband and was on the brink of poverty. She was blonde, shy, quiet and pretty. Her frail, petite frame— even smaller than his—made him feel like he *could* be her protector. Her son adored Norman. Norman proposed and bought a diamond ring for her. She accepted.

Norman had been postponing getting the HIV test. But after Claire accepted his ring, he knew he could not postpone it any longer. He took the test and in a week learned that he was infected with HIV.

I pressed Norman about the moment he found out he was infected. Did he cry? What did he say? What was he thinking? What did he do later? Where did he go? Norman never answered my questions, side-stepping them each time. All the years of his battle with hemophilia had left him no time for self-pity and despair. He appeared to have brought this same attitude to his HIV infection: it was a disability to be worked around, to be negotiated and overcome. If death was a possibility, it had *always* been a possibility. He did not dwell on death before and would not dwell on it now.

He told Claire at once, as soon as he knew he was infected. Their relationship had not yet been consummated. He explained to her the risks and what the future held, offered her the chance to back out of it, to come and see me and talk about transmission of the virus, about safe sex, even though, at this point, he himself had not come to see me. Claire saw no reason to see me, no reason to rescind her decision to marry him. He told me later that he had promised her "ten good years," which were more good years than Claire had had in her life up to that point.

Later, when I heard this, and when I came to know her, I wondered whether in her innocence, her simplicity, she had perhaps pictured ten years in which Norman would be in perfect health and then at the end of the tenth year suddenly drop dead? Was she informed enough about AIDS, or about hemophilia, to be prepared for disability, for prolonged sickness?

Norman had been married for two years and was known to have been HIV-positive for the same duration when he finally came to my office. He had sought no special medical attention for the HIV. His family doctor in Kentucky, a Parsi from Bombay, would call me from time to time to discuss Norman's case. The doctor had tried to get Norman to come and see me, but Norman's rationale was that since there was no treatment, he saw no point to the long drive down. Just as with his hemophilia, he had read and learned enough about the disease to know what could be done.

Issues of confidentiality and prejudice at the mines or in his social circle did not concern Norman greatly; he was too wrapped up in taking care of Claire and the little boy he had adopted. Others in the personnel office were aware of what Norman had; his good friend Sharon Phillips, the primary care nurse for the mine offices, was also in the know. If anyone else knew or suspected, Norman didn't really care.

He came to my office when he heard that AZT was now being made available outside of study protocols. His doctor insisted that AZT was out of his league and that Norman would *have* to come to me.

I remember the first time Norman walked into my office. He was a small man, about five foot three inches, and he held himself very upright. His face was serene and he seemed quite oblivious to his limping gait. In his lifetime he had seen so many doctors and been hospitalized so many times that the clinic held no awe for him. When he extended his hand to shake mine, he did so by bringing his trunk forward until his hand reached mine: his shoulder and elbow had a very limited range of motion. His handshake was firm.

When I examined him with his clothes off, I was surprised by the extent of the damage done by the hemophilia. The repeated bleeds into his joints had affected his growth and left him with a body disproportionately smaller than his head. Several of his joints were frozen or else had limited movement.

He had no complaints related to any of these findings, even though they were undoubtedly a source of chronic pain. He did complain of weight loss and fatigue; he was 15 pounds down from his normal 135 pounds. His temperature in our clinic was slightly elevated, and he said that low-grade fever had been going on for weeks. He told me his hair was falling out. I rubbed his hair between my fingers: it was dull and lusterless and felt brittle. When I tugged, a few hairs readily came away. When I made him lie flat on his back so I could feel his belly, his knees sat up off the bed a good six inches: he had flexion contractures in both hips.

After he was dressed, we talked about AZT. Norman was reluctant to begin. I obtained a CD4 count which came back at 180 cells/mm^3—the normal should have been about 1,000. The following week his doctor called me to say Norman had developed severe esophageal candidiasis. We admitted him and treated him. At that point Norman agreed to start on AZT.

I never saw a more dramatic response to AZT than I did with Norman. His hair stopped falling out and grew back thicker. His skin, which had begun to look waxy, regained a healthy pink color. He put on weight and I even kidded him about a trace of a paunch. He told me his energy level had quadrupled and he wished he had been on the drug before. It was a satisfying moment for both of us.

I often tried to compare Norman Sanger with other hemophiliacs I had taken care of. Many had a reckless quality to their lives, as if to compensate for all the admonitions they had heard to "be careful." One teen had insisted on riding dirt bikes, crashing often and once developing life-threatening bleeding in the splenic bed. Another hemophiliac I met in Boston had wanted to be a Green Beret but had been turned down. Instead, he took to wearing combat boots and fatigues and worked as a bouncer in a nightclub. One night he called complaining of high fever, but he refused to come in to be seen. His girlfriend said his fever was 105 degrees Fahrenheit. "Look, Doc," he said over the phone, "just call me in some extra-strength Tylenol, some Phenergan and I'll be all right. And by the way, call me in 1400 units of factor VIII—I've got a little bleed in my elbow." I called him the next day to see how he was; his girlfriend told me he had gone on a hunting trip.

Norman Sanger had none of this recklessness. But just like the other hemophiliacs I knew, he rarely ceded control to anyone. He started AZT only when he was ready to. If I recommended admission to the hospital, Norman decided whether to accept it or not. The recklessness I saw in the nightclub bouncer manifested in Norman in another way: Norman had no fear of death; death was something that I and all my other patients seemed to dread. It was the very thing that made AIDS so frightful, the *essence* of AIDS: the fact that it was a uniformly fatal disease. But this seemed to hold no fear for Norman.

Late on a Sunday evening in the spring of 1988, I admitted Norman Sanger to the Miracle Center with the diagnosis of probable *Pneumocystis* pneumonia. It had been a glorious day for a ride up to Roan Mountain, for a picnic, and even for tennis before the light failed. To have to come back to the house, summoned by my beeper, and to then put Norman in the hospital had been a reminder that the day had not been glorious for everyone

Monday morning I called Norman to tell him that my partner, Felix, would cover the Miracle Center that week while I worked the VA. I would not be by to see him that day.

Norman, who said he was feeling a little better, accepted this; he knew and liked Felix. Still, something in the tone of his voice stayed with me: he had not sounded himself. Later that afternoon, when I ran into Felix, he told me that Norman seemed discouraged, something neither of us had seen in him before. On an impulse, when I was done for the day, I decided to pay a social visit to Norman.

I stood outside Norman's room now. I could not hear the TV and I wondered if he was sleeping. I knocked gently and heard him say, "Come in." Norman greeted me and seemed pleased to see me, but he was much less animated than usual.

The curtains were drawn and the room almost dark but for the glow of the setting sun showing through the thick drapes. Wall oxygen was bubbling through a humidifier and being delivered to him through green nasal cannulae. His roast beef dinner lay untouched next to his bed. Norman was breathing rapidly, about twenty-eight breaths a minute, and a fine sheen of sweat had formed on his brow.

Despite the smell of the roast beef, I detected with alarm the faint and familiar scent of AIDS that I had smelled in Cameron Tolliver's room, a smell that I will always be able to identify, a smell that still fills me with dread.

Norman told me in a flat voice that he had had his bronchoscopy an hour ago. He had been kept "NPO"—nothing by mouth—in preparation for the bronchoscopy. Now he was asked to wait another hour until the anesthetic in the back of his throat wore off so that food would not go into his lungs when he tried to swallow. He was not hungry anyway, he said.

I asked him how the bronchoscopy had gone and he said, "All right, I guess."

Claire, his wife, sat next to his bed. I found myself studying her whenever I could, curious about this woman who knowingly married a man infected with HIV, a man who likely would die of his infection well short of the ten years he had promised her. I had never been able to engage her in conversation or draw her out. She had many opportunities to step out of the room and to quiz me about Norman's condition, but she had never done so, content, it seemed, to get all her information from Norman. For all I knew, even now she was counting on eight more years.

"You sounded really down on the phone this morning," I said. "I thought I would come and see you before I went home."

Norman looked at me and nodded. "Thanks for coming. Last night, after you left . . . was the lowest point," he said.

"You know you *are* entitled to be a little down," I said. "It would be superhuman to always—"

"—I want to be remembered for having had dignity. For courage. Sometimes it is so tough . . ."

"You *will* be remembered for those things—"

"No, you don't understand. All my life, that's all I've had, that's the currency I built up: *courage* and *dignity* with this difficult disease—diseases. That's what made me different. Other kids had blazing speed, or the height for basketball, or looks, or wealth or . . . But what I had was these mental qualities—useless to other people but critical to me. It was my thing."

Here he trailed off and I was about to say something when he continued: "And last night, for the first time since I was a little boy, I wondered whether I could keep it up, whether this disease would make me lose it all?"

I could not hold Norman's gaze. He was looking at me as if I was supposed to reply. As if, despite all his experience with medical people, for once he expected a pearl of wisdom to come from my mouth, something more than a platitude, something that would tangibly ease his mental anguish. I was distressed by what he had said. I had drawn strength from *his* courage and his dignity, had counted on them. Now it was almost as if he was asking me to lead the dance, and I feared I did not know how.

I spied an envelope tucked under the telephone on the night table. He had written on the back of it: three telephone numbers, all with a strange area code. Above the three numbers it was written: "Dad, California."

He saw me look at the phone numbers. "Every time I speak to my father I wonder, will this be the last time I speak to him? Is there something I must say now or will there be another chance? For so many years he and I have talked matter-of-factly, as if hemophilia or AIDS is just one of those things that we had to negotiate—all of us. But now I find I want to hear something different from him. I want to say something different to him, like 'Daddy, take care of me, don't let this happen to me. I'm just a little boy and I want you to take care of me . . .' something I never really said when I was a little boy."

I found these words heart-wrenching. I looked to Claire: her face was expressionless and she was looking at the floor.

I felt so out of place and awkward hovering beside Norman's bed, standing tall next to him, occupying this spot reserved for the doctor. If I could have sat down I would have, just as I used to sit on Will Johnson's bed. But Norman might have been uncomfortable with that. Claire was in the only chair on the other side of the bed. As a reflex, I reached for my stethoscope. I pushed the stethoscope back in my pocket, remembering that was not what I was here for.

I think Norman felt for my awkwardness. His glance expressed pity for me, sympathy for my wretched state, benign as it was.

There was nothing more to say.

I reached out to shake his hand to say goodbye.

As my hand touched his, I found myself sliding my palm around so that our hands were in a "soul shake," our thumbs hooked together. I covered both our clasped hands now with my left hand. I wasn't sure why I did this, except I wanted to convey to him how much I felt for his situation, how much he moved me, how I could not fathom how one man could bear all this suffering, how I kept thinking he was me and I him. And it was tearing me up even if he still had some strength.

My handshake took him a little by surprise and he looked carefully at my face again and said, "Thank you, Abraham."

Tears rushed into my eyes and I had to turn away. But not before he noticed. I could not control myself. I left saying goodbye over my shoulder, not even looking at Claire, because the tears were welling out onto my cheeks now.

When I opened the door, there was Felix, my partner, his back to me, studying the chart. He looked over his shoulder and was startled to see me. He was about to say something but caught sight of my eyes. I could not offer a word. I patted Fil's back and slid past him. I walked down the hall hoping that nobody would see me, swiping ineffectually at my eyes.

In my car I felt ashamed for crying. What kind of message did it convey when you broke down in front of your patient? Certainly not a message of hope. I prayed he did not misinterpret my crying as a sign that the end was very near. The end could be still very far away. But not eight years away.

On my way back to the VA I kept thinking about Norman's two "things": dignity and courage. The only two gifts he ever had, the two things he could control, the two things that he wanted most to be remembered by.

I decided not to go home. I parked near the gazebo, waited for my emotions to settle down.

I needed time before putting my armor back on again, resuming the role of husband, father and family man. I could not bring these feelings home.

Later, when I entered the house, I wondered if my clothes smelled of AIDS. Was this the scent my sons associated with their father? I showered quickly but I could not put the day behind me. All evening I paced, restless, filled with a nameless anxiety. In bed, I pretended to sleep, but could not. I stayed very still, but I knew that something coming from me, some visceral emanation—fear, terror—was keeping Rajani awake too. I felt her there, waiting, silent in the dark.

22

"IF YOU HAD TOLD me a year ago that my two best friends in this world would be Bobby Keller and Jacko, I would have told you you didn't know B from bull's foot."

We were sitting on the cinder-block steps outside Vickie's trailer. Vickie was smoking and I was puffing away too on one of her cigarettes. It had become a ritual every time I visited her; she loved the idea of seducing her doctor into a forbidden cigarette. Vickie had called to tell me she had something that Cameron Tolliver, the patient Sue McCoy operated on, had entrusted her to give to me. I had brought Vickie some prescriptions and had looked in on Clyde, who was sleeping, the TV blaring away as usual. I saw some ominous signs: a gauntness had crept in, there was not much flesh in the bare leg that showed under the sheet, his skin had taken on a darker, nut-brown hue.

It was the fall of 1988 and the wildflowers around Vickie's trailer were putting on a show. The Vickie McCray standing next to me was different from the one I first knew. She was a veteran of support groups and a busy volunteer at TAP. There was a fine stubble of hair peeking out from under her bandanna. I teased her that *I* was the one pulling my hair out now. Vickie's best friends were Bobby Keller—the most outrageously campy and funny gay male in Johnson City—and Jacko, a relatively new patient to my clinic. "If you ask me, what brought us all together was when Cameron Tolliver got sick. Cameron was one of those I liked right away in support group. Between you and me, he was the only one there who acted halfway normal the first time I went. He'd hardly talk, just listen. And when he said something, it warn't no smartaleck thing like Bobby Keller, say. You could trust it. Kind of like the quiet wife of a jawing preacher, know what I mean? After he had that gallbladder surgery at the hospital, why, he just kept going downhill. And all of us started to go round his place to help him. I mean there wasn't one person in support group that didn't go to see him and help out.

"His mind was clear right to the end. But he had that diarrhea so bad. Not many people could be around it; they'd come and 'How-are-you?' and 'Can-I-do-anything-for-you?' and light out of there faster than greased lightning. But Bobby, Jacko and I, somehow we just couldn't leave. We got in there, put on them gloves and changed his diaper, washed him up. But as soon as you did it, but there he'd go again. It was terrible: like some faucet being turned on. You know he warn't eating nothing so it was like he was just shitting out his flesh, if you pardon my French. I hope to God that Clyde—or me—never have to go through that. Bobby Keller says he'd just as soon someone take a gun and put him out of his misery if he ever gets that bad. Is that going to happen to all of us? To Clyde? To me?"

I lied and shook my head. The way the virus could attack the bowels was remarkable. In Africa, wasting and diarrhea are such discrete and common manifestations of the disease that AIDS is referred to there as "slim disease." But even in North America, diarrhea is a common problem. And for some unfortunates like Cameron Tolliver, their entire fight with HIV is dominated by diarrhea. Cameron's gallbladder problem had occurred on a backdrop of diarrhea that barely ceased. Why some patients suffered so with diarrhea was quite mysterious.

Cameron's gift for me was two small polished stones, about the size of walnuts—"lucky" stones, he told Vickie they were. One was a shiny mahogany and the other a variegated green and brown stone with what looked like a third stone embedded in it. They were the kind of stones you might see in a shop that sells crystals and incense sticks. They were beautiful. I rubbed them together between my fingers, hearing them click together like marbles. They made me think of Mrs. Paez and her genuine pearls.

How I wished Cameron had been able to give them to me himself.

I wished that Cameron could have explained to me the significance of the stones. If he had an interest in stones and crystals, I had never known about it. In our encounters in the hospital, he had allowed me to dictate the pace and the nature of our interaction. His illness had dominated everything. So much of who he had been as a person I was now left to imagine. That was the way things worked. I knew everything about them—and nothing.

"He had something for each one of us, little gifts like that," Vickie said. "And the best part is he was living in this one room of his friend's house. The friend was hardly ever there, and the only reason Cameron stayed was 'cause he had been looking after his friend's old mother. She was in a wheelchair and real weak, and it came to a point where he was weaker than she was. The visiting nurses used to come and take care of the old lady, and Cameron would ask us to wheel her in so he could see her and make sure she was all right. Bobby Keller has been going over there about every other day checking on the old lady 'cause he knows Cameron up in heaven is still worrying about her. Bobby says he thinks it's not long before she's going to have to be in a nursing home."

Bobby Keller, the clown, whom Vickie had been so suspicious of when she first saw him in support group wearing his leather outfit, had revealed his sweet caring side to Vickie. And running with him nowadays, his buddy, was a new support group member, Jacko. Vickie said that Bobby and Jacko would come over to Vickie's trailer, help her clean house, go shopping for her, baby-sit Clyde while Vickie ran some errands.

Jacko was not a native of east Tennessee. He had lived in Sacramento until he was diagnosed with Kaposi's sarcoma (KS). I had assumed Jacko was his pet name, but I learned from Vickie much later that it was an abbreviation for Jackie O, a reference to his getup at a Halloween party some years ago, a nickname that he then adopted. He had a sister who lived in east Tennessee, and she took him in when he lost his job and his lover died. She was married with grown children; her husband was employed by ETSU. She freed up a bedroom for him and took care of his medical expenses until he finally qualified for Medicaid.

Although I had seen KS frequently in Boston, Jacko had the most florid KS of any of my patients in Tennessee. When he first walked into my clinic, it was difficult to see beyond the KS and discern the young man underneath. A fleshy, violaceous KS lesion hung down from his right eyebrow, almost covering his eye; more lesions were peppered over his face. When he opened his mouth, his palate was covered with a dark purple patch of KS and there were more KS lesions on his cheeks. One unusual KS lesion had grown out from the space between two teeth and hung down like a tiny parachute.

Jacko showed me the birth and evolution of a KS lesion. One day he came to my office with a little puffiness under his left eye and a yellow blemish with well-circumscribed borders under the eyelid. I would have sworn that he had been punched and that this was a four-day-old bruise that was going through its color changes. Jacko informed me otherwise: it was a new KS lesion "being born." He could recognize an even earlier stage, well before anything was visible externally, when he would feel a little tingling in that area. The next time I saw him, the original yellow bruise had turned purple and swelled up, becoming a perfect match to all the other lesions on his body.

KS was intriguing. This once-rare tumor had become epidemic in the era of AIDS. With AIDS, it was almost exclusively seen among gay men: it was extremely rare among intravenous drug users or hemophiliacs. Despite being a cancer, it behaved almost like an infection associated with fecal-oral transmission, much like amebiasis in gay men. Initial KS lesions, as with Jacko's, were often in the mouth or on the nose, as if to confirm this method of spread. The penis was another common site for a KS lesion.

Even though KS was disfiguring, if the patient was fortunate it remained largely a cosmetic problem. I generally did not make any attempt to treat KS unless I was forced to. Patients usually succumbed to other problems unrelated to KS.

Occasionally, the KS could suddenly erupt, with new lesions blossoming all over the body. This had happened to Jacko. The tumor formed one big confluent patch on his legs. It obstructed the lymphatic drainage of the right leg, causing the leg to swell and take on the appearance of a tree trunk whose bark was oozing. I began Jacko on chemotherapy for this reason. The once-a-week chemotherapy was mild in its side effects—no hair loss or severe bone-marrow suppression—but it did make Jacko's leg shrink gradually in circumference. It had very little effect on the size of the KS lesions elsewhere in the body.

While I was trying to find a dentist to see him and remove the broccoli-shaped KS lesion that hung down between his teeth, Jacko took matters into his own hands: he tied a loop of dental floss around the base of the tiny tumor and pulled the noose tight. The lesion lost its blood supply and dropped off.

Jacko had missed several clinic visits with me. I felt slight hostility from him. He was very close to Bobby Keller, and I wondered if Bobby had told him the story of how I put his lover, Ed, on a ventilator against Bobby's wishes. Bobby was friendly to me, but that incident always seemed to stand between us, something I had been forgiven for but that neither of us could forget. Jacko's hostility was directed not just at me but at all medical personnel. It was a barrier that neither Carol nor I had been able to penetrate.

I asked Vickie now how Jacko was doing; I told her how difficult it had been for us to get to know him. How he had missed several rounds of chemotherapy and had not answered our calls or our reminder post-cards.

"He's not doing that well, if you ask me. That KS is all over the place. He uses Avon foundation to cover it on his face. But it's not much use. Remember that last real warm weekend we had? Well, I invited him and Bobby over for a cookout. He asked me if I didn't mind if he wore short sleeves and shorts—he usually never goes anywhere except in long sleeves. I said I didn't mind at all, I wanted for him to feel comfortable. And when he came, I never realized how many of the KS things he had. I mean it's *all* over his skin, as if he's been spray-painted with it. And his left leg is still swollen. But that toe that used to hurt him real bad don't bother him no more. You know why?"

I shook my head. I remembered that one of the toes on his right foot was completely purple with KS.

"He said the other day, when he pulled off his sneaker, the toe just came off. Evidently it was just about dead. Said he picked it up and threw it in the garbage."

Vickie shuddered as she said this. I wondered if Jacko had gone the dental floss route on his toe.

"Now, I been around these gay men quite a bit," Vickie said. "But I think Jacko is the only one that is like real guilty about being homosexual. It still bothers him in support group that when we get done, everybody gets up and hugs everybody else. Of course Clyde, when he used to go, just marches out whenever he pleases. And old Ethan Nidiffer don't stay for no hugging. He just chugs on out of there; he hates it that people smoke in there 'cause it bothers his lungs. Jacko stays, but he doesn't care for all the hugs, though he'll do it anyway. He says he wished he'd never been born homosexual. That it is a cross he has to bear. He was always a loner according to his sister, someone who more or less tried to disappear into the background, if you know what I mean? And now, bless his heart, he can't disappear into the background even if he wants to."

I asked how she was coping with Clyde.

"Here we are talking about other people and meanwhile I've got me one here that's just about to drive me crazy! Clyde is slipping. There ain't two ways about it. Did you know we been to the Grand Ole Opry? And the Knoxville Zoo since I talked to you last?"

I shook my head.

"A couple of weeks ago, he ran off. Danielle and I went looking for him everywhere. None of our relatives would keep him without telling us, so we didn't know where to go look. Finally I get a call from the Salvation Army shelter that he is there. Lord knows how he got there. I go there and he says he won't come with me! No, sir! That he wants to go to the Grand Ole Opry before he dies, and I need to give him money and put him on a Greyhound. Now here's a man for whom a one-dollar bill is the same as a twenty-dollar bill, for whom Tuesday is the same as Friday. How am I supposed to let him go to the Grand Ole Opry alone? I says to him, come home and we'll talk about it, and I put my arm on him to take him away but he starts to hollering and they call the law. Well, the law comes over and says I can't take him if he didn't want to go. I had half-a-mind to tell them about the AIDS thing and I know they would have let me have him in a hurry. There was nothing I could do. I had to just drive away.

"The next morning I went and got a court order. I told the judge the way it was. I said, 'He's got AIDS and he's crazy as a loon. He no more knows his mind than a little baby does.' I get me the court order and go over to the Salvation Army and come to find out he's gone over to the Haven of Mercy!"

"How did he know about these places? How did he find his way there?"

"You tell me! *I* don't know! Beats the hell out of me. Makes me wonder how many other things about this man there must be that I don't know? When I get to the Haven of Mercy they tell me he just done took off. I looked all over for him, and when I get home he calls me from the bus station. Says I need to meet him there right now and give him money to go to Nashville or else he was going to commence a-walking. Son, I believed him. I promised him if he'd just come back with me, we'd go. That afternoon we packed the kids and drove our old junker out to Nashville."

Vickie grinned. "Spent money we didn't have but we had us a good ole time." She lit another cigarette. "We did it all. I mean *all*. Ernest Tubb's music store, Music Row, a show at the Grand Ole Opry. He saw Minnie Pearl—gave Clyde a big kick, it did. And I was glad I took him. When we got back, Clyde calmed down a lot. See this was something *real* important to him and I didn't know it. He knows he is going to die. Said it to me himself. After we came back from Nashville, he said there was one more place he wanted to go: the Knoxville Zoo. This time I didn't fight him. As soon as he said it, the next day we were off. God must be watching us 'cause the junker made it all the way and back for this trip, too, them tires as good as gone and eating oil like you won't believe. At the zoo, I got me a wheelchair and we pushed Clyde all over the place—me and Danielle. But he got real tired. On the way back he messed on himself in the car. It was a *long* trip, I tell you what. And I done cleaned the car a zillion times but I can't get the smell out."

Now Vickie swiped at tears with the back of her forearm. "I think now he is ready to die. He's gone to the two places he wanted to go to. And ever since we got back, he's taken to bed. He don't act like he wants to get up and go anywhere no more. We've had quite a few accidents. No real diarrhea, thank God. But enough where I put a diaper on him if he'll let me."

It was time for me to go. I took my leave of Vickie.

"Doc, before you go, seeing as much as you're interested in flowers, let me show you something." She pointed out a shrub on the other side of the road with red flowers on it. "Do you know what that is?"

We crossed the road and I examined the plant: a low shrub with peculiar wine-colored flowers on it. Vickie snapped off a flower and put it in my hand. It was more like a pod than a flower. The pod had burst open to reveal a brilliant cluster of bright red seeds within, shining like polished pebbles. I had never seen anything like it.

"It's called *hearts-a-bustin'*," Vickie said. She nodded emphatically when I looked at her in disbelief. "Oh yes, *hearts-a-bustin'*. It's also called 'swamp dogwood,' but I don't care for that much. 'Hearts-a-bustin': That's pretty much how I feel sometimes about what's happening to me."

23

ORIGINALLY, THE "OFFICE" for the Tri-City AIDS
Project was the dining table of an ETSU faculty volunteer. From
there it moved to Fred's sister, Bettie Lee's, dining table, where, with
the guest leaf inserted, the office had doubled in size. But there was an
acute need for a regular office with a business address, telephones, filing
space, storage space for brochures. This was particularly true if TAP was
to start receiving state and federal funds.

Fred and his sister, and later Bettie Lee by herself, did the searching
for office space. Downtown seemed to be the place to look, since the
fancy office parks near the mall or on the north side of town would be
altogether too expensive.

There were office spaces in the floors above the storefronts of downtown. Because the courthouse was nearby, a number of lawyers kept
their offices downtown, as did some accountants, chiropractors and bail
bondsmen. But not enough to keep the buildings at full occupancy.

"Our criteria for an office space were simple," Bettie Lee said to me.
"It had to be donated to us and it had to be over 700 square feet." A few
weeks of searching and it became apparent that there would be no space
donated. And with TAP's meager funds, in place of 700 feet, they
would have to settle for something a little larger than a broom closet.

"The first lead I had was when I talked to the secretary of a man who
owned a downtown building near the old Majestic Theater. When I
told her what TAP stood for, she says, 'AIDS—Ooooh! Scares me to

death.' But she didn't mind if I came and looked. And the space would have been all right for us. She had talked to her boss by then, and she wanted to clarify exactly what we would be using the office for. I said we had a support group but that it met mostly at the Episcopal Center and I didn't envision the support group meeting at the office. The office would be mostly for paperwork and for meetings of the board of directors."

The next day when Bettie Lee telephoned, the secretary put her through to the owner. He asked her, "Well, who exactly is coming here. Not people with AIDS, surely!"

Bettie Lee said, "Well, we don't really ask." She reiterated that the support group would meet elsewhere. The owner said he would have to do a poll of all the tenants and see what they thought of it. Bettie Lee called him back many times after that and was finally told by the secretary that they had done their poll and, unfortunately, the space would not be available for TAP. Other rejections followed.

Finally Bettie Lee found a place on Spring Street that had once been a studio for an artist, who had just moved out. The owner, a lawyer, had the same questions that Bettie Lee had answered over and over: Who exactly would be coming to the office? Would there be AIDS patients walking in there?

"Ultimately he did rent us the space, for which I was very grateful. We had no sign outside. Just a poster on the door. Our whole attitude then was defensive. I was conditioned by the way the town had reacted to the Connection not that long ago. You know: running them out of the neighborhood, smashing their cars when they parked there—*We don't want that element around, influencing our children*—that kind of thing. When we first opened the TAP office, I worried about things like a pipe bomb every time I unlocked the door. And I was so hurt by the questions being asked about just *renting* an office space. My *brother* has AIDS. And *of course* he would be coming to the office. These people were acting like he was radioactive or worse, that if he entered the building it would contaminate the whole place."

TAP's office on Spring Street was across the street from a rooming house. It was common for panhandlers to approach Bettie Lee as she came and left the office. In the small park opposite the office, she would see drunks and tramps fast asleep after having spent the night there.

The little office proved quite inadequate. It was a third floor walk-up. There *were* many persons with HIV who came by, but they struggled with the effort of climbing all the stairs. The ceiling was falling in, water was leaking into the walls, and the mold and moisture made it an unhealthy place to be. The sound of pigeons scurrying on the roof was incessant and the window ledge was white with pigeon droppings. If part of the goal of TAP was informing and educating the community of both TAP's presence and TAP's mission, a third-floor walk-up with an entrance from a back alley, with no sign outside, was hardly the way to go.

AT LEAST ONE TAP member—Clyde McCray—was slipping. The dementia was getting worse, making him act as if he had "old-timer's disease," according to Vickie. He had begun to have seizures. Vickie and the children felt helpless watching Clyde's eyes roll up and his body start flailing. The headboard slapped against the trailer wall like a grotesque musical accompaniment to his seizures. The only blessing was that after the seizure, after Vickie and Danielle had cleaned him up and held him and told him how much they loved him, Clyde would begin a long refreshing sleep. Vickie would go to the porch and have a quiet cry, burn up a half-pack of cigarettes before she could bring herself to go in again.

Clyde was back to diapers full time, and he rarely got out of bed. He would forget what he was doing and stop with his fork in his hand as if he had no idea what the instrument was for or how to guide the food to his mouth. Vickie would gently remind him and steer his hand with the fork in it so that it picked up the beans and went to his mouth. Sometimes, out of frustration at his condition, Clyde would begin to cry. Before he got ill, Vickie had never seen him cry.

When he cried, Vickie would hold him and rock him. Sometimes he would push her away, like a child throwing a tantrum, too angry to have its tears wiped.

Vickie called me and said that Clyde had become almost mute. "You have to prod him to get him to say anything. Danielle will go up to him and say, 'I love you, Daddy.' He won't say nothing. She says, 'Well? Do you love me?' Nothing. Then she'll say, 'Daddy, say: I love you, Danielle.' And he'll come out with 'I love you, Danielle.' Otherwise, nothing."

My partner, Felix, saw Clyde in the clinic. He took Vickie aside and told her that Clyde was fading rapidly. Did she want to take care of him at home? Would she want to consider a nursing home? Vickie was adamant that Clyde should die at home, in the bedroom, in the trailer with everyone around.

Felix told her what to expect. Clyde was likely to regress further, become totally dependent on her for all his bodily functions and eventually slip into a coma. Felix suggested it was probably time for Hospice of Johnson City to help provide care at home. A registered nurse would come out several times a week to check on Clyde. A trained volunteer would be assigned to the family to help deal with their emotional needs. There would be a nurse on call twenty-four hours, and Vickie would be trained in nursing skills such as taking his pulse, blood pressure and temperature. The word "hospice" shook Vickie and she began to cry. Hospice seemed so final, so terminal.

Almost on cue, the week after her visit, and once Hospice of Johnson City started to come by, the fevers and night sweats returned. Vickie was now taking vital signs, recording in a spiral bound notebook what transpired on her shift: how much fluid he drank, how many times he urinated, his level of consciousness, and his blood pressure. She had even picked up on words like "diaphoretic" and "dyspneic" and was using them in the diary and over the phone to Felix.

The only thing Clyde would eat was ice cream, and Vickie began to buy it by the gallon. He no longer talked at all. When the children came home from school, they simply climbed into bed on either side of him and they all watched television.

By the following week he barely recognized the kids or Vickie. He was taking so little fluid that hospice, under our instruction, had begun an intravenous line and administered IV fluids. I had talked to Vickie about the IV fluids. I said, "All it will do is prolong his life."

"I know that," Vickie said. "But I'm the one that takes care of him, has to watch him disappear piece by piece. And I can't bear to watch him shrivel like a prune, have his skin shrink onto his bones, have his urine output drop to nothing."

After the IV had been in place for three days, Fil called Vickie to ask how Clyde was doing. She said, "You can say he has more or less slipped into a coma. When I go into the room, I am afraid to come out again because of what I might find when I return. I am not sleeping: I am just going through each day like a zombie. Just functioning, just living and going on with the children's needs. I feel as he dies, a part of me is dying."

On a Tuesday, Clyde's vital signs were dropping all day. The nurse told Vickie that the time was getting closer. Did she want to say goodbye to him?

Vickie told me later: "All I could think was: Oh, God, it's here, it's here, the time is here. I sent my cousin to the school to fetch Danielle because Danielle had very much wanted to be there when her father died. Danielle was my partner, helping me take care of her Daddy all those days. We had kept Junior away when Clyde got real sick. Danielle said she wanted to be there when he died, no matter what. At fourteen I decided that she was old enough for that if that was what she wanted. We were both there at his side, talking to him, telling him how much we loved him, each one of us holding his hand.

"He opened his big eyes once and saw us both and for just a moment it seemed like it was the old Clyde behind those eyes. He wanted to say something to us but he couldn't. I knew he was scared—I'd been married to the man so long I could read his mind. I said to him, 'It's all right, sweetheart. Go on. It's all right. God loves you. He will take care of you. Jesus will take care of you. Go on.'

"He opened his eyes a few minutes later, as if he'd seen or heard something else right above him, and that was it. We were there when he took his last breath."

When Vickie called to say that Clyde had died, I thought of the television in his bedroom and how difficult it must have been for Vickie to finally turn it off. I imagined her sitting in the silence of the trailer and wanted to go to her. She had never been someone I thought of as a patient I was paid to help. She felt more like a sister to me. I had been pulled further and further into her world.

Now, as I put down the receiver, I could think only of all the inevitable calls to come and I wanted to run.

24

U P IN KENTUCKY, Will Johnson had finally retired completely from "the firm." The Johnsons were now being followed by the infectious diseases clinic at Duke. I still received regular updates from Will and from Sarah Presnell. Sarah went regularly to their house to draw blood for routine blood counts and then sent the results on to Duke. The Johnsons' medical charts, as always, were kept in a locked filing cabinet in Sarah's house.

Will began on AZT at Duke and responded dramatically. His weight shot up to 137 pounds from 116 pounds; he said the food he ate was finally "sticking to his bones." He had been bothered by an itching and scaling of his skin ever since he first became symptomatic; it had resisted all the creams and ointments that Sarah had prescribed. With AZT, his skin cleared up. Even his night sweats disappeared.

On the phone, he was elated, hopeful that with AZT he could survive a few more years until there was another medical breakthrough. Meanwhile, Duke had enrolled Bess in a study of AZT in patients without ARC (AIDS-related complex). The study was to see if AZT worked better if used earlier in the disease, before the patient developed.

The Johnsons were still expending a great deal of creative energy on maintaining their secret. Each visit to Duke required an overnight stay and meant they had to invent a reason for their absence. Theirs was a big social circle and they were among the town's best-known citizens. They had always lived their life publicly, and after the heart attack, friends, neighbors and church mates were even more solicitous. "Abe," Will said to me over the phone, "I believe it's easier for the queen to slip away unnoticed from Buckingham Palace than it is for us to be gone from home."

Their daughter lived close by. Their son, after a tour of duty with the Army Corps of Engineers, had returned home and had joined the firm as a junior associate. For their children, the Johnsons invented trips to various friends across the tristate area as explanation for their absences. Unaccomplished liars that they were, many times they felt obliged to actually visit their friends to render some truth to their alibi. They professed a sudden interest in bed-and-breakfast tours, a passion that kept them on the road quite often.

Incredibly, their son and daughter still had no inkling of the true nature of their father's illness. The son, Will Junior, later told me he went fishing with his father the month before he finally learned that his father had AIDS: "All my life I had taken my cue from my father: as long as he did not appear worried about his illness, I didn't worry either. I idolized my father, and still do. He was always the single most powerful influence in my life, the model of how I should be. He guided me into my career, into working at another firm to get a larger perspective, into returning to his firm. It was always his plan that I should eventually come back to the firm. I never questioned him and had complete trust that his vision for me would encompass my own dreams and goals. I figured that when he wanted me to worry about his illness, wonder why this cancer of his was so peculiar, he would let me know. It never occurred to me when I first met you to question you. After all, you were *his* doctor and he was quite satisfied with his medical care. That was all I needed to know.

"But on that fishing trip we had time on our hands. It was a real special time for my Dad and me to visit with each other, just as when I was a boy. We were talking about everything under the sun. I asked him what was going on with this illness of his, almost as a matter of curiosity—the way I might ask him how business was doing. I said I could see he was losing weight and he showed no signs of recovering the energy level that he had before. He thought about it long and hard and he said, 'Son, you could say I have a cancer of the blood system. Right now it isn't causing me too much of a problem. But the fact is, I will

probably eventually die from it. But it can be controlled for many years.'
I accepted that and had no cause to question it for the longest time."

It took an article in *Time* magazine for Will Junior to put together all
the facts that had been available to him all along: blood transfusions, the
mysterious viral illness that had followed the transfusions, the weight
loss and lymph node enlargement, the involvement of an infectious
diseases specialist like myself instead of a cancer specialist.

Will Junior called his sister at her house: "Sis, I think Dad has
AIDS!" He read to her from the article. She too had resisted putting the
facts together, but now the conclusion was inescapable. Lee Ann suggested that they wait and not do anything with their newfound knowledge. Maybe their parents had good reasons not to tell them. But Will
Junior could be as bulldogged as his father, and he could no longer live
without knowing, particularly if his father was doing it to spare them the
worry. It was exactly the kind of thing his father might do.

Will Junior decided to call Sarah Presnell. She was surely in on this.
Sarah was his age and went to the same church. Will Junior's children
and the Presnell children were classmates. When Sarah got on the line,
Will Junior asked her, "Sarah, does my Dad have AIDS?" There was
silence.

Sarah said, "Junior, I think you need to ask your Dad that question."

As it turned out his parents were away at their summer house in
Corpus Christi, Texas.

Sarah Presnell called them in Texas almost as soon as Will Junior
hung up.

"Will? Junior knows. I think he will be calling you."

Will Junior sat in front of his phone. He reached for the phone twice
to call his father, and each time put it down. He stayed in his office
without going home, without calling his wife to tell her he would be
late.

"As long I did not make the call to my father, there was still a chance
that my father might not have AIDS. If I made the call and had my
worst fears confirmed, there would be no going back to the innocence
of not knowing."

The hours passed and it grew dark outside. Will Junior could not
bring himself to leave his office. He could not walk into the hallway and
see the portrait of his Dad and the late Chuck Hoover, a portrait they

had commissioned out of pride in their friendship. The portrait showed a ruddy, robust, granite-jawed Will Senior, a far cry from what he looked like now.

Before Will Junior could make up his mind, the telephone rang. It was his father.

"Son, I know what's on your mind. Your mother and I have just put an overnight parcel in the mail to you. It explains everything. Please share it only on a need-to-know basis. I know you will share it with Rebecca and that is fine. But please reinforce with her the need to keep this to yourselves."

Will Junior's voice was choked up as he answered his father. "Yes, sir."

"Junior?"

"Sir?"

"It's bad news, son, real bad."

"Yes, sir."

"I'll talk to you tomorrow, Willy."

"Yes, sir."

What arrived the next day was the journal that Will and Bess had jointly kept. The package was addressed to Will Junior in his father's characteristic script: uppercase print, the first letter of each word taller than the rest. There was a brief cover letter and another package within. It told him to be sure and read it in a quiet place where he would not be disturbed for several hours.

He read his father's description of how Sarah Presnell had told them the news late one Friday night. And then Will Junior let out a cry: he had not been prepared for the journal to tell him that his mother was also infected.

Soon, Will Junior stumbled onto why his parents had decided to keep the awful news to themselves:

SHE [Dr. Sarah Presnell] ADVISED US EMPHATICALLY THAT SHE FELT WE SHOULD KEEP OUR CONDITION TO OURSELVES. BESS HAD NO SYMPTOMS AT ALL. MINE WERE VERY EARLY INDICATIONS OF ARC [AIDS-related complex]. NEITHER OF US HAD THE DISEASE ITSELF—AND MIGHT NEVER DEVELOP IT. IT WOULD TAKE BLOOD OR SEMEN TO INFECT SOMEONE ELSE. CASUAL

CONTACT WOULDN'T DO IT. IT COULD NOT BE TRANSMITTED TO SOMEONE USING OUR DISHES, EATING AFTER US, OR BY KISSING OR HUGS. THE ONLY WAY WAS BY TRANSFER OF BLOOD OR SEMEN DIRECTLY TO THE BLOODSTREAM OF ANOTHER. SHE FELT (AND WE AGREED) THAT THE THEN PREVALENT AND PATHOLOGICAL FEAR OF THE DISEASE ON THE PART OF MANY PEOPLE WAS SO STRONG THAT IT WOULD BE BEST TO KEEP OUR SECRET TO OURSELVES LEST WE BE SHUNNED, OR HURT OUR LOVED ONES, OR OUR CHURCH, OR THE FIRM.

The journal entries by his mother were radically different in tone and appearance from her husband's. Whereas his father's print was at times upright and at other times, perhaps because of the thought being expressed, slanted to the right, his mother's writing was a model of cursive script. His father's section had a wide left margin as if to leave space for formulas and calculations, and it was interspersed with photocopies of doctors' consultations, even some of my later correspondence, as though introducing evidence, building a case.

His mother, by contrast, had written an uninterrupted narrative, the left margin and right margin straight as plumb lines. Her section of the document was the fitting product of a magna cum laude graduate of the University of Virginia, an English honors student, a lady whose heroes and heroines were Blake and the Brontë sisters. Only the content of this remarkable journal, not the form, betrayed his mother's agony. Her very first paragraph explained the purpose of the diary:

> . . . we put our story on paper for the purpose of information to our loved ones in the future, should we choose or need to make this information known to you.

His father had not bothered with such an explanation. Instead, his father had begun as if visualizing that moment when the journal would be in his son's hands:

IT GRIEVES ME TO TELL YOU, BUT I MUST LET YOU KNOW THAT BESS AND I ARE INFECTED BY THE AIDS VIRUS.

The second paragraph of his mother's diary read:

So here goes—I feel like I am making a confession, and I will try to explain the circumstances and our reasoning about it all.

Much later came:

We hate not telling you and Rebecca, or Lee Ann and John about the biggest burden of our lives and pray that you will not hold this against us. We just couldn't see that it would serve any good to have you saddled with this burden too. It would be dumping our problems on you when you couldn't do anything about it. Still, we miss your caring and concern. We love you all more than anything else on this earth. We continually pray for God's guidance, our health, and for a cure to be found for this awful scourge.

There was a reference in Will's writing to the cost of all the deception that had to be set into play from the moment Will saw Sarah Presnell:

THUS BEGAN ANOTHER PART OF THE NIGHTMARE. I'VE ALWAYS FELT IT BEST TO BE ENTIRELY TRUTHFUL. IF I TOLD THE TRUTH I'D NEVER HAVE TO REMEMBER WHATEVER IT WAS I SAID. NOW I HAD TO LIVE A COVER-UP—AND SO DID BESS. IT PREVENTED US FROM RECEIVING THE PRAYERS & SUPPORT FROM THE SAINTS AND OUR FAMILY. . . . FATHER [Will Johnson's aged father] TRIES TO KEEP UP WITH WHERE WE ARE AT ALL TIMES—A REAL PROBLEM FOR SUCH INEXPERIENCED LIARS AS WE. I THINK IT WOULD KILL HIM IF HE KNEW. I PRAY THE LORD SPARES MY OLD MAN FROM THIS KNOWLEDGE.

Will Johnson anticipated his children's reaction when they finally found out:

YOUR QUESTION MIGHT BE—"WHY DIDN'T YOU TELL US, DAD?" YOU MAY FEEL RESENTMENT BECAUSE YOU'D FEEL YOU HAD THE RIGHT TO KNOW FROM THE BEGINNING—SO THAT YOU COULD DECIDE ABOUT HOW TO REACT—AND TO DECIDE YOURSELVES HOW TO DEAL WITH WHETHER YOU AND YOUR FAMILIES MIGHT HAVE BEEN AT RISK—AND TO ESTABLISH YOUR OWN POLICIES ACCORDING TO YOUR OWN JUDGMENTS. YOU HAVE THIS KNOWLEDGE NOW, OF COURSE, AND YOU WILL DO AS YOU THINK YOU MUST.

> THE DREAD OF SUCH A QUESTION FROM YOU, AND THE POS-
> SIBLE RESENTMENT WHICH MIGHT ACCOMPANY IT WHEN YOU
> LEARN ABOUT OUR HORROR, HAS CAUSED US TO CONSULT AGAIN
> WITH OUR SPIRITUAL COUNSELOR, REV. S_____ FOR EVEN
> MORE GUIDANCE.
>
> THIS CATCH-22 PROVIDES THE ESSENCE OF OUR STRUGGLE TO
> FIND THE BEST ANSWER AS TO HOW TO HANDLE IT. NOT THE
> PERFECT ANSWER, BUT THE BEST WE CAN COME UP WITH AND
> DO UNDER THE CIRCUMSTANCES. THIS IS THE GREATEST CRISIS
> OF OUR LIVES, NOT JUST THE DISEASE BUT THE COVER-UP.

Here Will Junior recognized words that were an anthem to his father,
words that his father had used with me:

> I PERSONALLY THINK THIS THING IS FROM HELL AND THE
> DEVIL HIMSELF. I DON'T BELIEVE GOD "LET IT HAPPEN." I
> SURELY DON'T UNDERSTAND IT, BUT I SEE IT AS AN EVIL ON-
> SLAUGHT—A TEST IF YOU WILL—AND I'M DETERMINED WITH
> THE HELP AND STRENGTH OF JESUS CHRIST, I WILL PASS THIS
> TEST. I REMIND MYSELF ALSO THAT IT MATTERS NOT SO MUCH
> WHAT HAPPENS TO US ALL AS HOW WE TAKE IT—AND WE'LL
> NEVER BE GIVEN TO ENDURE MORE THAN WE CAN BEAR.
>
> REV. S_____ REINFORCED OUR RESOLVE TO KEEP OUR PRI-
> VACY. THIS LETTER AND HISTORY IS BEING WRITTEN NOW, HOW-
> EVER, AT HIS SUGGESTION. HE SAYS FOR US TO KEEP IT ON
> FILE—IT MIGHT HELP YOU UNDERSTAND OUR HANDLING OF THIS
> IF YOU MUST KNOW LATER ON—AND EVEN IF YOU DISAGREE
> WITH US, IT MIGHT HELP REDUCE YOUR RESENTMENT IF YOU
> EVER HAVE TO KNOW.

It was a long while before Will Junior was able to go home and share
with his wife what had transpired. Everything in his life to that point in
time now seemed a preface to this nightmare. A few miles away, his
sister was reading a copy of the same journal.

25

IN THE SUMMER OF 1989, Norman Sanger died, bled to death. His friend Sharon Phillips, the occupational health nurse at the mines, left a message with my secretary giving me the news.

I had to find out more; I *needed* to know how he died. How did the man who said, "All I have ever had was courage and dignity—that was my thing," the man who had despaired about losing these qualities—how did he handle the end? I had witnessed a lot of deaths now. Some were triumphant, a victory over fear. Some people were apparently surprised by its arrival, never fully believing that it could occur. As an observer, each death still seemed fantastic to me, a feat of sorts.

If Norman had found a way, had stumbled on a path—or indeed, if he had not found a way—then I wanted to know. I was after something more intimate, something less elegant than Kübler-Ross's stages of denial, anger, bargaining, grieving and acceptance. I simply wanted to know how to accomplish a *good* death. I needed the knowledge to say (or not say): "When death approaches, have a fire going to ward off any chill. And you will be more comfortable wearing cotton. And your bed should be in the north room with the head of your bed facing west. And as for what you should eat, avoid lentils, take rhubarb if you like it . . ." If I could do little else, perhaps I could lead them to a proper end, the right punctuation to close a life.

I had always felt inexpert when a patient was near death. I knew I was not alone: the gallows humor evinced in comments like "the patient is circling the drain," or "about to transfer to Central Office," reflected the clumsy way all of us in the hospital dealt with impending death. Give me a patient with massive gastric bleeding or ventricular fibrillation and I am a model of efficiency and purpose. Put me at a deathbed, a slow dying, and purpose is what I lack. I, who till then have been supportive, involved, can find myself mute, making my visits briefer, putting on an aura of great enterprise—false enterprise. I finger my printed patient list, study the lab results on the chart which at this point have no meaning. For someone dealing so often with death, my ignorance felt shameful.

THAT SUMMER, when I found I had a lecture to give in Kentucky, I decided to use that trip to see Sharon Phillips, the nurse at the mining company where Norman had worked. They had been office mates. Sharon had become Norman's closest friend and had accompanied him many a time to Johnson City. I had the sense now that I could speak to her in a way that might be very difficult with Norman's wife.

Sharon met me at the Pizza Hut in town. She drove me to the city park; we walked as we talked. I told her on the phone when we set up our meeting that I wanted to know *specifically* about Norman's death. I needed to know so as to bring a sense of closure to it. But now both of us seemed hesitant to get to it, circling around it instead.

Sharon was in her forties. She had no accent to speak of. As an army brat, she had grown up in Okinawa, Louisiana, California and Texas before her parents returned to Lexington where the family was originally from. She was blond, wore no makeup and had a trim, muscular figure. In a part of the country where women can age rapidly—the result of smoking, early and closely spaced pregnancies, poor diets—Sharon was an exception.

Before she knew Norman well, she asked someone one day why Norman walked with a limp. She was told it had to do with hemophilia. Norman had first mentioned AIDS when he and Sharon were volunteering in a booth sponsored by the mine at the town health fair. They had time to chat in between taking people's blood pressures. Out of the clear blue, Norman said, "My biggest fear in life is having AIDS." Sharon had wondered why Norman would dwell on something like that. It hadn't struck her that Norman was at risk. The year was 1985.

After Norman's death it was difficult for her to believe that she was so late in having knowledge of AIDS penetrate her consciousness.

She found out later from Norman that he had already been tested and knew he was positive by the time they talked at the health fair. His statement about his biggest fear being that he would get AIDS had not been an abstract declaration; he had been talking concretely about the stages of HIV infection.

Sharon said, "I remember one morning when I went to work, my personnel supervisor asked me, 'Did you know that Norman is in the hospital with AIDS?' And I started to weep. My supervisor was shocked; she didn't know what to say. Neither she nor I had realized how deeply this little man who shared my office had affected me."

When Norman returned from the Miracle Center the first time, he seemed so small to Sharon. He tried to be his usual self, but he had never looked so fragile.

Sharon felt angry at herself, angry that she had let herself get so close to Norman. "I knew it was going to be a long battle and that I could not turn my back on him now. I think the word had got around the mine office by then as to what Norman had. Most people were very accepting, or else maybe they didn't understand too much about it. I would sit and eat lunch with him. And there were several who would refuse to sit at the same table or even refuse to sit with *me* because I was so close to him.

"At the time it was all happening, my biggest fear was that my memory of him, of his kind of bravery, would fade. The opposite of my Vietnam nursing experience where I want the memory to fade . . . but mostly it won't."

Sharon, in describing her ordeal with Norman, seemed to be capturing what I was going through with *all* my Normans: getting so close to them that I would regret it later, knowing that the intimacy made the ordeal of illness costly and painful to me. I was, like her, tainted socially by the association with my patients, even if most days I told myself I cared nothing about what others thought. Whatever efforts we made seemed to be happening in a vacuum: our little towns were unaware of the drama, the gallantry of their dying heroes; there was great danger that there would be no memory of the lives lost.

Sharon learned everything she could about AIDS and hemophilia so that she could be both a good nurse and a good friend to Norman. And yet whenever she went to see him, she had the sense that he was ministering to her. He had decided that *she* needed him; he was going to open doors in her psyche that she had long considered closed off.

I asked Sharon how Norman's wife, Claire, was faring after his death. "Claire moved away to join a distant cousin in California and to be close to Norman's parents. I think Claire made him very happy. But I don't know if she had a good understanding of the disease. One time Norman told me that they were supposed to go somewhere but he was really ill—throwing up and having fever. She was all dressed up and he finally said, 'Claire, I don't think I'm going to be able to go.' She sat down on the bed in a huff and said, 'When *are* you going to be well?' "

We had come to the edge of the park and Sharon pointed to a church. She said it was where Norman had worshipped. "One of the things that Norman taught me had to do with faith. I told him that I didn't think I could be a good Christian because I did things that I didn't think a good Christian would do. He said to me, 'You don't understand grace at all, do you? You don't *earn* grace and therefore you can't *lose* grace when you do something bad. If God grants His grace to you because of your belief and your faith in Him, He doesn't take that away when you mess up. You can't do anything to earn it or anything to lose it.' "

We stepped into the church.

"Two days before he died, he asked me to come here with him, and when we went in it was just the two of us. He broke down and cried these really angry tears and he just didn't want to leave. I didn't know what to say to him. Finally, when he got ahold of himself, he said to me, 'I don't mind dying. I'm going to be okay with death. It's just that I'm not ready to leave.' "

It was almost time for me to leave and we had not as yet discussed Norman's death.

"About a week before he died, he decided to stop taking his medications. By this time he was just wasting away and had high fevers. Nothing was really helping him. Although I saw him every day at work—when he was working—I was hesitant to bother him at his house. On the fourth of July he called me. He said he wanted to come to my house. My husband and he knew each other, but not very well. And whatever way my husband thought of Norman, he never perceived him as a threat, you understand? I don't think he felt the same sympathy for him that I did. He was puzzled by our relationship. It is a tribute to my husband that he gave me·room to have this connection with Norman.

"I had planned a big dinner for that night. I was going to make barbecue. I knew exactly what Norman liked and he didn't like onions, so I left them out. His favorite dessert was peach cobbler and vanilla ice cream, so I made that. When he and Claire got to the house, he was wearing thermal underwear and a long-sleeved shirt, even though it was the fourth of July. He was extremely pale and his voice was hardly audible. When I was clearing dishes I could hear him talking with my husband, and I realized that this was the first time my husband really recognized that Norman was about to die.

"I heard Larry ask him what he wanted to do, and Norman said something like, 'Larry, I just want to have fun. I want to have fun.' And Larry said, 'Are you talking about *now*, Norman? You want to do something right *now*?' And he said, 'No, I'm too tired now. But let's go to Gatlinburg, just the four of us and rent a chalet sometime. We'll get one with the whirlpool because I know Sharon loves a whirlpool.' And my husband's just sitting there saying, 'Okay, Norman. Okay.'

"We have this big backyard, about five acres. I used to tell Norman about this special spot at the edge of the property where I go to just meditate. It is my little spot and you can't see any other houses from back there, just mountains. You can hear the birds singing and nothing else. Silence. I told him that one day I would take him back there, we'd spread a blanket and talk. Now Norman said, 'I need to go back to your spot and sit there with you. I need to cry and I need to pray.' I needed Larry's help because he was so weak. Larry got on one side and I on the other. We walked him past my flower bed and I had these red gladiolas—for some reason that summer nothing came up but the bright red ones. He said, 'Those are the prettiest flowers I've ever seen.' Later at his memorial service I brought red gladiolas to the church. I said, 'Norman, this is where I go when I worry about you and I pray for you. This is where I sit and cry about you.' And he looked around and said, 'You are all around this place and you always will be.' He said, 'Keep praying for me and I will always come back here.' We sat there for about fifteen minutes, but then it was uncomfortable for him to sit on the ground because he was all bones by then."

As Sharon talked about her special spot, I recalled all the singular places *I* had come to associate with this disease: Vickie's trailer and the land around it, the Powell Valley cemetery where Gordon was buried, Essie's house at the foot of the mountain. I remembered the visceral, healing effect the mountains surrounding Powell Valley had on me. If time permitted I would stop at Gordon's final resting place on my return drive.

"We went back to the house and laid down by the pool and he was looking up at the sky and he said, 'You know, right now I don't hurt anywhere. I don't think I have a fever. I'm not nauseous. Everything is just right. I have the people that I love most in the world right here.' It seemed like he suddenly got a burst of energy from being in that spot. Suddenly he said: 'So, Sharon, what is it that you would most like to do? Make a wish.' It was like he had started a game or something. I said I always liked the idea of flying in a small plane but never had the courage. He said, 'Well, I know a friend and he has a plane and we'll arrange that.' Then he goes: 'Okay, Larry, your turn: what do you want to do?' Larry said, 'I want to go fishing. I want to take you with me and teach you how to fish.' Norman laughs and says, 'Okay. But I already know how to fish—I'll outfish you, but I'll go fishing with you anyway.' Then he asked his wife, 'Honey, what do you want to do?' And she says, 'I don't care. Whatever you all want to do.' And he paused there, as if she had thrown him off. He said something like, 'All right, okay, we'll do something.'

"He went on with his fantasy about what we're all going to do and the three of us were just sitting there looking at him, trying to figure out what we should say. He grew real quiet, like it had suddenly struck him that there was no point to these plans.

"Then he suddenly pipes up, 'Didn't you say you fixed some peach cobbler?' Claire and I and Larry were tripping over ourselves to go get him the ice cream.

"When it got dark, Norman wanted to see the fireworks. We all put our jackets on and drove up in our two cars to the crest of the hill. The fireworks were spectacular. Then we said goodbye. He said that he'd had a wonderful evening and he was going to see me at work tomorrow, which I very much doubted. After he died, Claire told me that just as soon as our car was out of sight, he had her stop the car and he threw up all his dinner. He had not wanted to do that in front of us.

"The next day he called to say he had made reservations at a chalet for the four of us. I couldn't believe he'd done that. I was enough of a nurse to know that he would never make it there. But he went on saying, 'Make sure Larry can get off work,' and I said, 'Okay, I'll take care of it.' He said, 'Do you know what the name of the chalet is?' I said, 'No.' He said, 'It's called Heaven's Gates.' He said that he wanted to come out the next day and visit my little private spot again, that it had given him a lot of peace.

"That evening about six o'clock, Claire called me and said that Norman was very ill and would I meet them at the emergency room. We jumped in the car. The route took us right past Norman's house, and the rescue squad ambulance was still parked out there. So we stopped and I went flying through the door. I knew all the rescue squad people and I asked them, 'What's going on?' They said Norman was in the bathroom with Donny, one of the rescue squad people. Norman had wanted to use the bathroom before leaving. And I thought to myself, 'Well it can't be too bad.' But then I went and looked down the hall and the whole bedroom and the entire hallway was covered with blood, soaked with blood. Apparently something had broken loose in his lungs and was hemorrhaging. He was coughing it up, spurting it up all over the place. I asked Claire, 'Has he had his factor VIII?' She said, 'No, I brought it in to him and he wouldn't take it.' I stuck my head in the bathroom and just then Norman was walking out on Donny's arm. He let them lower him down onto the stretcher.

"I got in the back of the ambulance with him. I was holding this trash can next to Norman and blood was pouring out of his mouth and nose into the trash can. Every time he coughed, blood was flying everywhere. He was coughing like crazy. In the ambulance he sat bolt upright and we put oxygen on him but he was still so pale and so blue. His hands were really cold and I remember thinking that everything I was doing was medically wrong. Here he was in shock and I was sitting him straight up. I should have taken his blood pressure, but I couldn't even think to do it. All I kept doing was washing his face, wiping his face

with a towel and saying, 'Norman, it's all right, it's all right." He didn't
have his shirt on, just his pajama bottoms, and he was so uncomfortable
and restless, but still he was conscious, though I don't know how alert
he was. My mind kept going back and forth: How do I help him die
comfortably? How do I save him?

"He was very, very short of breath, and every now and then his head
would loll back and his eyes roll back as though he was going to pass
out. Then he'd suddenly snap his head up again and try to look around
him. He'd see me and then he'd let his eyes roll again. And I kept saying
to him, 'Norman, go easy. It's okay. God's with you. It's okay.'

"All the time I was thinking, Why did he call the ambulance? He told
me never to let him die in the hospital. He had quit taking his medicines. Why did he call an ambulance? Was it fear?

"I said to him, 'I'll start your IV and get your factor VIII and we'll stop
this bleeding.' But by then he looked like he was about to lose consciousness. He had no pulse and his breathing was very shallow and
rapid.

"We were backing into the emergency room entrance now. And
when they took him out of the ambulance, he raised his head up again.
I remember the ambulance drivers as they moved the stretcher were
bouncing his head and I was trying to follow behind, holding his head,
keep it from bouncing. I screamed at them, 'Careful, for God's sake!'

"Claire was in the ER and I grabbed her by the shoulders and I said,
'Claire, you've got to tell them not to do anything.' But she was paralyzed and didn't seem to be hearing me, and finally when the doctor
stepped out and said, 'Who's the wife?' she said, 'I am.' The doctor was
someone I didn't know, someone from ETSU moonlighting up here.
He said, 'How vigorous do you want us to be?' and she said, 'Do
everything.' And I just rolled my eyes and said, 'Oh God, Claire.'

"Well, they worked on him for a couple of minutes and it was breaking
my heart. Here he was, he had seen a lifetime of hospitals, had his fill
of doctors and treatments. If he had any life or a conscious mind left in
him, all he would remember of the way he left this world was being shocked and having a tube run down his throat into his lungs and
being stuck with IVs and people jumping on his chest, cracking ribs and
setting up more bleeding in there. Thank God, in just a few moments the
doctor came out and said that it was all over, and I took Claire home.

"A lady from church and I spent a couple of hours just cleaning up the bathroom and bedroom so that Claire could go in there. I set up some pillows to sleep on a sofa in the bedroom. But Claire couldn't sleep and neither could I. In the middle of the night she turns to me and says, 'Are you asleep?' I said, 'No. I can't quit crying,' and she said, 'I'm the same way.' So we just both laid down on the couch and propped ourselves up and we started talking. And I had this Hershey bar in my handbag that Norman had given me—he was a chocolate nut. And I brought it out and we started eating it. And when we were done it turned out that Claire knew where Norman had a Hershey stash. She brought it out and we sat there eating chocolate like little schoolgirls. We thought Norman would have approved.

"Claire and I were just sitting on the sofa remembering all these things about Norman and I turned to her and said, 'You know where Norman is right now, Claire? He's at *Heaven's Gates.*"

ON MY DRIVE HOME I kept thinking of Norman's last hours. It wasn't at all what I had wished for him: the blood flying everywhere, the chaos and confusion of the rescue squad and emergency room, the paroxysms of coughing. Why did Norman go to the hospital? I imagined a vessel bursting in my own lung, the blood welling up the bronchus, into the trachea, spilling into the good lung, rising up to the larynx and threatening to drown me. All Norman's courage and dignity—his two assets—could not counter the sheer horror of that moment. He had undergone the jolting ambulance ride, the Code Blue in the emergency room, because he was *scared*.

I realized that I could have done much for him if I had been in his house. I would have pushed morphine—*large* doses. Morphine disconnects the head from the body, makes the isthmus of a neck vanish and diminishes the awareness of suffering. It is like a magic trick: the head on the pillow, at peace, while the chest toils away.

I would have sat with Norman and said to him, just as Sharon had said, "It's OK, it's OK. Go easy. God's with you." When I saw the faintest twinge of anxiety in his eyes or around the corners of his mouth, I would push more morphine.

That night, I pulled out Osler's classic textbook of 1892. The kind of medicine I needed to practice, the therapeutic advice I wanted, was surely to be found here in Osler's text. Osler knew what I was going through: few opportunities to reverse the underlying situation, but no lack of means to bring the patient comfort, at the very least the comfort of the physician's presence. I read: "By far the most important measure is absolute quiet of body such as can only be secured by rest in bed and seclusion . . . for cough which is always present and disturbing, opium should be freely given, and is of all medicines most serviceable in hemoptysis."

Norman's death increased my resolve to be a presence at the bedside when I could. And I would carry morphine with me always, have it ready at each bedside, at a moment's notice, ready to disconnect the head from the body's anguish.

26

THE NIGHT BEFORE Luther Hines reappeared in town, I had a dream in which once again I contracted HIV. The dream recurred so often—always in a different form—I thought of it as the "infection" dream. This time I was with my brothers, we were dressed in suits and ties, three Brooks-Brothers boys sliding along the marble walkways of a fancy mall. A lady in a lab coat—not a doctor, but a cosmetic-counter person—beckoned us into a room to have our blood drawn. I was being cavalier, teasing my brothers about how shy they were with needles. I groped the woman and my brothers watched with embarrassment. We walked around some more and soon the mall was dark and empty, and we struggled to find our way back to the lady in white. "You both," she said to my brothers, are fine. "But *you*," she said, pointing at me, "it's really strange, it definitely looks like it is—"

"Nooooo!" I screamed. I wept and said it was a mistake, but she shook her head, a little amused by my histrionics, as if one should be able to take this sort of news in one's stride—particularly as a *medical* man. My brothers tried to console me. I pleaded with Reji, my older brother, to please turn it back, to please let me do this part of my life over again. He was heartbroken: I was asking him for something that was not in his power.

I woke in a cold sweat. Each time I had this dream, I immediately recalled the last time I had broken the news of a positive test to a young man. I remembered my concern, my empathy, my encouraging and supportive tone, as if to say, "Don't worry, I know what you are going through, and it will be all right." But a dream like this made me feel like I had no idea what I was saying. In my waking hours I never understood the absolute terror of finding out you have HIV; in my dreams I understood all too well.

I shaved and dressed without much thought or enthusiasm; like an automaton I picked up my beeper and my wallet and my pen and my keys and distributed them on my person.

Halfway through the morning, I had ducked away with Rajani to go and see a house with a realtor. We had been looking for three months, my enthusiasm for this project waxing and waning. Rajani was keen on a new house. As quaint as our Mountain Home house was it lacked certain things: a bathroom on the ground floor, a dishwasher, the sense that we owned it and could alter it to suit us. At times it seemed like the most wonderful thing in the world for me to contemplate: my *own* plot in suburbia, my own lawn, amenities such as a jacuzzi, a garage with electric door openers, intercoms, central air and heat, central vacuum, a pool, none of which were to be found at the VA. And at other times, the two-car garages packed with lawn mowers and bicycles and shovel and pickaxe and skis, the tricycles sitting in the driveway, the flag flying proudly, the fleshy thighs and pastel-colored shorts of would-be neighbors bending over their flower beds, trowels in hand—it all seemed like a terrible trap. It was the *opposite* of my infection dream: I could see the danger, I was awake and I *had* plenty of time to back off, to not fall into a binding mortgage that would cut off my escape.

The realtor had picked up on my ambivalence some time ago. She eyed me warily, tried to box me out when she could. But Rajani had found a fatal flaw in this house that eliminated it from consideration. I breathed a sigh of relief.

By afternoon, when Carol greeted me, I felt my smile was rigid and false, my energy low, my mood black. And now here was another chart waiting, another young man. Carol's chirpiness only seemed to make it worse.

The chart said that I had seen Luther Hines two years before. As I read through my notes, I remembered a young man of slight build with sandy-brown hair, a pointed face.

Two years before, when he discovered he was HIV-positive, he moved back home from California. His family reacted to the news of his infection with indifference; they reacted to his physical presence with some discomfort, as if to say, why would you come back home with a thing like that? He took a job in Johnson City, but didn't care for it. When I first met him he had said this hick town—his home town—was too much for him; he was planning to leave. He thanked me for having seen him, but assured me that he would get the latest and best treatment back in California. He had left me feeling that the medicine we practiced here was from the Stone Ages.

I knocked and pushed open the door, curious why Luther had come back again.

I was shocked at what I saw: Luther sat in the corner, a small shriveled figure, leaning against the wall, looking like an abandoned cur, staring back at me sullenly, as if I had trapped him in this room, as if he was fully expecting me to kick him and he was readying his best snarl.

His lips were horribly crusted and fissured. There were angry sores at the corners of his mouth. From where I stood I could see the *Candida* growing in his mouth like cheesy curd that threatened to spill out. His face was covered with a swath of fluid-filled vesicles, each with a central little dimple on the top. This was molluscum contagiosum, a viral infection of the skin. Some of the lesions were as big as marbles; one of them hung down from the point of his chin and made him look like an old shrew. His shoulders resembled wire coat hangers that propped up his shirt. His nails were long and pale and seemed to hang down like a parrot's beak, as if the skeleton of the nail had softened. I could have superimposed his knobby skeleton, his sunken eyeballs, the taut starvation smile and the cheeks sticking to the teeth onto a *Life* magazine picture of a famine victim from Biafra or Ethiopia. His skin had turned dry and flaky. He was altogether a hideous sight.

I said something like, "Luther, what happened to you?"

He snapped back, "What do you mean what happened to me? I've moved back, that's all."

"But how do you feel? You look . . ."

"Nothing happened to me. I'm fine. I just need a refill on some medications."

Luther had brought no medical records with him. When I asked him if he would sign a release and let us get records from the doctors that had seen him, he balked. He came up with a litany of people who had seen him in California: each one was "an asshole" and "didn't know what the hell he was doing."

This caustic manner of his was new, part of what the disease had done to him. He had shown few signs of it before. He was looking at me like I was yet another asshole who didn't know what I was doing. And yet, here he was in my office, having come of his own free will.

With some coaxing, I established that his problems included:

Tuberculosis—He had taken treatment for six months and stopped for the last two weeks because "those pills were hurting me, I could tell."

Three episodes of Pneumocystis carinii pneumonia, including one that had resulted in his being on a ventilator. His lungs were so fragile that thrice his lungs had popped, allowing air to leak into the chest cavity and requiring the placement of a tube in the chest to reexpand the lung. The Bactrim tablets, which he was instructed to take daily to prevent a further episode of pneumonia, he had stopped taking because "I didn't think I needed them."

Severe esophageal candidiasis made it almost impossible for him to eat. The pills—ketoconazole—that he should have been taking he had run out of.

Severe malnutrition—A physician had put in a Hickman catheter which still dangled from under his collarbone. The entry site under the filthy dressing had a drop of pus welling out. Luther had not been getting any hyperalimentation feeding through the catheter for some months now, having fought with the doctor who put it in. He had not even bothered with the heparin solution he was supposed to flush the catheter with to keep it from clotting off.

When I examined him I found his weight to be ninety pounds, *with* his shoes on. He had a temperature of 103 degrees Fahrenheit. The appearance of his mouth was enough to turn my stomach. The sight in his left eye was diminished, and I saw a white splotch in his retina that was suspicious for cytomegalovirus, a major cause of blindness in AIDS.

His lungs sounded gurgly on both sides, and both his liver and spleen were grossly enlarged, giving a protuberance to his belly reminiscent of children with kwashiorkor. I wondered why the sheer tonnage of these organs did not offset his plummeting weight.

His legs looked like kindling under his hips. The skin of his legs was covered with scratch marks, several of which had festered into sores. As I examined him he continually drew his long nails against his skin, producing a raspy sound that made my hair stand on end.

"Luther, I'd like to put you in the hospital."

"What for? I'm not going to no hospital."

"*What for?* You need intravenous medication to clear up your mouth. I'm worried that there is an infection in your eye that may cause you to lose your eyesight. You look dehydrated. We need to get the catheter out . . ."

Luther disagreed. The thing he wanted from me was a prescription of Lomotil for the diarrhea. His self-image was so distorted that it was almost as though he did not see himself.

I asked him whether he was staying with his parents.

"Why should I? I don't need them."

We found out later through a social worker that his mother didn't want any part of him. And his dad had not even told his new wife about Luther; he didn't want Luther to come by.

"So where are you staying?"

"In an apartment off West Market."

"And who gets your groceries and cooks for you?"

He acted as if I had gone too far. He came rearing off the exam table. He shouted at me now, his face coming forward as if he would bite, his saliva spraying on me as he screamed: "*I* do. Okay? *I* do. I DON'T NEED ANYBODY'S HELP."

I told him about TAP and how they might be able to help him. But he dismissed this. He stalked out of the clinic with his prescription of Lomotil. Other patients stared after him.

Carol and I, looking through a side window, watched him walk down the road. He appeared to have no car. We kept wondering what kept him upright.

"Poor thing," Carol said.

For a fleeting second I thought Carol was referring to me, to how *my* day had gone, to the kind of patients I saw week in and week out, to the ambivalence that had crept into what I was doing, whether it was buying a house or treating this fatal illness.

———

THAT SAME WEEK Otis Jackson had a recurrence of the shingles and an acceleration of his psoriasis. He complained constantly of pain. He was frequently angry and bitter.

Fred demonstrated saintly patience well beyond what his sister, Bettie Lee, or anyone else was capable of when they took turns with Otis. Fred's father asked him at one point, "What keeps you there?" Fred answered, "If mama was sick and in the hospital, wouldn't you be at the bedside most of the time?"

Still, Fred and Otis's relationship was strained. The breakthrough, which Fred described to me, came near the end. "Till then I had no acknowledgment for my support of him, my sticking with him through thick and thin. At the time we met, we were both infected; I could have gone my own way. But the other night, he was really suffering, and he said to me that he was scared. I found out that one of the things that was really worrying him was the business of being 'saved.' His mother and father were fundamentalists and it was very important for him to be saved. And yet he didn't feel quite up to the spectacle of a baptism in his hometown; he was ashamed to mention it to me, but it was eating him up. Once I found out what he was worried about, I was able to convince him that it was enough for him to *want* to be saved, to feel repentance for his sins. I told him that was all he needed to do—baptism was simply a sight-and-sound ceremony added on. At that point, he seemed relieved and he let go of that fear and we never talked about it again. He thanked me for all I was doing and told me he loved me."

Over the phone Fred described to me how Otis was now bedridden, his eyelids open, but despite that, quite unresponsive. His eyes would make roving movements, examining the ceiling as if waiting for the Angel Gabriel to descend. He would make picking movements at the bedclothes. He would mutter under his breath. What Fred was describing was the classic "typhoid state," a dramatic state seen in the terminal phases of many illnesses but particularly in typhoid fever and other febrile illnesses. "Coma vigil" or "muttering delirium" was the name given to the strange state of consciousness. The picking at the bedclothes had its own name—carphology.

Under our direction, Fred was giving Otis morphine round the clock. Every day Fred would check in with us. Death, when it came, was peaceful, a striking contrast to Norman Sanger's death.

Fred told me later, "When he died I held him in my arms and I sang to him long after he stopped breathing because I had read that the brain goes on for a few minutes.

"He had wanted to be buried in his hometown, sixty miles away. After all was said and done, he still had a strong attachment to that place. By the time I drove up there, the funeral home had dressed him in a V-neck sweater with a T-shirt underneath. His hair was combed the wrong way and his hands were hidden under the sheet. We had exchanged rings before and now his ring was hidden under the cover, as if they did not want to show it."

Despite this, Fred felt very accepted by Otis's immediate family. It was an old-fashioned funeral, with all of them standing by the casket and greeting visitors. Fred's friends came, as did everyone from support group. But what surprised him the most was that his parents came too.

"What the preacher said was something of a blur to me. But he did at one point say something about 'bringing things on ourselves. The Lord is merciful but we have to live with the consequences of our sins.' And I almost lost it then. I wanted to go up and strangle him.

"I gave a eulogy but it was the hardest thing I'd ever done. Not just what I had to say, but where I was saying it. Nonetheless, I wanted to make my presence known. I didn't want to cause the family further trauma, but I wanted to carefully express my love for Otis, our relationship, our long battle against this disease. I remember the last thing I said in my eulogy was, 'Goodbye, little cowboy. We love you, we'll miss you.' Because Otis always liked cowboy stuff: boots, hats, spurs and chaps.

"At the end of the funeral, a very, very, old lady—a distant aunt of his by marriage whom he cared for very much—came slowly up to me and said, 'You all really liked each other, didn't you?' I answered, 'We sure did, we sure did.' This lady lived in a house without electricity, with a hand pump and as much poverty as you can imagine and here she was now saying to me, 'You know he really liked you. He really cared a lot about you. I don't know what anyone would have done without you. Thank you.' Here was this lady who was too simple, too plain to have all the prejudices the preacher had, for example. And when she said, 'I don't know what anyone would have done without you, Fred,' I just lost it, bawled like a baby, with her comforting me."

27

ONCE HE FOUND OUT HIS FATHER HAD AIDS, Will Johnson, Jr., made a trip down to Johnson City to see me. I suggested that instead of meeting in my clinic, we meet for lunch. I felt guilty about the role I had played in keeping Junior and his sister in the dark on what was happening with their parents, for having invoked "lymphoma" and "a kind of leukemia" to explain his father's hospitalizations. What could I say to defend myself? We were making up rules as we went along. I was improvising constantly to deal with the moral, ethical and social subtleties that were so much a part of this disease. There were so many new questions I had no training in handling. I was relieved that everything was now out in the open and I wanted to make amends for my role in the deception.

As I had predicted, Will Johnson's children and their spouses had rallied round their parents and had not for a moment considered any response other than that of complete support.

I met Junior at a Mexican restaurant in Johnson City. He was exactly my age. It had been a long time since I first saw him in his father's hospital room. I had forgotten how his blue eyes, just like his father's, developed a myriad of crinkles around them when he smiled. He was less animated than his father, had more of his mother's quiet nature. He spoke in a careful, measured southern drawl. He listened very carefully and only spoke when he was certain that you had said your piece. Will Junior's hand would hover over the salsa bowl, a nacho between his fingers, waiting to complete the sentence he had started, or waiting for me to finish what I was saying, before he dipped in.

I studied him. I was going through a phase of intense doubt as to my role as a doctor in the town, my goals in life; I imagined this was reflected on my face, in my posture. I envied Will Junior his good looks and his quiet self-assurance. This was a man who would fit in any-where. To hear that he had attended VMI like his father, that he had been part of an old institution with great tradition, added to my feeling of inadequacy. I had never lived in one place long enough to belong to anything with that sort of history. Maybe that was why I so treasured the old buildings on the Mountain Home grounds.

Shortly after Will Junior found out that his father had AIDS, he went back to VMI for Founders' Day at his father's request. "I drove there as if I had never been there," he told me. "I used a visitor's eyes. I requested a tour by a cadet at the visitors' center. This young, scrubbed cadet took me around, told me about the Rat Line, about the Rat Bible, about the battle of New Market, took me to the barracks, to the chapel, to the classrooms, to the library, told me all about the honor code—I didn't let on to him that I knew it all. I was *angry*. Angry about my parents' illness and the unfairness of it. Angry at the conviction with which this cadet was telling me things. I wanted to grab him by his shoulders and shake him and say to him, 'I've been here. It's all bullshit. There's a world out there that has nothing to do with square corners or Rat Bibles.' I wanted to scream at him, 'Do you know there is an AIDS virus out there that eats people up, and no spit or polish is going to keep it away?' I wanted to tell this kid, 'Use VMI as a model, but don't think this is the world, because it is not.' "

I understood Will Junior's sentiments exactly. I was angry too, angry at all the untouched lives that went on without knowing or caring, all the people that could ignore my patients' suffering.

Unlike his father, who had told me he had little time to waste on the past, Will Junior was seething with anger about Duke's failure to warn his father about the risks of blood transfusion so that he might have spared his mother this vile disease. I pointed out to him that it was a problem of the times, a failure of the national blood banking system, a failure of leadership, the FDA, Reagan. . . . He listened but said noth-ing; it was a difficult pill to swallow, being failed by his heroes.

His father's initial improvement with AZT had been short-lived, and soon the fever and night sweats had started again and he began to lose weight. It appeared that Duke had very little more to offer him.

"He called me from Duke the last time he was there. He said, 'I'm having these tests done on my lungs. They tell me it's either bad or real bad.' He laughed on the phone at his joke. Then he said, 'Son, I taught you how to live. Now, I'm going to teach you how to die. I'm going to show you how to execute an operations order on how to take care of final business.' He laughed again when he said that. It was a VMI phrase and I knew he was deadly serious.

"We went out to Corpus Christi—perhaps his last time at the beach house. I had not really understood till then what he meant by operations order, how much he perceived this as a battle. He would say to me again and again how much he *hated* Satan. It was Satan who gave him the disease in an effort to make him curse God. My sister would say to him that he should not say *hate*, as if the devil would take extra satisfaction in causing him pain or causing my mother pain for saying that. But it wouldn't stop him. He *hated* the devil."

I told Will Junior about his father's epiphany in the hospital room. How he felt Satan had appeared and Jesus had intervened.

"Oh, that has happened more than once. I heard him scream in the kitchen about a month ago. Apparently he had seen Satan, he said he could *smell* him there, and he had yelled at him to get away from him. It was so real that I kept looking for this other presence in the room, imagining I could feel it. We were walking on the beach one day in Corpus Christi; it was a nice sunny day and I was enjoying the feeling of sun on my skin. And he was leaning on me and walking—trudge, trudge, trudge. Then he stops and says that the sun on him felt like the fires of Hell. 'Christ is in my heart, but the virus—Satan—is in my blood. My ultimate victory will be when I die and go into the hands of Christ while this virus from hell will be sent down to the crematory and burned out of existence.' "

Will Junior said his father's walking had gradually deteriorated. It was now painfully slow. He could not pick up his feet, and it was trudge, trudge, trudge everywhere. He had a ritual of putting on clothes and going to the porch. Gradually he no longer changed out of his pajamas and he stayed in the living room.

They rented a hospital bed for him. The bed was placed in what had been Will Junior's room when he was young.

Will Senior became a very demanding patient.

"When you'd walk in there, Dad would say, 'Will, can you help me sit up.' 'Sure, Dad,' I'd say and get him situated just so. Then, 'Can you lower the window?' 'Sure, Dad.' Then when you were done with that it would be, 'Son, I believe your old man is ready to lie down now,' and then 'Son, I know your old man is driving you crazy but would you turn off the TV?' Then, 'Turn on the TV,' and then, 'Open that window, would you son?' It would just drive you bananas."

They hired a woman to come help. "She was this big, warm, compassionate country lady. She had been instructed about AIDS and the precautions to take. She took them in her stride. Of all of us, she was perhaps the best at handling Dad because she would just josh with him and take charge and baby him and get him situated, and for some reason he would give her less grief than he would us. He really liked her. He would kid her about her boyfriends and she would tell him how she was trying to 'rope' one in but how they were all skittish. My Dad would roar with laughter. But then last week—and you're not going to believe this—her son-in-law forbade her to come to our house."

Here Will Junior took a long sip of his beer and looked at me as if debating whether to say this to me. "Her daughter married this foreign physician. He got wind of what's wrong with Dad."

"How did he get wind of it? I thought it was top secret."

"To tell you the truth I think most people in town know what's wrong with Dad. Dad and Mom don't want to think so, but I think there's a lot that know. . . . Anyway, the foreign physician, he married this local girl—the daughter of the nurse's aide who looked after Dad. The daughter and her husband live in this big old house with a Porsche and a Jaguar parked outside. And the doctor, when he gets wind of where his mother-in-law is working, he tells her that he doesn't want her working with us and then being around his kids!" He stopped here, as if he was holding back.

"How does that make you feel, Will?"

He took his time answering. He asked the waitress for another beer for him and one for me. I didn't think I would be going back to work that afternoon.

"How does it make me feel? . . . I think: How can this guy come bleed off us hillbillies, live in a mansion, and then of all people he has that kind of attitude to AIDS?"

There was nothing I could say. It hurt me to hear this.

Will went on, "Mind you, when I broke my arm, my Dad took me to the ER and the guy who set my bone was Indian, just the nicest guy in the world. I was very pleased. But I know there is an underlying sentiment in the community about these doctors: they are so obviously foreign, so clearly not from the area. And they are so obviously well-off compared to the miners and such like. You can't help these thoughts. Have I upset you?"

"No. You see, I wrestle with this in my head all the time. I wonder if the patient is thinking to himself, 'Well, if this doctor is so damn good, why doesn't he stay in his own country and treat *his* people? God knows, they need him there.' The truth is that countries like India need money more than doctors, Will. There's enough doctors, particularly in India. But what good does it do to stick a doctor in a rural clinic when all he can stock there is sulfa and scabies ointment? So the doctors congregate in the cities and cater to the rich. Or they try to leave to come here. . . ."

"Don't get me wrong, Abraham," Will said. "We think the world of you, and none of what I said is against you. My Dad always said that it was part of Christ's intervention that when he came to Johnson City for treatment he should run into you. I think he meant in part your compassion, but also your foreignness—as if you were a messenger from another world."

We were quiet for a long time now. The lunch crowd was gone and we were on our second beers.

Out of the blue, Will Junior asked me, "What do you think of gay men?" I wondered whether his question was prompted by someone he had seen, a waiter or a customer perhaps.

"What do *you* think about gay men?" I asked, turning the question back on him.

"Well . . . I know statistically, there must have been gay men in VMI, but I didn't know any. And I have had a lot of hate for them after my Dad got ill. After all, they are the ones who donated the blood that allowed the virus to get in there, right?"

I was noncommittal.

He continued, "When I went to Duke one time, there was this gay man sitting next to Dad and Mom. I thought it was the strangest sight: my parents who are like angels, innocents, and this outrageous guy who was complaining and carrying on in a real hateful way, but you could tell where he was sick too. Well, when they called the man in, Dad turns to me and says, 'Junior, no one deserves this disease. No one deserves this suffering. It is not from God, or God's punishment. It's straight from the devil.' It was like Dad was reading my mind."

"I agree with your Dad," I said.

Will leaned forward and lowered his voice. "What I don't understand is how can they resist women? I mean, goodness, Abraham, you picture this gorgeous woman—a Raquel Welch, say—all perfumed and lying on a bed in a skimpy two-piece, and *say you never had sex in your life* and you open the door and there she is, just waiting for you—how can a man resist that? I can't imagine it."

"Maybe it doesn't work that way for gay men."

Three attractive Johnson City women headed for their car. We watched them drive away.

"Beats it all, don't it?" Junior said.

I asked Will Junior how his mother was doing.

He shook his head sadly. "Mom has no symptoms and Dad is requiring so much attention that sometimes we forget that she has this virus. The other night, I had just taken over from my wife in watching Dad. He was tossing and turning and had finally gone to sleep but he never slept more than twenty minutes at a time. I heard the alarm clock go off in Mom's room next door at three in the morning. And I knew she had put it on so that she could take her AZT—you know how it has to be taken around the clock. Well, I went in and said, 'Mom, let me get it for you,' and I got the pill and the water and she was crying. 'This is the first time anyone has done anything for me, the first time anyone has acknowledged that I have this awful virus too.'

"I am just amazed at their strength, at their love for each other, and the way they kept this secret from us for so long. I am haunted by this trip Mom, Dad, and my wife and I took to England two years ago. It must have been just after they knew they both had the virus. We were in Bath, England, at a place where they had their honeymoon thirty-five years ago. And that afternoon a waitress had looked at them and the way they were holding hands and looking at each other with so much love and asked them whether they were on their honeymoon. She said they looked like newlyweds. That evening at a restaurant in an old castle, a string quartet began to play 'Send in the Clowns' and the tears just poured down both their cheeks. They were looking at each other and smiling and crying at the same time. I knew it had always been their special song. And I was thinking, how sweet but how corny—you know what I mean? In a million years I would never have guessed what the significance was of the look they were giving each other.

"When we were leaving the Corpus Christi beach house for what would probably be my Dad's last visit there, I knew how significant the occasion was. This was the beach house Dad had bought when we were young. It has become such an important part of our growing up, of our memory of childhood. I made a special tape for them, and that night we drove out to the pier and I played the tape in the car as we stared out over the water at the lights off Padre Island and in the bay. We all cried. The tape had all their favorite songs on it. I just can't get that music out of my head."

RAJANI AND I HAD made an offer on a house in Roundtree. It was a great time to buy a house: so many of them sat on the market with sellers getting desperate. The house was fabulous, but secretly I hoped that we had made an offer the seller would easily refuse. I was now certain that I didn't want to buy a house. A fancy house would not solve our problems, only camouflage them. And Rajani had begun to sense my ambivalence about the house, though I had said nothing to her.

Rajani encountered the world of AIDS firsthand when Will Junior came to the house on his next trip to Johnson City. She knew of the Johnsons; I had spoken of them often. I think the disease became real for her when she saw how AIDS had shaken the world of this handsome young man, his beautiful wife, and their children. She took pains to put them at ease in our home, and I was grateful.

And then another time, Rajani and I were walking in the mall when we spotted Luther Hines walking—a miracle in itself. He strode purposefully in a jerky, unbalanced fashion, stopping every ten steps or so, to sit or to reach a hand out to the wall. People stared at him, at the crusted lips, the frondlike growths of molluscum contagiosum on his face, his impossible thinness. How could you not look? It seemed to defy all physical laws that he could be so upright. If anyone stared too long at him, he snarled: I saw two teenage girls rear back in fright, almost spilling their sodas. I pointed him out to Rajani as one of mine. I waited for her to say something, but his appearance had stunned her into silence.

ONE MORNING, I got word that the assistant medical administrator at the Miracle Center wanted to see me. As I walked up to the executive suites, I tried to imagine what the interview might be about. All around the country, hospitals were hiring ID physicians and paying them a salary to run the hospital's infection control and surveillance program and to see the infectious disease consultations. This made perfect sense, because so much of ID—certainly in the pre-AIDS era—was hospital-based.

The administrator was in his forties, the epitome of the MBA health management type. On his office wall were planning charts; the computer monitor on his desk had a clock ticking in the bottom right-hand corner and my name in a bar. On his desk was a picture of his wife and children.

"I appreciate your coming," he said. "I wanted to chat with you about the AIDS situation. What do you think the future holds? Are we going to see more patients?"

"Undoubtedly," I said.

"But is it really necessary for us to see them here? Do other hospitals—say, in Bristol and Kingsport—see as many cases?"

"I don't know about 'necessary.' Felix and I are the only staff doctors in infectious diseases in your hospital. We are both almost full-time VA. The main reason we are here is providing service to your hospital."

"Oh, don't get me wrong, we appreciate what you do here. It's just that AIDS patients sometimes are a big drain on our funds. Scotty Daws, who stayed in the ICU so long, for example, cost us about 250,000 dollars."

"Well, Scotty is a good example. I didn't admit Scotty; he showed up in your emergency room. He was admitted to neurology and I was consulted on the third day. He would have been your problem whether

I was here or not. In fact, we probably saved you money because we got him out of the ICU and to the floor as soon as we could."

The administrator looked skeptical. He was thinking that, but for me, Scotty might have died on day two and saved even more money. "Is it fair to say that part of the reason we have so many AIDS patients is because of your reputation?"

I shot back with a question of my own: "Isn't it true that as a community hospital that takes public funds, you really can't turn away patients like that?"

"I'm not saying we should turn them down. I don't know that we should attract them from other towns that have good-size hospitals."

"Well, the fellows we are training in infectious diseases are taking up positions in some of those hospitals. With time they may take over some of the case load. Then again they might not."

"Why not?"

"Because, as you pointed out, many of these patients don't pay. If you are losing 250,000 dollars on Scotty, you don't imagine I got paid for all the hours and hours I spent with him?"

"Well," he said, using the same phrase with which he had begun the interview, "I appreciate your coming."

I appreciate your coming. I made my way to the parking lot. As I started my car and looked at the Miracle Center through the windshield, I was furious and humiliated. I wanted to walk out—let them see if AIDS went away. They seemed to think *I* was bringing AIDS to this hospital, disrupting the precious bottom line, the perfect symmetry of the cancer center, the one-day surgery center, the birthing suites, all the high-tech smorgasbord of offerings to channel paying patients into the system. I wasn't a profit center. And my patients simply did not matter. I wanted out.

AS A REFLEX, I drove over to my friend Allen's service station. My frequent visits at the end of the day were therapy for me. He had been a patient listener over the years to the saga of AIDS: first its absence, then its appearance, now its abundance. His response to gay men had been the same stereotypical, knee-jerk response that I had once had. But over time, as the people behind the label became more apparent to him, he even extended credit and worked free on some of my patients' cars. His prejudice had vanished.

I told him what had happened. My desire to take a break, to change the arena, to start anew.

I expected him to protest that I should not think this way. Instead, he was silent, pensive.

"I don't blame you, Doc," he said at last. "I don't see how you do it day after day. Hell, my heart breaks when I blow an engine—but it's just an engine, it's not a life. I don't see as I blame you, though you know I wouldn't *want* you to leave."

We watched cars pull in and out. Allen held his cigarette pack out to me. I lit up and took so deep a drag I had to sit down to keep from passing out.

"You know what, Doc?" Allen said. "One day, about ten years from now, I'd say this town is going to be just like San Francisco. People won't pay no mind to gay or AIDS or nothing, people just won't think too much about it. It'll be like diabetes or cancer, you reckon?"

After Allen's, I drove to see Darryl, my motorcycle mechanic. I had always tried to keep AIDS out of our conversations. But today, as I told him what happened, he surprised me.

"You don't have to tell me nothing, Doc. My baby brother, who you never met—I come to find out he is homosexual. I loved him and protected him when he was young. But when I realized what he was, I hated him. But, see, I couldn't keep hating him because I had loved him for so many years before that. And I realized he couldn't help it, you know what I mean, Doc?"

I certainly did.

"So I just more or less one day told him I still loved him. I said, 'Be careful,' though I didn't really know nothing about AIDS when I said that."

"Does he live in town?" I wondered if Darryl's brother was someone I might have seen at the Connection.

"Hell no. He couldn't really live here and be homosexual, you know what I mean? He had to get away—I don't think he really wanted to, but seemed like he had to."

"Where is he?"

"San Francisco."

"How long has he lived there?"

"Let's see: he left in 1978 or so."

"Do you hear from him?"

"I haven't in years. We're not much for writing. After Mom and Dad died, we have all just kind of lost touch. And for the longest time I didn't have a phone. I have a sister in Cincinnati, Ohio, and another sister up in Massachusetts that I ain't heard from either. . . ."

"You ought to give him a call, tell him you still love him."

"Do you think he's still alive?"

28

J ULY 1989.

Rajani and the kids had gone to visit her sister in Washington, D.C., for the weekend. I was alone in the house.

The previous day, I ran into the pretty VA secretary with whom I regularly joshed and bantered whenever we met. She was walking up from the hospital to the domiciliary area, and I was heading the other way. This was the same woman who had been in the back of the VA squad car and offered me a ride the night I walked over to see the Johnsons for the first time. She looked radically different now. I complimented her: she appeared to have lost at least ten pounds and her arms looked sinewy and toned. She was wearing a tube dress. She said she had been working out at Gold's Gym. And eating differently. "High carbohydrate and watching my fat-grams."

Her new physique seemed to have given her personality a parallel change. She was bolder, more self-assured and confident—a state of being that seemed too much for our little town. We stood facing each other. Our rhetoric no longer seemed playful, but deadly serious. Like her makeup.

"I'm a new person, Abe," she said, turning her arms inward, so that I could see her triceps. "Last night I went and bought myself a little black dress. A crepe number. I have this mirror on my ceiling. I looked at myself and, damn, it made *me* hot."

I knew what I was supposed to say: something about wanting to see the little black dress. The thought of the little black dress, the delicious way she had said it, already seemed to alter the space we stood in, blocked out the cars passing by, the heat of the day. I was thinking of Will Junior's acid test for a gay man: send him through a door where a skimpily dressed voluptuous woman is waiting.

I was tongue-tied. "Oh," is what I finally came up with.

She seemed to be enjoying my discomfort. Before, we had dealt as equals. Now, I felt at a disadvantage. She came up close. "Face it, Abraham," she said. "We've got the hots for each other." She whispered, "I'm in the phone book."

Her hand came up from her side now and I froze, wondering where her fingers were going. She reached for the skin under my nipple and pinched me there. Pinched me hard. She strolled away, looking over her shoulder as if to see if I would follow.

All that day she loomed in my mind. I had even checked the phone book: yes, she was listed. And for the first time I felt I could even rationalize what I was tempted to do. All around me, my patients were dying; AIDS made things like bank accounts, compound interest, retirement funds, 30-year mortgages seem absurd. I felt like a death camp inmate: in this setting what did a friendly fling, a flying fuck, a quickie, matter? Lust was such a genuine and life-affirming emotion compared with the ambivalence, confusion and sadness I was experiencing.

At home I felt lonely. As if everyone had left me. But at the same time, I felt guilty for some reason, as if I had driven them off. What saved me that weekend from temptation was not just fear and loyalty to my family, but the fact that there was something else on my mind, something that hovered near the surface like a familiar name I was struggling to remember. There was a pattern in my HIV practice, a paradigm I could see but wanted to flesh out. I had carried copies of patient files and records from the clinic to my house. I kept feeling if I could concentrate hard enough, step back and look carefully, I could draw a kind of blueprint that explained what was happening here in Johnson City, Tennessee, and perhaps in the process explain what was also happening in every little community like ours across the country. And maybe work would make me forget the Little Black Dress and what lay underneath it.

Here we were in late 1989, and the picture of AIDS in our town had changed radically from the day when I walked into the Connection. In 1985 we were in our age of innocence: I was an AIDS expert with no AIDS in sight, a rookie looking for a challenge. Now, we had over eighty HIV-infected persons in our practice, we were AIDS-seasoned, and all sense of innocence had vanished. Including my own. Our little town in the heart of the country with 50,000 residents had a hundred-fold more cases than the CDC would have predicted for us. The belief that AIDS would not touch this town had been absurd—almost as absurd as the plan to bury the respirator when the first unfortunate young man had ridden down from New York and fallen ill with AIDS. The deaths seemed unreal now, so many I could not process what I was feeling. And meanwhile, new patients each week.

I began to think about the patients we were following. Our town's high-risk folks—gay men—were *not* infected: several surveys by Carolyn Sliger of the Health Department at both the Connection and New Beginnings had shown us that. Then where did our eighty-odd patients come from?

Spread out on my living room floor, I compiled a list of every person with HIV that we had seen in the office, the VA, the Miracle Center or the hospitals in our neighboring communities. I made a line-listing with three columns: patient name, address, and a blank column in which I penciled in what I knew about each patient's story, how and where he or she had acquired their illness. I consulted my personal journal, in which for four years now, usually late at night, I had written down the stories behind the medical facts I knew.

I went to Steven's room and took down the map from his wall. Steven loved maps and had a precocious knowledge of the world's geography. He knew India, Ethiopia, Boston, Tennessee, all the places that were significant in his life or that of his parents.

I traced out in pencil a map of the quad-state area—Tennessee, Virginia, North Carolina and Kentucky. I labeled this quad-state map: "Domicile." I penciled in tiny red cannonballs for the *current* residences of my patients.

The dots clustered around Johnson City and included Bristol and Kingsport—the Tri-Cities. But the dots also spilled over the ledge of upper east Tennessee into southwest Virginia and Kentucky and across to North Carolina. Big Stone Gap, Blackwood, Wise, Pennington Gap,

Pikeville, Whitesburg, Norton, Pound—our HIV-infected patients were tracking down from the small mining towns of southwest Virginia and Kentucky; they were coming up from the farming towns of east Tennessee like Greeneville, Morristown and Tazewell. They were even coming across the mountains from North Carolina.

Part of the explanation, then, for our high patient numbers was the large catchment area for our medical practice.

Next, I traced out the outline of the entire United States, leaving out all the detail within. I titled this map "Acquisition." I was after something different on this map: I wanted to locate the places where each patient *used* to live between 1979 and 1985. This was the period in time when most of them had *contracted* infection with the AIDS virus. I culled all the stories I had been told to try to arrive at this information. The sentinel patient, for example, the young man who had driven down from New York and come to the Miracle Center and died, he had almost certainly contracted his infection in New York City. I placed a dot there for him. Gordon, the prodigal son, brother of Essie, had come back from a prolonged residence in Florida; I placed his dot in Jacksonville. Otis Jackson had lived in San Francisco in the Castro district before returning . . .

As I neared the end, I could see a distinct pattern of dots emerging on this larger map of the USA. All evening I had been on the threshold of seeing. Now I fully understood. The paradigm was revealed.

I took the completed maps to the porch. I was proud of my handiwork. I poured myself a scotch and sat on the porch swing, staring at the two maps while moths swarmed around the porch light and threw shadows on the paper.

The dots on the larger map, the "Acquisition" map, were no longer confined to the rectangle of Tennessee and its neighboring states as they had been on the "Domicile" map. Instead they seemed to circle the periphery of the United States, they seemed to wink at me like lights ringing a roadside sign. Here was a tight cluster around New York City. Below that, a few dots around Washington, D.C., and then scattered dots on the eastern seaboard down to Florida, where a clump of dots outlined Miami, and single dots pointed to Fort Pierce, Orlando, Jacksonville and Tallahassee. The middle of the country—the heartland— was bare except for three dots in Chicago. There were isolated dots over

Houston and San Antonio and Denver and Salt Lake. But on the western seaboard the dots were clustered again in two spots: San Francisco and Los Angeles.

The numbers were small, but the two maps unequivocally confirmed what individual stories of Otis, Gordon and so many others had suggested: infection with HIV in rural Tennessee was largely an *imported* disease. Imported to the country from the city. Imported by native sons who had left long ago and were now returning because of HIV infection.

But if AIDS was a disease imported to east Tennessee, I needed to explain the dots that were clumped around Johnson City on *both* maps. These were patients who lived in the Tri-Cities *and* acquired their infection in the Tri-Cities—the "local-locals," as we came to refer to them.

The first name I wrote down—Rodney Tester—provided the clue to the "local-locals": he was a hemophiliac. Rodney Tester was the recipient of tainted factor VIII that, courtesy of an efficient manufacturing and distributing system, had been delivered to his doorstep in rural Appalachia as soon as it was available anywhere else in the country.

But there were still more "local-locals"—persons whose dots occupied the same position on both maps. There were blood transfusion recipients—persons other than the Johnsons—infected by a batch of tainted blood that had found its way into the blood bank of a regional hospital.

The remaining "local-locals" were partners of infected patients—Vickie McCray was in this group. There were also gay men like Raleigh, Ed Maupin and Bobby Keller who had not resided out of the area but had made frequent trips to big cities (or to highway rest-stops where they had met people from the big cities) and engaged in unprotected and high-risk sexual encounters. Finally, there were a few men like Vickie's husband, Clyde, and Jewell, who did not fit into any category. They may have contracted their HIV infection in Johnson City. Or else they were not entirely forthcoming about their travel and risk factors.

IT WAS AFTER midnight but I was still on the porch. I was too wired to contemplate sleeping. Here in our little corner of rural America, my patients, trickling in over the past several years in ones and twos, had revealed a pattern to me. Their collective story spoke of an elaborate migration. Did this paradigm hold true for rural Iowa or rural Texas just as it did for rural Tennessee?

The first step in this circuitous migration was a disappearance from home, a departure from the country. When I thought of departure, I thought of Hobart Carter. One of Hobart Carter's earliest memories was that of his brother telling him not to "walk like that." By the time I saw him, Hobart was in his late twenties, with a large head and an owl-like face. He carried himself very upright, almost tilting backward, making him appear taller than his six foot two. His protruding lower jaw only exaggerated his peculiar hip-swinging carriage. If that was not enough to make him different, he had started to lose his hair at the age of fifteen.

Was it any surprise that when Hobart Carter realized he was gay, he left home for the city at the first opportunity? Yes, the leaving could be construed as a search for a better job, a better education, a space apart from the family just like any heterosexual male might want. But clearly, his desire to leave had much to do with his awakening sexuality.

At home, his opportunities to meet other gay men would be limited and there would have been his parents to deal with: their knowledge, their attitude. His greatest fear was that he might embarrass them, bring them shame. Perhaps he needed distance from them to really understand if he was gay; to live independently was the only way to define himself. He had to separate, despite the part of him that might have wanted to stay.

The opportunity came when his uncle in California became sick. Hobart, who was eighteen by then and quite close to his uncle, volunteered to move there and take care of him. Hobart's father, a fireman and church deacon, recalls: "While he was in California, Hobart was working in a beer-and-sandwich joint called 'Thirteen Buttons.' I asked him on the phone one time, I said, 'Son, what does thirteen buttons mean? When I was in the Navy, thirteen buttons was a kind of coat navy men wore. Does it have something to do with sailors?' And he said, 'Yes, Father, it has something to do with sailors.' But even then, I didn't make the connection."

After two years, Hobart decided to move to San Francisco. He had a friend there and pretty soon he got a job as a night clerk in a very prestigious hotel in San Francisco. He worked that job for a long time and was happy with it, proud of doing what he did and doing it well. He sent his parents a picture of the hotel and a picture of himself working behind the counter. In it he was wearing a black tuxedo and a bow tie, together with an expression that seemed to say he had found not just a job but a city where he could be himself. He had arrived in Mecca.

San Francisco was perhaps the most comfortable place in America in the 1970s to live an openly gay life. On his days off, Hobart strolled up and down the Castro, shopped at the All American Boy or went for a drink in one of the bars. If he ate in a restaurant, he was surrounded by gay men. The "Castro-cut" which was popular then, exaggerated the natural male-pattern recession on either side of the widow's peak. It was, at least in part, a rebellion against effeminacy. Hobart's baldness, which had embarrassed him in Tennessee, now seemed desirable. It fit into the "clone" look (Levi's 501s, flannel shirts or Izods, lace-up boots) that most gay men seemed to be espousing at that time. Adopting the clone look of that town and that era—and gay men have continued to reinvent the look—seemed a way to signal a union with a community after years of alienation from the rituals and even the dress of the larger community. Hobart was no exception.

There was a point in the paradigm that I was constructing when parents became fully aware that their son was gay. With Hobart it happened years before he got sick. His father recalls:

"Hobart came home one vacation in 1977 and he and I were driving down this bypass just about a mile from the house and Hobart turns to me and says, 'Daddy, I want to tell you something that has been eating me up inside. I'm gay. I've had these feelings in me ever since I can remember, since the age of four or five.' Well, it hit me like a ton of bricks, for him to tell me that. Then Hobart says to me, 'Daddy, if you want to stop the car, I'll be happy to get out now.' I said, 'Why would I want to do that? I don't love homosexuality but I love you and I would never tell you to get out of my house.' We just kept a-driving and a-driving, and I was thinking about it and he was studying me. He asked me whether he should tell his mother and I said no, I better be the one to tell her 'cause you know how Mother is.

"I remember telling Hobart as we were driving around that I had known or suspected this for some time, even if I had never formed the words 'homosexual' or 'gay' in my brain. Hobart says to me, 'Why in God's name did you not say something to me if you knew, Daddy? I've been living with this burden for years and years, from the time I was a small boy. I wish you had said something to me.' I said, 'What would I say to you? And if you were not gay and I had suggested you might be, it would only have hurt you.'

"When we got home, we were at peace with each other. Like I said, it hit me like a ton of bricks, but all the same I felt like I understood my son and that his pain had been eased by telling me. I prayed for guidance on it. When I told Mother, it hit her like a ton of bricks, too. Even though she had suspected the same thing beforehand. Hobart called up his brother and told him as well. Jake and Hobart were never really very close, and after that it seemed as if they were even more distant."

For Hobart, this period of independence and self-definition in California coincided with what was the first period of true gay liberation in the seventies. Hobart was discovering and creating his sexual self and adult identity at a moment when gay men and women across the country were learning for the first time to accept themselves and celebrate this sexuality. For the men, particularly, the search for psychological liberation was combined with a period of sexual revolution, a period of rampant sexuality and exhilaration. The gay community had watched the straights experience the sexual revolution of the sixties. For years before that, they had waited in the closets, often sexually inactive. Now finally it seemed there was freedom, exuberance, fraternity. At this moment, sexual freedom was more than just an expression of lust, it was a celebration of all that had not been previously available.

But no one knew of the existence of the HIV virus, least of all Hobart in San Francisco. By the time he was aware there was a virus, it was already in him, subverting his immune system.

Hobart kept in touch with his parents irregularly. Before Hobart returned, before he fell ill, the Carters had a great desire to go west to San Francisco, a part of the country that they had not seen. Mr. Carter collected travel brochures and used to sit in the evenings studying pictures of the Golden Gate Bridge, Embarcadero, Fisherman's Wharf and imagining how it would be. Every time they made plans, Hobart waved them off. For one reason or another their visit at that time was not convenient. When Mr. Carter related this to me, he did so with sadness and deep disappointment. He and his wife had a hard life with very little variety. The prospect of visiting San Francisco was indescribably exciting.

"I sure would have loved to see that Golden Gate Bridge," Mr. Carter told me. His longing has stayed with me as a symbol of all the pleasures denied by barriers of sexuality and misunderstanding, barriers between parents and their own children. When I think now of the losses caused by AIDS, I am also haunted by the earlier losses, the times that might have been, the communication and sharing that for many will never be possible. I can picture Mr. Carter on his porch, years after his son's death, still fingering brochures and studying pictures of the Golden Gate Bridge.

THE FIRST TWO STEPS of the paradigm—leaving home and then the period of urban living—were followed by the long voyage back. Four months before I first saw Hobart in clinic, he was admitted to San Francisco General Hospital for an acute attack of shingles, and while there was found to be HIV-positive. When he recovered, the hotel job was gone, his rent was in arrears, and there were no friends willing to take him in.

He called his parents to say he was sick, he had lost his job, and he planned to come home. He told his parents over the phone that he had "the virus that causes AIDS."

To his parents this must have seemed terribly unfair: Mr. Carter had just had diverticulitis and bowel surgery. Mrs. Carter was not herself because of her own medical problems. Now, Hobart, who had never once invited them to San Francisco, was coming home with AIDS.

Hobart's mother was a stern woman. If her husband's face was expressive and warm, hers was an inscrutable mask, and only the wild expression in her eyes revealed her underlying torment. When I met her at her son's bedside, I worried that she was going to explode from all the tension: a husband just weeks out of surgery, a son with AIDS.

If the move back was hard on his parents, it was hell for Hobart. He was once again in the same family environment, the same town that he had once felt imprisoned by. The boyhood room where he had once dreamed of a different life now held him again within its walls. The crucifixes in every room, the framed needlepoint verses in the bathroom

and kitchen, the giant, somewhat gaudy rendering of Christ at Geth-
semane that dominated the living room harked back to a childhood that
had been difficult. His apartment in San Francisco had been like his
vision of the world: *his* art objects, *his* framed and signed Mapplethorpe
print, *his* color scheme and furnishing. All these affirmations of his own
identity sat in a box in a friend's basement in San Francisco, a friend
who was also sick and might have to vacate soon.

A few months after returning from San Francisco, Hobart had tried
to live in an apartment away from his parents. Rents in Johnson City
were so much cheaper than in San Francisco; he was able to use his
disability check, food stamps and wages from a part-time accounting job
to exist on his own for a while. But his worsening illness made him
abandon the apartment and move back with his parents.

THE PARADIGM—the circuitous voyage, the migration and return—
ended in death. The last time Hobart came to my office, he looked
anxious and apprehensive in addition to being wasted and thin. I knew
from his conversation that he feared death greatly. I had no idea how to
approach this but I felt reckless, willing to try. I sat him down and asked
him a series of questions: Where did he want to die? At home or in the
hospital? Who did he want with him at his deathbed? What did he want
done with his body? What did he want to do with his remaining pos-
sessions? What sort of help could I offer him to alleviate his symptoms
near death? What symptom did he fear most? Choking? Gagging? Being
wide awake? Thinking of Norman Sanger and his death, I told Hobart
how I might prescribe morphine and how it would make him feel. Did
he want cremation? Did he want an autopsy performed? What sort of
service did he want? What music did he want played? Did he want his
father to speak? Anyone else?

He had pondered each question at length, and I was convinced that
he had avoided these thoughts before. As he answered I served as his
scribe, jotting down his replies on a yellow legal pad. At the end I
handed him the sheet of paper. We had addressed all those issues about
his death over which he had some control. He left my office helped not
so much by the paper, but by the sense of having faced his worst fear
and talked about it, walked past it. I resolved after that to discuss death
with all my patients when it was appropriate. In many families I noticed

it was the last entry on the long list of things not discussed with their sons.

A few weeks after Hobart and I had our talk, Mr. Carter visited me to tell me that his son was fading rapidly. He picked up a prescription for morphine solution to help Hobart rest. Hobart would ask his father to come and lie down with him and hug him just as when he was a little boy. They would stay that way for hours. He said to his father, "Daddy, I love you. I hope you never grow old and die."

Mr. Carter replied: "If I die today, I don't mind. Because of my belief in the Lord I feel I will never die. What about you, Hobart? Is everything all right with you and the Lord?"

"Daddy, it was not for the longest time. But now it is."

It was at this point that he called his brother Jake in Germany and asked him for forgiveness. Jake was puzzled. "Forgiveness for what?" Hobart replied, "Forgiveness for everything I have done to you." He had made a similar phone call to me, to ask me to excuse him for any grief he had caused me. I assured him he had caused me none. I thought guiltily about the yellow piece of paper—had that been too much?

He told his father that he wanted his body cremated. He wanted his ashes thrown over the pond at a farm that his friends owned, a farm where he had house-sat for a few weeks.

On a Saturday morning, I was on the tennis court when the call came that Hobart had died. I went over to the hospital and picked up some "Tru-Cut" biopsy needles and small bottles of formalin. This was his idea. In death he had wanted to give me some clues as to what had gone on from an infectious disease point of view.

I drove to the apartment complex in Bristol where the Carters lived, a thirty-minute drive. For financial reasons, the Carters had sold the family home and moved into an apartment. Outside the building, children were playing. They paused to watch me enter the Carters' flat on the ground floor. Did they know a death had taken place? Did they know a child like them had attempted an escape, tried to create a new life, but after just a few years had it cut short?

The apartment was neatly furnished, with a gleaming white sofa in the living room and pictures of Hobart and Jake on the coffee table. Mr. Carter rose to greet me, gracious as ever. "Praise the Lord, Doctor, he is out of his misery," he said to me. Mrs. Carter sat heavily on the couch; she looked up at me but said nothing. Mr. Carter went back to ministering to her.

The visiting nurse was on the phone to the funeral home.

She pointed to a room with a closed door. Inside, Hobart lay on his back, his head slightly to one side, his mouth open, his eyes open. His fringe of hair had grown long and wispy since I last saw him. I pulled the sheet away from his body which was lean and emaciated. The unremittent fever had consumed the body, burned it down to this stringy remnant. There was the loud sound of sobbing in the next room and the sounds of children laughing and playing outside. Hobart's face was incredibly sad, the eyebrows raised quizzically.

I put on gloves. I percussed down his chest to find the liver and settled on an interspace between two ribs. I pushed the biopsy needle in, felt it pop through skin and then slide into the liver. I advanced the hollow inner blade, then pushed the outer sheath over the inner blade. I pulled the whole thing out and held the needle tip over the bottle of formalin. A tiny wormlike core of tissue slid out of the needle into the bottle.

I got three or four more pieces of liver. Stab. Stab. Stab.

Then spleen. Stab. Stab. Stab. Heart. Stab. Lung. Stab. Into formalin.

A small victory here: this virus had killed Hobart. But it was not going anywhere from here but to formalin or to the crematorium.

THE WEEKEND WAS DRAWING to a close. All thoughts of the Little Black Dress had faded. I hammered out a paper describing the paradigm. The two maps accompanied the manuscript. I submitted it to the *Journal of Infectious Diseases*. The editor for the AIDS section, Dr. Merle Sande of the University of California, San Francisco, an internationally known AIDS expert, called me when he got the manuscript. He loved it! He thought it was important. But would I, instead of including just facts and figures, please add in a few anecdotes, individual case studies? I was delighted to.

The paper was a beginning, a rough start on a larger story, the story of how a generation of young men, raised to self-hatred, had risen above the definitions that their society and upbringings had used to define them. It was the story of the hard and sometimes lonely journeys they took far from home into a world more complicated than they imagined and far more dangerous than anyone could have known. There was something courageous about this voyage, the breakaway, the attempt to create places where they could live with pride.

No matter how long I practice medicine, no matter what happens with this retrovirus, I will not be able to forget these young men, the little towns they came from, and the cruel, cruel irony of what awaited them in the big city.

29

THE WEEK BEFORE THANKSGIVING, support group was
much smaller than usual. Amazingly, old Ethan Nidiffer, despite
his emphysema and his infirmity, had not missed a single session; he
had even attended more often than Fred Goodson. Sitting next to him
was Jacko, the KS on his eye hanging down like a shade. Vickie McCray
sat next to Jacko. Fred Goodson was in his usual role as facilitator for
the group. Other persons with HIV showed up sporadically; many lived
much too far away to make it down.

At the last meeting, Luther Hines had shown up, stunning everyone
in the room by his appearance. (Vickie, when she called and told me
about it, said Luther had looked like a *Friday the Thirteenth* character.") Sheer willpower kept him upright. There was no muscle on his
bone. He had sulked and tugged at his Hickman catheter. He had
coughed without bothering to cover his mouth, a wet cough directed
into the center of the group. And when he was asked to speak, he had
launched into a tirade about me, about his parents, about persons with
AIDS in general. No one had wanted to stop him. It seemed a miracle
that a skeleton could harbor the energy to talk and also muster so much
hate. Finally, even he tired of it, and he marched out in disgust.
Raleigh, who had seemed determined to titter his way through every
support group meeting, was, for the first time since anyone could remember, shocked into silence.

Bobby said now, "I hope Luther don't show up. I swear I can't bear the sight of him. And I was sitting next to him. Talk about bad breath, *pheweee . . .*"

"Bad breath is better than no breath," said Ethan Nidiffer, puffing for breath even as he said it.

"In his case no breath might be a plus," said Raleigh.

"But where's little Petie Granger?" Bobby asked. "Haven't seen him for a while."

When Petie Granger came to support group, he usually sat between Raleigh and Bobby. He had been ribbed so much about his "back in Baltimore" utterance that he no longer used it.

"He called me four weeks ago," Jacko said. "I think he only calls when his folks go out. He said he was getting weaker. He said he thought he had so few T cells that he was giving them names."

Bobby Keller said, "We ought to all go pop in on him at home, pay him a visit."

"*Right*, Bobby. That'll be well received, his parents will *love* that," said Fred. "They don't even like him coming here. They don't care for it when my sister calls from TAP."

"Well I miss his 'positive thinking,' " said Bobby Keller, imitating Petie's unique hand and head movement and getting a laugh from Raleigh.

"You mean his whining, don't you?" said Ethan.

"Now you don't mean that, Ethan, as much as little Petie loved you, had the hots for you."

"He's not my type, Bobby. And neither are you." He looked at Raleigh now. "Or you. Especially you."

"Well, I wish I was somebody's type," Bobby said. "I tell you all, I am looking for a man. He has to have five things." Here Bobby held up five fingers. "One, he has to be younger than me; two, he has to have his own car—"

"—That rules me out," said Raleigh.

"—Three, he has to have his own place and not be living with his mother; four, he has to have money."

He stopped now and said nothing. Vickie couldn't take it anymore: "You said five. What's the fifth thing?"

Bobby was still holding up his little finger, "The fifth thing I'm not telling on account of a lady being present. But I'll tell you what, the fifth thing better be a whole lot bigger than this finger."

Even Ethan doubled in laughter and had to reach for his inhaler to get his breath again.

Vickie interjected, "If you all are quite done, I think I'd like to say something about the quilt. I am making a panel for Clyde. And I know Fred and Bettie Lee are making one for Otis. And I feel like we should make a panel for Cameron Tolliver. We should set up a night where we meet and make a quilt panel for him seeing as he has no one that will make one for him."

This was agreed on as a good idea. A night was fixed when they would all meet at Vickie's trailer and begin the job. Vickie had received all the instructions on how to make the quilt panel.

Only Ethan Nidiffer grumbled about it. "I tell you," he said, "I don't want my name on no quilt."

"Well, you have to be dead first, so don't worry about it," Raleigh said.

Fred intervened: "Coming back to something else we talked about. It would be a nice thing for us to do what Bobby said: not visit Petie, but we could call him. In fact, why not let us devote this meeting to those who can't be here. Let's call the members who are not here and just wish them well. Thanksgiving is coming after all."

There was some discussion and it was agreed that this was a good idea. Fred brought in a speaker-phone from the minister's office. He insisted if they were going to call, they should call *all* the members— even Luther. When Luther Hines picked up his phone and Fred explained that they were calling to wish him well, Luther said, "Wish me what?"

"Well, *harrumph*, just to wish you well, and Happy Thanksgiving and all that."

"WHAT THE HELL DO I HAVE TO BE THANKFUL FOR?" Luther yelled and slammed the phone.

"He ain't getting none of my turkey," Bobby Keller said.

Old Ethan was livid: "I ought to go up there and put him out of his misery with my shotgun."

The last phone call was to Petie Granger. It was a while before the phone was picked up.

"Hello?" a woman's voice answered

"Can we speak to Petie Granger?" Vickie asked. It had been agreed that she would do the talking since the family was suspicious of men who called.

"Who *is* this?"

"Vickie McCray from the TAP support group."

". . . Petie died two days ago . . . the funeral was this morning. . . ."

Vickie was unable to say anything. The woman on the other end quietly disconnected the phone.

There was a shocked silence in the room. Raleigh began to cry. Bobby put his arms around him. Everyone stood up, hugged each other—even Ethan participated in the hugging—and then one by one they shuffled out.

THE MORNING AFTER Thanksgiving, before I went to work, as I sat down for a rare home-cooked breakfast, Rajani suggested we go to counseling. And I had a shocker for her: I told her I thought we should leave Tennessee on a sabbatical instead.

We were both taken aback. I knew the marriage was in trouble. But I felt as if it was primarily because we were living in a war zone. I imagined this period in my life as a strange and horrible time, the way it must have been in England during World War II: Each time you saw a friend you wondered if he would return. There was a sweet nostalgia that crept into all your actions at such times. You looked at every building and wondered whether it would be around the next day, whether your neighbor would be there to greet you.

I said I wanted to think about counseling. I wondered where I would find time. Time—or lack of it—seemed to be the essence of our problem. How would a counselor find me a way to free up time, while taking up more of my time?

"You can make time. If you can find time for Allen, for tennis, for your patients, you can find time for this. If you want to do it," she said. She was shaken that I could consider leaving our town.

THEN, AT LUNCHTIME, a patient sitting two booths down in the smoking section of the VA cafeteria exploded. There was a flash, a bang and a scream—all at the same instant. I whirled around to see green nasal prongs trailing down from his ears, a mini–oxygen tank strapped to his wheelchair. He stared ahead with a petrified expression as if he had been struck by lightning. His hair and eyebrows were singed and still smoldered.

At dinner that night, the phone rang and I heard that Will Johnson in Kentucky had died. I went into mourning. I had to wait a week until Will Junior stopped in Johnson City before I heard the end of his father's story.

Will Junior told me he had asked his father a few days before his death, "Dad, are you scared?"

"Afraid of dying? No, I'm just angry. I'm afraid of the process. I'm afraid of what I have to go through to get there. I have these bad visions of choking to death or gagging."

Two days before he died he called Sarah Presnell. He said, "I'm in despair. I don't want to feel any more pain. Can we turn up the morphine? But before we do, I want twenty-four hours without morphine so that my head is clear and so that I can see the family."

In his twenty-four hours of lucidity, he said his goodbyes to his wife, children and grandchildren. The morphine was turned back on and he slipped into coma.

"The instant Dad died, we felt we had achieved a victory of sorts. It was like a touchdown, was the way I felt. Mom was weeping, but I think she felt the same way. What a life! And the suffering was over. We patted him, as if to say, 'Way to go, Dad. You fought long and hard. What a life, Dad! What a life!' I had a sense that I was sending Dad on to a better place. And it was a victory for him and a defeat for the devil. There were tears, a lot more tears to see how hard Mom was taking it, but there was joy in his death, in the end to his suffering."

Will Junior said he kissed his Dad's feet and his forehead. He remembered marching out of the room backward, not wanting to turn his back on his father's body. The body was taken at once to the crematorium.

"You know, as soon as the body left the house, and I was sure that Mom was OK, I drove into town to get Kiwi polish for my shoes. I

wanted to make sure my shoes were spit-shined for the wake and funeral."

"Why?" I asked. He looked at me sheepishly. "I guess I can't explain
it. It was my way of honoring Dad; it was very important to me. All I
can say is that Dad would have looked down and understood exactly."

"How exactly do you spit-shine a shoe?"

"You take the cloth and wrap it tightly around your finger. Then you
take a little polish and a drop of water, apply it to a section of the shoe
the size of a quarter, and you rub and you rub until a shine emerges.
You do this section by section. You need strong fingers, lots of elbow
grease, and lots of patience. But when you are done, those shoes are so
shiny you can look in them and shave!"

Will Johnson and Bess had planned their funerals, just as many years
before they had planned their wedding. They picked the hymns and the
verses from the Bible. They decided that the children should not participate and there was to be no eulogy. Will told his son that he did not
want the funeral to focus on him. Instead he wanted people to see the
glory of God.

The church was packed. The Brother Rats had their own little section, which Will Senior had reserved for them. His father had picked as
the opening hymn, "Onward Christian Soldiers."

The text was from Paul's letter to the Romans. It had to do with faith,
with unwavering belief in Christ. Will knew that so many of his business associates and his Brother Rats would be there and he wanted to
reach them with the message. The preacher took the congregation
through the text and he ended with this comment:

"It was here and nowhere else that Will Johnson put his confidence
and hope, his trust. And he asked me to tell you today what answer God
had for him. He knew that he would have many friends here today who
did not know this truth. That is why he chose this text and asked me to
speak to you frankly about it. This truth stands validated for Will now.
But what of you? It was *sure* for Will, it *must* be for you and me, too."

Only the immediate family went to the cemetery to bury the ashes.
They read Psalm 23 at the grave site. Each family member took turns
scooping ash out of the urn and placing it in the ground.

Will Junior told me when he dipped his hand into the urn, he could
feel his father's bones in his hands. And after he scooped up the ashes

and put them in the grave, there remained dust on his fingers. He brought his fingers to his mouth, kissed them.

"I wanted in this last act to be a part of my father, to have my father within me. Though I think my wife looked at me strangely, it seemed the most natural thing in the world for me to do."

"Did people know that he had died of AIDS?"

"There was no direct mention of it. But more than a few people knew. Some Brother Rats had come by to see Dad a few weeks before that; they knew and they told him they were with him.

"And the night of the funeral, my cousins from Washington, D.C., who had driven down to be there, were sitting in the cocktail lounge of the Holiday Inn. They heard some local say to another, 'Isn't it a shame that Will Johnson died of AIDS? And you know what? His wife has it too.' "

AFTER HER HUSBAND'S DEATH, Mrs. Johnson continued to lead a vital life. She would invite a grandchild over for a day and bring all her attention to the child from morning to evening. She continued to play the piano in church until she was too weak to go on. After the Sunday church service, she would do as she had always done, invite people— newcomers in particular—to lunch at her home, where she would have had a pot roast in the oven. But when she was asked by her son or daughter how she was doing, she would answer, "I am brokenhearted. Just brokenhearted." And then, in just a few months, she wasted away. She began to have severe diarrhea. She seemed mad with the world, something no one had seen in her before.

Each day was a painful wait for the end to come. AZT, which had been made available to her early through a clinical trial, seemed to have lost its effectiveness on her, and she now quietly stopped taking it.

A few weeks before her death, she called her son and daughter into her room. She said to them, "I want you to know that I am quite ready to meet the Lord face to face. I want you to know that everything is all right. I am now consigning your care to His hands, and He will look after you and guide you." She then asked her son and daughter to take her to the cemetery. She wanted to see the plaque in the ground with her husband's name on it that had recently been completed. She was so weak that Will Junior and his sister had to support her every step.

"It was the most awful walk for my sister and me. We knew that very soon—maybe even in a week—we would be making this walk again, but instead of supporting our mother between us we would be carrying her ashes."

She was in a coma for many days. Every hour she would groan, and Will Junior and his sister would take turns holding her, kissing her.

When it appeared that the end was very near, everyone put hands on her just like they had done for their father. She was resting against Will Junior's chest letting out little "hoooos. . . ," each one louder than the next. They became more forceful, as if she was giving birth, as if she was trying to get out of her body. Just as for Will Senior's death, they urged her on her voyage, coaxed her free from a body that, though familiar, was diseased and wasted.

But when she died, the weeping was more intense, the sense of victory less acute than when her husband had died. Will Johnson was the fighter—the metaphor of battle and victory that he espoused had come to a head at the time of his death. He had won the fight. For Bess Johnson, her infection, her illness and even her death were quieter, more tender and tragic.

Will Junior, tears flowing uncontrollably, kissed his mother's forehead and her feet and backed out of the room, making a square corner into the kitchen. He had work to do on his shoes.

Whereas Will Johnson's funeral had been forceful and the message potent, Bess Johnson's funeral was much more poignant. There was no eulogy. She had wanted the hymn "Holy, Holy, Holy" sung. The congregation had then recited the Apostles' Creed, ending with, "I believe . . . in the forgiveness of sins, the resurrection of the body, and the life everlasting."

She had asked that the sermon be from John 11, verses 25–27: ". . . I am the resurrection and the life: he that believeth in me, though he were dead, yet shall he live. And whosoever liveth and believeth in me shall never die."

After the reading of Psalm 23, the service ended with the hymn, "All Hail the Power."

Will Junior and his sister, orphaned by this terrible virus, made the trip to the cemetery once more. They took turns scooping the ashes into the ground. Once again Will Junior kissed the ash off his fingers.

VICKIE MCCRAY HAD started going to church, a different church than the one her cousins attended.

For a while she liked the preacher. She had confided to him about her infection, and he had taken the news well and was full of sympathy. Then, a few weeks later, he called her and asked her if she was willing to stand up at church and tell the congregation that she had AIDS.

He said to her, "Let us carry your burden for you. It will also allow us to introduce this topic to the church."

Vickie had answered him, "And why would you want to use me as a specimen?" Danielle begged her not to even dream of it because so many of her classmates went to the same church. Vickie told the preacher, "What I would like to do is keep coming to your church and get to know the people and tell them when I'm ready."

The preacher persisted: "I feel like my congregation would support you. I know my congregation. I know what they will do."

"Oh no you don't. 'Cause you just done lost one member of your congregation."

Meanwhile Vickie was more and more active with TAP—Tri-City AIDS Project. She was crisscrossing the county, going up to see Bobby Keller every other day, taking care of Jacko. Jacko was deteriorating, losing more toes, having the KS lesions growing both without and within, squeezing out his life.

She said to me, "I'm beginning to believe that I was given this disease for a reason. I was just this everyday, typical housewife, taking care of the children, cooking meals for everyone, and waiting for my husband to come home after each evening's work. I didn't get the chance to go out much. I didn't go to bars. I didn't meet very many new people. My life just revolved around my family. We never had vacations, though we did go camping quite a lot. We went to big places where we could fish and swim, and we had a good time. But as I look back on my life and compare it to the way it was then and now, I say, 'Wow!'"

It was indeed a TV movie sort of transformation. Vickie's hair had grown back fully. With Clyde's insurance money, she had bought a four-year-old Camaro and was applying for a housing loan to move away from Tester Hollow to a subdivision of Kingsport. She was creating a new self.

"I feel like a bear that's been in hibernation, you know what I mean? I have become a person I didn't know existed inside of me. I know I can make friends. I know I'm respected after people get to know me. And my heart is so full of love to give to them who need it. I'm so active in every organization I join. I'm now on the board of TAP! Can you believe it? An old country hick like me? I'm living my life to the fullest and thanking God for each day that I'm here. Life is so precious, Abraham, and there's so many people that don't realize it. So if anything, this disease has made me take a long look at how things were before I got it and afterward. I'm more of a complete person than I ever was." Here she pounded her right fist into her cupped left hand. "I set goals for myself that I'm determined to fulfill. I am somebody. I'm happier now than I've been in a long time. I enjoy life more now."

I couldn't believe what Vickie was telling me. There was something a little desperate here, a measure of denial. But the new life she had created was one she was justifiably proud of. So was I. I just had a hard time getting the future—her future—out of my mind.

Vickie read my thoughts. "But I'm also realistic. I know that what I have is like a time bomb waiting to blow up in me and cause this terrible AIDS to begin. But I can't let it rule my life, get into my train of thought all the time and take away the best fight that my body possesses, and that is 'positive thinking.' I'm going to fight this disease with lots of laughter on account of, you know, it will boost my immune system."

I nodded. I believed laughter did a lot more than most things I prescribed.

She went on: "I've had a lot of sad times and probably a lot more to get through. But it helps having very special friends to talk to. I appreciate Carol at your office and I appreciate you. But my friends in support group are even more special to me because they know what I'm going through. They've been through it themselves. But I tell you what, Doc, there's much more to life than sitting around waiting to die. There's so many people with this disease that I've seen just give up on life, give in to this disease, and let it take over their lives.

"After I lost Clyde in that most horrible way, how much more horrible could anything else in my life be? I'm not scared of death one bit. And when it comes, I'll deal with it. I've made arrangements for my kids—I have a cousin what is well off and wants them both. Meanwhile, Doc, guess what: I have just enrolled in nursing school!"

I gave Vickie a big hug. I was so proud of her. I had watched her transition from housewife to household head to widow and now to nursing student. I told Vickie that I would come from the end of the earth for her graduation.

"Why? Won't you be here?"

"I might not, Vickie. I might not."

She shook her head as if she did not want to think about it.

I asked Vickie the question that had always nagged me: How was it that she managed to retain so much love for Clyde? In her journals, her poems, which she shared with me, and in the pictures on the wall, she had memorialized him. Yet this was the man who had cheated on her constantly with both women and men. He had had an affair with her own sister. This was a man who gave her a disease that might take away her life, make her children orphans.

Vickie's face took on that same teary-eyed, somewhat shamed expression as when she had exposed her scalp to me in clinic three years before.

"I don't know. I can't explain it. You know, when I caught him with my sister, what I had done is drive out to the store and then before I got there, I turned around and coasted home, cutting the engine off so they couldn't hear. And sure enough, her car was right there. I just bust in there and let them both have it. I remember I took my ring and threw it at him. It was the worst moment of my life.

"And then no more than two weeks later we're back together and he's sleeping with me. And I was thinking, 'How does this man have the nerve to sleep with me again when he knows I can just slice it off with my knife and hand it back to him and say that's what you get for sleeping around?'

"See, Abraham, I don't understand how he was able to attract those women, how I even forgave him. Why, he hardly spoke a word—he was backward, to tell you the truth. And I don't know why I still love him, but I do.

"It's almost like I'm still looking for him. I'll be driving and I'll see a dark-haired man with a mustache and my head will spin, as if it might be him. It's the strangest thing, Abraham."

30

I LIE AWAKE AT NIGHT, the household fast asleep around me.
I am now plotting the unimaginable, the sacrilegious. No: not the
Little Black Dress. Worse than that: I am thinking of how I will leave
my Mountain Home, leave Tennessee. Steve Berk has suggested I take
a leave of absence rather than quit. I have been looking for a research
or scholarly project to pursue outside Johnson City. I have told my
patients and they have accepted it quietly. But I worry that they think
I have betrayed them.

It was a crazy day: Roly-poly, jolly Bobby Keller died.

And Luther Hines is in the hospital refusing to die.

And Jacko is at home, near death. Vickie reports that one by one his
toes are falling off. I have a notion that one toe—perhaps the last one—is
attached to a guy wire that holds up his viscera. When the last toe falls,
everything within will collapse. The lungs and heart will crash through
the diaphragm onto the liver, breaking it free from its ligaments, carrying
the spleen in its fall, and the whole lot go crashing to the pelvic floor.

Fred the bear and Vickie McCray—I think of them as the brave
generals who lead the battle charge and will never admit defeat—are
doing well. They report the casualties to me.

The "infection" dream is so frequent that many mornings I wake up
and, even when I have shaved and showered, I am still having to
convince myself that I am uninfected. Perhaps my insomnia of the last
six months is an attempt to avoid the infection dream.

Idly, in the silence of the night, unable to sleep, I percuss my body, map out my organs, take an internal poll: liver, spleen, heart, lung— how do you feel? Do we leave or not, guys? I think of Hobart Carter and how I went to his house to biopsy his organs. I had percussed his Christ-like corpse just as I am percussing myself now to find my liver. Did his liver in death sound different from mine in life?

I was taught how to percuss the body so long ago: it was the first day of June 1972. That night, like tonight, lying flat on my back, the sheets pulled away and the lights off, I percussed my liver. I started just above my right lung, high, at the level of my nipple, pressing the middle finger of my left hand against my skin. I cocked my right wrist and let the fingertips fall like piano hammers: *thoom, thoom.*

"Resonance!" I said to myself, picturing the air vibrating in a million air sacs, a million tiny tambours.

I moved down an inch: *thoom, thoom.* Farther down and farther still, and then suddenly, *thunk! thunk!*—dullness. I had reached my liver, airless and solid.

I returned to my nipple: *thoom, thoom, thoom, thoom,* and then *thunk!* I lightened my stroke: there was no longer any sound but there was still a vibration in my stationary finger—the pleximeter finger— which told me where the air sacs ended and where, high under my rib cage, under the domed diaphragm, my liver began.

I traversed my liver, following its dull note into the belly until the *thunk! thunk!* was replaced by a sharp and high-pitched *tup! tup!*— "tympany!" It was the air that had been trapped in the loops of my bowel. No longer confined to little sacs, it was free to vibrate like the air in a conga drum—*tup! tup!*

As a young medical student, I percussed everything in the joy of discovery. I percussed table tops, to find the stony dull circle where the leg joined the underside. I percussed plaster walls, looking for studs. I percussed tins of rice flour and the sides of filing cabinets. But in the dark, just as tonight, it was my own body that I percussed. As I drifted to sleep I saw myself as if transparent, my viscera, both hollow and solid, shining through my skin.

But tonight, unlike those medical student days, sleep hovers far away and I continue sounding my body. I think of my hero, Charles Leit-head, who taught me percussion. He was professor of medicine at the

Princess Tsahai Hospital in Addis Ababa, Ethiopia. I was a third-year medical student. It was only a few years before Haile Selassie was deposed and the country came unglued.

Professor Leithead, who favored dark, pin-striped suits and Edinburgh ties, was bald except for a fringe of gray-white hair that hung long over his collar. Half-moon, tortoise-shell glasses were perched on the very tip of his nose.

At the time that I came under his preceptorship, I harbored secret fantasies of specializing in heroic neurosurgery, high-risk perinatology, surgery of the open-heart-and-transplant kind—as did my two fellow students, Tom and Arsalon. We were convinced that it was only by specializing in these fields that we could achieve the Dr. Kildare-ish charisma that we all secretly sought. As it turned out, most of us who met Charles Leithead found a higher calling than surgery or perinatology: we became internists.

We met Leithead in the hospital every other afternoon for a bedside tutorial. Leithead was about six-two but had a way of slumping his shoulders and bending his knees when first introduced to the patient, as though trying to make himself more human. After introductions, he would sit by the bed and hunch forward, crossing his legs English style, and then—as if that had not been enough—would hook a foot behind the calf of the other leg so that he was now double-twisted, vinelike, a seated caduceus. The spectacles would come off and he would bend over as if studying the tile pattern on the floor. The professor's command of Amharic was good enough, we suspected, for him to understand most of what transpired, but we translated for him nevertheless. The corners of his mouth would twitch or his chin draw up as though he was going to cry as we gravely described the case before us.

One case I remember was that of Woizero Almaz. I described to the professor how her symptoms unfolded. Almaz, having squatted beside the market road to pee, noticed that her water was taking a dangerous course. Emerging from the perimeter of her skirts, the narrow ground-stream had crept toward a nearby coil of rusty, evil-looking barbed wire. Ever since her water had touched the wire, Almaz had suffered pain in her hips, night sweats, fever. I asked more questions, but Woizero Almaz looked only at the bald pate while answering. Her gaze remained rooted on the Great White One. When I finished my history, we all looked at each other while our preceptor continued staring at the floor. Finally he spoke.

"Ask Woizero Almaz for me, would you, if . . ." And the questions, in a strange Yorkshire accent, would then emanate from this twisted vine, each piercing some protected enclave that the patient—her eyes bugging out—had not thought fit to share with us. Now, terrified at the clairvoyance of this foreigner with the white mane and the black serpent of a stethoscope coiled in his hand, she spewed out reams of history, well beyond the tales of barbed wire and bad humors and evil miasma that we had heard thus far. Other patients had been known to throw in cries for forgiveness.

Leithead rose to examine the patient, bringing his head close to inspect her skin and her bony landmarks, then stepping to the foot of the bed and squatting to "sight" down her body to see if both sides of the chest rose and fell equally, only then probing with his fingers. He percussed smoothly, rhythmically and rapidly: quick strokes—*thoom-oom-ooom*—before moving on, each triplet melodic and crisp, mapping out the borders of the lung, the edges of viscera, a silhouette of the heart. Finally, almost as an afterthought, he put his stethoscope on her skin. All this was done with great economy of time and motion, as if this was not an examination but some sort of bloodless surgery. Now, having understood the case, he would demonstrate each of his findings to us, letting us see and feel and hear what he had experienced, leading us in Socratic fashion to a diagnosis. "Never forget," he would say, "inspection, *then* palpation, *then* percussion, finally auscultation." He would look at us curiously and ask: "Which is the least important instrument in our armamentarium?"

"The stethoscope, sir!" we would bark out.

"And why is that, pray?"

"Because, sir," we would chant, "by the time you have looked, felt and percussed, you should know what you will hear!"

I LEAVE THE HOUSE AT 5:30 a.m. I pick the *Press* off the front porch and scan the first page before placing the paper back on the doormat where Steven will discover it in an hour or so and take it up to his mother.

A fine mist is in the air creating halos around the street lamps and making every tree look ghostly, as if a shrouded figure stands behind it.

In a few weeks there will be frost to scrape off the windshield, gloves to be worn.

Under the streetlight, I see the silky tracks left by the snails on the pavement, a slimy carpet they roll in front of themselves. The snails seem unaware that warm weather is over. I study the paths of their wanderings, their drunken meandering out of the hedges, up the foot-path and then looping back. They crisscross each other and I bend low to see if I can tell which traveler has gone most recently. I wonder if there is an order to this confusion of interweaving lines. Is there a set of rules that snails the world over follow, a code that if broken reveals an intricate pattern underneath this chaos?

I stop at the vending area next to the VA domiciliary canteen; I am starting so early that the Miracle Center's coffee and doughnuts will not be out. For a quarter, I get coffee and the bonus of my horoscope printed on the paper cup.

I see the shadowy figure that I know to be old Bill Mulrooney stand-ing by the door to the mess hall. He wears a tasseled, broad-beamed hat. In the morning mist he can pass for Lee at Appomattox waiting to surrender to Grant. When I come closer, I notice he is sniffling in the cold.

Bill's goal in life is to be first in the chow line. For years he has had no competition. Recently another old veteran, Edward Harless, a trans-fer from the Murfreesboro VA, has started to compete with him. On one or two mornings I have seen them race-walking and then finally running flat-out to the door while the rest of the VA sleeps.

Bill Mulrooney is a Bible nut. This morning he calls out to me: "Hey, Doc. You know the shortest verse in the Bible?"

"*Jesus wept*, Bill. *Jesus wept.*"

THE VENDING MACHINE ROOM this morning smells strongly of stale cig-arettes. In two hours the smoke will be so thick that you cannot see the far wall. If they ever tear the building down, the smoke will be found to have penetrated the heart of each brick. A few insomniacs and a few of the early risers who need that first cup of coffee to get their bowels going are seated in the booths. By midmorning, there will be no place to sit, as a dozen men will be stretched out on the seat cushions, their legs jutting out of the booth, sometimes snoring loudly.

I look for and find Red sitting in his favorite corner booth. He sits attentively, his hands on the edge of the table, as if at any moment someone is going to put a test paper and a No. 2 pencil before him and tell him to begin.

My guess is that Red is only in his late thirties—very young by VA standards—with a baby face and yet with hair that has turned completely white. If you ever ask him why he is called Red, he will say, "Well, I tell you. Back when I was younger, I used to work for the CIA, I had red hair and they used to call me Red."

"What kind of work did you do for the CIA?"

"I don't rightly remember. See they took me and brain-wash-ed me is what they did. Brain-wash-ed me." Here he will make a scrubbing motion with his hand.

"Why? How?"

"I don't know why, Doc. They put this metal thing on my head and I believe they shocked me?"

"How do you remember that?"

"It's about the only thing I still remember." Then he will smile, come close and whisper conspiratorially: "But they don't know I still remember that!"

Last summer he told me that *they* were sending him to the Murfreesboro VA.

"Who?"

"The CIA boys!"

"Why?"

"They say I'm mad."

"You are?"

"No, Doc. I don't think so." Here he will look around, lean close and whisper, "Between you and me, they know I'm remembering too much."

Two weeks before, I had seen Red in this room after a long absence. I had approached him with delight, pleased to see him in one piece, though looking a little older, the shoulders drooping a little more. He had looked at me blankly when I walked up. He stuck out his hand and said his name was Red. He had no memory of me. We had started all over again. He told me why he was called Red, told me about the CIA. The part he could still remember.

IN THE MIRACLE CENTER intensive care unit, the chief resident discusses the readings taken from a Swan-Ganz catheter that sits inside the heart of a Mr. Tobias. The students and interns are wrapped up in the medical issues of his heart attack, in the urgency of a situation that has lost all its urgency for me. The debate goes from a pacemaker to digitalis. While they debate, I picture Sir William Withering, the discoverer of digitalis, holding foxglove in his hand and wondering if it really cured dropsy, as his patients claimed, or merely created that illusion. Secretly, I believe it was the word, *foxglove*. Listen to it: *fox* and *glove*. What incongruous images: how impossible not to smile. I would like to think that it was the sight of those long tubular flowers spilling from his fingers, purplish and vibrant, that made him pursue his investigations.

We are nearing Luther Hines's room. I know. I can smell it. There are so many distinct smells in medicine: the mousy, ammoniacal odor of liver failure, an odor always linked to yellow eyes and a swollen belly; the urinelike odor of renal failure; the fetid odor of a lung abscess; the acetonelike odor of diabetic coma; the rotten-apple odor of gas gangrene; the freshly-baked-bread odor of typhoid fever. But this new smell that is not yet in the textbooks tops them all. Now, the redolence is so strong my nose wrinkles. I ask the students and residents if they smell it? They look at me strangely; one student, an obliging fellow, says, "I *think* I do."

It is the smell of unremittent fever in AIDS, fever that has gone on not for days or weeks, but for months. It is the scent of skin that has lost its luster and flakes at the touch, creating a dust storm in the ray of sunshine that straddles the bed. It is a scent of hair that has turned translucent, become sparse and no longer hides the scalp, of hair that is matted by sweat, and molded by a pillow.

Luther Hines, who had walked into my office looking like death so many months ago, a blocked Hickman catheter hanging from his collarbone, a face covered with smallpoxlike clusters of molluscum, and big curds of *Candida* in his mouth, has managed to elude death for so long. He had become my poster boy, a walking testament to how will and belief can make up for lack of muscle, how anger can overcome blindness. He had been blind for weeks now from cytomegalovirus infection but had still continued to sortie out of his apartment, get rides to the mall, take cabs to our office, cuss out the people he bumped into.

When Carol and I first saw him stumble angrily out of my clinic, refusing admission, heading out to the parking lot, we had given him three days.

Instead he had lived on his own for months, making us all dance around him, punishing us all: hospice, social work, TAP, his parents. When he showed up in clinic it was without an appointment. Nothing was good enough for him: If you went to see him in the emergency room at midnight and you wanted to admit him, you were insulting him. If you did not go see him and had the resident see him, you were insulting him.

I had become immune to his performance, almost admiring of it. I could see beyond it and marvel at his unique kind of courage. So now his performance reached for greater heights: squeezing pus from his Hickman catheter onto his finger and wiping it on his shirt, digging in his mouth for a chunk of yeast to display the inadequacy of your treatment, popping a molluscum lesion between his fingernails. Luther did not believe that HIV was killing him. He believed that our inability to treat the symptoms that bothered him, our prescribing the wrong medications, was at the root of his problem. I almost believed him: Maybe if we could put together the right concoctions we could give him ten good years.

On his deathbed now, Luther looks worse even than he did when he was up and about. His mother and father are in the room, pressed into one corner by our entry. Luther's lips are cracked and his mouth is filled with white patches. He inhales air noisily and erratically into his windpipe, dispensing with the niceties of nostrils, lips or cheeks because of his air hunger. Wisely, many weeks ago, he vetoed a ventilator—it surprised me. I thought out of spite he would say "do everything." But even he had no stomach for that; he had been on a ventilator for a long spell in California.

A wavy frost line has formed over his forehead. Like the remnants left by waves on a beach, the salt from his sweat has condensed on his brow. His skin is hot to the touch.

I call out loudly, "Luther!"

There is a barely perceptible raising of his eyebrows, a turn of his head, but the eyelids remain half-set. Underneath the lids, the eyeballs are roving, as if scanning the ceiling, searching for someone. This is "coma vigil," the same as Otis Jackson displayed before he died. In the preantibiotic era, when nothing could be done for most fevers, physicians painstakingly described the features of the "typhoid state," a terminal event. Luther has not only the "coma vigil" of the typhoid state, but also "muttering delirium" and "floccillation"—picking at the bedclothes. Since there is little I can do for Luther, I too point out to the residents the features of the typhoid state. They are not greatly appreciative: Numbers from a Swan-Ganz cardiac catheter have more allure for them.

The medical students and residents are quiet, hovering around the bed, uncomfortable because death is staring at them. I am uncomfortable too, and I am angry all the time now. This is what I think when I lie awake at night: I want to start all over again. I don't ever want to leave AIDS work—what else will I do? The battle of white blood cell and antibody and T cell with virus or bacteria continues to fascinate me. I want to start in a new community with a new set of names and faces.

When I began in Johnson City, I was ambitious, fascinated by the virus and by my patients. I maintained no distance, denying to myself that this was a fatal illness. The future, when all my patients were dying, seemed remote and vague. I convinced myself that I could handle that. But I simply did not understand how devastating it would be to watch. All the stories that I have painfully collected have come to haunt me with their tragic endings, as if I am the author and must take full responsibility. In a new place I can begin again from a wiser and more careful vantage.

The students and residents are waiting on me. I have been lost in thought. What am I supposed to do here, at this bedside? I have, for which I will always be thankful, the ritual of the examination. I put my hand on Luther: his pulse is difficult to detect, a faint thread under my finger. His belly is scooped out and hollow. I can feel the liver, and on the left side the spleen; both are much enlarged. As I press down on his flanks, I feel his kidneys slip under my palm with each breath he takes, pushed down by the descent of his diaphragm.

I palpate Luther's neck, armpits and groin for lymph nodes. I flash my penlight into his pupils, nose, mouth. I pull out my stethoscope and listen over his neck, heart, chest, belly, and femoral arteries. I unsheathe my tendon hammer and tap his biceps, then his triceps. I move down to elicit the knee and ankle jerks. Then I flip the hammer over and use its pointed end to scratch softly at the soles of his feet, noting the brisk flexion of his toes and the extension of his big toe.

I have saved percussion for last.

I percuss his chest, and the sound of his right lung is disturbing. Only at the very top, near his collarbone, do I hear the *thoom* of resonance. Below that, from above his nipple to his belly, it is dull; the sound is indistinguishable from the *thunk* of the liver. The lung has been transformed from a spongy, light, pliant organ to a solidifying, consolidating mass. The sounds of my percussion on his body fill the room. *Thoom, thunk, thunk, thunk, tup, tup, tup.* I glance at his parents. They listen to the sound of their son as if mesmerized. Once more: *thoom, thunk, thunk, tup, tup*—even Luther seems to pause in his delirious muttering, his floccillation, to listen to the music of his body, to relax, to smile.

My tools—the hammer, the flashlight, the stethoscope—are scattered on his bed. As I pick them up one by one, I realize that all I had to offer Luther was the ritual of the examination, this dance of a Western shaman. Now the dance is over, and the beeps and blips of monitors register again, as does the bored voice of an operator on the overhead speaker summoning someone *stat*.

We exit the room and in the hallway our little group is subdued. We have six more patients in the intensive care unit to see. We move on resolutely, wheeling the silver chart rack in front of us. My heart is heavy. I am already thinking of nightfall, of the comfort of my bed, my body.

31

DECEMBER 31, 1989. New Year's Eve.

Betty, my technician, watches silently as I pack the books in my office and take down my diplomas from the walls. Everything is almost ready for the movers. The last hamster has been given away. The fluorescent lights hum quietly over my head as I walk down the hall one last time.

At home, room after room is stripped down and the stacks of boxes grow higher and higher. My two boys crawl all over the cartons, excited by the activity around.

During the last few clinics I have said goodbye to all my patients. It was difficult and painful. Felix, who will take care of them for me, has convinced the four University Physicians Group primary-care internists to share the HIV clinic load with him: HIV infection at ETSU has now officially become a primary-care disease.

On the glass pane of the front door of our house I have pasted a bumper sticker that reads: IS THIS HEAVEN? NO, IT'S IOWA. Iowa is where I am headed. My clinical commitment will be in the University of Iowa outpatient AIDS clinic. Along with ten other full-time infectious diseases faculty, a social worker, a nurse practitioner, and four fellows, I will be part of an established AIDS team. I will have no responsibility for in-hospital care. I see it as a cooling-off period—a year at the most—before I reenter the fray somewhere else. I have no ambition to do anything but AIDS care. It is my metier. It has found me and will not let me go.

To my tennis buddy, Earl, I leave my Datsun Z; I cannot afford to carry insurance on it. He says whenever I return, it is mine to use. Allen takes my Ford LTD station wagon and works on it for a whole day, replacing belts, flushing out the radiator, changing plugs and points, adjusting the timing, assuring himself that it will carry us safely to Iowa. The car has 110,000 miles on it already.

Both Allen and Earl are certain that I will be back. Allen takes me out into the country and walks me through the six acres that extend behind his barn. It is a perfect plot: trees on one side, a pond, a clearing for a house, a spiraled slope to cut into for a driveway, and an uninterrupted view of the mountains. "You know I'd never sell this in a million years; I won't even listen to offers people make. But if you ever want to buy it, it's here for you. Remember that when you get done in Iowa, Doc."

Rajani is reluctant about this move; she senses, I think, that this is perhaps our last chance. She has agreed to come because she is trying to make herself believe that once I am removed from the maelstrom, I may become someone she can live with again. Rajani believes that safety can be found in the old conventions. But I have come to believe that human life is fast and fleeting, and that our moments of true safety are rare. I fear that this has made me a difficult companion.

By nine in the morning, the movers have loaded the van. We walk around the bare house in shock. Empty rooms. The old house takes back its character. Our presence has been temporary. The place will be whitewashed outside, painted within and the wooden floors polished. Soon it will fill with other voices; the house has seen so many of us come and go.

Our suitcases are on the rooftop carrier of the station wagon. My friend Jay Mehta and his wife, Meena, surprise us by coming by, bringing us a hot breakfast. I am so touched by all of today's acts of kindness. I feel them deeply. We sit on the window seats by the bay windows and eat puri and potatoes, using the plates and spoons Meena has brought. Meena is Rajani's closest friend and I catch her glancing at me with curiosity as if to say, "What is going on with you? Why are you putting Rajani through this? Why leave a perfectly secure job?" I can't explain.

Jay and Meena are longtime residents of Johnson City, the senior-most members of the Indian community. When Rajani and I first came, theirs was one of the first houses we were invited to. Now, the love they show us makes it doubly painful to leave. I push back tears. Before they depart, they bless us formally, wish us God speed. Meena and Rajani hug like sisters. They part reluctantly.

After the Mehtas drive away, I walk around the house with my two boys. They are excited by the prospect of a new geography, new toys, new rituals. They think it is a nice game as we go room to room and say, "Goodbye Steven and Jacob's bedroom, goodbye Daddy's study, goodbye porch, goodbye fireflies . . ." We get in the car and the goodbyes continue: goodbye oak tree, duck pond, and one final stop behind the hospital so Steven can say goodbye to the cranes. We wave at the domiciliary residents on the benches. When we leave the portals of the VA, we say, "Goodbye, Mountain Home."

Rajani's eyes glisten like rain-streaked windows. All around us the morning is so quiet. Only the sounds of the boys break the silence between us. I have only myself to blame for all these goodbyes.

We drive all day with many a pit stop. There is not much traffic on the road—who would move house on New Year's Eve? We sing in the car, drink Cokes, tell stories: Rajani and I work hard—too hard—so that the kids don't feel our sorrow. As the hours pass we leave Tennessee behind us, head north into Kentucky, on into Indiana.

By nightfall we are about to enter Illinois. The back seat is folded down and we have converted the rear cargo area of the station wagon into a cozy nest of sleeping bags and pillows; the two boys are curled around my wife. All three are fast asleep.

Now my familiar Tennessee starscape is behind me. Orion and a Triple-A road map guide my way. It all happened so suddenly. I left my own country, my beloved Tennessee. Perhaps my perennial migrations, almost hereditary, are a way to avoid loss. With deep roots come great comforts. Yet deep attachments are the hardest to lose. Maybe that is why drifters avoid them.

Somewhere in Illinois I feel the weight of five years lift away. It is nearly midnight, the threshold of a new year, a new decade: the '90s. I feel my belt now and assure myself one more time: there is no beeper there! No electronic summons that might sound its shrill alarm, jar my soul, make my heart race. I feel a lightness in my midriff: I tell myself that the umbilical cords that fastened me to eighty-plus HIV-infected people in Johnson City have detached. I feel so guilty over this sense of liberation. I feel such pain when I think of their faces.

I have lived for five years in a culture of disease, a small island in a sea of fear. I have seen many things there. I have seen how life speeds up and heightens in climates of extreme pain and emotion. It is hard to live in these circumstances, despite the acts of tenderness that can lighten everything. But it is also hard to pull away from the extreme, from life lived far from mundane conversation. Never before AIDS and Johnson City have I felt so close to love and pain, so connected to other people. How can I pull Rajani across the gulf of our experience?

WE HAVE NOW crossed into Iowa. The sky is rich and huge. My eyes are numbed by mile after mile of dark prairie. A sign says the next exit has a rest stop; after that you hold it for fifty miles. I have shot past the exit before it registers that I need to pee and have just lost my chance.

It is midnight or nearly so. It seems fitting to stop and welcome the 1990s in. I pull over onto the side of the road, the wheels crunching on gravel before the car rolls to a stop. The engine is on, the parking lights on, and in the back the family sleeps; I debate whether to wake Rajani and wish her a happy New Year. I decide against it: she looks too peaceful to disturb.

The wind is biting cold, hinting perhaps at what the Midwest has in store for us. I walk out onto the stone border of a field; I move slowly. The black horizon is so huge, the world so limitless here.

I look up at the stars. I feel connected: legs to earth, shoulders to sky. I squint my eyes and see the lines that link stars to make constellations, feel their umbra extend down to me, connecting me with this parcel of land that I stand on. Everything is united: my children, the clouds, God, the moon, the mother of my children, the Ford station wagon that will overheat soon if I do not get back and keep going. Under this sky I am connected to all I left behind in Tennessee, all the friends and the patients who wished me luck.

I linger outside my car, my gaze directed skyward. My watch tells me it is now the first day of 1990. I suck on the ice-cold air. My guilt, my shame, about leaving is diminishing. At least for the moment.

I press my nose against the glass of the Ford's rear window and peek in. I see my two sons snuggled up against their mother, each with a leg thrown over her. I want to join them and hope that I have not somehow forsaken my place.

I climb back into the car. I pull off the shoulder and ease the long nose of the Ford back onto the highway. As the needle reaches 65 miles per hour, I think of the young man from New York who six years ago headed to Johnson City. I think of his distress, his suffering, as he sped home, struggling to breathe.

I think if his voyage were to happen today, he might find a community in Johnson City better equipped to deal with him, to accept him. I have faith in the town and its people.

I remember the acts of human kindness that illumine our world.

Author's Note

I AM DEEPLY INDEBTED TO MY PATIENTS and their families for giving me so much of their time, their assistance and their stories. Their excitement for this undertaking and their support and urging have been invaluable. I would like to have acknowledged each one by name, but I cannot.

Many persons assisted me in researching this book; in particular I thank my dear friends in Tennessee: Debbie Byers, Anand and Madhu Karnad, Jim and Barbara Farnum, Earl and Janice Greene, Allen Hawkins, Martha Whaley, Lana Renfro and Joyce Larimer. Also thanks to Carolyn Sliger, Colin Baxter, Carol Ware, and the many doctors and nurses at both the VA and the Johnson City Medical Center who gave me their time and talked about this period in the history of our community. For bringing me a new level of understanding of AIDS, I thank Frank Robinson, Mary Kay Bearden, James Searcy, Jim Wilson, Della Nabhan, Sandy Pomerantz and John Chappie. Stuart Levitz, Jo Seibel, Kris Davis, Irene Connelly, Hilary Hirst and Karen Marasco read the manuscript or parts of it and gave me helpful advice. And thanks also to Bill, Jim and Bob. Connie Brothers of the Iowa Writers' Workshop served as friend, guide and reader. Sandra Hernandez, Deb West and Melanie Whiley assisted me in manuscript preparation. During 1992 I was supported by the Copernicus Society of America in the form of a James Michener Fellowship.

I was blessed in having Mary Evans, my literary agent, "discover" me in Iowa; it was her encouragement that led to the book proposal for *My Own Country*; George Hodgman, my then editor at Simon & Schuster, had a singular vision of the story to be told and coaxed it out of me. To both Mary and George I will be eternally grateful. Eric Steel, my new editor at Simon & Schuster, has shepherded me through the completion of the manuscript, and his calmness and quiet confidence have been soothing. Early on I was fortunate to have the advice of Robin Desser at Vintage as my paperback editor.

Lastly, I am grateful to John Irving, who gave me advice, friendship and the wonderful example of his work ethic.

Abraham Verghese
El Paso
November 1993

ALSO BY ABRAHAM VERGHESE

*"A winner. . . . Filled with mystical scenes and deeply
felt characters. . . . Verghese is something of a magician
as a novelist."*
—USA Today

CUTTING FOR STONE

Marion and Shiva Stone are twin brothers born of a secret union
between a beautiful Indian nun and a brash British surgeon.
Orphaned by their mother's death and their father's disappearance, bound together by a preternatural connection and a shared
fascination with medicine, the twins come of age as Ethiopia hovers on the brink of revolution. Moving from Addis Adaba to New
York City and back again, *Cutting for Stone* is an unforgettable
story of love and betrayal, medicine and ordinary miracles—and
two brothers whose fates are forever intertwined.

Fiction/978-0-375-71436-8